The Competition of Ideas

Bronze sculpture of W. Glenn Campbell, on display in the Stauffer Auditorium. The bust was commissioned by the late William E. Simon. Photograph by Jim Milton.

The Competition of Ideas

How My Colleagues and I
Built the Hoover Institution

W. Glenn Campbell

Jameson Books
Ottawa, Illinois

Jameson books are available at special discounts for bulk purchases for sales promotions, premiums, fund raising or educational use. Special condensed or excerpted paperback editions can also be created to customer specifications.

Cover and book design and production by Catherine E. Campaigne
Cover photograph of Hoover Tower by Jim Milton

For information or other requests please write:
Jameson Books, Inc
722 Columbus Street
Ottawa, Illinois 61350
815-434-7905 • FAX 815-434-7907
E-mail 72557.3635@compuserve.com

Jameson Books titles are distributed to the book trade by LPC Group, 1436 West Randolph Street, Chicago, IL 60607. Bookstores should call 800-243-0138. Individuals who wish to order by mail should call 800-426-1357.

ISBN 0-915463-89-X
Library of Congress Catalog Control Number: 2001 130148

Manufactured in the United States of America

First Printing January, 2001

1   2   3   4   /   03   02   01

To the late President Hoover and late David Packard,
the late William E. Simon and to Richard M. Scaife,
who made it possible for my colleagues and me
to build the Hoover Institution.

Contents

Tribute

M Y ACCOMPLISHMENTS AT THE HOOVER INSTITUTION WOULD not have been possible without Rita Ricardo-Campbell at my side. Rita received her Ph.D. in economics from Harvard in 1946, and we were married on September 15 of that year. In 1948 I received my own Ph.D. from Harvard, so we were well prepared, when the time came, to manage and expand the Hoover Institution as a partnership.

The time came thirteen years after our wedding, in September 1959. We disembarked from the U.S.S. *United States* and were invited to meet with Herbert Hoover in Room 31A of the Waldorf Astoria Hotel to discuss my appointment as director of the Hoover Institution. President Hoover specifically asked that Rita come with me, because this affected her too. I remember that he stressed the excellence of the public schools in the Palo Alto area and reminded us that if we came to Hoover, we would avoid the expense of sending our children to private schools.

So we went to California, where our third daughter, Nancy, was born on July 14, 1960. That September Rita accepted a teaching position at San Jose State University. The following year she could have had a tenured job teaching at San Francisco State, but that was not her only offer. Mr. Hoover asked her to take over the direction of the Institution's archives because, simply stated, he trusted her. He was concerned about unauthorized access to the restricted area of the archives, and he counted on Rita to deal with that issue. She also designed and introduced the first combined-file computer search system in a major archive, designed and

chose new furniture for the very small second-floor offices, and deco-
rated and furnished the new ground-level offices.

After that, she coordinated the interior design projects for the newly
established Herbert Hoover Memorial Room and the Milbank Reading
Room in the Tower; placed portraits of the Russian royal family by Russia's leading artists in the de Basily Room; and devoted many hours to
overseeing the building, decoration, and landscaping of our second building, dedicated to First Lady Lou Henry Hoover.

On September 1, 1968, Rita was named a Senior Fellow along with
Roger Freeman, Milorad Drachkovitch, Stefan Possony, Lewis Gann, Peter
Duignan and Richard V. Allen. Only Rita and Peter Duignan are still asso-
ciated with the Hoover Institution. All the rest, except for Richard V.
Allen, who runs a consulting firm in Washington, D.C., are now deceased.

In the 1970s Rita worked with Senior Research Fellow Darrell Trent
and an architect to plan and decorate our third building, the Herbert
Hoover Federal Memorial Building, which was dedicated in July 1978.
Her good taste, wise selections, and firm management saved the Hoover
Institution several million dollars. From 1974 to 1995 Rita served as the
only female director of the Watkins-Johnson Company, and as the first
female director of the Fortune-500 Gillette Company from 1978 to 1990.

Her record of public service is equally impressive:

- 1967—Appointed by Gov. Ronald Reagan to be the commissioner
  for the State of California on the Western Interstate Commission
  on Higher Education.
- 1970–71—Became commission chairman.
- 1970—Named a member of the newly created Presidential Citizens Advisory Council on the Status of Women.
- Early 1980s—Appointed to President Reagan's Economic Policy
  Advisory Board.
- Early 1980s—Named to the National Council on the Humanities.
- 1988—Appointed to the President's Committee on the Medal of
  Science. Served two three-year terms.

Her versatility notwithstanding, Rita retains her academic focus. In
1977 she published *Social Security: Promise and Reality* and in 1982 *The
Economics and Politics of Health*. She contributed to and, with Senior Fel-

low Ed Lazear, edited *Issues in Contemporary Retirement* in 1988. Her most recent book, *Resisting Hostile Takeovers: The Case of Gillette,* was published in October 1997.

Rita Ricardo-Campbell has excelled in every facet of her life—as a scholar, as a public servant, as a designer of the Hoover Institution's physical structure, and as a wife and mother. I could not have been so successful in fundraising to build the Hoover Institution's endowment if she had not been at my side helping me and advising me on everything from policy to staff appointments.

Acknowledgments

IT IS NOT CUSTOMARY FOR RETIRED DIRECTORS OF INSTITUTIONS like the Hoover Institution to write such books as this. Manifestly, such work is within the province of the professional historian. In the instance, if the job fell to me, it was largely because our most qualified candidates—Peter Duignan and Dennis Bark, along with economist Martin Anderson—were unable to make time for it.

Upon deciding to undertake this project, I was helped immeasurably by the Senior Fellows and Senior Research Fellows who were appointed in the 1960s and 1970s and were directly involved in building the Hoover Institution. I want particularly to thank Martin Anderson, Dennis Bark, Richard T. Burress, Robert Conquest, the late Milorad Drachkovitch, Peter Duignan, Milton Friedman, the late Lewis Gann, Robert Hall, Alex Inkeles, Seymour Martin Lipset, George Marotta, Thomas Gale Moore, Ramon Myers, the late Stefan Possony, Alvin Rabushka, Thomas Sowell, Richard Staar, and Edward Teller.

I want also to express my appreciation to all the people who formed my support staff from the early 1980s to the present: my administrative assistant, Martha Perez, and her predecessor, Louise Doying; Robin Warfield and Janette Aut; my research assistant, Suzi Kosher; and our student assistants, Reagan Demas, Michael Korns, and Jim Graham. Their dedication and outstanding work are in no small way responsible for this book.

Origin of the Hoover Institution

A Vision of Peace

WHEN HE WAS CROSSING THE NORTH SEA LATE IN 1914, Herbert Hoover was fascinated with a book by Andrew Dickson White, famed president of Cornell University. White lamented the difficulty of studying the French Revolution because of the disappearance of contemporary documents and fugitive materials. Mr. Hoover resolved not to let this happen to the records of the vast war that had just burst forth in Europe.

Mr. Hoover, then approaching his fortieth birthday, was a highly successful engineer, not an historian. His determination to preserve the historical material was spurred by a deep, lifelong vision of peace. Admiral Lewis Strauss explains:

> Half a century ago, Mr. Hoover came to the conclusion that man's best hope of peace would be to have the lessons of previous mistakes constantly before us and never to be allowed to forget them. All other means, alliances, covenants, pacts and solemn treaties had been abortive. "I have not forgotten," he once wrote regretfully, "that my ardent support of the League of Nations and the World Court, at least as an experiment in preserving peace, had failed." What was needed was a storehouse of blueprints for peace, for while "nations can blunder into war," he said, "they cannot blunder into peace."

From that time fifty-five years ago, as Mr. Allan Hoover has told us, his father began to collect, on a worldwide basis, the original records of men and governments, even while wars and revolutions were raging. "He did not intend his growing archive to be a mausoleum of documents

1

but, on the contrary, a place of living research, where the mistakes of governments, so costly in human lives and misery, could be studied and remembered and where the courageous efforts of a few men to avert wars, would likewise never be forgotten. It is in accord with this concept of Mr. Hoover's that Glenn Campbell and his staff have so brilliantly conducted this Institution."[1]

Professor William Mosely of Columbia University, in his remarks at the same anniversary dinner, added this perspective:

> I was struck in reading back into the history of the founding of the Institution how even in the midst of World War I and of tremendous exertions for mankind, Herbert Hoover saw the need for gathering the materials, for bringing them together and making them available systematically to scholars who would endeavor to answer some of the previously unanswered questions about the past and, in that way, try to avoid some mistakes in the future.

If the "exertions for mankind" were tremendous in World War I, those of Mr. Hoover personally were extraordinary. At the invitation of the Belgian government, he headed the Committee for the Relief of Belgium, which saved millions from starvation. Baron Louis Scheyven, Belgian ambassador to the United States, was among those who had been fed as a child by Mr. Hoover's wartime relief work. The ambassador remembered, and expressed his gratitude at the dedication of the Lou Henry Hoover Building October 9, 1967:

> In 1918, from his headquarters, King Albert, my grandfather, signed a decree proclaiming President Herbert Hoover "friend of the Belgian people."
>
> This exceptional honor was conferred upon him for outstanding services. My people and I remain deeply indebted to President Hoover. Not only did he organize food relief for our long-suffering population during World War I, but he also contributed, in a very substantial way, to bringing closer together the American and Belgian educational intellectual elites.

---

1. Remarks on the occasion of the Hoover Institution's Fiftieth Anniversary Dinner, November 17, 1969. These and other quoted remarks in this section are quoted more fully in Chapter 10.

And may I add a personal word of gratitude to former President Herbert Hoover a gratitude on two counts.

During the First World War, I was a small child belonging to a large family of thirteen. And every morning, I remember receiving at school together with other millions of Belgian children a loaf of white bread, the only white bread my brothers and sisters and I would have received, would have eaten, during the First World War which lasted, as you remember, over four years. For that, especially, I am deeply grateful.

When the United States entered the war on the Allied side, Herbert Hoover returned to Washington, D.C., to serve as the U.S. food administrator for President Wilson. After the guns fell silent on November 11, 1918, Hoover became a key member of Woodrow Wilson's delegation to the Paris Peace Conference. It was then that he founded what became the Hoover Institution on War, Revolution and Peace, and personally collected one of the future Institution's most valued treasures, the Paris Peace Conference Collection. This historic letter authorized and funded the founding effort:

Paris 20 June 1919

Supreme Economic Council
Office of The Director General of Relief
Prof. E.D. Adams
Hotel Montana, Paris

Dear Prof. Adams:

This is to confirm the offer which I made to Dr. Wilbur to find $50,000 at his demand or the demand of anyone he appointed to undertake the work for the purpose of sending a representative to Europe for the collection of historical material for the Stanford University Library. This fund to be entirely at the disposal of Dr. Wilbur or his agent for any purpose of expense for purchase of documents or otherwise that will contribute to the library's strength with regard to a documentary history bearing on the war. The fund is available at any time on demand.

Faithfully yours,
Herbert Hoover

Mr. Hoover's vision of a collection of contemporary materials on World War I, housed in a library at Stanford University, his beloved alma mater, became a reality as soon as practicable after the war, in 1919. It was realized first through his personal enterprise and later through a cooperative effort with Stanford faculty and friends, and with agents throughout Europe. Here began the Hoover Institution, and in the next seventy-five years it would become the preeminent national and international research library in the United States for the study of twentieth-century political, social, and economic affairs.

Hoover Institution Purposes and Principles

The mission of the Hoover Institution was set forth in a remarkable essay by Herbert Hoover himself, in 1959, forty years after he had founded it. The Institution was at the time under threat of reorganization or takeover, which Mr. Hoover vehemently opposed. He set forth his case in these plain words:

> During this century there developed forces and events which, as never before in our national life, have had so profound an effect on our independence, our form of government, our social and economic system, and the setting of the American people in the international world.
>
> Here in this Institution is the greatest amassing of the records of these forces and events, which exist in the world. Its upbuilding and preservation have become doubly precious to the world because of the wholesale destruction of libraries and historical material during the Second World War. Over fifty organizations and sixty nations have contributed to the building up of this two score millions of documents, books, and items covering the two great wars and their aftermaths.
>
> Here are the records of the causes of war, their destructions, and their consequences to mankind.
>
> Here are unique military records which have and can contribute to the defense of the United States.
>
> Here are the records of nations striving for independence and constitutional protection of the liberties of men.
>
> Here are the records of men's strivings, their ideals, and their negotia-

tions and failures to make and sustain peace in the world from these two world wars.

And here are the documents which record the great drama of superlative sacrifice, of glory, of victory, of sorrow, of death, which inspired the idealism of men in both the making of war and the hopes of peace.

Here are also the most complete existing records of revolutions to Communism, Nazism, Socialism, aggressive nationalism, the concentration of power in governments, their reduction of men to slavery, their denial of government by their people, their denial of the dignity of the individual man, and their destruction of the foundations of religious beliefs through atheism and agnosticism.

And here are the records of the lowest of trickery and conspiracies to overthrow the governments of free men and the repeated violations of promise and agreements.

Before the purposes of the Institution can be summarized, there must be some review of the purposes of the American people which must be sustained by this Institution. It scarcely needs to be stated that this Institution supports the Constitution of the United States, its Bill of Rights, and its method of representative government.

Both our social and economic systems are based on private enterprise from which springs initiative and ingenuity. Freedom in our economic system is limited by provision of law that there shall not be hurt to others through harmful monopoly or unfair competition.

But the American system goes far beyond the provisions of the Constitution and laws. Our people hold concepts of voluntary and cooperative associations far beyond the range of government.

In the social and intellectual advancement of our people, such associations contribute great institutions devoted to religious, educational, and scientific purposes; they provide for the sick, the aged, and the dependent children. In the economic field, our associational activities create skills and the diffusion of knowledge among the people. Ours is a system where the Federal Government should undertake no governmental, social or economic action, except where local government or the people cannot undertake it for themselves.

A purpose of this Institution is to support these great associational activities.

The purpose of the Institution must be, by its research and publications, to demonstrate the evils of the doctrines of Karl Marx whether Communism, Socialism, economic materialism, or atheism thus to protect the American way of life from such ideologies, their conspiracies, and to reaffirm the validity of the American system.

The overall mission of this Institution is, from its records, to recall the voice of experience against the making of war, and by the study of these records and their publication to recall man's endeavors to make and preserve peace and to sustain for America the safeguards of the American way of life.

This Institution is not, and must not be, a mere library. But with these purposes as its goal, the Institution itself must constantly and dynamically point the road to peace, to personal freedom, and to the safeguards of the American system.

And finally, among the many other materials in the Hoover Archives is the record of the compassion of the American people, who, by self-denial and long hours of labor, provided the margins of food, medicines, and clothing which, in the wars of the present century, have enabled over one billion, four hundred million human beings to survive who otherwise would have perished.

These principles I share, with few quibbles and no reservations. They are, however, not infrequently regarded with scorn or disgust from the other side of the ideological barricades. In enclaves of the political left, political correctness is in and academic freedom is out. Thus, relations between Stanford and the Hoover Institution have often been strained in recent decades, sometimes with costly damage.

Herbert Hoover took a nonconformist, conservative view, which also retains influence at the university. Stanford Associates is an organization founded by a small group of Stanford supporters in 1934. By 1953 its numbers had grown to nearly six hundred, and it had created the Uncommon Man degree to honor those who have given unique and outstanding service to Stanford. (The university does not grant honorary degrees.) The Associates' degree acquired its name from one of the most widely quoted statements ever made by President Hoover. Rejecting the popular "cult of the Common Man," he said: ". . . most people are holding fast to an essential fact in American life. We believe in equal opportunity for all, but we know that this includes the opportunity to rise in leadership—in other words, to be uncommon."

The Hoover Institution is the home of the uncommon scholar. In witness, I was delighted to hire the late Sidney Hook, gentlemanly and scholarly expositor of John Dewey and Karl Marx. Professor Hook later on touched me and yes, surprised me with these kind words:

> Glenn Campbell's achievements represent one of the highest peaks of educational statesmanship in modern times. He has transformed a modest research and archival institution into an internationally famous center for the incubation of seminal ideas in the area of social thought.
>
> Glenn will probably be surprised to hear me say, and there are others on the Stanford faculty who will be even more surprised, that his accomplishments are a consequence of his faithfulness to the highest liberal traditions of the past. Never concealing his own conservative allegiance, he has nevertheless taken as his primary criterion of eligibility for membership in the Hoover Institution family, intellectual excellence. Glenn has been far more faithful to the philosophy of Justice Holmes and its stress on the importance of a free market in ideas than have his detractors.[2]

The Work

The story of my life intertwines with that of the building of the Hoover Institution on War, Revolution and Peace.

The Hoover Institution was founded on the campus of Stanford University on June 20, 1919. Still centrally located on the campus, the Institution now is housed in three buildings: the Hoover Tower, the Lou Henry Hoover Memorial, and the Herbert Hoover Federal Memorial. At the start of my directorship, only the Hoover Tower had been built. Most of its 96,000 square feet of space housed library stacks and archives, and the building as a whole badly needed renovation.

We completed that work in the mid-1960s, but the need for additional space was already pressing. Over the next several years that need was met. In October 1967 the Lou Henry Hoover Building was dedicated,

---

2. Letter to Emil Mosbacher, Jr., with regrets at being unable to attend a celebration of the 25th Anniversary of my directorate at the Hoover Institution, July 18, 1984.

and in July 1978 the Herbert Hoover Federal Memorial. Between the two a courtyard consisting of two small pavilions created a unified complex. These two newer buildings together house a library devoted to political, economic, and social change in the twentieth century. It is used by Stanford students and faculty, resident Hoover scholars and staff, and scholars from throughout the world who come to consult its outstanding collections of works on Africa, the Middle East, East Asia, Eastern Europe, Russia, Latin America, North America, and Western Europe. In 1998 dollars the Lou Henry Hoover Building would cost approximately $30 million and the Herbert Hoover Memorial $30 million.

The International Studies Program, the Domestic Studies Program, and the National Security Affairs Program sponsored by the Hoover Institution publish both the results of basic research and current public policy analyses by economists, political scientists, sociologists, educators, lawyers, and historians. The National, Peace, and Public Affairs programs each year recognize the work of promising young scholars and provide them with the opportunity for advanced postdoctoral research. Journalists selected as Media Fellows are also invited to spend time at the Hoover Institution.

Out of all this research come seminars, conferences, books, journal articles, lectures, interviews, and magazine articles. Hoover staff members also give expert testimony to congressional committees, consult with departments and agencies of the federal government, and engage in a wide variety of other public service activities. Some scholars are jointly appointed to the Hoover Institution and Stanford University—or another university—and they teach courses, offer seminars, and direct Ph.D. dissertations.

Scholars in most academic research settings must devote much time and energy to writing grant applications. This struck me as a less-than-optimum use of their time and energy, so during my years as director, Hoover scholars rarely had to concern themselves with obtaining grants. As a result, they had more time for scholarly pursuits and for sharing their ideas through essays, opinion pieces, and editorials written for widely read newspapers and magazines.

In 1960 three or four scholars served on the Hoover Institution's staff, and we were publishing one or two books a year. By 1989 the staff boasted one hundred scholars in addition to fifteen or twenty National,

Peace, and Public Affairs Fellows in residence, twenty or so visiting scholars, and half a dozen Media Fellows receiving Hoover grants. More than twelve hundred scholars from forty states and as many foreign nations used our library and archives, and we published about twenty-five books a year.

In 1989, my last year as director, Hoover generated more than five hundred op-ed articles. These appeared in the *New York Times, Los Angeles Times, Chicago Tribune, Wall Street Journal, Washington Post, San Francisco Chronicle, San Jose Mercury, USA Today,* and the *International Herald-Tribune;* in major newspapers in Great Britain, Germany, France, Italy, Japan, and other Far Eastern nations; in a variety of publications in the countries of Africa; and in such prestigious journals as *Foreign Affairs.* The combined circulation of these publications was over sixty-five million.

When this op-ed outreach started in the mid-1970s under the direction of Research Fellow George Marotta, only about a dozen such essays were printed each year. Along with this phenomenal increase in publication, more and more Senior Fellows and staff members were invited to appear on radio and television discussion shows. These articles and appearances bring our research results to the attention of the average reader and viewer, and provide a forum for our scholars' views of current public policy issues. The Hoover scholars themselves deserve the credit for their energy and dedication in this endeavor.

I believe that the success of the Hoover Institution can largely be attributed to a competition of ideas. Of course, it resulted in strong differences of opinion among our scholars, and the Senior Commons Room was the scene of many heated disagreements and discussions. This was healthy, for an atmosphere of mutual respect prevailed, and out of strong views, many new understandings and insights were forged.

At Stanford, however, the Donald Kennedy administration took a very different approach. Kennedy was a pioneer in the movement toward "political correctness," and under his aegis notably few Hoover scholars—no matter the excellence of their credentials—were invited to teach at Stanford. This was particularly true in the departments of history and political science, but it extended even to the department of philosophy in the case of the world-renowned and world-class philosopher Sidney Hook. Indeed, this quarantine continues to be applied to Robert Conquest,

Milton Friedman, and Edward Teller, whose ideas are presumably considered contagious.

The Director's Role

I came to the Hoover Institution as its director on January 1, 1960. For the previous six years I had been research director of the American Enterprise Association (AEA). In that capacity I had worked with a number of scholars on the AEA's advisory board: Charles C. Abbott of the Harvard Business School, later first dean of the Darden School, the University of Virginia's graduate school of business; Milton Friedman of the University of Chicago; Herrell de Graff of Cornell; Gottfried Haberler of Harvard; Stanley Parry of Notre Dame; and David McCord Wright of the University of Virginia. I had also collaborated in various ways with Felix Morley, former president of Swarthmore College (and editor of the *Washington Post* in the 1930s); Roscoe Pound, former dean of the Harvard Law School; Karl Brandt of the Food Research Institute at Stanford; Earl Butz of Purdue; Edward Chamberlin of Harvard; Gregg Lewis of the University of Chicago; Raymond Moley of *Newsweek;* and Roger Freeman, who prepared studies for us.

From my experience with these scholars, I knew that if their research was to remain innovative, useful, and policy-oriented, I had to work for them rather than attempt to direct their activity. Good self-starter scholars do not need supervision. At the Hoover Institution, I extended this same freedom to our curators and librarians. I did not, for example, guide or second-guess the curators' decisions about additions to our collections. The result was an atmosphere of collegiality that I hope Hoover will always retain. If a director favors—or appears to favor—any particular discipline or any specific area of collecting, the staff and the scholars may find themselves drawn into factions jealous of one another's perquisites and pay.

I defined as my primary functions the acquisition and provision of funds to support the work of the Institution, and the selection of the finest scholars, curators, and librarians. Management by objective was my general style, modeled on the approach made famous by William Hewlett and David Packard in building the Hewlett-Packard Company.

In practical terms this meant that I would meet—usually once a year, sometimes every two years—with key Senior Fellows and curators who had imagination and good ideas. We would agree on our objectives for the coming year and for the next several years, and I would present those objectives to the other Senior Fellows, the Senior Research Fellows, and the Research Fellows. I'd answer any questions, entertain suggestions, and then get out of their way and concentrate on fundraising while they set about implementing the objectives. Thus, as we tended to our diverse employments, we pulled together to develop a new vitality for the Hoover Institution.

2
From a Canadian Farm
to Washington, D.C.

I HAD BEEN DIRECTOR OF THE HOOVER INSTITUTION FOR TWENTY years when Ronald Reagan was elected president—a triumph for the conservative ideas he expounded so ably as well as for himself. It was thus an emotional moment when, early in 1981, President-elect Reagan rose to address the Institution's Board of Overseers and their guests at the Sheraton-Carlton Hotel in Washington, D.C.:

> Hoover's excellence has emerged in large part because of Glenn Campbell. It is he who has worked so hard and planned so well. It is he who has maintained such high standards of academic excellence in finding the best scholars available. It is he who has worked to provide a challenging and stimulating environment in which superior scholarship can take place. It is he who has raised the financial resources necessary to develop a fine research institution. And, it is he who has effectively and fairly administered this "brightest star" in the constellation of think tanks.

This was heady stuff, and as I listened I could not help thinking what a long way it was from a Canadian farm in Lobo Township, Middlesex County, Ontario, to that hotel ballroom.

Undoubtedly I got some of my ideas about organization early. Large families have to maintain order and I was the youngest of seven children, coming along on April 29, 1924, and christened Wesley Glenn. I had four brothers named Milton John, Alfred Duncan, Graham Stuart, and Edwin Bruce, and two sisters, Marjorie Grace and Evelyn Blanche. My father's name was Alfred (Red Alf) Edwin Campbell. Mother's was Delia, *nee* O'Brien.

13

Mother was a remarkable and hard-working woman. She bore seven living children and had at least one miscarriage that I know of when she had to have an emergency appendectomy about 1908. In those days this was dangerous and very painful surgery, and patients frequently did not survive. She nearly had another miscarriage in May 1921, when my grandfather Campbell committed suicide as a result of unbearable headaches (probably a brain tumor). In the aftermath of his death, my mother pitched in to help with the harvest on my grandfather's farm, and she fell and broke her ankle. Nevertheless, my sister Evelyn survived and was born normally.

My brother Graham was born about three months prematurely. Although his organs were developed, he weighed only about three or four pounds. At that time doctors gave premature infants little chance of survival, especially when they were born at home, as Graham was. My mother told me she would sit up with him all night, keeping him warm and placing poultices on his chest to keep his lungs clear. She brought him through, and he lived to be seventy.

My own earliest memories are all happy ones. My father was a good farmer. Shortly after my birth he bought the larger, 150-acre McCready farm on the fifth concession. (For American readers, a concession is a subdivision of a township in the province of Ontario.) This he added to the 60 acres across the road that he'd bought about 1920 and the 50-acre farm about a mile away on the same concession where my brothers and sisters and I were born. The "50" was bought about 1906, when my mother and father were married. After their marriage they built a new house to replace the existing log house. In 1912 or 1913 they had a one-day barn raising in which, by custom, all their neighbors helped. The outhouse at the "50" was a "three-holer" with a small hole in the middle for little children. That certainly came in handy for the six little Campbells!

About 1925, our family moved to the McCready farm, which had a large brick house and much larger barns and implement sheds. Since the telephone line ran that far, we also had a party-line telephone. But like our previous home, the McCready house lacked indoor plumbing and running water. We took baths every Saturday night in a movable tub filled with water heated on the wood-burning stove in the kitchen. The outhouse was a "two-holer" next to some lilacs, which bloomed profusely in the spring—and which gave my mother an abundant supply of switches to punish naughty children.

I fondly remember the 1927 Model T Ford my father drove and accompanying my eldest brother Milton as he drove the horse and cutter on winter trips to the "50" where I was born. He went there to feed and water the cattle, and he always gave me a task to do—something like pushing straw though a trap door, even though, being very small, I was not good at it. My sisters tell me that my father bought his first Model T in 1922 and drove it through my mother's flower garden in front of the house at the "50," all the while hollering "Whoa." Drivers' licenses were not required in those days.

By 1930, about the time I began school, electric lighting had been installed in the house and barn, and the Model T was replaced by a Model A. Later, my father installed water in the barn for the cattle and other livestock, but none in the house for Campbells. A cistern under the house caught water from rain or melting snow for baths and laundry. Drinking water came from a pump attached to the windmill. Either my mother or one of the children would fill a pail and carry it to the house. As far as my father was concerned, this arrangement was completely adequate. It was not until March 1942, after his death of a stroke at the age of sixty-four, that the house finally got running water.

The back of the farm bordered on a wood (we called it a *bush*) consisting mostly of maples and beech trees, plus a few ash and poplars. Around the first of March when the sap started to run in the maples, we tapped them and hung buckets to collect the sap. At least once a day, the sap was collected and poured into barrels on a large sled drawn by two horses. It was then taken to a homemade brick oven where the sap boiled to reduce it to syrup. The thick liquid was put in cans and taken to the house to be finished—"sugared off"—by my mother on a stove in the woodshed. We children loved to make sweet maple-sugar cakes with farm-fresh eggs and butter, but I doubt that they were good for our cholesterol count. Of course, neither were the bacon and eggs we had every morning for breakfast, after we'd eaten our porridge.

I attended School Section Number 2 (sometimes known as the Gold Creek School), a one-room country school about half a mile from our home. Our teacher, Sarah Evans, taught all eight grades. My brothers and sisters and I always walked to school, summer or winter—no matter how high the snowdrifts were. Each morning before classes began, we stood and repeated the Lord's Prayer. When I came to the United States and became a citizen, I was puzzled as to why some people considered praying in school to be such a controversial constitutional issue.

Having all eight grades together was an advantage, because students could listen to what was being taught to the next grade and thus skip grades if they were so inclined. By the time I was ten, I was in seventh grade, and I could undoubtedly have passed the high school entrance exam by the time I was eleven. However, my mother and father were very anxious for me to win the medal given by the local member of the Canadian Parliament to the student who received the highest high school entrance grade in Middlesex County. I studied hard, passed with the best grades, and received the J. C. Elliott Medal in June 1936, just after my twelfth birthday. My sister Evelyn had won the medal two years earlier.

At the end of the school year, we always attended the Poplar Hill picnic along with students from several other elementary schools in Lobo Township. During the morning and early afternoon, we competed in various games. I usually did well in the running races, the three-legged race, and the find-your-shoe race. The last year I participated—when I was twelve—I won four dollars, largely because I won the eleven-to-thirteen race and placed second to Cecil Guest (who later became a good friend) in the thirteen-and-over race. Hot dogs and ice cream cones cost about five cents apiece; that was a small fortune, but I had money left over for my savings account at the Bank of Montreal. Later in the afternoon there was a baseball game, usually Coldstream against Strathroy, and in the evening a variety show. Until I started to go to movies on occasional Saturday nights, this was the event of the year for me.

Like most farm families, we had dogs. Our fox terrier slept behind the kitchen stove in the winter to keep warm. He was a pleasant dog, and we liked playing with him, but my mother was given to remarks like, "Get that flea-bitten dog off my couch!" When Sport was about sixteen—eighty to ninety in human terms—he was killed by a bigger dog in a fight over a female. He was replaced by a collie puppy, which one of us named Snort. As Snort grew older, his favorite sport was chasing the cars that passed on the gravel road. One day when he was fully grown and about five or six years old, we were playing on the front lawn and heard what sounded like a car. "Sic 'em!" we urged Snort. Unfortunately, that sent Snort into the path of a truck, which ran over him and killed him instantly. After that we had no more dogs on the farm while I lived there.

Until we were about fifteen my mother and father insisted that we all attend Sunday school and the subsequent church service at the local Presbyterian church in Komoka, Ontario. We also took part in all the various activities typical of farm children of my generation. In 1932, with my mother's guidance, I won the Timothy Eaton Trophy for the best flowers, fruits, vegetables, pies, and other exhibits at the September Lobo Township Fair in Poplar Hill. In 1938, with my brother Edwin's help, I had the best baby beef steer at the Ilderton Fair. In 1940 my partner Archie Crawford and I won the Inter-County (Province of Ontario) Trophy for judging beef cattle in a competition staged at the Ontario Agricultural College in Guelph. We also won a medal for judging swine. The County agriculture representative, W. K. Riddle, was very helpful to all of us boys in these and other farm-related matters.

Every year at Lobo Continuation School, we had a "field day," an athletic meeting with two nearby high schools, Ailsa Craig and Ilderton. In 1938 I won the Junior Championship Cup for boys fifteen years of age and under. I did particularly well in the 100-yard dash; the long jump; the hop, skip, and jump; and the three-person relay race. During the winter the Gold Creek Community Club held a meeting at the school about once a month. We sang sentimental songs about life's pleasures and sorrows. One I remember in particular included the line, "When the dawn comes over the cowshed, I'll be seeing Nellie home." We began each meeting by singing "God Save the King" and ended it with "Auld Lang Syne." During the meeting there was always a reading or a skit or two. Each year some of the meetings were given to production of and rehearsals for a play that the older, unmarried members put on about the end of March. The club also took up collections for presents for newly married members. When Rita Ricardo and I got married in 1946, club members sent us a check for twenty-five dollars, along with their best wishes for our future happiness.

When you live close to nature, springtime is special—the more so after the long northern winter. Every spring for many years my good friend Arthur McLaughlin and I got up early and went "birding"—counting how many birds had returned from the south. From age eight to about fifteen I rode horseback, using an English saddle, from our farm to the McLaughlin farm. On Saturday nights we frequently visited my brother Edwin's friend Kenneth Livingston.

Spring on the farm fascinated me because it was then that turkeys, ducklings, and goslings were hatched, and calves and lambs were born. In some years, one of the mares might foal. In the spring, too, the sheep were driven to a "sheep dip" so that the ticks, which had accumulated during the previous year, could be killed. Then the animals were sheared of their wool, and the curly crop was sold to a wool merchant.

In summer, when our work was finished, my brother and I, along with the neighbor boys, frequented the swimming hole in Gold Creek. This "pool" was formed by damming the creek so that it formed a very small lake about five feet deep. In the wintertime we skated and played hockey on frozen ponds. On Sundays, the only non-work day of the week, we played baseball in a pasture, with stones or pieces of wood serving as bases.

Once we turned five or six, my father would give us boys various tasks—hoeing potatoes, corn, turnips, and mangels; picking potato bugs; cleaning the stables; driving the horses; and helping load and mow the hay, oats, barley, and wheat. I also helped my mother care for her vegetable garden and flowers. Canadian Thanksgiving Day (in the middle of October) was a school holiday, but we'd spend the whole day digging potatoes, with a noon break for Thanksgiving dinner. By the end of the day those of us who were still in school, and not doing heavy manual labor regularly, had aching backs.

My mother raised turkeys, and as the youngest boy, I was required to help. I enjoyed the job. At Christmastime mother killed them, plucked them, and sold them in the marketplace in London. From the sale of the turkeys she made enough money to buy Christmas presents for all of us, plus enough for our shoes and clothes for the upcoming year. Each New Year's Day we feasted on a goose my mother had raised for the traditional New Year's dinner. I also raised rabbits and sold them at the London market as pets for city children.

From the time I was five till I was fifteen, I helped drive the cattle from the farm barns to pasture in the spring and then back to the farm barns in the late autumn when the snow started to fall. For many years we took them about ten or twelve miles to pasture them on an Indian reservation at Muncie, Ontario. In August we drove the grass-fattened steers and heifers about five miles to a place where they were weighed and loaded on trucks to go to the slaughterhouse in London. On most Saturdays my parents sold farm produce at the London market—potatoes, eggs, ducks, chickens, and my baby rabbits, along with turkeys at Thanksgiving and Christmas, and geese just before the New Year.

In 1932 or 1933 my father bought my brother Duncan a used Model A Ford with a rumble seat so that he and my eldest brother Milton could stop fighting over who would get the car for their dates. In September 1934 Duncan became the first male in the family to get married. His bride was Irene Sutherland of Komoka, and at threshing time, August 1935, my first nephew, Ronald Campbell, was born at the "50," where Duncan and Irene were living.

That same year (1935) my father bought a Ford V8 and gave the Model A to Milton, who was about to marry Janet McCallum, a nurse. My father also helped Milton purchase a hundred-acre farm on the seventh concession. Three years later my father received such a good offer that the Ford V8 was traded in for a 1938 six-cylinder Chevrolet, the car for which I got my first driver's license at fourteen. This was also the car that the family drove during World War II and for several years afterward while new cars were still unavailable because of pent-up demand and decreased production during the war.

In the fall of 1936 I entered the Lobo Continuation School, about five miles from our farm. In the fall and spring I drove a horse and buggy, and in winter a cutter (a one-horse sleigh) equipped with bells for the horse. Evelyn rode with me the first year, and so did the local cheese-maker's daughter, Ruby Shellington. The horse was part mustang mare from western Canada, and one of my brothers had named her Ruby. Like my brother Edwin (Bill) before me, I enjoyed racing other horses—especially in the winter.

By 1937 only Evelyn and I were left at home, and the following year she left to attend the London Central Collegiate Institute for fifth form (more or less the Canadian equivalent of the first year of college in the United States). In the fall of 1938 Campbell Fletcher, Rena Henderson, and I drove to school together. By combining the third and fourth forms, I was able to graduate at the age of fifteen.

Readers may wonder why I have not mentioned the Great Depression. The answer is simple enough: it didn't really affect us. My mother and father abhorred debt. By 1930 the mortgage on the McCready farm was paid off and all the farms were free of debt. To stay out of debt, my father always paid cash for new cars or farm machinery, or for improvements to the barns or houses. He sometimes borrowed from the bank in the fall to buy "feeder cattle," but the loan was always paid off the next year when the cattle were sold. On a family farm it is easy to see the connection between one's own knowledge and labor and the success of the enterprise—you literally reap what you sow. My father was a good farmer, and our land was good. We had no great problems.

These lessons were made plain one evening in the early 1930s when my father came home and told us that the bank was foreclosing on a neighbor's farm. He was sympathetic, but realistic. "He never was a very good farmer," father said. "I think he'll do better as a tenant farmer with someone telling him what to do."

In the fall of 1939 I entered the London Central Collegiate Institute in London, Ontario. Like my two sisters before me, I boarded in London during the week and came home on weekends. I had a heavy course load that first year to cover all the required areas. Fortunately, I got straight As, so I did not have to take the finals administered by the Ontario Department of Education.

The University of Western Ontario

In the fall of 1940, when I was sixteen, I entered the University of Western Ontario in London. I was lucky, because all my brothers had had to go to work on the farm after graduation from high school. This was particularly unfortunate in the case of my eldest brother, Milton, who was both a good athlete and a good student at Mt. Brydges High School. My next eldest brother, Edwin (Bill), did return to college after farming for about ten years and received a degree in veterinary medicine. Unfortunately, he died of leukemia a few years later, in the fall of 1955.

My father did not believe in sending girls to college, so my sisters Marjorie and Evelyn went to the London Central Collegiate Institute, then to the London Normal School to become elementary schoolteachers. My mother was delighted because she had always wanted to become a schoolteacher. Evelyn, with her straight A record at the London Central Collegiate Institute, could have done very well at the University of Western Ontario, but there was no way to convince my father that he should pay for a daughter to go to college. Had she gone, I am sure that she would have had a brilliant career in whatever field she chose. Instead, both she and Marjorie married successful Ontario farmers.

When I entered the University of Western Ontario in 1940, all freshmen were interviewed by the registrar, Dr. K. P. R. Neville. He gave me two pieces of wise advice which I remember to this day. The first was that figures do not lie, but liars can figure. The second was that there were three things most male students at Western did in those days. One was study and get good grades, the second was have a good time—which meant parties and girls—and the third was participate in athletics. He said that a young man could do two of these and do them well, but not all three. When I first enrolled at Western, I was hoping to qualify for a Rhodes scholarship at Oxford, which would require considerable attention to athletics. However, Rhodes scholarships were canceled for the duration of World War II, so I concentrated on my studies—plus parties and girls. I also joined the debate team, and in my senior year I was elected president of the Economics Club and treasurer of my fraternity.

The summer after my freshman year was the last one I spent on the farm. I was seventeen. As in the three preceding summers, I did a man's work under my father's stern tutelage. He was a great organizer, leader, and delegator. (Years later, when I was director of the Hoover Institution, I realized from whom I had inherited these talents.) In late August and early September I toiled at picking tobacco leaves to earn extra spending money. It was terribly dirty, sticky work, and it left me determined to find an easier way to make money.

In March 1942 my father died of a stroke. His will was a typical farmer's will, made out by the one lawyer in the nearby town of Strathroy. My legacy consisted of enough money to complete my education, plus one thousand dollars.

My second year of college like the first, went well academically. As summer approached a fellow student named Don Evans invited me to be his assistant at his summer job. He worked at the bar of a pleasure boat, a paddle wheeler named the S. S. *Kingston,* whose home port was Toronto. It traveled Lake Ontario to the port of Rochester on the U.S. side, on to Kingston, and down the St. Lawrence River all the way to Cornwall on the Canadian side. Don was a reserve officer in the Canadian Officers Training Corps (COTC), in which I was a corporal. He was about twenty-two and thus old enough to work in a bar, and though I was only eighteen, I looked old enough and no one questioned me. I made enough money that summer (between $500 and $600) to buy nice clothes, to live at my fraternity house (Alpha Kappa Psi) and to enjoy student life.

By then I was majoring in economics and political science with a minor in history. My principal professors in economics and political science were Dr. Mark K. Inman (a Harvard Ph.D.), Dr. Walter B. Harvey (a Chicago Ph.D.), and Col. Edward Reilly, who had an M.A. from Chicago but had never finished his dissertation. I also had three very fine history professors: Dr. Albert Dorland, the chairman of the department, who taught modern European history; Prof. Fred Landon, who taught an excellent course on U. S. history; and Dr. James Talman, who taught Latin American history.

In the fall of 1942, because of the war, there was a shortage of harvest labor in western Canada. Able-bodied young men—despite the fact that it was the middle of the fall semester—were encouraged to volunteer, so several of my fraternity brothers and I took the train west. It was the first long trip I had ever taken, and it was exciting to travel through northern Ontario, see Winnipeg and Manitoba, and finally end up in northern Saskatchewan. From there we were dispatched by train to Cut Knife, where the famous Canadian rebel, Louis Riel, made his last stand in 1883. Riel, part French and part Indian, was a skilled commander who had completely overpowered the legendary Royal Canadian Mounted Police and the local militia. He was finally defeated by British regular troops sent west to quash the revolt. My father was five at the time and remembered watching the troop train go west from the family farm in Caradoc Township.

My companions and I were sent about three miles outside of town, to a farm owned by a man named Dan, who had moved there from North Dakota. I think he was the most pessimistic man I ever knew. *Everything* was against him, including the weather and the Indians. My two fraternity brothers, Bill Buggs and Cameron Phillips, and I worked along with the regular farmhands. We worked for six days, loading oats onto a wagon drawn by two horses and hauling the load to the threshing machine, which separated the oats from the straw.

The Indians refused to work on the seventh day, Sunday, for fear of offending the "Great Spirit," so Dan and the three of us worked all day Sunday harvesting oats. When we woke up Monday morning, it was snowing. The Indians simply said, "We told you so." We stayed for the rest of the week, usually walking into Cut Knife Creek during the day (the main attraction there was the mill owner's daughter, Esther Bradburn) and returning before the evening meal. When the snow continued to fall for several days, we collected our pay and returned to London.

Back at Western, I switched from the COTC to the University Naval Officers Training Division (UNTD). In May of 1943, as soon as the spring semester was completed we were sent to HMCS *Deepbrook* in Nova Scotia. Soon after we arrived, they sent us out rowing a lifeboat with only the little sailors' hats to protect us from the sun and salt air. Being light-complexioned, I ended up with a severe case of sunstroke. I might actually have died that evening without the careful attention of Dr. Cram. The MD was the older brother of Jack Cram, a classmate of mine who was also in the UNTD, and he looked after me closely all night in the base infirmary as my fever rose to 106 degrees. At last it broke. I remember only two things about that night—feeling so sick I wished to die, and overhearing Dr. Cram tell the nurse to watch me carefully because if the fever did not break within half an hour, I might get my wish.

I had a recurrence of sunstroke in the late spring or early summer of 1947, when I neglected to wear a hat while playing golf at Harvard with my friend Robert Baldwin. I went to the doctor's office where I passed out and had convulsions while he was examining me. He admitted me to Mount Auburn Hospital in Cambridge where he did a spinal tap to check for spinal meningitis. I was then only recently married, and my very worried wife, Rita, hardly slept that night. Not until about midnight, when I was visited by a young intern, did I remember my previous bout with sunstroke. The intern said, "That's it!" and no one took any further interest in me. I was discharged the next day, but because of the spinal tap it took me about a week to get my sense of balance back. Only years later did I discover just how serious these episodes really were. I mentioned them during a medical examination for insurance purposes, and in answer to my question, the doctor said the fatality rate for such severe cases of sunstroke in the spring of 1943 was about 60 percent.

In early June 1943 I got a call from my fraternity brother Bob Davis suggesting that we go west to work on the Alaska highway. (Davis claimed to be a descendant of Jefferson Davis, the president of the Confederacy, who had taken refuge in Toronto after the defeat of the South in the Civil War.) On the westbound train Bob met a man who invited us to stay at his home in Edmonton on our way northwest to cross the Peace River. We accepted the invitation and spent a day or two visiting the capitol and the beautiful campus of the University of Alberta on the banks of the North Saskatchewan River.

After we reached the town of Dawson Creek, we crossed the Peace River—still close to flood tide in mid-June—on a raft attached to cables. We then proceeded by truck to our assigned positions. I was placed at Mile 159 (in British Columbia, 159 miles northwest of the Peace River crossing), and Davis was stationed about fifteen to twenty miles farther on. We were employed by the U.S. Public Roads Administration, so this was the first time I received a paycheck from the U.S. government. I was given a beginner's job of rear chainman on a survey team, which meant that after reaching the proper spot, I drove in a stake with a sledgehammer to mark the spot before we moved on.

We worked all summer in a cloud of dust thrown up by the trucks carrying gravel for the road. As a result I developed a dust allergy that persists to this day. We were so far north that darkness fell only between 1 or 2 AM and 5 AM. We played a lot of bridge and poker after dinner to fill those bright evening hours. Finally the summer ended and we left Mile 159, riding in the back of an empty truck to the Peace River crossing, then boarding a train to return to London.

The previous spring I had applied for admission to law school at Osgood Hall in Toronto and had been accepted. When I returned to London, however, I decided to spend my fourth year at the University of

Western Ontario, so I requested and got a refund of my $25 admission fee. Former Treasury Secretary William E. Simon told me a few years ago that *not* becoming a Canadian lawyer was one of the three good decisions I made in my life. The second was getting my Ph.D. at Harvard—because that's where I met and married Rita Ricardo. The third was becoming the director and builder of the Hoover Institution. Mr. Simon was kind enough to add that most people are lucky if they make *one* good decision in their lives.

I had an excellent and enjoyable fourth year at Western and graduated with honors in economics and political science. By March 1944, I was nineteen and facing military service. In Canada both the air force and navy were volunteer services, but I had earlier been turned down by the air force. Only the army drafted people, so I decided to volunteer for the paratroopers. On March 17 I was examined at Woollesly Barracks and rejected for poor eyesight. (This was well before the June 1944 D-Day landings in Normandy.) Shortly after that I resigned from the navy because my poor eyesight would have precluded sea duty, and I prepared for graduation in late May. Had I been accepted by the paratroopers, I would have arrived overseas in the fall of 1944 in time for the disastrous campaign that Field Marshal Montgomery arrogantly mounted against the Germans at Nijmegen. In a combination of poor planning and bad luck, a number of Canadian paratroopers were dropped right in the middle of crack German divisions. The casualty rate for these paratroopers was about 60 to 70 percent. (Their story was the basis of the film *A Bridge Too Far.*)

The Harvard Years

In the meantime I had applied for acceptance to several graduate schools and for a number of fellowships. In mid-June I was accepted and received an Austin Fellowship for the summer semester at Harvard, the university from which my mentor Prof. Mark Inman had received his Ph.D. Harvard was then on a trimester system because of World War II. Soon thereafter I boarded a DC-3 for my first plane trip, traveling from London to Ottawa to visit my girlfriend Madeleine Bradley before leaving for the United States. I also hoped to get a labor exit visa. Our local member of Parliament, Robert McCubbin, had already tried to get such a visa for me and had been turned down because I was considered "essential labor" to the war effort.

McCubbin had already found me a job with the Canadian government. However, Harry Bradley, Madeleine's father, who had a fondness for beer and spirits, was a racing commissioner for the Province of Quebec. He said he could get me into the United States easily. "Your passport is in order," he told me, "and you have a permit to take U.S. currency out of the country." In his opinion, all I needed to do was take the train to Montreal. French Canadian officials would be interested only in my currency permit because that was all they had to turn in to the federal government. On the other hand, he warned, if I were unlucky and got an English official, I would have a problem. In that case, he had some friends who would get me across the St. Lawrence River at Cornwall—which, needless to say, would have been illegal.

Following Harry Bradley's advice, I'd barely gotten seated on the train and had not yet time to conceal the excess currency I was carrying when a French Canadian official strode down the aisle and asked for my passport and currency permit. I was sure he saw my excess currency, but apparently he decided that it was simpler to ignore it. He collected my currency permit, stamped my passport, said "Merci," and continued down the aisle. From then on I crossed the border several times without a problem with emigration and customs officials.

My train arrived in Boston on July 4, and I proceeded to Harvard Square in Cambridge. At first I couldn't figure out why so many banks and stores were closed, because July 1 is the national holiday in Canada. At Divinity Hall, where I was to reside, I was let in by the caretaker who informed me that it was Independence Day, but he agreed to let me into my room and give me a key since I had no other place to stay.

On July 5, 1944, Professor Burbank assigned me to a theory course with Professor Leontief, an international trade course with Professors Haberler and Harris, and a money-and-banking course, plus a reading course in the history of economic thought with Professor Schumpeter. In late July, I was waiting to see Professor Schumpeter when a very beautiful young woman with a gorgeous tan swept into his office. Professor Schumpeter arose and, in proper Viennese tradition, bowed, kissed her hand, and said, "Miss Ricardo, what can I do for you?" Their conversation lasted about half an hour while the other students and I waited our turns with varying degrees of patience.

Joseph Schumpeter was a brilliant economist and is generally rated with John Maynard Keynes as one of the two best economists of the first half of the twentieth century. In his money-and-banking course, I learned that the real, and perhaps the only, case for the gold standard is that people cannot trust governments. The gold standard prevents governments from inflating currency in order to engage in deficit spending and debt growth. Schumpeter had a wide range of interests, from literature and the arts to horseback riding to history to economics. The doctrines of Karl Marx fascinated him intellectually but he was never in any way a Marxist as some people at the University of Chicago apparently thought. He had written what I consider the best book on economics, *The Theory of Economic Development,* by the time he was thirty. The last book he completed before his death was *Capitalism, Socialism and Democracy,* in which he explained why, in his opinion, capitalism tends to self-destruct. He was basically correct in some ways, but he was wrong, as we now know, in his view that socialism and central planning could work. At the time of his death, he was working on a *History of Economic Thought,* which his wife, Dr. Elizabeth Boody Schumpeter, finished. Professor Schumpeter is reported to have said that when he was a young man he had three ambitions: to be the greatest lover in Europe, the greatest horseman, and the greatest economist in the world. Later in his life he admitted that he never became the greatest horseman.

The summer semester ended in late September. Fortunately, my grades were all As, so my fellowship was renewed for the fall semester. My courses consisted of economic history with Professor Usher, economic statistics with Professors Crum and Frickey, economic theory with Professor Haberler, and public finance with Professor Burbank, who held the David A. Wells endowed professorship. This was one of only two endowed professorships in economics at Harvard at that time. The other was the Henry Lee Professorship, made famous by Prof. F. W. Taussig, who held it for many years.

My grades were As again, so my fellowship continued for the spring semester, which consisted of the second halves of my first-semester courses. That spring I became very friendly with an older graduate student,

Raymond Bressler, who was already an associate professor at the University of Connecticut. We spent many a late afternoon in a student hangout called Cronin's, drinking beer and discussing our courses, our professors, women, and the state of the world in general.

At that point, I had a hard choice to make: Should I take all my examinations, or should I chance taking my Ph.D. orals at twenty-one? I chose the latter option. The subjects I presented were economic theory, economic history, and economic statistics (all compulsory), plus international trade. My examiners were Professor Leontief as chairman, along with Professors Crum, Usher, and Haberler. I passed, so the only exam I had to take was in public finance, for which I received an A.

That summer I took a job in the Canadian Department of Finance. There I worked for Dr. Kenneth Eaton, the assistant deputy minister of finance, and his assistant Harvey Perry. Most of our time was spent running estimates of what the postwar Canadian income tax system would yield under various assumptions of gross national product, tax rates, etc. I also carried on correspondence with Rita Ricardo, who was working on Nantucket Island as librarian of the Maria Mitchell Library. During my tenure with the Department of Finance, I met the Honorable John Bracken, leader of the Progressive Conservative party, and John Diefenbaker, a Progressive Conservative party member from Saskatchewan. Both of them urged me to return to Canada after I got my Ph.D. at Harvard and serve as an economic adviser to the Progressive Conservative party.

I returned to Harvard in September of 1945, supported by the Henry Lee Fellowship in Political Economy. The amount was $1,000, the largest fellowship the department of economics offered at that time. I had a relatively light course load and was able to spend considerable time with Rita Ricardo. Since the fall of 1944 I had been living in Adams House, a great improvement over Divinity Hall. In the winter of 1946 I became a tutor at Leverett House.

My First Trip to California

That December my good friend Alfred Nicholls, having received his Ph.D. in economics from Harvard, was returning to Los Angeles, and he invited me to accompany him in his drive across the country. Since it was winter, we took the southern route. From the Pennsylvania Turnpike, we headed west, picking up Route 66 to Los Angeles after we crossed the Mississippi River. We broke up the long trip with a few diversions, the most memorable being the Grand Canyon in all its beauty and majesty. Finally, we crossed into California and reached Nicholls' wife's home, which lay across a park from Bing Crosby's house near the UCLA campus.

In those days UCLA was, I believe, still known as the southern branch of the University of California. There were very few buildings, and Westwood was a pleasant, sleepy little village. I attended a tennis exhibition between Donald Budge and Bill Tilden, and a dinner dance on a blind date with Howard Hughes's confidential secretary, a very pleasant person who confided some of the reasons for her employer's penchant for privacy. I returned to Boston on a DC-3, which made two landings for fuel before it arrived at Logan Airport sixteen to eighteen hours after leaving Los Angeles. During the fuel stops, passengers dashed into the terminal to buy food and bring it back to the plane.

Back at Harvard

In September 1945, when I succeeded my friend Raymond Bressler as president of the Harvard Economics Club (for graduate students), Rita Ricardo was elected secretary. Early the following January Professor Burbank called me to his office and told me I was spending too much time chasing "that girl." He was going to deal with that by putting me to work teaching. He directed me to resign my fellowship and become a Teaching Fellow. I had yet to receive $500 of my fellowship money, and I suppose that today a student in this situation would sue the economics department. Anyway, at twenty-one, I became a Teaching Fellow. I mention my age only because Harvard's left wing has always made much of the fact that the English socialist Harold Laski taught at Harvard when he was twenty-one. The full-time salary for a Teaching Fellow was, I believe, either $2,500 or $3,000, and very few Teaching Fellows taught full time.

Meanwhile, Rita started teaching at Radcliffe College under a Harvard appointment. We were both working on our Ph.D. dissertations when we became engaged in March 1946. In June Rita received her Ph.D., and during the summer she worked at the Maria Mitchell Library on

Nantucket for the last time. I taught summer school at Harvard and made two or three weekend trips to see her. On September 15, Rita and I were married in Boston by a justice of the peace with Thomas Baker as my best man. My beautiful bride wore a lovely blue suit, and a corsage that I had given her. Her father gave a luncheon for us after the ceremony.

For our honeymoon we took a DC-3 to Montreal, Rita's first plane trip. As we were embarking, some of my students sent a message to the stewardess (they were not yet "flight attendants") congratulating "Dr. and Mr. Campbell" on their wedding. This greatly puzzled the stewardess, and the immigration official in Montreal. He asked me if I was in the United States for postgraduate studies (my passport was British), and I answered, "Something like that." Everyone obviously assumed that the message was wrong, that we must in fact be "Dr. and *Mrs.* Campbell."

We quickly cleared immigration and customs and proceeded to a dinner dance at the Mount Royal Hotel. We stayed there about two days, and then took a train to Komoka, Ontario, where we were met by my brother Edwin and taken to the family home on the fifth concession. My bride was warmly welcomed (perhaps to her surprise) by my mother and brothers and sisters, plus their wives, husbands, and children. Rita was also surprised that the house lacked indoor plumbing. Apparently she had never really believed my stories about the outdoor privy next to the lilacs and how it built character—particularly in winter.

Married Life at Harvard

After a few days at the farm, we returned to Harvard. Housing for married students was scarce because of the number of returning veterans, so we were very fortunate to obtain a small suite in the university-controlled Hotel Brunswick, located near Copley Square in Boston. Later we found out that we had the suite George Herman (Babe) Ruth had occupied when the New York Yankees played the Red Sox at Fenway Park in Boston. The suite consisted of a pleasant sitting room, a large bedroom, and a bathroom with a large tub and a pull-chain toilet. Although it was minimally furnished, it had no kitchen so we bought a toaster, plus a hotplate for making tea or coffee. It was my pleasure to teach my bride how to make coffee.

At the Hotel Brunswick, we would get up; dress; breakfast quickly on orange juice, toast, and coffee; then take the subway to Harvard Square. If either or both of us had a section (usually between fifteen and thirty students) of economics to teach, we went directly to the classroom. After class we sometimes met at an inexpensive local restaurant for a late breakfast of bacon and eggs. Other times, I went to Leverett House where I was a tutor and got a free lunch, while Dr. Ricardo-Campbell went to the Littauer Center Library. In the evening we ate in Harvard Square or returned to Boston for dinner. At the end of the month, if we were short of money, we skipped breakfast and had bacon and eggs for dinner at an inexpensive restaurant near the hotel.

In the fall of 1946 Rita became a Harvard instructor at an annual salary of $3,500, and she was reappointed for the fall of 1947, undoubtedly the first woman to teach economics at Harvard on a regular appointment. Meanwhile, I became a full-time Teaching Fellow at $3,000 a year. I continued to teach a section of elementary economics, and I also handled the graduate students in public finance for Professor Burbank (grading and a once-a-week section meeting) while doing the same with the undergraduates. At the same time, I mounted an all-out effort to complete my dissertation, "The Impact of Social Security Expenditures on Canadian Government Finance." I finished it in time to present it to the department of economics. The committee for my oral defense consisted of Professor Burbank, as chairman, and Profs. Dan Throop Smith and J. Keith Butters from the business school. They gave me an excellent (*summa*) and in June 1948, at the age of twenty-four, I received my Ph.D. My degree was signed by *Jacobus (James) Bryant Conant, Praesus,* and *Payson Sibley Wild, Decanus.* My MA, which I had received in 1946, was also signed by James Bryant Conant, president, and Payson Sibley Wild, dean of the Graduate School.

In the spring of 1947 we managed to get an apartment at 1716 Cambridge Street. We accomplished this in the time-honored Cambridge way—by bribing the person who oversaw the building's renting and maintenance with a payment equal to the first month's rent, in addition to the landlord's required one-month down payment. That summer, I taught summer school again while Rita spent her time decorating the apartment, learning to cook, and cleaning the apartment—all of which left her little time for research. In fall I continued as a Teaching Fellow, teaching one section three times a week and acting as an assistant in Professor Burbank's undergraduate public finance course. My duties involved meeting with students once a week and grading their papers.

I was appointed an instructor in the department of economics in the fall of 1948. Since Harvard's nepotism rules at that time did not allow a husband and wife to teach in the same department, Rita investigated jobs elsewhere, and she was offered jobs by two colleges and one university. Wellesley College offered her an instructorship at a salary of $2,700. The Brown University offer came from Chelcie Bosland, chairman of the economics department, but it was temporary—to cover the leave of a second-rate, very prolabor union professor named Philip Taft. The third offer, from Tufts College, was obviously the best—an assistant professorship in economics at a salary of $3,500, per annum, the same amount I received as an instructor at Harvard. Assistant professor was also the highest rank held by a woman on the Tufts faculty at that time. (There was a dean of women, but she did not teach.)

In early July, at my insistence, we bought a new Hudson Super Six for Rita to drive to Tufts. It cost $2,500 and used up practically all the savings she had accumulated at the Boston Five and Dime Savings Bank. On the other hand, the car lasted ten years, so I guess we got a good return on our money. Rita had taken driving lessons from me, which caused considerable tension in our marriage since she was not the best student and I was *definitely* not the most patient instructor. Nevertheless, she passed her driving test in late August 1948.

On January 14, 1949, Prof. Armen Alchian sent Rita and me the following letter:

> Dear Campbells:
>
> You may remember from our conversation at Cleveland that I said I would write you more details about UCLA as soon as they became available. They are not yet available, though I don't want to delay writing you and asking you to send us your vitae, bibliography and references from people at Harvard or Tufts. These records will of course come in handy in the process of converting some of the people here. They will also help in the attempt to see if something can be arranged for Mrs. Campbell at one of the nearby universities.

From preliminary conversations I am quite hopeful. I could almost say optimistically that something might be arranged, but until we have your letters of reference, it will be quite difficult for me to press your case.

I hope you will send the material even though you regard the probability of coming as very slight. I have no information yet about the summer possibility. My general lack of information is due not to my neglecting to try to get some, but is due rather to the inability, unwillingness, or neglect of the department to get around to making decisions.

I am glad that I had a chance to get acquainted with you in Cleveland and hope that we will be seeing more of each other in Los Angeles.

Cordially,
/s Armen Alchian/

P.S. I have delayed this letter a few (12!) days since information seemed to be precipitating from very recent developments (e.g., B. M. Anderson's death). Please send me immediately a statement of your fields of interest and also fields of training. I refuse to state to the department what they are since I may misrepresent them in my eagerness to press your case. Could I be excused for being so rude as to ask to have you send a statement immediately?

[9 hours load is maximum—pay $45–4800 assistant professor—+7% retirement—housing available—etc. etc. etc.]

In the fall of 1949, with the departure of Dr. Phillip Bradley from Harvard, I became the chief section man in the elementary economics course. A year later Rita and I moved to 27 Grozier Road in Cambridge, the small house previously occupied by the Bradleys. Rita was pleased that we at last had enough space outside to grow some flowers and vegetables (primarily marigolds, petunias, radishes, cherry tomatoes, and lettuce).

We remained at Harvard and Tufts, respectively, through 1950–51, but there were two differences for me: Prof. Arthur Smithies replaced Professor Burbank as the new chairman of the department, and, to compensate for the inflation resulting from the Korean War, my salary was increased to $4,000 per annum. In the meantime, in addition to UCLA's offer, I had received some inquiries about my availability for positions at other colleges and universities. One was from Lee Bach of the Carnegie Institute of Technology in Pittsburgh. On May 24, 1950, I replied to Professor Bach: "I have decided to remain at Harvard for another year. I wish to thank you, however, for your willingness to consider me as a candidate for a position in the Department of Economics at Carnegie."

I received the following letter, dated February 7, from George Taylor, chairman of the Economics Department at Amherst College:

> Dear Dr. Campbell:
>
> Professor Chandler and I enjoyed meeting you on our recent trip to Harvard and wonder if you would be interested to come up to Amherst some day next week to look around the place and meet the other members of our department. We should, of course, be glad to cover your expenses for such a trip. I should tell you that a decision has not yet been made as to whether we shall appoint an assistant professor or an older man at the associate professor level but for the former position you now stand at the head of the list. If under these circumstances you would care to make the trip, we should be glad to have you. One day is about as good as another for us although, probably, if it is as convenient for you, Wednesday should be avoided.

I responded promptly to Professor Taylor's invitation: "Thank you for your letter inviting me to come to Amherst College next week. I plan to make the trip next Thursday." Following that visit, on February 21, Professor Taylor wrote me that the board of trustees had surprised both him and the president by authorizing them to make an appointment at the associate professor or full professor rank. Then on April 3 he informed me that they had appointed James Nelson of Oberlin College to the position. At the time I was very disappointed, but with hindsight I know it was one of the best things that ever happened to Rita and me.

Professor Burbank died unexpectedly in February 1951, and my world changed completely. I really did not want to remain at Harvard. With the appointment of John Kenneth Galbraith as a professor and with Professor Smithies as chairman, the economics department was falling under three pernicious influences— Keynesianism, the control of Edward S. Mason, and the presence of mediocre persons Mason and Smithies appointed as assistant professors, such as Carl Kaysen and James Duesenberry.

Still, I value my time at Harvard. I had a number of students who went on to hold important positions. Perhaps the most famous was Paul Volcker, who took a graduate course in public finance from me and in the late 1970s became chairman of the Federal Reserve. In those days (1951) *summa cum laude* was an infrequently given honor. During my teaching years at Harvard, I had only one *summa cum laude* student— Phillip Areeda, who went on to the Harvard Law School, again graduated *summa cum laude,* and became a distinguished senior professor, holding the famous Langdell Chair at the Harvard Law School. Other students included William C. McConnell and Berton Steir who founded a coffee-vending business among other enterprises and subsequently became millionaires. McConnell now lives in retirement in Florida and Steir is in Boston. Both contributed to the construction of the Lou Henry Hoover Building.

In many respects, the two most important students I had in the elementary economics course were George Putnam, Jr., who is now head of the Putnam Group of Mutual Funds, and Charles Slichter, who became a professor of physics at the University of Illinois and was the senior member of the Harvard Corporation (the governing body) until June 30, 1995, when he resigned at the age of seventy.

At the U.S. Chamber of Commerce

With the help of Dr. Phillip D. Bradley and Charles Cortez Abbott of the Harvard Business School, I started to look for a position elsewhere. Because of the draft for the Korean War, enrollments were down, and there were very few positions open in the academic world. With Professor Abbott's help I prepared, for the first and, I hope, the last time, a *curriculum vitae* setting forth my qualifications and experience.

Professor Smithies apparently developed a bad conscience over the years, because Harvard let me go at a time when it was emphasizing teaching. In the *Crimson Guide for Freshmen,* I had received high ratings in both 1950 and 1951. In fact, the 1951 *Guide* gave me the highest rating possible, namely, that I was an excellent teacher with a fine sense of humor. In any event, after I had accepted Dr. Emerson P. Schmidt's offer to work as an economist at the U. S. Chamber of Commerce, I received a letter dated June 8, 1951, from Dudley Dillard, head of the Department of Economics of the College of Business and Public Administration at the University of Maryland. He inquired about my availability and said that Professor Smithies had suggested he write to me. After receiving my response, he wrote: "I was disappointed to learn that you have a previous commitment which makes it impossible for you to consider an appointment at the University of Maryland."

Professor Smithies and I crossed paths again, in 1976. I was in Washington as a member of the National Science Board, and had arranged in advance for a taxi to take me from the Cosmos Club to foundation headquarters at 18th and G Streets. When I came out for my taxi, there was Arthur Smithies, smoking his trademark smelly pipe and waiting in the rain for a taxi. I introduced myself and asked if I could give him a ride. He was going to CIA headquarters in Langley, Virginia, and my destination was on the way, so the cab took me to the foundation, I paid my share of the fare, and he went on to Langley. That night, Dennis Bark and I were holding a reception at the Cosmos Club for former National and Public Affairs Fellows located in Washington, D.C. A former National Fellow, Dr. Allan Goodman was, like Smithies, a consultant to the CIA, and he told us an interesting story. He said that Smithies told him that years ago they had done a terrible thing to me at Harvard—that is, they had let me go for political reasons. I asked Goodman to tell Smithies the next morning that I was well aware of their outrageous behavior at the time, but that, as it turned out, getting kicked out of Harvard into the real world was probably the best thing that ever happened to me. Without that, I would probably never have become director of the Hoover Institution, a Reagan-appointed regent of the University of California, and a Nixon appointee to the National Science Board, nor would I have had so many other opportunities for public service. I might even have ended up as an insular, snobbish, liberal Harvard professor.

Clearly, political correctness was already alive at our leading universities in the 1940s and the 1950s. Considerable evidence exists that it began in the 1920s and 1930s. In those days it was primarily ideological. In the late 1980s and early 1990s, it took the form of requiring the curriculum to include black studies, Chicano studies, women's studies, etc., to reaffirm and reenforce the prevailing left-wing bias of professors.

In response to my *curriculum vitae,* I received a number of good job offers. One came from Walter Hoadley, chief economist for the Armstrong Cork Company of Lancaster, Pennsylvania. Another was from Dexter Keezer, director of the Department of Economics of the McGraw-Hill Publishing Company in New York. The third offer—the one I accepted— was for a position with the U.S. Chamber of Commerce in Washington, D.C., at a salary of $7,500 a year. It came from Emerson P. Schmidt, the Chamber's chief economist. I recall that Dexter Keezer wrote to warn me that, by middle age, a marriage involving two career persons becomes "singularly stark and dreary." Little did he realize that in the course of her distinguished career, Rita would bear three beautiful and intelligent daughters, all of whom are successful career women. Each of the three now has one son and one now also has a daughter. These children are, and will continue to be, sources of great pleasure to Rita and me.

In September 1951, we moved to Washington and found an apartment at 525 Argyle Drive in a Virginia development called Culmore. Later that fall in Washington, D.C., Rita met the person who had employed her first at Harvard. Prof. John T. Dunlop was a public member of the Wage Stabilization Board, established after the outbreak of the Korean War. He told her that it very much needed economists of her capability on the staff, and he assisted her in being appointed to a level-12 position, which, as I recall, meant a salary of about $7,600 per annum. By spring 1952 she was promoted to a level-13, and her salary rose to $8,500 per annum.

Europe in 1952

In August, my wife and I took our first trip to Europe, something we had planned for a long time. In New York we boarded the *Liberté,* a converted German liner which the French received as reparations for their famous passenger ship the *Ile de France,* sunk by the Germans during World War II. To save money we traveled second class, but on a French liner in those days, that made little difference as to food and wine. The crossing took about five days, and daily we enjoyed wine at lunch and dinner, along with excellent food. Evenings we went dancing, and a nice English-woman, the wife of an English bandleader, taught me the samba.

We landed at Plymouth, England. I was traveling on a British passport since I was not yet an American citizen, but my wife had a U.S. passport so it took her about half an hour longer to go through immigration and customs (on our return to the United States, it was my turn to wait). We then took the train to London, where we had our only hotel reservation of the entire trip.

We spent several days in London visiting Windsor Castle and Eton; watching the changing of the guard at Buckingham Palace; touring the Tower of London, built in William the Conqueror's time, later used as a prison, and now the place where the Crown Jewels are kept; and walking through Westminster Abbey and Saint Paul's Cathedral. Everywhere we went, we found reminders of the devastation of World War II German bombing. Thanks to Emerson Schmidt we also had the special treat of a gourmet luncheon with the chief economist for Lloyd's Bank.

After a few days we rented a car and traveled north to the English Lake District made famous by Wordsworth and Keats. On our journey north, we stayed at small inns that did not require reservations. When we arrived at the Scottish border, one of the tellers at a local bank thought I was a Scot returning home—in a way, I was. We proceeded across the lowlands toward Edinburgh, stopping at a Scottish inn. Great Britain was still rationing, and I remember overhearing the proprietor say to another person that he should be given an additional ration allotment because he had two Yanks staying at his establishment. The next morning we arrived in Edinburgh and stayed at the inexpensive Temperance Hotel on Princess Street, the only hotel we could get into without a reservation. We visited the Old Castle, attended the world-renowned Scottish tattoo, and went to Holyrood Palace, the residence of the British sovereign when he or she is in Edinburgh. We also took a day-trip to Stirling Castle, near the place where the Battle of Bannockburn was fought in 1314. There the English army, led by Edward II, was defeated by Robert the Bruce, supported by all the Scottish clans. (Among the most important of those clans were the Campbells.) After that devastating defeat, the English never again tried to invade Scotland.

Next we proceeded west by car because I was very anxious to visit Argyllshire, the area from which my ancestors had come. We also went to Glasgow, where, it seemed, every other butcher shop in the downtown area was owned by a Campbell. This greatly amused my wife. By the time we made it to the shores of Loch Lomond, it was early September and raining so much that we decided to turn back without crossing Loch Lomond into the land of the Campbells. In due course, we returned to London via the Scottish border area made famous by Sir Walter Scott as the locale of the brutal border wars between the English and the Scots.

After we returned to London, we booked passage on an overnight boat to Rotterdam. In Holland we visited the Hague and the quaint area where Dutch cheeses were made, then took the train to Brussels, where we stopped overnight. The next day on the train to Paris we met a Dutch ship's engineer who visited the French capital frequently. I mentioned that I had a carton of cigarettes I could give him, and he told us about an inexpensive hotel on the Left Bank. We had barely checked into the hotel and started unpacking when he appeared at the door to receive his cigarettes, and also to take us for a drink in the Place du Tetre and to show us how to use the Underground.

In Paris we viewed all the noted landmarks—Notre Dame Cathedral, the Eiffel Tower, Napoleon's Tomb, Versailles, and, when it rained, the Louvre. By then we were running short of traveler's checks. Since I came from Canada, I had insisted on using Cook's Traveller's Checks. We went to Cook's, but it refused to issue us more. A Cook's representative did, however, suggest that we go to American Express, and there we purchased more traveler's checks. I have used American Express Traveler's Checks ever since and avoided Cook's.

We rented a Renault and drove southwest through the countryside. The French peasants were farming much as they must have done in the Middle Ages, everyone living in small towns where the houses were attached to the cowsheds. We reached Dijon in a rainstorm and stayed overnight in this town at the center of the Burgundy wine region. We enjoyed an excellent dinner with plenty of fine, inexpensive Burgundy.

From France we drove to Geneva to visit the League of Nations building and the Institute for Graduate International Studies, and to take the funicular part way up the side of the Jungfrau. Then we proceeded to Germany through the German-speaking area of Switzerland. Each night we stayed at pensions that were parts of private homes.

In West Germany we visited Heidelberg University, which had not been damaged much by World War II. My method of proceeding through West Germany was to approach the highest-ranking American officer I could find and ask for directions. I remember in particular staying in Wiesbaden, in a place with goose-down quilts on the beds. In that part of Germany much devastation from Allied bombing was evident.

Leaving Germany, we traveled through Luxembourg back to Paris, where we turned in the Renault and took an overnight train to Florence, Italy. We visited several museums in that center of the splendors of medieval and Renaissance art. We next took a bus to Rome, where we stayed at a small hotel and found an excellent restaurant. I remember in particular the proprietor's daughter asking if we were on our honeymoon, because her parents told her that when Americans got married they went on honeymoons. We said no; we had been married for several years, but we were enjoying our trip so much that it *seemed* like a honeymoon. In Rome we visited all the famous sites we had read about in school, including the Vatican and the Sistine Chapel, the Colosseum, the Forum.

We moved on to Naples by bus and saw how poverty-stricken World War II had left the Italians. Pimps were openly soliciting business, and approached me even though I was with my wife. A day trip to the boot of Italy brought us to the area of Mount Vesuvius, which was being excavated. For a small "honorarium" our guide would let tourists look inside at the pornographic pictures. Finally, it was time to board one of the Four Aces—cargo ships that also carried a limited number of passengers. Ours was called the *Excalibur,* and we spent about sixteen days aboard her en route to Boston. On the way we stopped at Pisa to see the Leaning Tower and at Barcelona to visit its magnificent cathedral. Observing the many beautiful women on the streets, I noticed that the most beautiful of them resembled my Spanish wife. The ship also stopped briefly at Marseilles, giving us time to visit the low-cost housing designed by the famous architect Le Corbusier. Then we headed through the Strait of Gibraltar and across the Atlantic Ocean to Boston. We enjoyed the eight-day crossing very much because it gave us an opportunity to get better acquainted with the other passengers and also to engage in deck sports every day. One passenger, David Newsome, was a State Department career officer traveling with his wife and children. He later served as ambassador to

Libya, Indonesia, and the Philippines, and as undersecretary of state for political affairs. After his retirement in 1981 he became a professor at Georgetown University.

When we arrived in Boston in late October 1952, after a diet of European newspapers predicting that Adlai Stevenson would win the election, we were surprised that virtually all the Irish pubs sported "I like Ike" signs. The Boston Irish were historically Democrats, and I became convinced that the Republican candidate, General Eisenhower, would win in a landslide. In the November election, in addition to the presidency, the Republicans won majorities in both the House and the Senate—something they would not do again until 1994 and 1996. After visiting Rita's mother and father, we took the train to Washington, D.C., and proceeded by taxi to 525 Argyle Drive.

All in all it was hugely exciting. We have been abroad many times since, but no later trips to Europe produced the memories of that first one. In addition, it was one of the few trips abroad that we paid for entirely by ourselves.

Becoming an American Citizen

By April 1953 it was clear to me that I was never going to live in Canada again, so that month I took my citizenship examination at the Alexandria (Virginia) Courthouse. Two American citizens, my wife and Dr. Phillip D. Bradley, promised to support me if I became an indigent. (I don't know whether this is still required for naturalization.) In any event, from that time forward I have traveled on a U.S. passport, though under British law I have dual citizenship.

After a year at the Chamber of Commerce my annual salary was increased to $8,100, and Rita became an economist for the House Ways and Means Committee (specifically, for the Social Security Subcommittee, with Carl Curtis of Nebraska as chairman and Wilbur Mills of Arkansas as ranking minority member). She was paid about $9,500 a year, a level-14 rate. While she was working with the Ways and Means Committee, my wife and I discovered that she was pregnant. She continued to work and during committee hearings the courtly Congressman Mills frequently brought her mid-morning milk to her. She resigned at the end of the year to prepare for the birth of our first child. After the long hours she had been working, she badly needed the rest. Besides, we were spending much time looking for a house to purchase.

At the American Enterprise Association

In the meantime, William Baroody, Sr., and I had been searching for higher-paying and more-interesting jobs than those we held at the Chamber of Commerce. Several people I knew from my Harvard days, particularly Prof. Charles Abbott, Dr. Phillip Bradley, and Sinclair Weeks (the first secretary of commerce in the Eisenhower administration), were looking for young people who could revitalize an organization that had been founded in 1943 but that had fallen into slothful and ineffective ways. It was called the American Enterprise Association.

In January of 1954, Allan D. Marshall of the General Electric Company became president of AEA, and on February 1 William Baroody, Sr., became executive vice president at a salary of $15,000 and I became director of research at $13,000 a year. During the rest of the 1950s my salary gradually increased to $20,000. It was a time of major changes for Rita and me. On March 21 we made our first offer on a house at 8612 Beech Tree Road in Bethesda, Maryland. The next day Rita gave birth to Barbara Lee, and in April we moved into our new home. Almost two years later, on January 25, 1956, our second daughter, Diane Rita, arrived. A few months after Diane's birth, Dr. Rita Campbell returned to work as an AEA consultant, doing bill analyses and special analyses for members of Congress and members of the Eisenhower administration. Our family lived in the house on Beech Tree Road until March 1960, when we sold it and moved in April to the home in Los Altos Hills, where we still live.

At the American Enterprise Association I worked closely with many professors from numerous prestigious universities, including Milton Friedman of the University of Chicago Department of Economics; Paul W. McCracken of the University of Michigan, who was later named chairman of the Council of Economic Advisors; and Roscoe Pound, who served as dean of Harvard Law School for twenty years. I was able to observe how they operated and to learn a great deal from them. For example, they taught me that if innovative and useful policy-oriented research was to be done by eminent scholars, I would have to work *for* those scholars, not attempt to direct their activity. By seeking out the top people in their fields, I built an invaluable base for future policy formulation. The advisory board concept gave me the opportunity to approach any academic luminary, and I knew that if I selected good, self-starter scholars, close supervision would not be necessary. What they wanted was a good income so that they would not have to "waste their time" raising money. In addition to our other jobs, therefore, Baroody and I handled AEA's fundraising.

At AEA I also had the privilege of meeting and getting to know a number of important senators—Gordon Allott of Colorado, Barry Goldwater of Arizona, Everett Dirksen of Illinois, William Knowland of California, Dan Thornton of Colorado, Frank Carlson of Kansas, Jack Kennedy and Leverett Saltonstall of Massachusetts, Richard Russell and Walter George of Georgia, and Homer Ferguson of Michigan. Among the congressmen I got to know were Gerald Ford of Michigan (later, president of the United States), Melvin Laird of Wisconsin (later Nixon's first secretary of defense), Carl Curtis of Nebraska (later Senator Curtis), and William Miller of New York, who was Barry Goldwater's vice presidential running mate.

In 1958 at its Princeton meeting I became a member of the Mont Pelerin Society. It was a great honor for me, and I have always been glad that I joined.

Newsweek Magazine

By early 1959 Raymond Moley was urging William Baroody and me to put together a wealthy group to buy *Newsweek* magazine. Vincent Astor (who held at least 60 percent of the controlling shares) was not in good health, and if he should die, Moley believed, his estate would undoubtedly sell the magazine to some left-wing group because Brooke Astor did not like conservatives.

We got Harvey Peters interested in buying *Newsweek* on behalf of the Allen-Bradley Company, so Baroody, Peters, and I went to New York City to meet with Raymond Moley and Vincent Astor. The night before the meeting, Mr. Astor died of a massive heart attack, and our plans were aborted. *Newsweek* magazine was later sold to the *Washington Post,* and Moley's concerns about its ending up in left-wing hands came true.

A Professorship

During our stay in Washington I received three offers of professorships in economics—one from Emory University in Atlanta, the University of Virginia at Charlottesville, and Wabash College in Crawfordsville, Indiana to succeed John van Sickle as chairman of the department of economics. None of these offers particularly appealed to my distinguished spouse. The second and third in particular would take us to relatively small towns where job opportunities for Ph.D.s in economics were rare. In those days the University of Virginia simply did not hire female professors, and Wabash College was an all-male college and hired women only as secretaries, dietitians, etc. In fact, Wabash College *still* does not employ female professors.

3
Director of the
Hoover Institution

I N THE LATE 1950S IT BECAME INCREASINGLY CLEAR THAT THE
American Enterprise Association would not satisfy my career hopes.
I began looking for something else, preferably a position closer to
Academe and to the forums of ideas in collision. The two things fore-
most in my mind at the time were Rita and the prospects for a profes-
sorship in economics at a major university.

Harvard, plainly, was not about to come through with an offer, so I
chose Stanford, where I had been offered the directorship of the Hoover
Institution. I had no idea, of course, that I would hold this position for
almost thirty years, nor that my services could in some degree help turn
Hoover toward the path to grow into one of the greatest think-tanks of
all time.

The Institution had changed direction more than once. At its founding, it was only a tiny room in the Stanford University Library, housing
a small collection of war memorabilia in the library. From that beginning
it grew into a well-known research center, and the changes were reflected
in various changes of its name.

When the Institution was founded in 1919, it was known as the
War Library. In the early 1920s it was renamed the Hoover War Library,
and around 1938 it got the grander title of the Hoover Library on War,
Revolution and Peace. That was the name it bore when the Hoover Tower
was dedicated on June 20, 1941, near the end of Ray Lyman Wilbur's
long (1916 to 1943) tenure as Stanford's third president. On September
19, 1946, Donald Tressidder, Stanford's fourth president, with the approval
of Herbert Hoover and the board of trustees, changed the name of the

Institution for a fourth time, to the Hoover Institute and Library on War, Revolution and Peace. In 1957, three years before my arrival, the Hoover Institution on War, Revolution and Peace got its fifth and final name change. By then it had formulated a defined organizational structure: The Hoover Institute and Library on War, Revolution and Peace was organized as a separate division of Stanford University.

An Advisory Board advised the university administration regarding the Institute and Library.

The chairman of the Hoover Institute and Library would be responsible to the university president and function in a manner similar to department heads throughout the university.

In addition to the chairman, the president would appoint other officers as circumstances warranted.

This last name change recognized the fact that Hoover had become a research institution as well as a library. Harold Fisher was then chairman of directors of the Hoover Institution, having succeeded Dr. Ralph H. Lutz in 1944 after Lutz suffered a heart attack and retired. Harold Fisher had worked for Mr. Hoover in the American Relief Administration (ARA) and had accompanied the Hoover Collection to Stanford in the 1920s. What Mr. Hoover did not realize when he approved Fisher's 1944 appointment was that the man had moved far to the ideological left, while Hoover himself remained as conservative and private-enterprise-oriented—and as big a believer in private solutions to problems of poverty, sickness, and education—as he had always been. Witold Sworakowski told me that in the late 1940s, while Stalin as dictator of the Soviet Union was populating the Gulag, Fisher used to make speeches in which he stated that the United States had more *economic* democracy, but the Soviet Union had more *political* democracy.

By 1952 Herbert Hoover had had enough of Fisher and his left-wing speeches and appointments. Mr. Hoover had played a key role in the appointment of Stanford University President J. E. Wallace Sterling in 1949, and Sterling persuaded him to appoint Dr. C. Easton Rothwell as director and to allow Fisher to retain his old position as chairman until his retirement in 1955. Mr. Hoover, pleased that Sterling had done his Ph.D. dissertation at the Hoover Library under the direction of Ralph Lutz, acquiesced, but that was the last time he would yield to Dr. Sterling's manipulations.

In any event, Dr. C. Easton Rothwell of the Brookings Institution was appointed deputy chairman in 1947. His most noted achievement to date had been his service in the State Department during World War II, culminating in 1945 when he attended the founding of the United Nations in San Francisco as Alger Hiss's deputy. Professor Sworakowski was also present at the founding as the representative of the Polish government-in-exile (the noncommunist pre-World War II government). One day a representative of Polish intelligence came to him and asked him not to give any documents to the secretariat when Alger Hiss was on duty. Asked why not, the intelligence officer replied that Hiss was a Soviet agent!

The 1955 Presidential Library Act

In 1955 the United States Congress enacted legislation permitting the creation of presidential libraries to be built with private funds but maintained with federal appropriations. The act was passed to accommodate former President Harry S Truman, who had agreed to give his papers to the National Archives on the condition that they be kept in Independence, Missouri. While the legislation was being formulated, Speaker of the House John McCormack of Boston made a special trip to New York City to meet with Mr. Hoover. They agreed that presidential libraries might also be located on college or university campuses—though Mr. Truman's is not—and this provision was incorporated into the final bill. For many years Hoover had maintained his personal archives (including the papers of his presidency) at his own expense in the Hoover Tower, intending someday to give his papers to Stanford University. After the 1955 act was passed, Mr. Hoover altered his plans and determined that the Hoover Institution would house his presidential library.

About two years later Rothwell proposed that a Hoover library be established on the top floors of the Tower. In that way the Hoover Institution would receive a sizable sum of money—about $100,000 a year—from the federal government. This would greatly ease the Institution's financial problems. Mr. Hoover, however, recognized immediately that Rothwell's plan would lessen, if not eliminate, the former president's influence on Institution affairs. He gave various reasons for rejecting the idea, but all of them added up to no.

In early 1956 the Hoover Institution launched a $2.5 million endowment campaign under the chairmanship of Alonzo Peake, a Stanford graduate in geology and a retired chief executive officer of Standard Oil Company of Indiana. Within two years, the project had clearly failed, largely as a result of Mr. Hoover's noninvolvement. He was remaining aloof in response to the duplicity of Sterling and Rothwell. They had, in his view, allowed left-wingers to take over the Hoover Institution. On March 20, 1958, a Special Committee of Trustees of the Hoover Institution was created at Mr. Hoover's request. James Black was chairman and the committee members were Mrs. Allen E. Charles, George A. Ditz, Mrs. Roger Goodan, and Ira S. Lillick. After he became board president in July 1958, David Packard became an ex-officio member.

On May 8, 1958, Director Rothwell presented the Black committee with a comprehensive memorandum suggesting a number of fundamental changes. The most significant item was the proposal that Stanford should henceforth assume "full responsibility" for the Hoover Institution's "total budget." In addition, all existing endowments should be allocated toward current operations. Rothwell had created a blueprint for making the Hoover Institution fully dependent on Stanford University and for effectively ending its existence as an independent entity. What's more, this plan would have required the trustees to violate their fiduciary responsibilities by spending for current operations endowment funds which Mr. Hoover had obtained in good faith in the 1920s. Fortunately, Stanford trustees such as Ira Lillick, Herman Phleger, James Black, David Packard, and Thomas Pike took their fiduciary duties very seriously. It was easy for Mr. Hoover to defeat Rothwell's proposal.

In order to clarify the position and the mission of the Institution, Mr. Hoover prepared a statement with the help of Dr. Arthur Kemp, who had been his research assistant from 1947 to 1949 while the ex-president was chairman of the first Hoover Commission. Dr. Kemp had gone on to become a professor of money and credit at Claremont Men's College in 1953. Hoover released his statement on May 20, 1959, with the approval of the Black committee and the less enthusiastic approval of President Sterling:

Special Committee on the Hoover Institution

Wednesday, May 20, 1959
10:00 a.m.

A meeting of the Special Committee on the Hoover Institution was Held on Wednesday, May 20, 1959, at 10:00 o'clock, in the offices of the Board of Trustees, at which were present the following:

Committee members: Mrs. Allen E. Charles
                    Mr. George A. Ditz
                    Mrs. Roger Goodan
                    Mr. Ira S. Lillick
                    Mr. David Packard

Others: J. E. Wallace Sterling, President

Upon motion duly made and seconded, the Committee approved the following recommendation of the President of the University and recommends that it receive the approval of the Board of Trustees:

That the Trustees adopt the following resolution which is submitted with the recommendation of the President of the University, the endorsement of the President of the Board and of the Trustee Chairman of the Committee on the Hoover Institution, and the approval of Mr. Hoover:

That the status of the Hoover Institution on War, Revolution and Peace, its purpose, its management, and its policies shall be clarified, the Trustees of Stanford University resolve:

Paragraph 1. The Trustees feel that there should be in their records a statement of the scope, the importance and the purposes of the Hoover Institution. To this end Mr. Hoover has prepared for them the following statement:

This was the statement quoted in full in Chapter One, Section Two. Here I shall repeat only its final three paragraphs pertaining to the Hoover mission.

The over-all mission of this Institution is, from its records, to recall the voice of experience against the making of war, and by the study of these records and their publication to recall man's endeavors to make and preserve peace and to sustain for America the safeguards of the American way of life.

This Institution is not, and must not be, a mere library. But with these purposes as its goal, the Institution itself must constantly and dynamically point the road to peace, to personal freedom, and to the safeguards of the American system.

And finally, among the many other materials in the Hoover Archives is the record of the compassion of the American people, who, by self-denial and long hours of labor, provided the margins of food, medicines, and clothing which, in the wars of the present century, have enabled over one billion, four hundred million human beings to survive who otherwise would have perished.

Paragraph 2. That the Trustees' Resolution of September 19, 1946 on the Hoover Institution on War, Revolution, and Peace is rescinded.

Paragraph 3. That the Hoover Institution on War, Revolution, and Peace is an independent Institution within the frame of Stanford University. Its relation to the University is that the President of the University will propose all appointments, promotions, and the budget of the Institution directly to the Board of Trustees. There will be no reference to any faculty committees between the President and the Trustees.

Paragraph 4. That the resources of the Institution in so far as available shall be devoted to the preservation and enlargement of its collections.

Paragraph 5. That the doors of the Hoover Institution on War, Revolution, and Peace are to be open for research by competent and qualified scholars.

There are many collections which have been given to the Hoover Institution by donors with restrictions of time or otherwise as to their use. Adherence to these restrictions must be strictly maintained in order that the Hoover Institution continue as a sanctuary for such collections.

Paragraph 6. That the dynamic purpose of the Hoover Institution is that it should constantly prepare and publish objective collections of documents and materials upon events, negotiations, or actions, which can give guidance to thought on public policies. The names of the staff who prepare these objective publications of documents should, as hitherto, be noted on the publication.

The members of the staff of the Hoover Institution must be free to publish statements or books of the results of their research work in which they give their "interpretation" or opinion. If the writer of this type of publication wishes to state that he is a member of the Hoover Institution, the publication must carry a declaration that the Institution does not assume responsibility for statements in the publications.

Qualified scholars from outside the Hoover Institution must be free to publish anything they wish from the unrestricted documents and records and to mention their source. But such publications by persons outside the staff of the Hoover Institution must not carry any implication of the Institution as to the authenticity of the facts or opinions they present. Otherwise, the Hoover Institution will be involved in controversies over such publications or be assuming responsibility for them.

Paragraph 7. The Director of the Institution shall be recommended to the Board of Trustees by the President of the University for appointment by the Trustees. He shall have been previously approved by Mr. Hoover. Such recommendation of the President shall not require approval of the Advisory Board of the Academic Council of Stanford University.

The Director must be a man who reflects the purposes of the Institution. He should be of an age which gives him a substantial period of service before the retirement age of 65 years.

The Director shall be responsible, through the President of the University, to the Trustees for:

(a) recommending appointments to and supervising the staff of the Institution;

(b) directing and supervising the library functions of the Institution which include acquisitions, processing and cataloging, use and security of the collections and reference materials; directing and supervising the research and publication program of the Institution;

(c) preparing and administering the annual budget of the Institution.

The Director shall have tenure as long as he satisfactorily discharges his responsibilities. This is administrative tenure, comparable to that of the President of the University, and not academic tenure for which faculty members are eligible.

The staff of the Hoover Institution is responsible to the Director and through him and the President to the Trustees. Appointments to the staff of the Hoover Institution shall be considered as administrative rather than faculty appointments, and shall not carry academic tenure.

Paragraph 8. The Director and members of the staff of the Institution:

(a) shall be eligible for retirement benefits made available by the University to the non-faculty members of the University staff. The Director,

Assistant Director, the Librarian, and the Curators may be eligible, alternatively, to retirement benefits made available to regular faculty members of the University, and, if so, may opt for this eligibility;

(b) shall be eligible to participate in the benefits of health and insurance programs sponsored by the University;

(c) shall be eligible, under University regulation, to lease University land on which to build and own private homes for their own occupancy.

Paragraph 9. That gifts made to Stanford University and designated for support of the Hoover Institution shall be used for that designated purpose and no other. The funds available to the Hoover Institution from such gifts, be they income from endowment or gifts for annual expenditure or gifts for special purposes on a special schedule, shall be made part of and shown in the annual budget of the Institution.

The University receives many benefits in reputation from the Hoover Institution, and the members of faculty and students have available to them the unique collections of the Institution. The University shall provide from its General Funds additional support for the Institution. This additional support shall be not less than $125,000.00 per annum, barring presently unforeseen financial adversity which would oblige the Board of Trustees to reduce total University expenditures.

The President of the University and the General Secretary's Office shall continue to include support of the Institution in their solicitation of funds.

The Institutional cost of providing retirement benefits shall be borne by the University.

Paragraph 10. The purpose of the Advisory Board of the Hoover Institution is to maintain interest in the Institution, to aid in securing support to the Institution, and to advise on policies of the Institution. The Advisory Board comprises eminent men and includes the President of the University and the President of the Board of Trustees. The Chairman of the Trustees committee on the Institution is to be a member of the Advisory Board.

David Packard
Acting Chairman

Early in 1959 C. Easton Rothwell announced his intention to resign, effective April 1, to become president of Mills College. Mr. Hoover believed that he had a commitment from President Sterling to make Witold

Sworakowski acting director. Once again, he was double-crossed, and Philip H. Rhinelander, dean of Stanford's School of Humanities and Sciences, was named acting director instead. Between that date and my appointment on January 1, 1960, Sterling tried unsuccessfully to dump his weak dean on the Hoover Institution as its director. By then he had realized his mistake in hiring Philip Rhinelander from Harvard. In fact, he had already appointed Dr. Robert Wert as vice provost for Undergraduate Studies.

President Hoover's Notes

After I had written about my appointment as director as I remember it, I found, among old notes and papers in my study, Mr. Hoover's own version, taken from meeting notes kept by his secretary Bernice Miller:

Monday, June 29, 1959
    Dr. W. Glenn Campbell was recommended to Mr. Hoover by Mr. Raymond Moley by letter.

Wednesday, August 26, 1959
    Mr. Hoover communicated with Admiral Lewis Strauss. Mr. Hoover wrote President Sterling. He listed Dr. Campbell among others, but stated regarding him (Campbell): "I am investigating further, but at the moment he seems most promising."

Sunday, August 30, 1959
    Admiral Strauss telephoned Mr. Hoover about Dr. Campbell getting F.B.I.[1] clearance, and comments of the members of the Board of the American Enterprise Association. Dr. Campbell in England.

Thursday, September 3, 1959
    Mr. Hoover wrote Mr. Henning Prentis and Mr. Colby Chester regarding Dr. Campbell.

---

1. This was not necessary, but after his experiences with Fisher and Rothwell, Mr. Hoover thoroughly checked my appointment through J. Edgar Hoover.

President Sterling wrote Mr. Hoover: "The lines I had out on Campbell produced only a skeleton." President Sterling attached a short sketch from the reference library dated 9/3/59.

Sunday, September 6, 1959
Mr. Hoover wrote President Sterling: "I am making further inquiries as to Dr. W. Glenn Campbell."

Wednesday, September 9, 1959
Mr. Prentis replied enthusiastically by telephone and by letter. Mr. Colby Chester replied enthusiastically by letter.

Thursday, September 10, 1959
Mr. Henry Bodman wrote glowingly to Mr. Hoover of Dr. Campbell.

Monday, September 14, 1959
Mr. Packard had breakfast with Mr. Hoover. They discussed foundations.

Wednesday, September 16, 1959
Miss Miller telephoned the AEA to find out when Dr. Campbell would arrive in New York, and asked that he call on Mr. Hoover when he arrived in New York.

Thursday, September 17, 1959
Stanford Board of Trustees met in San Francisco.

Friday, September 18, 1959
Mr. Hoover wrote President Sterling as follows:

The outstanding man as to experience and with the enthusiastic recommendation of important men is Dr. W. Glenn Campbell. When Mr. Packard was here I gave him the list of those recommending him. He [Campbell] is returning to New York from Europe in a few days and I have arranged for him to call upon me.

I want to size him up personally and find out his availability if he is offered the appointment by you. He, of course, in any event will want time to study the job.

Tuesday, September 22, 1959

Dr. and Mrs. Campbell called on Mr. Hoover in New York, at Mr. Hoover's request, on their arrival from Europe. Mr. Hoover records their discussion as follows:

On September 22, 1959, I saw Campbell and his wife. Greatly impressed; asked him if he was available. Described Library, its work, gave him copy of pamphlet, list of Trustees of University, and my form letter to Foundations; assured him a minimum of $300,000; explained I already had:

Fleischmann	$50,000 a year
Pews	50,000 a year
Milbank	25,000 a year
Expected Sloan	50,000 a year

$175,000 a year in addition to an income of $200,000 annually from the University and endowment income. Felt certain he would have an income of about $400,000 with which to work.

Wednesday, September 23, 1959

Mr. Hoover wrote Mr. Felix Morley regarding Dr. Campbell.

Thursday, September 24, 1959

Mr. Raymond Moley wrote letter to Mr. Hoover regarding Dr. Campbell.

Sunday, September 27, 1959

Mr. Hoover wrote Dr. Campbell—offered $2,000 to move.

Monday, September 28, 1959

Mr. Ray Henle had lunch with Dr. Campbell—approved him. Told him about Hoover Institution.

Friday, October 2, 1959

Dr. Campbell came in to see Mr. Hoover. He said that he was available, but Mr. Hoover told him the University must make the appointment.

A few hours prior to Dr. Campbell's visit, Mr. J. Howard Pew had telephoned Mr. Hoover, upset at Campbell's leaving AEA.

Mr. Hoover telephoned Ray Henle.

Saturday, October 3, 1959

Mr. Henle reported to Mr. Hoover that he thought it would all work out.

Mr. Hoover wrote to President Sterling and gave him a full statement of his conversation with Campbell. Mr. Hoover also sent President Sterling a full copy of Dr. Campbell's qualifications. (A duplicate copy of letter and attachments was sent to President Sterling in Washington, to be held for his arrival on October 8.)

Sunday, October 4, 1959

Mr. Hoover wrote Dr. Campbell that President Sterling will be in Washington October 8 and 9.

Tuesday, October 6, 1959

Mr. Hoover wrote to Mr. J. Howard Pew regarding Dr. Campbell.

Dr. Campbell wrote Mr. Hoover that he will see President Sterling on October 9.

Wednesday, October 7, 1959

Mr. Hoover wrote to Mr. Black and sent Dr. Campbell's qualifications to him. He stated, "I think we have a Director for the Library." Mr. Hoover also sent Mr. Black Dr. Campbell's recommendations. Mr. Hoover continued to Mr. Black, "Wally is to see Campbell in Washington and I can see no remote reason why he should object."

Mr. Hoover wrote the same letter to Mr. Packard as he wrote to Mr. Black, and sent the enclosures also.

Friday, October 9, 1959

President Sterling saw Dr. Campbell in Washington.

Saturday, October 10, 1959

President Sterling telephoned Mr. Hoover about meeting with Dr. Campbell.

Monday, October 12, 1959

Dr. Campbell wrote to Mr. Hoover that he had had a pleasant visit with President Sterling on October 9, in which President Sterling invited him to visit Stanford before making an offer. Dr. Campbell said that he would go to California at the earliest possible date.

Dr. Campbell said in his letter to Mr. Hoover: "Now that I have given you my word that I will accept the position, I am as anxious as I am sure you are that the formal appointment be made as soon as possible."

Tuesday, October 13, 1959

Mr. Hoover telephoned to Mr. Packard and twice to President Sterling that he hoped President Sterling would propose and approve Dr. Campbell's name at the Board of Trustees meeting on October 15.

President Sterling wrote to Mr. Hoover as follows:

> I'm hardly more than back from Washington, where I had the pleasure of a visit with Dr. Campbell. This I have reported to you by telephone. Let me add that I very much like the cut of his jib; I also like the questions he asked me about the University, the Institution, you and myself. I'm delighted that he can arrange for an early visit, because I think it portends the high probability that he would be able to join us soon.
>
> In my discussion with him in Washington, I did not go deeply into the area of fringe benefits because that sort of discussion can be conducted more effectively when he is here and can literally see what we are talking about. Ann and I expect to have his wife and him as our guests next Monday and Tuesday, October 19 and 20.
>
> After talking with you on the telephone today, I called Dave Packard, and have arranged to call a meeting of the Trustees Committee on the Hoover Institution so that they may recommend to the Board that I be given authority to finalize arrangements with Dr. Campbell. This is all on the strength of his letter to you in which he says he accepts, a statement he did not make to me in Washington.

Wednesday, October 14, 1959

Mr. Hoover wired President Sterling the text of Dr. Campbell's availability letter of October 12.

Mr. Hoover telephoned Dr. Campbell that the Board of Trustees would probably appoint him at their meeting on October 15.

Mr. Hoover telephoned President Sterling to present the matter.

Mr. Hoover wrote to Mr. Ira Lillick as follows:

> I think the Stanford Board will tomorrow authorize Wally to appoint Dr. W. Glenn Campbell, Director of the Institution. Wally has approved

him. Campbell has agreed with me to accept, and I have informed Wally of it.

Campbell and his wife will be going to Stanford on a visit—probably next week.

Thursday, October 15, 1959

The Stanford Board of Trustees action—Instructed President Sterling to appoint Dr. Campbell.

Mr. Packard called Mr. Hoover from Palo Alto and advised him of action of the Board approving the appointment of Dr. Campbell.

Friday, October 16, 1959

Mr. Hoover wrote to President Sterling: "I had the welcome news from Dave as to the Trustees' action on Campbell. That ends a chapter."

Mr. Ira Lillick wrote Miss Miller (Hoover's secretary) as follows:

So that you may be otherwise informed, the calling of the meeting by a notice to its members was by a telephone message from Wally's office [on October 14] that there would be a meeting of the Committee [of Trustees on Hoover Institution] at 11:45 AM on the following day [Thursday, October 15]. Mr. Ditz, as I think you know, is abroad, but the other members of the Committee were present, including Fred Glover, who acted as secretary, Wally and Dave Packard. (Jim Black returned to the City yesterday morning, I believe.) Dave, in a brief statement, recited what was hoped might be done by the Committee, and Wally then covered, comparatively briefly, the background attainments of Dr. Campbell, and followed with the statement that the Chief was enthusiastic about the Doctor and that he, Wally, felt his selection would turn out satisfactorily to all concerned. The Committee then unanimously resolved to recommend the appointment of Dr. Campbell as Director.

In the afternoon at the meeting of the Board of Trustees, Dave said that the Hoover Institution Committee had unanimously approved the appointment of Dr. Campbell as Director of the Institution, and further said that the minor changes that had been agreed upon between the Chief and Wally in the Resolution that had been passed at the previous meeting of the Board of Trustees were acceptable. Dave then asked Wally to supplement what he had said, if Wally cared to do so. Wally then briefly reviewed the situation and stated that it would be desirable to have the Board of Trustees pass a Resolution formally approving the recommendations that had been made to the Board by the Hoover Institution Committee. I think the other members of the Committee with me breathed a sigh of relief as well as a mental blessing that agreement had been arrived at with respect to the permanent Director.

In passing, it seems to me that the whole tone of Wally's letter of September 21st to the Chief evidenced friendly co-operation as well as such a very definite expression of appreciation for what Mr. Hoover stands for publicly, is doing, and what he has always continuously done for the University. What with Dave Packard and Jim Black on the firing line, we can look forward to the Institution finally coming into its own.

Monday, October 19, 1959

Mr. James Black wrote to Mr. Hoover: "I understand our prospective Director is to be on the campus this week, and you will note from the minutes of the last Trustees' Meeting that Wally was given authority to employ him."

Monday and Tuesday, October 19 and 20, 1959

Dr. and Mrs. Campbell visited Stanford University and stopped at Sterling's.

Wednesday, October 21, 1959

Mr. Hoover had asked Miss Miller to telephone Mr. Black that he (Hoover) was fighting against a good deal of misrepresentation as to the Institution. That Mr. Hoover had seen Mr. Sloan and Mr. Rusk endeavoring to clear up some of this stuff. Mr. Hoover asked Miss Miller to ask Mr. Black if he thought it a good thing if Mr. Hoover had Mr. Heald of the Ford Foundation in.

Friday, October 23, 1959

President Sterling had breakfast with Mr. Hoover in New York. Mr. Hoover's memo on their conversation:

Wally said Campbell was a second-class man and wanted to know if my mind was fixed. I said it was, that Campbell's appointment had been recommended to the Trustees by both him and me, and that they had authorized him to make the appointment. I stated that I simply could not reopen the subject. He said he would make the appointment, but evidenced no enthusiasm.

We discussed my foundation drive. I found he was urging Rockefeller and Ford Foundations to contribute to other University programs.

Miss Miller in San Francisco, tried to telephone Mrs. Sterling. Talked with Judy Sterling.

Saturday, October 24, 1959

Miss Miller spoke from San Francisco to Mrs. Ann Sterling early AM. In course of conversation Mrs. Sterling said that the Campbells had been with her. (Mrs. Sterling was lukewarm about them.)

Monday, October 26, 1959

President Sterling had breakfast with Mr. Hoover. Mr. Hoover's memo on their conversation:

I asked Wally if he had made the appointment of Campbell. He said no; he had caught Campbell in a lie and could not have a liar on his staff. [The alleged "lie" he claimed to have caught me in had to do with whether Mr. Hoover had earlier offered me the job and I had accepted. He kept questioning me on this and I repeatedly answered with the truth, namely, that I had told Mr. Hoover of my availability and that I would accept the job if he, Wallace Sterling, offered it to me.]

We sifted the matter out and he agreed it was an honest misunderstanding. I insisted on his making the appointment as authorized by the Trustees. He again demurred and I read to him his appraisal of Campbell in his letter to me of October 13, and that he had recommended him in these terms to the Trustees. I pointed out the embarrassment he had put the Trustees and me in.

He promised to make the appointment.

At noon Mr. Sterling telephoned Miss Miller for Dr. Campbell's telephone number. President Sterling told Miss Miller he rates Dr. Campbell B-plus. He got irate about "lies" and "fibs." President Sterling said he doesn't have the background to run the Hoover Institution—"no languages, no history, no library experience." Miss Miller said that Easton Rothwell had no such training in languages or libraries either. President Sterling snapped, "We'll not make comparisons." President Sterling did agree to call Dr. Campbell and said that he could probably help Dr. Campbell get on his feet. Miss Miller told President Sterling that she thought he could. She continued, stating that Sterling had studied in the Library and knew all its workings, etc.

Miss Miller and President ended on a happy note.

6:30 PM Miss Miller telephoned Dr. Campbell to find out confidentially if President Sterling had called Dr. Campbell during the day. Dr. Campbell said President Sterling had telephoned about 4:00 PM and offered him the Directorship and said that he would write Campbell a formal letter either Friday or Monday upon his return to Palo Alto.

Dr. Campbell is going to accept.

Dr. Campbell coming in to see Mr. Hoover on October 27 at 4:00 PM.

Tuesday, October 27, 1959, 8:00 AM

Miss Miller telephoned Dr. Campbell. Suggested he call on Mr. Hoover later in the week. Mr. Campbell to arrange for an appointment by telephone on Wednesday, October 28, for the end of the week.

Miss Miller telephoned President Sterling to say that Mr. Hoover thought there were some projects outside the Institution that have not been covered and where Mr. Hoover could possibly help. Therefore a need for another meeting and breakfast on Thursday, October 29, was set. Mr. Hoover also would need some advice from President Sterling on some foundations.

President Sterling confirmed to Miss Miller that he had made the appointment of Dr. Campbell.

Second Set of Notes

As I said, when I compared Hoover's notes with my own recollections, I was amazed at the similarity of the two versions. Here are my recollections:

In late June 1959 I received a telephone call from Raymond Moley (the man who coined the phrase "New Deal" for the administration of Franklin D. Roosevelt). Mr. Hoover and Mr. Moley had had dinner together the previous evening in Mr. Hoover's suite in the Waldorf Towers.

Moley read me the names of the various people Mr. Hoover had on his list and then asked me for my reactions. I informed him that in my opinion most were able people. However, there was one problem: virtually all were near or over the age of sixty-five, which I understood to be the retirement age at the Hoover Institution. Moley then asked me if I had any interest in becoming director of the Hoover Institution at Stanford. I answered, "Probably not," but added that I had never turned down a job I had not yet been offered.

Late in August my wife and I set sail for England on H.M.S. *Queen Elizabeth.* Our destination was the Mont Pelerin Society meeting at Oxford where we were scheduled, jointly, to give a paper. We traveled second class because we were returning first class on a new ship—the U.S.S. *United States*—and we wanted to save some money for the American Enterprise Association, which was paying for our trip. At the meeting Rita became a member of the society.

The program chairman was Prof. John Jewkes, author of *Ordeal by Planning,* a famous book on the disastrous results of the Labour government's policy. He gave a dinner one evening at Merton College, which was his own Oxford college, and I had the pleasure of sitting next to Henry Luce, the founder and long-time publisher and editor of *Time, Life,* and *Fortune* magazines. I told Mr. Luce that I had been an admirer of his distinguished spouse ever since she, as a member of Congress, coined the term "Globaloney" to describe some of Eleanor Roosevelt's silly statements about the postwar world. I also admired her comment about the horse that kicked Sen. Wayne Morse of Oregon in the head (though that particular witticism cost Clare Boothe Luce the ambassadorship to Brazil for which President Eisenhower had nominated her).

Ralph Harris (subsequently Lord Harris) and Arthur Seldon of the Institute for Economic Affairs of London handled the secretariat for the meeting. All the greats of the Mont Pelerin Society were there, including several subsequent Nobel Prize winners in economics: the president of the society Friedrich von Hayek, Milton Friedman, George Stigler, and James Buchanan (I did not know it at the time, but all these Nobel Prize winners would later be involved with the Hoover Institution), plus Ludwig von Mises, Jacques Rueff (President de Gaulle's economic adviser), Peter Bauer (now Lord Bauer), and Wilhelm Roepke of Geneva. Rita was, I believe, the second female member of the society, the first being Rebecca West.

While we were in England, I called William Baroody, who informed me that former President Hoover had been checking up, inquiring as to whether I was qualified to be—and would be interested in becoming—director of the Hoover Institution.

Rita and I boarded the U.S.S. *United States* in late September for the trip back to New York. About a day before landfall we received a seagram from Mr. Hoover asking us to call on him as soon as we got off the ship. After clearing customs we took a cab to the Waldorf Astoria Towers. There we were greeted by Mr. Hoover's secretary, Bernice Miller, and very shortly thereafter by Herbert Hoover himself. After introductions, Mr. Hoover told Rita that this would affect her also, so she should accompany us into his living room.

About thirty seconds later, Mr. Hoover asked me to become the director of the Hoover Institution. He knew we had two small daughters, so he launched into his praise of the public schools in Palo Alto. Perhaps twenty minutes into our discussion, I asked him if I might have some time to think the matter over, he agreed, and we left. Later that day we caught a train to Washington, D.C., and a taxi to Beech Tree Road.

I discussed the directorship with William Baroody in the next few days, and he urged me to accept the offer if it was forthcoming. I also discussed the matter extensively with Rita, who simply said that I should do what I thought would be best for my career. Returning to New York City, I told Mr. Hoover I would be willing to become director of the Hoover Institution if I were offered the job. He in turn informed me that President Sterling was coming to Washington, D.C., very shortly and would like to meet with me at the Hay-Adams Hotel. We met for coffee one morning in early October. Wally (we were already on a first-name basis—at his insistence) strongly urged that my wife and I come to Stanford to see the Institution and to meet the faculty involved with it. I agreed and he invited us to stay at the Hoover House (the president's house).

We arrived at the beginning of the third week of October and were escorted around the Hoover Institution and introduced to Witold Sworakowski, Thomas Thalken, and other high-ranking Hoover Institution employees. We also had lunch with members of Stanford's history department (notably Gordon Wright, who was department chairman at that time), members of the political science department, and Robert

Walker, chairman of the Stanford Overseas Program. On the evening of October 20 we were taken to dinner by a former AEA staff member and his wife, Dr. and Mrs. Virgil Salera. It was a great relief for Rita and me to get away from the stuffy, hostile atmosphere of Stanford and relax with friends. The next night, the eve of our departure, Sterling invited me to come to his study after dinner. He made it very clear that, as far as he was concerned, I was Mr. Hoover's choice and that I would not be welcomed at Stanford either by him or by the key members of the faculty and administration (for example, Gordon Wright, Robert Walker, Merrill Bennett, Dean Philip Rhinelander, and Vice Provost Wert). He pressed me to tell him whether Mr. Hoover had already offered me the job. Each time I told him the truth, to wit, that I had assured Mr. Hoover I would accept the job *if* he offered it to me.

Sterling offended me with some derogatory remarks about my qualifications. I had a Ph.D. in economics from Harvard, and he had a Ph.D. in history from Stanford. In those days a Ph.D. from Harvard was generally considered superior to one from Stanford. In addition, though he was much older than I was, my scholarly output was much greater than his. Finally, he annoyed me so much I told him that if I were to be known as "Mr. Hoover's candidate," that was perfectly fine—I knew of no person whose recommendation I valued more highly. Then I decided to call his bluff. I said it was obvious to me I was not welcome, and I was going back to New York to ask Mr. Hoover to release me from my commitment to accept the job if it were offered. Sterling was not pleased. He was afraid that the "Chief" (as he called Mr. Hoover) and his friends among the trustees would blame him.

That evening when I went up to bed, Rita was already there, having run out of things to talk about with Mrs. Sterling. I suggested a walk, since this might be the last time we'd visit Stanford University. As we strolled, I rehearsed my conversation with "Wally." The next morning after breakfast, Sterling asked me to meet him in his study. He expressed concern that he had given me the impression last night that I was not welcome. I agreed that he had. He explained that actually he *very much* wanted me at the Hoover Institution, that after I had gone to bed he had made some telephone calls to Hoover and Stanford scholars well acquainted with the Institution, and they all said they wanted me. I thanked him, told him I would think about his offer, and Rita and I returned East. I reported my experiences to Mr. Hoover and he told me not to worry—he would take care of things.

Apparently, however, Sterling made one more attempt to dissuade Mr. Hoover and the trustees from supporting me. In this he proved to be a man lacking in courage, as well as in adherence to the truth.

Under date of November 6, 1959, I received the following letter:

Dear Glenn:

I am just home from my various travels, and write to confirm the substance of our telephone conversation when I was in New York.

As I told you, the Stanford Trustees have authorized me to finalize arrangements concerning your appointment as Director of the Hoover Institution, and I have discussed these arrangements with Mr. Hoover, who approves of them. With this letter, then, I formalize the offer to you of said Directorship, with a salary of $18,000 per annum and eligibility for other benefits including T.I.A.A. participation, for which regular members of the Stanford Faculty are eligible. You will have administrative tenure, as I have, which means that you hold your appointment at the pleasure of the Trustees. You will not have academic tenure—nor do I.

I understand from both Mr. Hoover and you that your costs of moving will be underwritten to the amount of $2,000. This is agreed to.

There remains the matter of when you would be able to assume office. Our strong preference is to have you take office as soon as possible. When we last talked on the telephone, I asked you to ponder this matter, and you said you would let me know at your earliest convenience the best schedule you could work out. I look forward to having this schedule from you as soon as possible so that we may announce the effective date of your appointment and work out the pro-rating salary for the period in which you may be part-time in Washington and part-time here. Let me repeat that we are eager to have you full-time here at the earliest practicable date. All best wishes,

Sincerely yours,
J. E. Wallace Sterling

cc: Mr. Hoover
    Mr. Packard
    Mr. Black

On November 20, 1959, I received this telegram from the staff of the Hoover Institution: "WE WARMLY WELCOME OUR NEW DIREC-TOR." This pleased me very much, because some of the staff had long been loyal to my predecessor. Now they were transferring their loyalty to me, largely, I believe, because they knew I was Mr. Hoover's choice.

I was able to arrange my affairs so that on January 1, 1960, at the age of thirty-five, I became director of the Hoover Institution. On September 1, 1989, at the age of sixty-five, I became counselor. The intervening twenty-nine-plus years were for the most part very fulfilling.

Accepting this new position meant taking a $2,000 salary cut, but I agreed to this for two reasons: First, Mr. Hoover very much wanted me to accept the post. Second, I relished the challenge of trying to build the Hoover Institution into something important, even though I knew I would be working in a hostile environment. As I recall, Mr. Hoover offered two other arguments to entice me to Hoover: I could always travel first class in airplanes, and I would always be able to keep my special parking place behind the Hoover Tower. If prime, reserved parking is, as one hears, a matter of great moment to members of Congress and business executives, it is equally important at a large university. At that time parking spaces at Stanford were still free (the huge parking space behind the old library is now taken up by the new Green Library), but the coveted spots were those closest to the back of the Tower. When Stanford started charging for parking places, I always paid for mine even though I wasn't required to do so. I was sure there would come a time when someone would argue that I should lose my parking space because I'd never paid for it.

4
Working with Herbert Hoover

W HEN I WAS APPOINTED DIRECTOR, ONE OF THE FIRST ITEMS of business was the renovation of our only building, the Hoover Tower. The ground-floor staff room was our first project. It was painted and refurnished in 1961, and Dr. Rita Ricardo-Campbell obtained and hung some large travel posters to brighten its appearance. This staff room remained in use until early 1979, when the Herbert Hoover Federal Memorial Building, with its Senior Commons Room and its spacious staff room, was opened. That was also the year (1961) when we renovated and refurbished the ground-floor offices for the Chinese and Japanese curators, their cataloguers, and the rest of their staffs.

As we expanded the Institution's research staff, the use of its library increased, requiring further renovation of the Hoover Tower. In 1964 part of the newspaper collection was moved from the ground floor to the fifteenth floor, and the rest was put into temporary storage until a new building could be completed. Thirteen well-furnished research offices were constructed in the cleared space, along with rooms for researching current newspaper and microfilm collections, and a large Research Reading Room equipped with thirty-two carrels and generous shelf space. The second-floor offices were painted and refurbished in 1966.

In 1965 the Lou Henry Hoover Room, containing memorabilia of the former First Lady, was redecorated and rearranged for a more attractive display and for more secure placement of valuable items. For example, her Ming vases were rescued from the top of a rickety table that would have collapsed in a sizable earthquake, and given a safe setting.

A reading room for visiting scholars on the opposite side of the Tower rotunda, identical in size to the Lou Henry Hoover Room, was formally dedicated as the Herbert Hoover Room. Its exhibits displayed the broad range of Mr. Hoover's activities during fifty years of public service. Its contents included:

- A chronology of the major events of Herbert Hoover's life and a list of the major positions he held under five presidents of the United States
- The desk and chair Mr. Hoover used as secretary of commerce and the chair from which he presided over cabinet meetings when he was president
- The president's handwritten draft of a letter to well-wishers upon his election in 1928, plus communications to him from King Albert of Belgium and President Masaryk of Czechoslovakia
- Handwritten drafts illustrating the development of a Hoover speech, along with his presidential appointment diary
- Gifts of appreciation to Mr. Hoover from the people of war-torn countries aided by his relief programs, including flour sacks embroidered by Belgian women and children
- Awards bestowed on the former president—for example, his credentials as a Stanford graduate and trustee, a selection from the more than one hundred honorary degrees granted him by other colleges and universities, and the U.S. Mint silver medallion commemorating his service in the nation's highest office

The dedication of the Herbert Hoover Room on July 20, 1965, brought messages from all over the world testifying to the international respect in which the man was held. Former President Eisenhower noted that "his interests were so broad and his productive activities so varied that there is scarcely anyone who does not have a special reason for cherishing his memory." Eisenhower's predecessor, Harry S Truman, said in a telegram that Mr. Hoover's "record as the great humanitarian of this century will long endure in the hearts of men." The speakers at the July 20 dedication ceremonies were Stanford President J. E. Wallace Sterling, Trustee David Packard, and Allan Hoover.

Working with Mr. Hoover

Until President Hoover's death in October 1964 I was pleased and fortunate to have his help in fundraising and other matters. After the trustees approved his May 1959 resolution establishing the Institution's independence and removed the "left-wingers," Mr. Hoover launched a fundraising campaign which started an increasing influx of gifts to the Institution. Part of his reason for this effort was his desire to attract a young and energetic scholar with vision, leadership, and a backbone to the job of director.

Among the "left-wingers" Mr. Hoover referred to were Mary Wright, curator of the Chinese Collection, who became a professor of history at Yale; Nobutaka Ike, curator of the Japanese Collection; Robert North, a research associate; and Christina Harris, curator of the Middle East Collection. These became full-time members of the political science department at Stanford, continuing to enjoy joint appointments. Rita and I always considered Christina Harris's political and economic views quite well balanced, but she was often criticized for her pro-Arab positions.

My predecessor, Dr. C. Easton Rothwell, and President Sterling had used joint appointments to frustrate Mr. Hoover's plan to make the Hoover Institution more ideologically balanced. All the people in question had tenure in their university departments. One powerful argument Mr. Hoover used to interest me in the director's job was that—in addition to his fundraising drive, which he expected would raise at least $1 million in gifts and pledges—there was almost $2 million in endowment money, so a new director need not worry about funds for traveling around the world, obtaining valuable collections, taking part in important scholarly conferences, or meeting leading statesmen and scholars. Since the market value of the existing endowment was about $9 million on August 31, 1959, there was indeed sufficient financing for all these activities. However, the expense of traveling extensively would probably have precluded the construction of two additional buildings, and the endowment and expendable funds would not have grown to $128 million, as they later did, plus $5 million in pledges and $10 to $20 million in potential bequests. Even more important, my colleagues and I would not have been able to appoint so many distinguished scholars or institute such programs as the National, Peace, and Public Affairs and the National

Security Affairs programs. Nevertheless, in retrospect, there have been times when I wished I had followed the course he outlined.

The Major Task of My First Years

Once appointed, I quickly worked out my vision for the future of the Hoover Institution—to turn it into a well-balanced scholarly institution where ideas of all varieties (except totalitarian ones) were welcomed and respected. This vision always had the enthusiastic backing and encouragement of Mr. Hoover. Over the years, the Hoover Institution was visited by a number of so-called scholars from totalitarian countries such as the Soviet Union and the People's Republic of China, virtually all of whom were obviously doing research on behalf of the secret police in their countries.

In time I came up with a ready answer to the numerous questions about my policy as it related to ideology. I said that I would appoint a communist if we could find one who was a genuine scholar and not a propagandist. The closest we ever came was the appointment of Bertram Wolfe, a first-rate scholar who had been a communist in his youth but had reconsidered when he saw Stalin's effect on the Soviet Union. We also appointed Sidney Hook, who always claimed to be a Marxist but who was also a world-class philosopher; some Mensheviks, such as Boris Nicolaevsky and Anna Bourguina; and one or two people who'd been Trotskyites in their youth, such as Seymour Martin Lipset.

To the best of my knowledge, Hoover is the only major think-tank that has managed to turn from a left-wing organization into a well-balanced and scholarly one that fosters a true competition of ideas.

Of course, some institutions have turned in the other direction. In the 1960s, for example, the Brookings Institution shifted from the balanced policies of president Harold Moulton to the left-wing focus of new president Robert Calkins, largely because of a $15 million grant from the Ford Foundation ($10 million for endowment and $5 million expendable over a ten-year period). In effect, the Ford Foundation's left-wing staff simply bought the Brookings Institution. The Ford grant was part of a $20 million campaign which Calkins and the Brookings trustees undertook to celebrate the fiftieth anniversary of Brookings' founding in

1915. Shortly after the campaign began, Mrs. Brookings died, leaving about $8 million to the institution. Thus, with just two gifts—the Ford Foundation's obviously being the controlling one—the campaign exceeded its goal.

Kermit Gordon, who succeeded Calkins as Brookings' president, was a well-meaning but weak man who had served in relatively high posts—member of the Council of Economic Advisors and then director of the Budget Bureau—in the Kennedy and Johnson administrations. Bruce K. MacLaury, who followed Gordon as president of Brookings, strove to bring it back to a reasonable balance and to restore the competition of ideas, but he did not fully achieve his goal. The current president, Michael Armacost, an old friend from his days as a White House Fellow, will, I am sure, complete the transition, and Brookings may well give the Hoover Institution more competition in Washington, D.C.

Salary Discrimination at the Hoover Institution

I was surprised to find that salary discrimination was rampant at Hoover. My predecessor, C. Easton Rothwell, a nice man and a good leftist, had been paid $17,000 a year. The next highest paid staff member was Mary Wright, curator of the Chinese Collection, who received about $8,500 (half the director's salary) until she left Hoover to become a professor of history at Yale shortly before I took over. One of the persons Mr. Hoover referred to as a "left-winger," she had circulated around the San Francisco area, giving speeches to explain that the Chinese Communists were simply "agrarian reformers." This infuriated Mr. Hoover because she gave the impression that she spoke with his approval. He received many letters from long-time friends in San Francisco who wanted to know why he had changed his mind about the Chinese Communists, and—if he *hadn't*—why he was sanctioning Wright's behavior.

The salary discrimination was directed for the most part against Eastern European refugees and Asians, most of whom were also refugees and women. Polish refugee Witold Sworakowski, who served as assistant director (the second highest post at the Hoover Institution), and Phillip McLean, the long-serving but not very competent librarian, each received about $8,000 in salary. The curator of the Chinese Collection, Eugene

Wu, was paid about $5,000, and Tomatso Takase, the curator of the Japanese Collection, was paid slightly less. Joseph Bingaman, the assistant librarian, was receiving $5,220 a year.

I increased the salary of Agnes Peterson, curator of the Western European Collection, to $5,500 in 1960–61 and the salary of Barbara Lasarev, a very competent librarian, to $3,360. I raised the salary of Peter Duignan, the new curator of the African Collection who also served as a research associate, from $6,000 to $7,500 that year. I was surprised that my $18,000 salary was *double* that of anyone else on the staff, especially since I'd been hoping to match the $20,000 I'd been getting at AEA.

By fiscal 1970–71, the inequities were corrected, but not without a considerable struggle on my part. I had particular difficulty raising the salaries of employees like Professor Sworakowski who—in President Sterling's view—had been too loyal to Mr. Hoover and then to me. Peterson's salary was increased to $14,200, Lasarev's to $7,632, and Duignan's to $22,000. Dr. Milorad Drachkovitch, whom I had appointed in July 1961, was making $23,500; Dr. Lewis Gann, appointed in 1964, was paid $15,000; and Dr. Richard Staar replaced Witold Sworakowski (who, when he retired in 1969, was being paid $24,000) as associate director for library operations at a salary of $26,000. Because of Sworakowski's encyclopedic knowledge of our collections, and to compensate for the salary discrimination he had suffered for so many years, I arranged to retain him as a paid consultant until his death in 1979.

My own salary for 1970–71 was $30,500. There were two reasons why it did not much exceed the salaries of the Senior Fellows. First, I firmly believed in paying them their market value, so the Hoover Institution was always a very collegial, productive place, a place that a Senior Fellow need not leave in order to receive a reasonable income. Second, President Sterling had systematically practiced salary discrimination against me during the 1960s, so I knew how it felt.

During the 1970s President Richard Lyman also worked to overcome the previous salary discrimination. He set my salary at $35,000 for 1972–73, and by 1979–80 it was $58,500. President Donald Kennedy did not begin to practice salary discrimination until 1984–85, and once Board President James Gaither took over, he persuaded Kennedy to set my salary at $125,000 for 1988–89 (almost a 20 percent increase over the previous year). When Hewitt Associates compared my salary with those paid the heads of comparable research institutions in 1987, Hewitt concluded that I should have received $175,000 that year.

A Hoover TV Series

When I arrived at the Hoover Institution, Professor Sworakowski was already producing an important television series entitled "The Red Myth." There was campus opposition to it, but I immediately gave him my full support and also enlisted Mr. Hoover's. The program was a tremendous success in the United States and even in the Soviet Union.

The series chronicled the history of communism from Karl Marx to Nikita Khrushchev and drew from the wealth of material housed in the Hoover Institution libraries. The series aired on over fifty public television stations and some commercial stations. Because of numerous requests for written transcripts of the series, Stanford University, the National Education Television Foundation, and Radio Center in New York produced a narrative account based on the television series. That account, written by Stephan Baffrey, presented the salient points of the dramatized television shows in a literary format. Professor Sworakowski initiated the production of the television series, selected the documentary material for the scriptwriters, acted as consultant during its production, and as host of the series supplied the preface.

My First Hoover-Stanford Controversy

A controversy concerning the Trustees Resolution of May 1959 arose in March 1960, less than three months after I came on board. Raymond Moley had recommended me to Vice President (and presidential candidate) Richard Nixon to be director of research for his 1960 campaign. I was in New York for a meeting of the Advisory Board of the AEA at the University Club, and was seriously considering accepting the Nixon job if it were offered. Of course, I would have had to resign as director of the Hoover Institution and would probably never have returned to California.

A telephone call from Assistant Director Sworakowski informed me that we were under attack at the Hoover Institution and that Stanford

President Sterling was doing nothing to defend President Hoover or me. Because of my commitment to Mr. Hoover, I dismissed any thoughts of assisting the Nixon campaign and returned to the Hoover Institution. I assured Mr. Hoover that Sterling and his supporters would have to carry me out in the same way the army, on FDR's orders, had removed Sewell Avery as CEO of Montgomery Ward during World War II. I was confident that they lacked the courage to do that.

On April 1, 1960, President Sterling addressed the Academic Council, which responded with open hostility despite his attempts to assure the members that the founder (Hoover) could not live much longer and that things would then change to their liking. Such promises notwithstanding, the Academic Council voted 78 to 73 to ask the Advisory Board to establish its own committee to devise "A statement of the scope, importance and purposes of the Hoover Institution." The report of this committee—known as the Wright committee after its chairman, history professor Gordon Wright—follows:

May 6, 1960

Professor E. R. Hilgard, Chairman
Advisory Board, Stanford University

Dear Professor Hilgard:

Two weeks ago the undersigned faculty members were appointed to serve as a drafting committee to propose "a statement of the scope, importance and purposes of the Hoover Institution" for submission to the President and his transmittal to the Board of Trustees.

The drafting committee's proposed statement is attached hereto. At the risk of seeming to offer presumptuous and unsolicited advice, the committee members would like to make several observations which they consider to be relevant:

(1) The committee views its statement as supplementary to the Trustees' resolution of May 21, 1959 on the purposes, management, and policies of the Hoover Institution. Paragraph 7 of that resolution declares that "The Director must be a man who reflects the purposes of the Institution"; but the resolution contains no explicit statement of what those purposes are. The committee hopes that the Board of Trustees will accept the attached

statement as the official statement of the scope, importance, and purposes of the Hoover Institution.

(2) The committee hopes that its statement will be given wide public circulation. It believes that both Stanford University and the Hoover Institution have been damaged by the circulation of an unofficial brochure [there was nothing unofficial about it; President Sterling had simply *called it* unofficial] purporting to express the aims and purposes of the Institution. The committee is convinced that this damage cannot be undone except by providing friends of Stanford, and the public generally, with a new brochure that contains an officially sanctioned statement of the Hoover Institution's purposes. The committee's draft has been intentionally worded in such fashion as to serve this kind of public-relations function.

(3) The structural relationship between the Hoover Institution and the rest of the University, as defined in the Trustees' resolution of May 21, 1959, remained outside the terms of reference of the drafting committee. The committee members suggest, however, that changes are desirable in that structural relationship at some appropriate future time. The committee shares the conviction of many faculty members that a closer integration of the Hoover Institution with the rest of the University would prove to be of mutual benefit. The committee regards the Hoover Institution as one of Stanford's greatest assets, but it believes that the full scholarly utilization of this unique resource cannot be achieved until a close working relationship is established between the Institution's staff and the University's academic staff.

Respectfully submitted,
Merrill K. Bennett
Bernard F. Haley
David S. Nivison
Gordon Wright (Chairman)[1]

---

1. Bennett was director of the Food Research Institution, Haley a professor of economics, Nivison professor of philosophy, and Wright professor of history. Bennett, Haley, and Wright are now deceased.

President Sterling tried to get me to accept the committee's statement, but out of loyalty to Mr. Hoover I respectfully declined. There was
nothing necessarily wrong with the statement itself, but it was written
and would have been used in an insulting context. To make it more difficult, all this occurred while I was driving my car from Washington,
D.C., to California. On June 2, after we had discussed the matter over
the telephone and agreed that we were both under attack, Mr. Hoover
sent a long letter to the trustees, declaring that he did "not believe that
the Trustees will countenance such an insult." Mr. Hoover's letter was so
important that it is reproduced here in full:

> A twelve-year-old issue as to the relationship of the Hoover Institution
> to the University, its purposes, its policies, its management, and its rela-
> tions to the faculty has been revived by a group of the faculty.
>
> During recent years consideration of these subjects for action by the
> Trustees has been held within the President of the Board of Trustees, the
> President of the University, myself, and more recently, the Chairman of the
> Trustees' Committee on the Hoover Institution, working out successful
> solutions of these matters. In consequence, some of my fellow Trustees are
> probably not fully familiar with this subject.
>
> Of primary importance in the understanding of these matters is the forty-
> year background since I founded this Institution at Stanford. For these rea-
> sons the time has come when I believe I can be of service to my fellow
> Trustees by giving a review of these backgrounds, and also that I give some
> samples of misunderstandings and misrepresentations due in part to unfa-
> miliarity with the facts.
>
> ### The Background
>
> At the time I founded the Institution and during its first few years cer-
> tain conditions and policies were defined by me and accepted by the Uni-
> versity authorities under the leadership of President Wilbur. These were:
>
> 1. That the Institution shall be an independent institution within the
> framework of the University, where the President of the University approves
> the appointments and the budget, and recommends them to the Trustees.
>
> 2. That there shall be no control of the Institution by the faculty or fac-
> ulty committees at any time.
>
> 3. That the publications of the Institution shall be limited strictly and

solely to factual documentation concerning historical events, negotiations, and actions that illuminate phases of history.

4. That these publications shall also include purely factual documentary volumes, which will give guidance to the American people from the lessons of past experience. (As Santayana has aptly phrased it: "Those who cannot remember the past are condemned to repeat it.")

5. That the doors of the Institution shall be open for research and study to all qualified scholars.

These policies, mentioned in paragraph 3 and 4 above, were insisted upon by me to avoid discord over racial and religious questions, or statements of opinions, which inevitably lead into conflicts over academic freedom, freedom of research or inquiry.

All of these basic principles are confirmed in the early records of the Institution which will be furnished to the Trustees.

In 1948, a new regime as to publication policies was instituted by the Director of the Institution—so-called "interpretive" history. These publications carried the imprint and authority of the Institution. Over seventeen such publications were issued. A series of disagreeable incidents followed, as to which I can furnish the facts to the Trustees if they so desire. These publications and statements brought forth both public and private protests.

At the July 30, 1956 meeting of the Advisory Board of the Institution, I made a motion that the policy of solely objective documentary publications should be restored. The motion was supported by President Dinkelspiel of the Board of Trustees and by President Sterling, and was carried unanimously at this meeting.

On May 8, 1958, the Director of the Institution made an extensive report and many recommendations, which he sent to each of the Trustees. He proposed a reversal again from the factual, documentary publication policy to "interpretive history." He proposed the use of endowment funds for current expenditures (most of these endowment funds were under contract by the donors that only the income therefrom was to be used for current expenses). He proposed changes in the purposes and management of the Institution, the introduction of faculty control, and generally the reversal of the original basic principles of independence of the Institution and policies of management.

On August 25, 1958, I made a fully documented report on the Director's proposal to the Trustees. For the reasons stated above, my documented report was limited in its circulation.

As a result of my report, President Packard and Chairman Black initiated negotiations with me as to a complete reorganization of the purposes, policies, and management of the Institution. I naturally urged the restoration of the independence of the Institution within the original limits as stated above, and the reestablishment of the policies of publication and management which had prevailed during the first twenty-six years of successful management and productive work.

I also, at the request of these Trustees, prepared a statement on the "purposes of the Institution." I submitted a draft to President Packard, Chairman Black and President Sterling, all of whom made suggestions and minor amendments, which I adopted.

An agreement on the policies, purposes, and management of the Institution was achieved, and a resolution was unanimously passed and adopted by the Board of Trustees on May 21, 1959.

Because of my faith in the Trustees' resolution of May 21, 1959, carrying into effect this agreement, I transferred, subject to certain conditions, the Hoover Archives, containing the largest private collection of modern historical documents in the United States, to the Hoover Institution. This arrangement was accepted by the Trustees on September 17, 1959.

The financial gifts to the Institution for current expenditures had reached a low ebb due to loss of confidence in the Institution by many of its friends. With the background of the Trustees' resolution of May 21, 1959, I undertook to raise financial support for the Institution from national Foundations and my friends. At the present time this support has reached over $1,250,000 in cash and commitments with additional important contributions in prospect.

Correction of Some Misunderstandings and Misrepresentations
The Trustees are amply informed as to the agitation on the Campus during the past four months.

I have little inclination to discuss these incidents and I have made no public statements in respect to them. However, an analysis of two of these samples may be helpful to my fellow Trustees.

There is a travesty in these agitations to which I refer only because they have had wide circulation.

After forty years' advocacy of academic freedom and freedom of research in public addresses, two of which were made on the Campus, and after having received eighty-five honorary degrees from universities equally zealous of academic freedom as Stanford, I was astonished at statements being made that I was restricting academic freedom, etc.

All of which was based on a tortuous and distorted argument over a short paragraph in my statement on "the purposes of the Institution."

Among the statements which have been made by a group of the faculty is: "It believes that both Stanford University and the Hoover Institution have been damaged by the circulation of an unofficial brochure purporting to express the aims and purposes of the Institution."

This "brochure" was printed on September 7, 1959, and contained: that part of the minutes of the Board of Trustees meeting of May 21, 1959, which pertained to the Hoover Institution; my statement as to the purposes of the Hoover Institution which had been included with the Trustees' resolution of May 21, 1959; and minutes of the Trustees meeting of March 20, 1958, establishing the standing Trustees' Committee on the Hoover Institution.

In sending out the "brochure" it was accompanied by a letter of appeal for financial support which stated the fact that the Trustees had recently reorganized the Institution.

In correction of the implications and misunderstandings of the above faculty statement, I may cite the following facts:

On September 9, 1959, I wrote President Sterling that I was undertaking a personal appeal for financial aid for the Hoover Institution. On September 10, I wrote to Chairman Black about my drive, enclosing several copies of the brochure. On September 14, I showed President Packard a sample of the letters I was writing to foundations, and gave him several copies of the brochure. And, also on September 14, I wrote President Sterling that I had given my solicitation materials to President Packard and that he would show them to President Sterling.

Far from "damage," the clearing of the air with this "brochure" contributed substantially to the success of obtaining more than $1,250,000 for the Institution.

Over and above all this, it seems to me that the action of the Trustees on

May 21, 1959, which is of such importance to the Institution, to its supporters, and to the American people, should not be withheld from their knowledge.

It might easily be assumed that I know the purposes of the Institution, since I founded it. But a group of the faculty has demanded that the Trustees expunge my statement on the purposes of the Institution and substitute a statement on its purposes to be prepared by them.

I do not believe that the Trustees will countenance such an insult. A member of the Board of Trustees has requested that I further analyze certain faculty recommendations and statements. I regret that I do not have the time to undertake personally this task more than is shown in the samples above. As the members of the Board know, I am now approaching my 86th year and have great responsibilities aside from the Hoover Institution in the administration of educational, scientific, and charitable institutions—to say nothing of my hope of finishing some historical publications of importance to the American people.

However, I have requested my secretary, Miss Bernice Miller, a graduate of Stanford University, and her staff, who are familiar with all these events, to prepare an extensive and documented record of the backgrounds, discussions, agreements, and recommendations of the past on this subject, including documentary proof of the statements in the letter.

I regret, although greatly condensed, that this letter may be over-long. But fidelity to agreements concerning the Institution, the preservation of its integrity, and its potential service to the American people are of high importance to the University and to our country.

Yours faithfully,
/s Herbert Hoover/

This letter put an end to the efforts of Professor Wright and his friends to get revenge. Wright had long coveted the position of director of the Hoover Institution. Indeed, I was told on reliable authority that he had been *promised* the job by Sterling and several influential faculty members. The Senate Committee had called for major "structural change" in the Stanford-Hoover relationship "at an appropriate time," which all understood to mean at the death of Herbert Hoover. This, combined with the trustees' apparent acceptance at their June 1960 meeting of

Sterling's own needlessly insulting statement about how *he* would administer the Hoover Institution, caused Mr. Hoover to take a drastic step.

Other 1960 Changes

In April or May of 1960, the Hoover librarian came to see me in a very agitated state. According to him, African curator Peter Duignan was collecting *economic* material and "everyone knows that such material has nothing to do with War, Revolution and Peace." I looked him straight in the eye and said, "Are you aware of which field I got my Ph.D. in?" He answered, "Yes," and I continued, "From now on, instruct *all* curators to collect economic materials that have to do with War, Revolution and Peace—and there is *a lot of it.*" This probably explains why our library does not contain a copy of the late Friedrich A. von Hayek's seminal work against socialism, *The Road to Serfdom.* Actually, the librarian's attitude did not surprise me. He once claimed that regular acquisitions did not cost us anything because they were *already provided for in the budget.*

Among other unsound practices was the librarian's policy of charging only the original cost if students or faculty members lost books they had checked out. In fact, the lost books cost Hoover more than that because of the time our librarians spent searching for the prices of pamphlets or books purchased in the 1920s for $.50 or $1.50. As soon as we began charging replacement costs, it was curious how many fewer books were lost.

I discovered in early 1960 that, over the strenuous objections of Professor Sworakowski, Acting Director Philip Rhinelander had approved the sale of twenty or thirty thousand duplicates to a midwestern university for about a dollar apiece. Rhinelander's contention was that this was all they cost us, but in fact we could easily charge four or five dollars for each duplicate, and so we did. Over the years we've received millions of dollars from the sale of duplicate books. (During my tenure as director, Hoover took in $7,558,000 in receipts from sales of publications and duplicate books, and $1,454,000 in receipts from sales of microfilms.)

One amusing result of the March 1960 controversy over Mr. Hoover's statement about the evils of the doctrines of Karl Marx was that in April we received an unsolicited contribution of $15,000 from Mr. Hoover's long-time friend Joseph P. Kennedy. Strangely, when I mentioned this to faculty members hostile to the Hoover Institution, they did not seem as amused as I was. Nor were they pleased when I informed them that I had first been recommended to Mr. Hoover by Raymond Moley, the Columbia University professor of public law who, at the request of the president-elect in 1932, organized the famed "Brain Trust" that advised Franklin D. Roosevelt's administration.

Protecting the Academic Integrity of the Hoover Institution

The unreasonable attacks mounted in March of 1960 made me quite angry at first. Professors were saying that I would not support and build the library and archives, which was entirely untrue. So I decided that, if Mr. Hoover at his age was willing to fight for the Institution, I would do the same, even after he had passed away. I persisted despite intermittent opposition and takeover attempts by leftist faculty and presidents like Donald Kennedy. Some University of Chicago people had a theory about my persistence. George Stigler, the 1982 Nobel Prize winner in economics, contended that part of the reason I worked so hard to build the Hoover Institution was that I was reacting to the negative and hostile atmosphere at Stanford.

In June 1960 Vice Provost and Mrs. Wert, on President Sterling's instructions, held a cocktail reception at their home to welcome Rita and me to Stanford. Rita was well into the eighth month of her third pregnancy—Nancy Elizabeth would be born on July 14—so she had to go out and buy a new maternity dress. It became painfully clear shortly after our arrival that we might as well have saved the money and stayed home. Nearly everyone, including our hosts, was there under duress. The only friendly people were a professor of medieval history and his wife, William and Eleanor Bark. We spent most of our time talking with them and learned that Eleanor had been a Stanford classmate of David Packard's wife, Lucile.

The friendship that began that evening has lasted a lifetime. Just before Christmas 1965 William Bark, accompanied by his son Dennis, brought some of his specially baked Christmas bread to Rita and our daughters and me. It was excellent— particularly served with cognac. Dennis Bark was home from the Thunderbird School in Phoenix, Arizona, where he was studying international trade. At one point William mentioned that he would really like Dennis to go to the Free University of Berlin and get his Ph.D. with Hans Herzfeld, a distinguished professor of history. I remembered that the Relm Foundation of Ann Arbor, Michigan, had granted me the right to nominate one promising student per year for graduate study, and it would pay for his or her schooling. So Dennis Bark did indeed attend the Free University of Berlin where he received his Ph.D. (*summa cum laude*) in history and political science in the spring of 1970. Eventually, to my great satisfaction, he came to the Hoover Institution.

President de Gaulle of France and Professor Sidney Hook

In June 1960 Charles de Gaulle of France visited the United States. Mr. Hoover had sat beside him at a dinner in his honor in New York City, and they had discussed the World War II French Resistance Collection at the Hoover Institution. President de Gaulle expressed great interest in seeing it, but was told by his aide-de-camp that his schedule on the West Coast called for him to visit only the new Stanford Medical School. Nevertheless, the general expressed interest in meeting the new director of the Hoover Institution, so I had the pleasure of a private conversation with this great man about our World War II French Resistance Collection. I also issued a warm invitation to him to visit the Hoover Institution the next time he came to the Stanford area, and he said that he would do so.

In fall of 1960 Rita and I met Sidney Hook—who was spending that academic year at the Center for Advanced Study in the Behavioral Sciences at Stanford —at a cocktail party at Professor Sworakowski's home on campus. Professor Hook expressed outrage about the attacks on Mr. Hoover and me and told me that if they ever recurred I must let him know; he and his friends would respond to these attempts to restrict free speech and to engage in what we agreed could only be described as "academic McCarthyism."

The Bohemian Club

Since the beginning of the twentieth century, several U.S. presidents—Theodore Roosevelt, Dwight Eisenhower, Richard Nixon, Gerald Ford, Ronald Reagan, and George Bush—have been members of the Bohemian Club. Former President Jimmy Carter spoke at the Lakeside at the Bohemian Grove recently, as did Attorney General Robert F. Kennedy in 1964. Carlos Romulo of the Philippines, a long-time honorary member of the club, has made more than one speech at the Lakeside. When I became a member of the club, King Gustavus Adolphus of Sweden was listed as an honorary member, and since I have been a member, Charles, the prince of Wales, has visited the San Francisco club.

Many leading jurists, such as Chief Justice Earl Warren, have also been members of the club, as have several secretaries of state (most recently, Henry Kissinger, George Shultz, James Baker III, and Warren Christopher) and secretaries of treasury (Henry Fowler from the Kennedy-Johnson administration, William E. Simon, James Baker III, and Nicholas Brady). There are also many corporate CEOs, including Thomas Watson, Jr., of IBM, David Rockefeller of the Chase Manhattan Bank, Maurice R. Greenberg of the American International Group, Fred Crawford of TRW, and David Packard and William Hewlett of Hewlett-Packard. University presidents have included Robert Gordon Sproul and Clark Kerr of the University of California, Kenneth Pitzer of Rice and Stanford, Chancellor Roger Heynes of Berkeley, and Lee Du Bridge and Harold Brown of Cal Tech. (Du Bridge became science adviser to President Nixon and Brown became secretary of defense to President Carter.)

I became a member of the Bohemian Club in January 1961 with Herbert Hoover as my lead sponsor and Charles Kendrick, a former Bohemian Club president, as seconder. In July I had the pleasure of meeting former Vice President Richard M. Nixon again at Cave Man Camp. One weekend, he and long-time Bohemians Bill Thompson and George Alexander replayed his famous Kitchen Debate with Nikita Khrushchev. Thompson played Khrushchev, Alexander (who speaks both Russian and English) was the interpreter, and it was one of the funniest exchanges I ever heard. Mr. Hoover regularly spoke at the Lakeside on the last Saturday of the Encampment, the last time in 1962 when he was almost eighty-eight years old.

I was grateful that Mr. Hoover arranged for me to become a member of Cave Man Camp. Most members were celebrities, a nice mixture of intellectuals, public servants, and businessmen. In addition to President Nixon, there were Herbert Hoover, Jr., who was a very successful businessman before he joined the State Department under Secretary of State John Foster Dulles in the Eisenhower administration; Lawrence Kimpton, president of the University of Chicago; and Wallace Sterling, president of Stanford. Cave Man member Lowell Thomas was already a newsman at the beginning of World War I. He went to the Middle East and was arguably the person who made Lawrence of Arabia famous. A great storyteller as well as a great newscaster, he got to know almost every president of the United States from Woodrow Wilson to Richard Nixon. At a luncheon at Cave Man Camp, Thomas once told us about the time he sat next to ibn-Saud, the first king of Saudi Arabia, at a state function there. During the meal the king asked him, "How many wives do you have?" Lowell said, "One, Your Majesty." King Saud was puzzled because under Muslim law a man is allowed four wives at a time, plus a harem. Lowell explained that in the United States it was illegal to have more than one wife. The king thought that unfair, so he did an unusual thing for an Arab monarch: he offered his good friend his pick of the harem for the evening. Thomas declined gracefully.

Other distinguished members included Roy Howard of Scripps-Howard and his son Jack; Mr. Hoover's best friend for many years, Jeremiah Milbank, Sr., on whose yacht Hoover used to sail when he was president; and Gen. Albert Wedemeyer, author of the Wedemeyer Report on China, compiled for President Truman in response to public criticism of Gen. George Marshall's report. Frank Prior, the CEO of Standard Oil of Indiana, Mr. Hoover's younger son Allan, and Herbert Hoover III (Pete) were also members.

Between 1965 and 1967 Richard Nixon spoke at the Bohemian Grove in Mr. Hoover's old position, at 12:30 PM on the last Saturday of the Encampment. His 1967 talk was particularly memorable. He stood at the lectern with no notes and in thirty minutes gave a brilliant commentary on all the many trouble spots of the world—the Soviet Union, the People's Republic of China, the Middle East, and Latin America—

then presented his proposals as to what the United States should do in each area. Being able to discuss these problems and the proposed solutions with him was particularly helpful to me when I returned to the Hoover Institution.

Lenin's Letters

During the negotiations for the Limited Nuclear Test Ban Treaty signed in Moscow on August 5, 1963, Secretary of State Dean Rusk called our home on a Sunday morning in July. Rita was busy making pancakes for the children and herself. When Rusk asked for me, she explained that I was at the Bohemian Grove. My name went up on the message board of the Bohemian Grove with a request to call Secretary of State Rusk. A lot of practical jokes were played there, so when Jack Howard told me about the note, I was skeptical. I called Rita, who confirmed that Secretary Rusk had indeed called while she was cooking breakfast. By the time I called Washington, the secretary was out.

I reached him on Monday, and he told me that during the treaty negotiations the Soviets had requested copies of Lenin's letters, letters they knew were in the Hoover Institution's collections. I explained that the Russians had been trying to get those letters for years, but since Rusk was making the request on behalf of the United States government, I agreed to provide copies that he could pass on. Then I consulted Sworakowski, who bitterly resented the communists for replacing the elected government of Poland (for which he had been a Foreign Service officer) and forcing it into exile. Thus, he took great pleasure in providing the Soviets with copies of letters that *he knew they already had in their possession* —including what he and I called the "I Am Not a Crook" letter, which Lenin wrote to a fellow communist in New York City who had accused him of using party funds for private high living.

Distinguished Foreign Visitors

On April 16, 1967, Princess Beatrix of the Netherlands visited the Hoover Institution and was given the usual tour by Professor Sworakowski and me of our special rooms and unique holdings. On May 9 our visitor was His Imperial Highness, Crown Prince Akihito (now Emperor Akihito) of Japan. I vividly recall one awkward moment of that visit: the crown prince and I were on the fourteenth-story platform where I was showing him the Stanford campus. When we got off the elevator, I pushed the hold button. Dare Stark McMullin—a former staff member whom I had retired early, with Mr. Hoover's approval—was also on the platform, but I assumed she would be courteous to the crown prince. Just as he, his party, and I turned toward the elevator to go back down, McMullin stepped into the elevator, released the hold button, and let the door shut on the crown prince and me. I don't imagine anything like that had ever happened to him before, but he was very polite and much less upset than I was. In due course the elevator came back up and we took it to the main floor where we toured the Lou Henry Hoover Room and the Herbert Hoover Room, after which he thanked me and left.

That July Ludwig Erhard, former chancellor of West Germany, visited the West Coast at the invitation of his long-time friend Karl Brandt. I arranged for him to speak at the Bohemian Club, and Rita and I invited many important San Francisco business people, including Claire Giannini Hoffman (daughter of the founder of the Bank of America) to attend the luncheon. As soon as the president of the Bohemian Club received his invitation, he called to ask if it would be possible for the chancellor to visit the Bohemian Grove and address the members. Erhard was famous throughout the world at that time as the "father" of the German postwar economic miracle. As the economics minister for Chancellor Adenauer he had removed price and wage controls—which the representatives of the U.S. State Department had insisted on keeping—over a weekend while the military governor, Gen. Lucius Clay (who was unofficially sympathetic to this action), was away. The tremendous German postwar recovery basically dates from that 1948 decision.

Erhard came to the Bohemian Grove accompanied by Karl Brandt, who acted as his translator when he spoke at the Dining Room Circle. His impromptu speech was well received, and his visit brought another deluge of visitors to the Cave Man Camp. After he spoke at the Bohemian Club in San Francisco early the next week, Professor Brandt, the chancellor, and I drove to Sacramento in a large, air-conditioned Mercedes for a meeting with the new governor, Ronald Reagan. It was a hot and humid day in Sacramento, and the chancellor was wearing a heavy blue wool suit. Since we had to park the car about a hundred yards from the governor's office, Mr. Erhard was sweating and puffing profusely by the time we got there. He was greeted warmly by Governor Reagan, who looked cool and comfortable in a light summer suit. When the governor said proudly, "We think we have the most beautiful state capital in the United States," the chancellor replied in English, "Yes—and also the hottest!" In the governor's air-conditioned office, we were able to exchange views on many problems of the world, particularly those of Eastern Europe and the Soviet Union.

After this meeting we took a small plane back to Palo Alto and then drove to Karl and Anita Brandt's house for dinner. After dinner we took Chancellor Erhard to the faculty club because he was speaking in Dinkelspiel Auditorium at 8:00 that evening. He gave an excellent speech, "The European Economic Community with a View to the Future." The next morning he was very unhappy that the only food available at the faculty club was a continental breakfast. He wanted bacon and eggs, so Rita took him to Tressidder Union, where he ate a hearty breakfast before flying back to West Germany.

In 1968 the pretender to the throne of Yugoslavia, King Peter, visited the Hoover Institution at the invitation of Milorad Drachkovitch, who hoped to get him to agree to give us his papers. However, Drachkovitch himself agreed that his fellow Serb was weak and indecisive, and as far as I know, we never got a decision—or any papers—from the late King Peter. In 1969 we were visited by another famous Serbian, Milovan Djilas, who had been a close associate of the Croatian communist General Tito during World War II. Djilas had broken that association when he saw Tito, Stalin, and other communists living in luxury while the common people got very little.

When I became director Robert Paul Browder and Alexander Kerensky were already at Hoover working on a project on the Russian provisional government. This project, along with one by Jan Triska and Robert M. Slusser on Soviet treaties, was financed by a grant of approximately $100,000 which Mr. Hoover had obtained from his long-time friend J.

Howard Pew. The Triska and Slusser book, *A Calendar of Soviet Treaties, 1917 to 1957,* was published by Stanford University Press in 1959. The second project was published in three volumes by the Stanford University Press in 1961 and was titled *The Russian Provisional Government 1917 Documents: Selected and Edited by Robert Paul Browder and Alexander Kerensky.*

Much to my surprise, I learned that Acting Director Philip Rhinelander had unnecessarily subsidized the Stanford University Press to the extent of about $40,000 to publish these volumes. This led to my decision to set up Hoover Institution Press in 1962. Since both of these books enjoyed good sales, they should have been published without a subsidy, and I never again allowed Stanford University Press to publish a Hoover book or a book of conference proceedings, unless published without subsidy.

Alexander Kerensky

In the fall of 1960, shortly after I moved to the eleventh floor of the Tower, I was visited by a very angry former prime minister of Russia's 1917 Provisional Government. Alexander Kerensky stomped into my office, banging the floor with his cane and demanding to know why I had moved his research assistant, Nucia Lodge, from his office to an office next door. I explained that I thought he was entitled to an office of his own, but if he insisted on having Mrs. Lodge in the same office, I would be happy to move her back. I did so, and they went on talking to each other in Russian for as long as Kerensky was here. Professor Sworakowski once told me that Kerensky had confided in him his reasons for not putting Lenin, Stalin, and Trotsky in jail for treason: Kerensky was a lawyer, and all his life he had been protesting the way the czar treated his enemies. Therefore, even though he was convinced the three of them were involved in treasonable behavior, he could not bring himself to suspend the right of habeas corpus and jail them. In neighboring Finland, the former czarist general Baron von Mannerheim immediately suspended habeas corpus and jailed all communist conspirators. As a result, he remained the head of the Finnish government until his death, and Finland remained a free country despite a Soviet attack that came without warning in 1940.

Kerensky returned to Hoover briefly in late 1967 to discuss selling his papers to the Institution. He had an offer from the University of Texas at Austin, but the price, according to Witold Sworakowski, was well above their value, so we did not engage in a bidding war.

The Hoover Presidential Library

In December 1960 Mr. Hoover formally deeded his presidential papers to the U.S. government to be placed in a presidential library in West Branch, Iowa. He consulted his lawyer, Northcutt (Mike) Ely, but neither of them discussed it with me.

Unfortunately, Mike Ely behaved the way lawyers sometimes do, particularly when they want to please a very important client, and made the arrangements without determining who actually owned the papers. In one telephone call I could have told him two things he did not know: that Mr. Hoover had promised me he'd locate his presidential library at the Hoover Institution; and that, at the time of my appointment, Mr. Hoover had already given his papers to Stanford for the Hoover Institution. In any case, Hoover had made his decision. The faculty's antipathy toward Herbert Hoover and the Hoover Institution, coupled with weakness or hostility on the part of the university presidents, had cost Stanford dearly—for the first, but not the last, time during my directorate.

I did my best to persuade Mr. Hoover not to divide his papers between West Branch and the Hoover Institution, but it was obvious to me that I had no support from President Sterling. David Packard tried to help, but I gave up early in 1961 when it was clear that Mr. Hoover would not change his mind. I was simply irritating him by being the sole person at Stanford actively concerned with trying to keep his presidential library at Hoover.

This was a particularly difficult period due to the petty hostility of the faculty that I have touched on. Why should I fight Stanford's battles? Why should I fight to retain the presidential library of the only Stanford graduate ever to become president of the United States? In addition to the question of prestige, a good deal of money was at stake. If the Hoover Presidential Library had stayed at the Hoover Institution, we would in 1996 have been receiving about $2 million a year in federal funds.

We were, however, winning battles on other fronts in the 1960s. The $1.8 million Lou Henry Hoover Building was dedicated in October 1967, and by 1970 endowment and expendable funds had increased from $2 million to $12 million.

The Minutes of the Late July 1960 Meeting

I prepared this presentation to demonstrate to President Sterling that he and Vice President for Finance Ken Cuthbertson were not the only people who could draw up ten-year plans:

> Dr. Sterling called the meeting to order at 10:00 AM. Present were Clarence Bamberger, Herbert Hoover, Ralph H. Lutz, Edward D. Lyman, A. C. Mattei, Jeremiah Milbank, J. Roscoe Miller, Robert L. Minckler, Sidney A. Mitchell, George G. Montgomery, David Packard, Thomas Pike, J. E. Wallace Sterling, Arnold G. Stifel, Robert E. Swain, William B. Wright and W. Glenn Campbell, Witold Sworakowski and Thomas T. Thalken from the Institution staff.
>
> Dr. Sterling stated that since the Director's report covered the Institution's program for the past year as well as plans for the years ahead, he would confine his remarks to the general plans of the University for the next ten years as they related to the program of the Hoover Institution. The University is planning a major fundraising campaign with a target of 40 million dollars or more. It will include a vigorous effort on behalf of the Hoover Institution. Dr. Sterling stated that it was his hope that a substantial portion of the approximately $5 million in additional funds needed by the Institution during the next ten years, according to Dr. Campbell's report, would come from this drive.
>
> Dr. Campbell opened his report with some general comments on the importance of the Hoover Institution as a center of learning. He then turned to a discussion of Mr. Hoover's fundraising campaign of the past year. Everyone agreed that this was a remarkably successful campaign and that it should serve as a model for a continuous campaign on behalf of the Institution.
>
> Mr. Hoover stated that the drive had been directed principally toward the medium-sized and smaller foundations as well as corporations so as not to interfere with the University's approach to the major foundations. He further stated that one of the lessons of this campaign clearly pointed to the advisability of expanding the Advisory Board in order to increase the

number of persons who have a direct influence on corporate and foundation giving. He suggested the names of eleven persons. The Board unanimously accepted this proposal and recommended that the eleven persons named in Mr. Hoover's memorandum be invited to join the Advisory Board.

The Board also agreed that each member present would send in additional suggestions for Board membership and that Advisory Board members not present should be requested to do likewise. Mr. Packard suggested that some of the persons who are on the University's list of prospective donors should be invited to join the Advisory Board.

Other promotion possibilities discussed included the suggestion that we should hold occasional exhibits of rare and interesting Hoover Library holdings in various cities throughout the country, as had been done at various times in the past; that we publish a brochure containing an outline of the Institution's history, a description of its operations and library and archival holdings, and a synopsis of its research and publications program, and that we publish "occasional papers" prepared by the curators which would contain extracts, with appropriate commentary, from valuable and interesting materials in the Institution's holdings.

Dr. Campbell presented the budget for 1960–61. He reported that virtually every employee would receive a salary increase in 1960–61. He also reported that the funds presently uncommitted (some $57,000) in the research and publications budget would be used to pay the salaries of the two senior research directors to be added to the staff, as well as for new projects. The budget for 1960–61 was approved by the Board.

The Board discussed at some length the section in the Director's report on financial requirements and resources of the Hoover Institution for the next ten years and noted the magnitude of the sums involved.

The research and publications program of the Institution was outlined briefly by Dr. Campbell. The Board endorsed the proposals to add two senior scholars to the research staff and in recognition of the national and international status of the Hoover Institution, to appoint a group of eminent scholars from other institutions in the United States, as well as abroad, to act as a consulting task force on research to the director. It was also reported that the Institution hopes to be able to offer some post-doctoral research fellowships for visiting scholars.

During the discussion of library acquisitions, use and service, Mr. Hoover reported on the acquisition of the excellent Kohlberg archive on modern China which was bequeathed to the Institution in the spring of 1960. The Board recommended that the Institution should try to purchase the library and files of the National Republic Publishing Company—a vast collection of documents on Communist activities in the United States.

Mr. Sworakowski explained the reasons why it was felt that a regular acquisitions budget of $23,000 plus a special acquisitions budget of $10,000 were sufficient to acquire enough new material to preserve the library's collections.

The report on the Herbert Hoover Archives was presented by Mr. Thalken. He outlined the progress that had been made during the past year in reorganizing the Archives with the intention of making them accessible to scholars, as well as future plans. Mr. Hoover expressed his approval of this program.

The meeting was adjourned at 12:00 noon at which time the Institution staff presented Mr. Hoover with a picture of the Hoover Tower and an album of photographs of the Lou Henry Hoover Memorial Room in honor of his 86th birthday. The Board members and I (no other staff was invited) then went to the Lou Henry Hoover House (President's home) for libation and luncheon at the invitation of President and Mrs. Sterling.

A year later, in July 1961, Rita and some other wives were so annoyed by the failure of President and Mrs. Sterling to invite them to the luncheon that they held their own luncheon at the Woodside Hotel. Mrs. Sterling was very upset when she learned of this, so spouses *were* invited to the 1962 luncheon at the Lou Henry Hoover House. However, President Sterling billed that hospitality to Hoover Institution. From that year until the end of his presidency in August 1968, President and Mrs. Sterling continued to invite wives—and continued to send the bill to me. The sting was partly soothed by the pleasures of these lunches, especially by the opportunity to talk to Kosta Boris—Mr. Hoover's butler at the White House—and his wife, Essie. Succeeding Stanford presidents— Kenneth Pitzer and Richard Lyman—also invited spouses to the luncheon, and they *didn't* bill the Hoover Institution! After the dedication of the Herbert Hoover Federal Memorial Building in 1978, these July luncheons were held there, in the Mark O. Hatfield Courtyard.

On August 2, 1960, Mr Hoover wrote to me:

My Dear Dr. Campbell:

I wish you would express to the staff of the Hoover Institution my gratitude for the gift of the beautiful picture of the Tower. It will have a prominent place among my *Lares* and *Penates*.

With all good wishes to you and everyone there.

Yours faithfully,
/s Herbert Hoover/

Shortly thereafter, Mr. Hoover invited Rita and me to a dinner party at his suite in the Mark Hopkins Hotel in San Francisco. Charles Kendrick and his wife, Joseph Moore and his wife, plus Bernice Miller and a few other long-time Hoover friends were there. Our host regaled us with stories of his mining days and other highlights of his career. His favorite mining story was set in a mine shaft in Burma. He and his companions were crawling through the shaft on their hands and knees when one of them noticed tiger tracks going in ... but none coming out. They quickly reversed direction and, still on hands and knees, backed hastily out. At one point in the evening, Charles Kendrick said, "Chief, since leaving the White House, you have developed a fine sense of humor." Mr. Hoover fixed him with a steely glance and said, "I *always* had a sense of humor. I just didn't think that the president of the United States should behave like a comedian." Everyone left that evening impressed at what a warm and caring person he was—and what a fine sense of humor he had.

He was genuinely interested in his associates. After we moved to California, he invited Rita and me to bring our daughters to meet him. Barbara and Diane shyly shook hands with him (Nancy, the youngest, was an infant in her mother's arms). Mr. Hoover did his best to put them at ease by asking the two older girls what they had had for breakfast. "Pancakes," they answered in unison. Mr. Hoover said *he* liked pancakes too. He asked each girl how many she'd eaten and then listened attentively to her eager answer.

Settling in as Director

At the Hoover Institution I was assigned a large office in the general area where the de Basily Room is today. The archives had appropriated all the space on the eleventh floor after C. Easton Rothwell left to become president of Mills College. Within a few months I found this location most unsatisfactory. I was constantly interrupted by staff members who wanted my approval on insignificant details—a practice my predecessor had encouraged. When the Hoover Tower was dedicated in 1941, President Wilbur, soon to become Chancellor Wilbur, took the office built for the director because it had a door leading to his good friend Herbert Hoover's office. Professor Lutz's office was then on the twelfth floor.

While Mr. Hoover was in California, I got his approval to move Thomas Thalken and the archives from the eleventh floor to the tenth and twelfth floors, and I took the eleventh-floor corner office. I moved Witold Sworakowski to another corner office and asked Ralph Lutz to occupy yet another corner office so that I would have easy access to his wise counsel and his knowledge of the history of the Hoover Institution.

I remained in that office for about twenty years, until early 1980. Then, with the approval of Allan and Herbert Hoover III, I moved into the large oak-paneled office that had been specially built for Mr. Hoover on the eleventh floor. When Alger Hiss visited the Hoover Institution at the invitation of Director Rothwell, he had used this office and had sat in Mr. Hoover's presidential chair and worked at his presidential desk. Dr. Rothwell had done likewise, but that furniture was moved to West Branch, Iowa, in 1962 at Mr. Hoover's request.

Professor Sworakowski told me that Mr. Hoover refused to go to the Hoover Tower until my predecessor, Easton Rothwell, moved Alger Hiss out. During Hiss's first trial, his lawyers wanted to call the director of the Hoover Institution as a character witness. Dr. Rothwell, somewhat panicky, went to New York to ask Mr. Hoover what he should do. Mr. Hoover told Rothwell that, since he really did *not* know Hiss that well, he could honestly tell the lawyer that, as far as he knew, Hiss might have been a communist agent. Rothwell was never called as a character witness.

The First Attempt to Fire Me

President Sterling was on sabbatical leave during the fall quarter of 1960. In early December I received a very discourteous message from him concerning information on the Hoover Institution that I had prepared for Mr. Hoover to use in his ongoing fundraising campaign. In effect, Sterling said he would "take care of [fire] me" after he returned. I was so angry and so tense that I'm afraid I was not a very jolly father for our three young daughters at Christmas.

On December 25 Mr. Hoover wrote the following letter to President Sterling:

> Yours of December 20 was a most gracious note. And it gives me the opportunity of wishing for Ann and you a Merry Christmas and a Happy New Year. For my sake, that of the University and of the Institution, please go easy with Dr. Glenn Campbell.
>
> Whatever disturbance there may have been over Dr. Campbell's statement, I am wholly to blame. It seemed to me that having been asked to put on the drive for corporation contributions, a statement from him was necessary. I approved it. And in fact, introduced the paragraph objected to, as I considered it necessary to appeal to the business world. Some one of your faculty objected, as Dr. Terman can inform you, and he also can inform you of my reply to him.
>
> Dr. Campbell has proved to be a scholar of high historical attainments and a fine administrator. He has also proved to be a good collector of funds for the library.
>
> At my time of life I find that I need less worries and more sleep. The slump in business of course directly affects corporation donations for charity and education, as such grants are mostly dependent upon the 5 percent income tax deduction. The 5 percent is decreasing with the reduction in profits and donations have been more restricted out of fear for the future. But as I have carried that major burden of finance outside of the University's contribution for over forty years, I must continue to do what I can.
>
> Dave has agreed to go fishing with me the late part of January. I have a job to do in Florida by way of dedicating an important public works. And to comply with a personal request of Senator Kennedy and the Senate Committee on Arrangements, I have to interrupt fishing to attend the Inauguration.

As I have said, I wish Ann and you all the joys of the Season.

Yours faithfully,
/s Herbert Hoover/

On New Year's Eve I suffered excruciating stomach pain and was rushed to the Stanford Hospital by my neighbor Dr. Richard L. Wilbur. I spent the New Year in the hospital and had one further attack in 1961. Ever after I have referred to the ailment as my "Sterling Stomach."

The Otis Pease Memorandum

A June 13, 1961, memorandum from Coe Associate Professor Otis Pease (who subsequently became a Stanford trustee, largely because of his friendship with Provost Lyman) reveals the full extent of the unfounded mistrust and suspicion of and the disrespect for President Hoover himself by the Stanford administration and many on the faculty. This plagued my life at the Hoover Institution for the first few years. In counseling tactical retreat to the Hoover critics, Professor Pease stated:

> We haven't enough to go on yet. True, no one likes Campbell, and all are of the opinion that his continued command of the library will be disastrous. But Wally [Sterling] surely knows this now, and I take it that he is determined to settle for a short run policy of care taking in the library in order to gain a long run freedom from both Mr. Campbell and his fairy Godfather.

Because of firmness by David Packard and virtually all the other trustees, plus my own determination, Sterling stood no chance of making good on his promise to get rid of me after Mr. Hoover's death.

The Hoover Papers

In April 1961 I received this letter from Mr. Hoover:

> My dear Dr. Campbell:
> I have your most kind letter of the twenty-ninth.
> It has seemed to me that the first thing to do is to get the Archives back.

I am in hopes that the Trustees will act on this matter at their next meeting.

   If then your ideas can be carried out with the National Archivist, it should effect what we want and clear up any other questions. But for the present we will have to wait.

With kind regards,
Yours faithfully,
/s H.H./

My proposal was that, since Mr. Hoover's papers were being divided, the presidential library should be located at West Branch, Iowa, *and* at the Hoover Institution. Unfortunately, however, Mike Ely had already given the store away when he let Mr. Hoover sign a deed of gift to the National Archives in late December 1960. My only options were to become the director of the presidential library at West Branch or to remain as director of the Hoover Institution. It took me only about two seconds to decide. I had been born and raised on a farm near London, Ontario, so the cornfields, rain, heat, and humidity of West Branch, Iowa—not to mention the snow and cold in the winter—held little attraction for me, and none for my spouse. There still remained the matter of getting the Stanford trustees to return to Mr. Hoover the papers he had given to both the Hoover Institution and the National Archives. I could have blocked this, but I decided I had no right to stand in the way of Mr. Hoover's desires. Board President David Packard and I met and agreed that the trustees should return all the papers to Mr. Hoover. Packard accomplished this, but then the National Archives and the people at West Branch tried to get all *our* Hoover papers, particularly those of the U.S. Food Administration, which Mr. Hoover had headed at the request of President Wilson. Having already agreed that his presidential papers and those from his tenure as secretary of commerce should go to West Branch, I said no to sending the Food Administration, the Committee for Relief of Belgium, and the American Relief Administration papers. In the confusion surrounding this division of papers, West Branch did get some that belonged to the Hoover Institution, including the Hugh Gibson papers and some of Ray Lyman Wilbur's papers. Whether we ever got these papers back, I do not know.

Dr. Ricardo-Campbell, Archivist

When Thomas Thalken left as Hoover's archivist in the summer of 1961 to take a job as librarian of a new university in Dallas, Witold Sworakowski and I had a real problem. For years the left-wingers on the Stanford faculty had wanted access to Mr. Hoover's archives because they hoped to find something incriminating about him. They also knew that he was working on what he called his "magnum opus," a criticism of the New Deal and an examination of all the legally questionable things FDR had done to get the United States into World War II—with Stalin as an ally. Fortunately, Eileen Shaw, Thalken's secretary, who remained when he left, was completely reliable. Finally, despite her reluctance, Rita agreed to take the job, and I notified a delighted and relieved Mr. Hoover. She had had an appealing offer to teach at San Francisco State and considered it for a long time. She finally decided that, with three small children, it was just too far to commute several times a week. But it would be an easy commute to the archives.

Mr. Hoover was staying at the Mark Hopkins Hotel in San Francisco when he wrote me this letter on August 1:

> This is purely personal. You suggested that Mrs. Campbell would temporarily take charge of the Hoover Archives.
>
> I hope she will consent to make it permanent. It should not require but a few hours a day if she has any needed staff. It would strengthen the whole Institution.
>
> With kind regards,
>
> Yours faithfully,
> /s Herbert Hoover/

On August 31, I wrote to President Sterling:

> Dear Wally:
>
> Effective September 15, 1961, I propose to appoint Dr. Rita Ricardo-Campbell as Archivist of the Herbert Hoover Archives. I am calling this appointment specially to your attention in view of the family relationship involved.
>
> Mrs. Campbell's appointment would be on a three-fifths basis and she would be compensated at the rate of $5,400 per annum. This means that

her rate of pay on a full-time basis would be $9,000 per annum, which is less than the $9,500 per annum she received some eight years ago as an economist for the House Ways and Means Committee, which is the last time she worked on a full-time basis. I might also point out that this compensation will be little more than enough to pay the additional income taxes and household help costs that her working will necessitate.

Mrs. Campbell has a degree in library science (the only one in the family) in addition to her Ph.D. in economics from Harvard. She has taught at both Radcliffe and Tufts colleges.

This appointment has the approval of the Founder of the Hoover Institution.

cc: The Honorable Herbert Hoover

On September 5 Sterling sent me the following memorandum:

I have your letter of 31 August about your wife's appointment as Archivist for the Hoover Archives. I note that the Founder approves.

Family relationships do indeed create a sensitive situation in this kind of context, as you have noted. They evoke questions, occasionally from Trustees. Before I approve the appointment, I shall have to have more information as to what other candidates for the position you have considered, and how you evaluated their credentials.

The rate of pay you recommend seems high, given comparable positions and salaries in the University. I note that Thalken's salary, after several years direct experience, is budgeted at $9,600 for this year, as against $8,400 last year. I understood from Thalken's report that most of the basic archival work was done. Is my understanding correct?

Whatever the compensation may be in its relation to your family's domestic administration is a matter that is essentially irrelevant to a budgeting consideration.

On October 6, I replied:

Your statement during our conference on Wednesday morning, that I was using improper procedures in the proposed appointment of Dr. Rita Campbell as archivist of the Herbert Hoover Archives, concerns me very much.

In the first place, I think the record shows that I had no intention of appointing Dr. Campbell to this post even on a temporary basis without the approval of the appropriate Stanford authorities. She has been doing some work in the Hoover Archives at my request and as my deputy, but solely on a "pro bono publico" basis. I assume that it is not necessary to obtain the approval of the Board of Trustees of Stanford University for this.

I see nothing improper in obtaining the approval of the Founder of the Hoover Institution prior to the submission of this appointment to the Board of Trustees of Stanford University for their approval, as it is my clear understanding that this appointment requires the approval of Mr. Hoover.

You also stated that I had not conducted a proper search. I am firmly of the opinion that I did conduct a proper search. When the special circumstances of this position are taken into account, I find it difficult to see how one can argue otherwise. I discussed the vacancy with several persons including Dr. Arthur Kemp and Mr. Hoover. I also canvassed the roster of persons within my knowledge and acquaintance who might be considered qualified for the post. Everything pointed to Dr. Rita Campbell as being the best qualified person for the post. When the special requirements of this position as well as the salary limitations are also taken into account, the evidence for this conclusion becomes, in my opinion, overwhelming.

On October 12, 1961, I wrote to Mr. Hoover:

I had hoped not to bother you with the enclosed correspondence between Dr. Sterling and myself concerning Mrs. Campbell's appointment to the Archives. However, in view of the way the situation has developed, I feel you should be fully informed on the matter.

To say that I am disgusted would be putting it mildly. Perhaps I did not handle this appointment in an ideal manner. However, I do not feel that it justifies Mr. Sterling's behavior. In any event, it only redoubles my desire to do a good job at the Institution which in my opinion is what is really annoying Mr. Sterling.

I am also enclosing copies of a letter and supporting information on the Archives which Mr. Sterling requested for use at the October Trustees' meeting. When he discussed the matter with me, his obvious intent was to try to show that your Archives had been a burden on Stanford University.

Mr. Hoover replied on October 18:

> I have your letter of October 12.
> Disgust is a weak word for this action. Please keep me advised. I will be able to report promptly to you on anything that happens elsewhere.

> With kind regards,
> Yours faithfully,
> /s Herbert Hoover/

President Sterling grudgingly approved Rita's appointment effective November 1, managing to delay it for six weeks, which made no real difference to Rita and me. It was just another example of Sterling's pettiness in anything involving Mr. Hoover or me, not to mention his two-faced behavior. With the advantage of hindsight, I now understand that I was in the middle of an ideological tug of war between the conservative Hoover and the liberal Sterling. Since I was basically a nineteenth-century liberal (one who favors limited government, low taxes, and free trade), my sympathies were virtually always with Mr. Hoover.

Conversations with Hoover

I had uncounted interesting conversations with Mr. Hoover, usually at breakfast. He did not like to eat alone, so when I came into town from the West Coast, I would struggle up at 5:30 AM California time and meet him in his suite at the Waldorf Towers. One time I asked him why John Maynard Keynes had such nice things to say about him in his book *The Economic Consequences of the Peace,* in which Keynes was very critical of the 1919 Treaty of Versailles. Hoover's answer was simple: because he agreed with Keynes about the treaty. He added, though, that John Maynard Keynes was about the most arrogant man he had ever met—and that he had met a lot of them.

Another time, during cocktails before dinner, the discussion turned to President John Kennedy and a possible Kennedy-Kennedy ticket in 1964. There was much speculation that JFK was going to dump Lyndon Johnson from the ticket and replace him with his brother Robert, putting Attorney General Kennedy in line to run for the presidency when his brother's two terms were over in 1968. Mr. Hoover said, "Only time will tell if something like that works out." He then added, "Roosevelt would have liked one of his sons to succeed him but unfortunately, he did not have very good material!"

Mr. Hoover also knew W. K. Kellogg, founder of Kellogg Cornflakes, who financed the 1931 White House Conference on Children. Mr. Kellogg was a strong-minded businessman, but he was rather careless when it came to trustees for his foundation. He had appointed his accountant, his dentist, his doctor, and his lawyer as his trustees. He used to come to Southern California from Battle Creek, Michigan, in winter. One year when Kellogg was quite elderly, Mr. Hoover urged him to replace his trustees with people "of substance." Kellogg agreed to do so as soon as he returned to Battle Creek. Unfortunately, he passed away on his way back to Michigan. The people he appointed and their successors have been running his foundation ever since—and none of the money has ever come to the Hoover Institution.

One morning in 1962 I told Hoover about two students I'd had at Harvard, William C. McConnell and Berton Steir, who went into the vending-machine business. While I was still at Harvard, they issued convertible debentures in the amounts of $5,000 each. I said that if I had bought one of them, it would have been worth $150,000 after they merged with a group of other companies and went public in 1962. The old gentleman looked at me and said, "If I was to cry over every missed opportunity in my life, there would be a river of tears running down Park Avenue." That ended that.

At one breakfast I found him not feeling well and somewhat grumpy. I told him I couldn't understand why he felt as he did because I'd spent the previous day with a gentleman older than he was, Dean Roscoe Pound of the Harvard Law School. Mr. Hoover asked how he was, and I reported that the dean said he was having some trouble "moving his circumstances."

"Well," Hoover shot back, "how is he from the neck up?"

I said he was just fine, and Mr. Hoover's mood quickly improved.

The 1962 Contract

On May 1, in a letter to Thomas Pike, president of the Stanford Board of Trustees, Mr. Hoover offered to transfer to the board title to the Hoover Archives now in the custody of the Hoover Institution upon the basis of the 1959 Resolutions, provided that:

Paragraph 7 of the Trustees resolution of May 21, 1959, relating to the purposes, managements and policies of the Hoover Institution on War, Revolution and Peace is amended to read as follows; all other provisions of that resolution to remain unaffected:

Paragraph 7. The Director of the Institution shall be recommended to the Board of Trustees by the President of the University for appointment by the Trustees. He shall have been previously approved by Mr. Hoover, and after Mr. Hoover's demise, by the Trustees of the Hoover Foundation, Inc., a New York Corporation. Such recommendation of the President shall not require approval of the Advisory Board of the Academic Council of Stanford University.

On May 17 the Stanford University Board of Trustees approved the proposed changes and accepted Mr. Hoover's offer to transfer his memorabilia to the trustees. In a letter dated May 23, Wallace Sterling advised Mr. Hoover of the trustees' action and stated: "I am delighted at the successful completion of these negotiations, which will maintain these important and valuable records in the Hoover Institution."

Getting Mr. Hoover to insist that paragraph 7 be amended seemed one of the most difficult assignments I had ever undertaken. I knew that Sterling and the left-wingers on the faculty hoped to get rid of me after Mr. Hoover's death and take over the Institution. Nevertheless, it seemed a little ghoulish to be raising that concern with Hoover himself. However, as soon as I mentioned that this needed to be done because no human being was immortal, he quickly put me at ease and suggested that I get together in Washington, D.C., with Mike Ely to work out the details. Ely and I turned the agreement into a contract, with an offer by Mr. Hoover and an acceptance by Stanford. It is interesting to note that for the last thirty years, successive trustees and presidents of Stanford have tried to act as if that 1962 contract did not exist.

The July 1962 Advisory Board Meeting

A Stanford University News Service release of July 30, 1962, after the Advisory Board meeting earlier that month, reported:

Private gifts and pledges totaling $2 million have been received by the Hoover Institution of Stanford University for an enlarged program of research on international communism and related topics, Institution Director W. Glenn Campbell announced Monday (July 30).

The funds, obtained during the past three years, currently support studies of the Chinese Communist economy, Communist penetration in Africa, development of the Communist International (Comintern), and preparation of teaching material on communism for college, high school, and adult education groups.

A history of Chinese communism and a study of the world Communist movement are now in the planning stage, Campbell told the summer meeting of the Institution's Advisory Board.

"We feel that we now have the most comprehensive program of studies of communism and related revolutionary movements to be found in any American university," he said.

"Our holdings on the Russian and Chinese revolutions and the growth and spread of communism throughout the world are generally considered the outstanding collection in this field in the Western world. This collection serves the needs of scholarship by providing indispensable source material for study and research."

Started in 1919, when Herbert Hoover offered $50,000 to Stanford "for an historical collection on the Great War," the Institution's library of current materials on political, social, and economic trends of the 20th Century today are valued at more than $25 million. (During the early 1920's, Mr. Hoover had donated a further $100,000 of his own funds.)

Major contributors to the Hoover Institution's expanded research and publications program include the Fleischmann Foundation of Reno, Nevada, which has made a five-year pledge of $250,000 for research and publications; the Lilly Endowment of Indianapolis, Indiana, which has contributed $100,000 to further studies on international communism and related movements; the Relm Foundation of Ann Arbor, Michigan, which will provide $138,000 for a history of the Comintern; and the Andrew W. Mellon Educational and Charitable Trust of Pittsburgh, Pennsylvania, which has provided $100,000 to assist in the purchase of important historical collections.

Principal acquisitions of the Hoover Institution during the past year were the Confidential Prints on Africa of the British Foreign Office and Colonial

Office, described as the most valuable single source on African affairs in this country, and microfilm copies of the Chen Cheng Collection. This collection, never before available to Western scholars, includes more than 1,100 documents concerning the Chinese Soviet Republic (commonly known as the Kiangsi Soviet) from 1931 to 1934.

In his Board report, Campbell noted that publications of his staff during the past year have included a three-volume history of *The Russian Provisional Government, 1917,* and separate books on *White Settlers in Africa, The French Fifth Republic,* and *A Forward Strategy for America.* Major new books on *Theory, Law and Policy of Soviet Treaties* and *The Chinese Communist Movement, 1937–49* are now in press.

In the near future, the Institution will publish research papers on Comintern training schools, Comintern purges of foreign leaders, and U.S. foreign policy implications of the current Chinese economic crisis.

The Institution's staff has been strengthened by several notable appointments, Dr. Campbell added. These include:

Dr. Stefan Possony, director of the International Political Studies Program;

Dr. Milorad Drachkovitch, director of the history of the Comintern project;

Roger Freeman, senior staff member with special reference to problems of government finance and taxation; and

Dr. Y.L. Wu, director of the project on Communist China as an economic power.

Research Associate Peter Duignan of the Hoover Institution will edit a series of studies on Communist activity in Africa.

In the future, the Institution plans a history of the Communist Information Bureau (Cominform), successor to the Comintern, and an analysis of the Council for Mutual Economic Aid (Comecon), Russia's response to the Marshall Plan.

Several studies of Western Europe also are in the planning stage. These will cover such topics as inter-governmental liaison, obstacles to supranational organizations like the European Economic Community, Western Assistance to underdeveloped nations, and a European-wide survey of fascism.

Today the Hoover Institution has more pro-Mussolini and anti-Mussolini data than can be found in Italy. It also has what is believed to be the most complete record on Hitler and the Nazi movement available in the U.S.

Every year, hundreds of students and scholars use the Institution's collections. During the past year, Campbell reported, Hoover library users came from 50 U.S. and 16 foreign colleges and universities. To date, more than 65 books have been published by the Stanford University Press and others, reporting the findings of Hoover scholars.

After the July Advisory Board meeting Mr. Hoover sent this note: "That was a splendid report. I would like three more copies."

The same year, 1962, the Herbert Hoover Presidential Library in West Branch, Iowa, was dedicated on August 10, Mr. Hoover's eighty-eighth birthday. Former President Harry S Truman was a speaker, as Mr. Hoover had spoken at the dedication of the Truman library in 1957. I was privileged to be present at West Branch along with members of Mr. Hoover's family and a select group of his closest friends and admirers.

1963 Report to the Advisory Board

After more than two years as director I put what we had accomplished at Hoover in concrete terms:

> The new brochure covering the history, present status, and future plans of the Hoover Institution on War, Revolution and Peace was released in January of this year. I am pleased to report that it has received an extremely favorable reception. Because this booklet covers both the research and publication program of the Institution as well as library activities at some length, this report will deal almost exclusively with financial matters and should be considered as a supplement to the brochure.
>
> During the past three years, we have devoted our efforts to three main tasks. First, to recruit a first-class team of scholars for the staff; second, to assure the availability of the necessary funds to plan Institution expenditures on an efficient, long-term basis so that they would no longer vary widely from year to year depending on the amount of money immediately available, as they did in the 1950s; third, to implement a research and publications program in the field of public and international affairs which in its scope, intensity, and quality would unquestionably rank among the finest in the country.

Notable staff appointments of the past three years include:

Dr. Stefan T. Possony as Director of the International Political Studies Program;

Dr. Milorad Drachkovitch as Senior Staff Member and Director of the History of the Communist International project;

Roger A. Freeman as Senior Staff Member in charge of problems of government finance and taxation;

Dr. Rita Campbell as Archivist of the Herbert Hoover Archives;

Dr. Y. L. Wu as Research Associate and Director of the project on Communist China as an Economic Power;

Dr. George Rentz as Curator of the Middle East Collection;

Dr. Branko Lazitch as Research Associate and co-director of the Communist International project;

Boris Souvarine as general advisor on the history of the Communist International;

Dr. Andrew Kobal as Research Associate in charge of the processing and organization of the Okhrana Collection (the archives of the Czarist Secret Police);

Richard Wraga as Research Associate working on studies of the World Communist movement; and

Karol Maichel as Curator of the East European Collection.

Thanks in large part to the efforts of Mr. Hoover and members of the Advisory Board, more funds have been raised in the past three- and-a-half years than in the preceding 15 years. In the summer of 1959 Mr. Hoover embarked on a campaign to raise funds for the Institution. During the period from June 1, 1959 to date, the Institution has obtained approximately $2.5 million in cash receipts and pledges. Almost $1.8 million of this amount counts as matching money for the $25 million Ford Foundation grant to Stanford University. Since the Ford Foundation grant is on a $1 for $3 basis, this means that these contributions to the Hoover Institution will earn an additional $600,000 for Stanford University.

In my report I also noted that the operating costs of the library were steadily increasing. These costs had in the past been funded by grants, but I proposed that an endowment be created from which such funds could be drawn. According to my estimate, this endowment would need to be at least $1,000,000 and might comprise several smaller funds. I also proposed other endowments of at least $300,000 each to support the best curators for the five area collections. I added that Hoover would need an annex building to hold both special collections and offices for staff and visiting scholars. This building, according to my estimate, would cost at least $1,000,000.

Traveling

Since he and Mrs. Hoover had traveled around the world several times before August 1914, Mr. Hoover always urged Rita and me to go to the various areas where the Hoover Institution collected materials, areas where our scholars were studying political, social, and economic change in the twentieth century. Thus, in 1962 Rita and I took our third trip to Europe. Bea and Bill Baroody accompanied us on the S.S. *France* to Cherbourg, and then we went on to Paris. The primary purpose of the trip was to attend a meeting of the Mont Pelerin Society in Knokke, Belgium. Stephen du Brul, chief economist of General Motors Corporation, had arranged for a car and driver for us since GM had a plant in the Flemish area of Belgium. We took the train from Paris to Brussels, where the driver met us and drove us to Knokke. Midway through the meeting we had a day off to tour Brussels. It was a very pleasant excursion, and we had a wonderful time at dinner that evening with Bea and Bill Baroody, Ralph and Josie Harris, and Ted Herz and his wife. Unfortunately, we spent so long at dinner that all the buses taking Mont Pelerin Society members back to Knocke had left. The car and driver were still there and could take a maximum of four people, so he took the four women and the rest of us took a taxi back to Knokke—which is about a hundred miles from Brussels, so the ride cost us the equivalent of $100 in U.S. currency. We finally got back to Knokke about 2 AM. After the meeting, the Baroodys went on to Rome to have an audience with the pope, and Rita and I returned home on the S.S. *France* because we wanted to be home with our children for a few weeks before leaving for the Far East in October.

While we were planning our first trip to the Far East, Dr. K. N. Chang came to my office in the Hoover Tower and told me that the Far East was his sphere of influence as the United States was mine. To my great pleasure, he planned practically all our trip and arranged introductions to important and interesting people.

In those days the longest-range jet was a 707. Ours landed first in Honolulu, where we stayed overnight at the Halikulani Hotel. The next morning another 707 took us to the Haneda Airport in downtown Tokyo. We went to Mount Fuji, stayed at a Japanese inn, and had a sulphur bath together (very refreshing and exhilarating, but also somewhat enervating). We visited the National Diet Library at the request of Eugene Wu, curator of our East Asian Collection, to make sure that our exchange program was proceeding well. We also moved from our inn to the New Japan Hotel (which has since burned down) near the emperor's palace.

From Tokyo we took a plane to Taipei, where we stayed at the Grand Hotel and were royally entertained by Dr. Chang's long-time friends and colleagues. I remember in particular Gen. Chen Ching hosting a dinner for us. In those days a properly polite guest always toasted the return of the Nationalist Chinese to the mainland. I did so, and the general (who also served as vice president to Generalissimo Chiang Kai-shek) declared that when we came to Peking, we must be guests at his home there. We also visited the magnificent collection of Chinese art which was in temporary storage far out in the country. The Nationalists had taken these treasures with them when they were forced off the mainland in 1949.

We visited Madame Chiang Kai-shek, a Wellesley graduate who spoke perfect English. She would not tell us where her husband was, but the next morning when our guide picked us up he asked my wife to bring a hat with her. When we got to the airport we were informed that the plane was going to Quemoy, where the generalissimo was on maneuvers with his troops. We did not *have* to go because it was somewhat dangerous, but having come this far we decided to go on. In due course we met with the generalissimo and spoke to him through an interpreter. We were delighted when he insisted that the three of us have our pictures taken together.

We were then invited to the Officer's Mess where we drank several toasts with much *gambe*-ing ("bottoms up"). I could do this in those days because I ordinarily drank gin martinis. What the Chinese served was considerably stronger, but if I paced myself, I could keep up with them. It was a matter of pride to the Chinese to try to drink a foreign visitor under the table. After lunch we went outside and released some propaganda balloons, letting the winds carry them from Quemoy across the strait to the mainland.

At the end of our stay in the Republic of China, we gave a party for all our new friends at the Grand Hotel. We invited government officials, professors, and librarians, and the Hoover Institution had excellent relations with the Republic of China from that day forward. Our next destination was Hong Kong, where once again Dr. Chang had many friends. We stayed at the Island Club, which faced the bay and had been the German embassy before World War II. What I remember most is that the club assigned a Chinese man to take care of us, and he insisted on unpacking my wife's clothes and also on repacking them. In the process, he consistently mixed up her carefully planned color combinations. In addition, there was a water shortage, so he had to heat the water and bring it in pails for my wife's bath. Then he wanted to hold her robe and towel for her while she bathed. I asked her to pay no attention because he was really only interested in the tip he would receive when we left—which would be based upon how much service he had given us!

A friend of Dr. Chang's held a cocktail party for us at a local hotel, and we met a number of important Chinese who in subsequent years would be important to the Hoover Institution. We also met the rector (president) of the University of Hong Kong and visited the New Territories, where we saw the makeshift housing built by Chinese escaping from communism. Unlike the Soviets, who had built the Berlin wall and put up electrified fences to keep Eastern Europeans from escaping, the Cantonese Chinese could leave easily—and they *were* leaving by the hundreds of thousands each year.

We flew back to Tokyo and met Dr. Chiaki Nishiyama, who had received his Ph.D. studying with Friedrich von Hayek at the University of Chicago and whom we had met at Mont Pelerin Society meetings. This time we stayed at the Palace Hotel. The president of Rikkyo University, where Professor Nishiyama taught, gave a dinner in our honor, our first experience of being attended by geisha girls.

Rita and I took our first and only trip to the Middle East (Athens and Delphi; a Greek island cruise to Delos, Santorini, Crete, and Mykonos; Lebanon, Syria, Egypt, Jordan, and Israel) in 1965 after attending a Mont Pelerin Society meeting at Stresa, Italy. Our only trip to South Africa took place in spring of 1968, and our only trip to South America in August 1969 (to Colombia, Peru, Bolivia, Brazil, and Venezuela). All these trips were very helpful in discharging my duties at the Hoover Institution. They also made Rita a much more valuable adviser.

Letters from President Hoover—1964

In 1964 Mr. Hoover sent me a number of very nice letters, some of which are included here for what they reveal about his loyalty and his genuine interest in and concern for his friends.

April 17:

> I was sorry not to see you when you stopped in Tuesday morning. I wanted to tell you again that in our jubilation over the generous gift of the Scaife family I realized how much is due to you for your continuing loyalty and endeavors in making this possible. [Richard Scaife had just informed us that he was donating $750,000 on a one for one matching basis for a new building.]
>
> I send heartfelt appreciation to you and your colleagues at the Institution for your loyal and devoted service. I am deeply grateful to all of you.
>
> Yours faithfully,
> Herbert Hoover

June 25:

> I want to commend you and your staff for the magnificent job you are doing at the Institution.
>
> In the administration and expansion of the Library you have kept constantly in mind its original purpose—the promotion of individual freedom.

I am deeply grateful to you and your colleagues for your devotion and dedication to this task.

Yours faithfully,
/s Herbert Hoover/

On August 27 Mr. Hoover's secretary wrote to me:

Mr. Hoover wants you to have this watch to remember his ninetieth birthday and his affection for you. [Mr. Hoover was always interested in new technological developments. This watch was a Bulova Accutron, which used a battery and a tuning fork, the first real breakthrough in watchmaking since the Swiss had invented the ticking clock centuries earlier. I still wear it proudly.]

But he says time can never truly record the extent of your loyalty and devotion.

On August 31 I wrote to thank Mr. Hoover:

Your gift of that handsome wristwatch has touched me deeply. I shall always cherish it.

It is impossible for us to express how much your friendship and constant encouragement have meant to Rita and me. Nothing pleases us more than the knowledge that the job we are doing at the Hoover Institution meets with your approval.

I am proud to be associated with this great Institution that you have done so much to build up and I want to assure you that I will always do everything possible to see that it is a credit to the famous name that it bears.

With best wishes,
Sincerely yours,
W. Glenn Campbell

The Death of President Hoover

When Mr. Hoover passed away on October 20, I immediately called Rita, and she flew to Washington, D.C., to join me. Former Treasury Secretary George Humphrey was in Washington and offered us a ride with him and his wife on the M. A. Hanna plane on Friday morning. We had a quick lunch on the plane before we landed and were met by Humphrey's car and driver and taken to the Waldorf Astoria.

Rita and I proceeded to Room 31A, where we met the family and certain long-time friends such as Jeremiah Milbank and his wife, Kitty. In due course Senator Goldwater joined us, and we crossed the street to St. Bartholomew's Church for the New York City service. I was to enter the church first and sit on the aisle in case there were an assassination attempt on Senator Goldwater. (In those days presidential candidates did not have Secret Service protection, so the senator had only his body-guard, Charles Justice.) However, the army colonel in charge of the service was new to the job and did not know where friends of the family were to be seated.

Meanwhile, President Johnson arrived with his Secret Service entourage, Mrs. Johnson, and Sen. Hubert Humphrey. Johnson took over the seating of his party, making the colonel even *more* nervous. Finally, we were seated in the third row, two rows behind President Johnson and his party and one row behind Senator Humphrey. In any event, I ended up on the aisle with Senator Goldwater on my right and Rita on his right. Since President Johnson entered the church early, the Secret Service immediately had to lock all the doors, leaving hundreds of Mr. Hoover's long-time friends and admirers out on the street even though there were still plenty of seats in the church. Fortunately, a loudspeaker system enabled them at least to hear the service.

When we left the church, Senator Goldwater, Rita, and I joined former Vice President and Mrs. Nixon, the Hoover family, and other close friends to return to the Waldorf Towers. The next morning the coffin was removed from the church at 8:45, placed on a horse-drawn caisson on Park Avenue with brief but impressive military ceremonies, then taken to Pennsylvania Station. Rita and I were among the many friends and family members on the funeral train when it left at approximately 9:35 that morning. During the train ride I visited the Nixons' compartment to discuss some aspects of the closing days of the Goldwater campaign.

In Washington Mr. Hoover's body was taken to the rotunda of the Capitol, where on Saturday afternoon it received appropriate military honors and the placing of the wreath by President Johnson. On Sunday morning the coffin was removed and flown to Iowa for his burial in West Branch, where he'd been born. President Johnson did not make Air Force One available to the Hoovers. Instead, he offered the "Sacred Cow," a slow propeller plane used by President Eisenhower. We flew on Senator Goldwater's campaign plane, a new Boeing 727 jet, and arrived in Iowa about an hour ahead of the plane bearing Mr. Hoover's body. As we drove into West Branch, the road was lined with folk waiting to welcome Herbert Hoover home for the last time.

5

Institution Building

Fall 1959 to 1970

Fundraising in 1959 and 1960

THE FUNDRAISING CAMPAIGN MR. HOOVER STARTED IN THE LATE summer of 1959 produced $1 million, including pledges of $50,000 a year for five years from the Max C. Fleischmann Foundation of Reno, Nevada. Mr. Hoover's long-time friend Lester Summerfield was instrumental in obtaining this pledge; in 1963 Mr. Hoover wrote Mr. Summerfield requesting a $1 million grant for a new building, and suggested that it be named for Major Fleischmann. We did not get the building grant, but the original pledge was renewed for another five years in 1963, so it totaled $500,000 over ten years.

Hoover supporter J. Howard Pew of Philadelphia also pledged $50,000 a year for five years, as did Alfred P. Sloan, with whom Hoover played pinochle regularly. Another close friend, Jeremiah Milbank, gave $125,000 over a five-year period. In addition, there were contributions from several corporations—Socony-Mobil Oil, Pacific Gas & Electric, Standard Oil of California, the Crown Zellerbach Foundation, the National Bank of Detroit, the Foundation of the Litton Industries, the Harnischfeger Foundation, and the Union Pacific Railroad Foundation. Some of these were brought in by Mr. Hoover himself; some I solicited through my own previous contacts.

Mr. Hoover also obtained two other important contributions. One consisted of $100,000 from the Andrew Mellon Foundation of Pittsburgh

117

for a Special Acquisitions Fund.[1] This fund's purpose was to commemorate both Andrew Mellon's and Herbert Hoover's years of public service. The other contribution was $99,500 worth of stock in the Varian Company from Mr. Hoover's long-time friend and Stanford University professor of chemistry, Robert Eckles Swain. That money established what is today the Robert E. Swain National Fellowship Endowment Fund, which over the years has been supplemented by further gifts from the Swain family and by unrestricted gifts allocated to it.[2]

President Sterling and the Coe Bequest

In the 1950s President Sterling managed to prevent the Hoover Institution from receiving a major bequest. William Robertson Coe, a friend and admirer of Mr. Hoover, died in 1957. The part of his will pertaining to Stanford reads:

> Eight per centum to LELAND STANFORD JUNIOR UNIVERSITY, Palo Alto, California, to be held by it and maintained by it as a separate fund known as the William Robertson Coe Fund, and managed, invested and reinvested by it and the net income used and applied by it to establish and maintain a Program of American Studies designed as a positive and affirmative method of meeting the threat of Communism, Socialism, Collectivism, Totalitarianism and other Ideologies opposed to the preservation of our System of Free Enterprise, including a Summer Refresher Program of American Studies for selected teachers and professors patterned after the existing program at the University of Wyoming.[3]

Apparently Mr. Coe concurred with Mr. Hoover's condemnation of the doctrines of Karl Marx in his May 1959 trustees statement. President Sterling and a number of faculty members, on the other hand, took exception to Mr. Hoover's statement.

It is now almost universally recognized that both Mr. Hoover and Mr. Coe were ahead of their times. Unfortunately, Mr. Hoover had introduced President Sterling to Mr. Coe. Even though Mr. Coe clearly

---

1. As of August 31, 1989, the market value of this fund was in excess of $376,000.
2. Its market value was $707,251 as of August 31, 1989.
3. Market value of that bequest was $4,827,480 as of August 31, 1989.

wanted this bequest to go to the Hoover Institution, President Sterling convinced him that there was no need to specify the Hoover Institution in his will, because Stanford would see to it that the Institution got its fair share. The Institution's fair share turned out to be zero, and today three Coe Professorships are held by Paul David in economics, Donald Kennedy in history, and Albert Gelpi in English. These men—particularly the latter two—have not been notable for following the terms of Mr. Coe's will. In addition, Stanford no longer honors Mr. Coe's will in respect to summer refresher courses for high school teachers.

In contrast, Mr. Hoover raised many millions of dollars for other Stanford schools in addition to the Hoover Institution. In fact, he was directly involved in raising about $50 million (in 1989 dollars) for other programs at Stanford, despite the way the university sometimes treated him.

For example, in the early 1960s Mr. Hoover and Dean Ernest Arbuckle of the business school worked jointly to obtain a $1 million gift from the Sloan Foundation for a new business school building. Mr. Hoover also served as honorary chairman of Stanford's $100 million fundraising campaign (the Plan of Action for a Challenging Era—PACE—Campaign), Stanford's first major fundraising campaign in my years as director.

Ford Foundation Gifts to the Library

In early 1962, thanks to the efforts of John McCloy, the Hoover Institution received a $500,000 Ford Foundation grant for strengthening the Hoover library system over the next five years. Getting this grant was a learning experience for me. One Saturday morning Mr. McCloy called me at home and told me how to send the Ford Foundation an application that would bypass the staff and go directly to the Executive Committee, of which he was chairman (he was also chairman of the board of trustees). McCloy had been Mr. Hoover's guest for dinner the previous evening, and during dinner he'd asked Mr. Hoover how his Institution at Stanford was doing. Hoover replied that it would be doing better if it received some help from the foundation of which McCloy was chairman, and McCloy replied, "We give to just about everyone else, so I don't see why we cannot give to your Institution." Obviously he was a man of decisive action, hence his Saturday telephone call!

Peter Duignan and I quickly put an application together and rushed it to Mr. McCloy, bypassing President Sterling and the chairman of the Stanford International Studies Committee, Carl Spaeth (both of whom opposed Hoover's receiving any money from the Ford Foundation). They wanted the full $2.5 million grant the Ford Foundation had promised Stanford to go to the faculty in International Studies. At the suggestion of Mr. Hoover's secretary, Bernice Miller, McCloy took his own secretary with him to record the minutes. Despite all these precautions, the staffs at both Ford and Stanford tried to prevent the Hoover Institution from receiving the $500,000, so determined were they to use some—and preferably all—of the money for other purposes. Fortunately, Mr. McCloy's minutes made that impossible.

In 1967 we received $386,000 out of a $700,000 Ford Foundation library grant to Stanford University for the continued support of our library system over a five-year period. Dr. Howard Brooks, the vice provost, played an important role in securing this grant.

Handling Fundraising

Herbert Hoover died in 1964, but for the first four years of my directorate I benefited greatly from his advice and assistance. My predecessors had, on occasion, disagreed with him, and some had sent off critical—not to say cranky—memoranda to let him know. I'd been brought up to respect the wisdom of my elders and to try to learn from them, so I never responded in that manner.

Indeed, at our very first meeting at the Waldorf Astoria Towers in New York City, he convinced me of the validity of his favorite quote from Santayana: "Those who cannot remember the past are condemned to repeat it." He and I agreed that my role was to build on the contacts I already had in order to bring in new contributors. These new contributors would supplement the gifts provided by his admirers and supporters.

By 1964 we had received over $425,000 from one of my contacts, the Relm Foundation of Ann Arbor, Michigan: $114,000 to support Duignan and Gann's *Colonialism in Africa* project, plus an additional $74,100 for various other Duignan-Gann projects; $164,400 for Milorad Drachkovitch and Branko Lazitch's *Lenin and the Comintern* project; and

$75,700 to support Roger Freeman's groundbreaking work on school finance. Freeman's grant also allowed him to move from Claremont Men's College to the Hoover Institution. At the request of the donor the grant funds were also switched to Hoover.

Freeman had made a tremendous reputation for himself at the Institute for Social Science Research in Washington, D.C., of which I was a trustee. There he produced two fine books, *School Needs in the Decade Ahead* and *Taxing for the Schools.* He was working on a third book, entitled *Crisis in College Finance? Time for New Solutions,* when he came to Hoover, and that volume was published in 1965.

In 1965–66, we received $24,000 from the Relm Foundation for a research assistant for Prof. Stefan Possony. In the case of the various grants from the Relm Foundation, it could be said that Peter Duignan acted as my director of development for *Colonialism in Africa,* Milorad Drachkovitch for the *Lenin and the Comintern* project, Roger Freeman for his work on school finance, and Stefan Possony for his projects. Between 1964 and 1968, we received $73,000 from the Relm Foundation for the appointment of Karl Brandt (former director of the Food Research Institute) as a Senior Research Fellow. An internationally known scholar, he had also succeeded former Food Research Institute Director Joe Davis as a member of the Council of Economic Advisors in the Eisenhower administration. After he returned from Washington in early 1961, he served as director of the Food Research Institute for four years until his retirement in 1965. Professor Brandt was the first scholar to receive the title Senior Research Fellow. Our ground-level renovation made it possible to give him an office that also served Senior Research Fellow Larry Diamond in the course of things and in which, almost thirty years later, important scholarly work is still being done.

In 1960 a sizable gift ($100,000) came from the Lilly Endowment of Indianapolis, another of my American Enterprise Association contacts; $35,000 from Mr. Harry Bradley of Milwaukee and—from 1961 to 1969—$50,000 a year in unrestricted funds from the Allen-Bradley Company of Milwaukee, of which Mr. Bradley was a founder, for a total of $535,000. Harvey Peters, general counsel for the Allen-Bradley Company, obtained that gift, and asked me if I could arrange an appointment for Harry Bradley with Mr. Hoover. I did, and afterward Mr. Hoover wanted to know what kind of nut I had brought in to see him. "A rich one," I said. Mr. Hoover sighed and said the man ranted and raved about the state of the country and the world for almost an hour—and wanted Hoover to straighten everything out. When I told him that we had got a contribution of $35,000 and I was sure we would get more, Mr. Hoover said with a twinkle in his eye that he guessed it was worth it.

We brought in many smaller private gifts during the 1960s, plus $55,000 from the CIA for processing Hoover records on espionage. Those records were still valuable, because the Soviet spying agencies had copied the methods used by the Okhrana (the czarist secret police), which used their Paris embassy as their European espionage headquarters.

While raising money, we were also seeking top-grade personnel. In late 1961 or early 1962 Peter Bauer, whom I had known since the fall of 1956 and who was already considered by many the world's leading expert on the underdeveloped countries of the world, visited the Hoover Institution to evaluate current programs and suggest future ones. Bauer was very impressed by the long-range potential of the Hoover Institution, particularly the work of Peter Duignan. He made some valuable editorial suggestions on the first book Duignan wrote with Lewis Gann, *White Settlers in Tropical Africa*.

Bauer and I agreed that I should try to get Emerson P. Schmidt's son, Prof. Wilson Schmidt, to become research director of the Hoover Institution. I had worked for Emerson Schmidt at the U. S. Chamber of Commerce, and Bauer had known him since 1956, when we all served on a Senate Foreign Relations project. We invited Wilson Schmidt and his wife to visit the Hoover Institution in 1962, but after much agonizing over whether or not he should accept the job with us, he finally declined.

Peter Bauer became Lord Bauer while Margaret Thatcher was prime minister of Great Britain, and served as a member of the Hoover International Studies Advisory Committee until the committee was disbanded in 1990.

The 1966 Fundraising Campaign

When, in 1966, the Scaife family gave us a million-dollar endowment pledge with a two for one matching requirement, they ensured the success of our fundraising effort. Campaign co-chairmen David Packard and Thomas Pike prepared a brochure containing a letter from President Hoover's two sons, Herbert, Jr. and Allan. One of the gifts we garnered was a bequest from Ira S. Lillick, a close friend of President Hoover and a Stanford trustee since the 1920s, who contributed generously to both Hoover and the Law School. Mr. Lillick's personal contributions totaled $517,367 over ten years.[4] Some of these gifts were directed to an expendable fund and to the building fund, but most went into an endowment.

We reported on the progress of the campaign at the Advisory Board meeting on July 21, 1969. The total amount raised in contributions was $5,378,897, plus $985,984 in pledges, for a total of $6,364,881. The success of the campaign far exceeded our expectations. The market value of the Scaife family challenge grant alone (we divided this money equally between library and research) was almost $3 million by 1989.

This was not the first time Richard Scaife had been generous in assisting Hoover. As noted earlier in passing, our first pledge contacts with the Scaife family were made in December 1963 and pursued in most agreeable circumstances. I had met with Richard Scaife and Daniel McMichael through Frank Barnett, president of the National Strategy Information Center. In spring 1964 I suggested that Mr. Hoover invite Richard Scaife to join us for lunch at the Waldorf Towers. At that luncheon we discussed the recent excellent progress of the Hoover Institution and our need for a second building. Following that luncheon, Mr. Scaife, with his associates Dan McMichael and Charles Ford, visited the Hoover Institution, and we met with David Packard at the Pacific Union Club in San Francisco. Mr. Packard eloquently seconded my appeal for a second building. In addition to library and archive space, we sorely needed new offices for the growing number of scholars, plus seminar rooms for meetings.

The Lou Henry Hoover Building

We got exactly what Mr. Packard and I asked for, namely, a pledge from the Scaife family of $750,000 on a one-for-one matching basis to fund

---

4. The market value of the Ira and Stella Lillick Curatorship was over $1.6 million as of August 31, 1989.

construction of a new building at a cost of $1.5 million. This pledge was made in honor of Mr. Hoover's ninetieth birthday on August 10, 1964. In extending this generous gift, the Scaife family said, "All of us have been tremendously impressed with the effective work being performed at the Institution. We feel that this work is so particularly important to the preservation of our Western Civilization that anything the Scaife family can do to assist is a source of pride to us." In June 1964 Mr. Packard won the trustees' agreement to use $500,000 in earned matching funds from the Ford Foundation's $25 million PACE campaign grant. Jeremiah Milbank, Sr., then agreed to contribute the remaining $250,000 to cover the estimated building cost.

During the campaign to raise the matching funds, I wrote to former Postmaster General James Farley, who was then an executive at Coca-Cola International. Mr. Farley wrote back to say that although he was not able to contribute at this time, he wanted me to know that he treasured his long friendship with Mr. Hoover and regretted all the nasty charges he and his associates had made against President Hoover in the 1932 campaign.

By mid-August the "match" had been raised and we received the Scaifes' $750,000 check (the largest check I had ever seen in my life up to that point). I proudly took the check home to show to Rita, who was also working at the Hoover Institution then as well as caring for three small girls and contending with babysitters and maids. She neatly deflated any expanding ego in me by wondering why, if I was so smart, I didn't bring home a similar check made out to me personally.

The Scaifes did not want the building named for them, but they did request that, if possible, we choose Charles Luckman Associates as our architect. The firm had designed a Scaife building in Pittsburgh which they liked very much. Naturally, I wanted to clear the matter with Mr. Hoover, so when I was in New York in late spring I brought it up over cocktails. He looked at me sternly and said, "Is that the fellow who designed that glass monstrosity on Park Avenue [the Lever Building]?" I assured him that Mr. Luckman understood that buildings at Stanford conform to the Spanish-mission style, with red tile roofs and arches. Besides, Luckman would not actually design our building, nor had he designed the building on Park Avenue. I explained that Luckman was basically the salesman for his firm. Mr. Hoover considered all this, then said wryly that he guessed that for $750,000 the Scaifes were entitled to select the architect.

The J. N. Pew Jr. Trust generously contributed $100,000, and by the time Mr. Hoover died in October 1964, we had an additional $50,000 or larger contributions from supporters such as David Packard and Dudley Swim. We received a pledge for $50,000 from Todor Polich, a Serbian immigrant who was a successful contractor in Southern California and whose sons had graduated from Stanford; $25,000 from the Kresge Foundation; $25,000 from the Chauncey & Marion Deering McCormick Foundation; $25,750 from Ruth Baker Pratt, besides many others who are listed on a plaque in front of the building. We had ample funds in hand, including $1,000 each from Allan Hoover and Herbert Hoover III, and $1,000 from Rita and me.

By 1967 the $500,000 in matching gifts approved by the Stanford trustees was not needed, so in accordance with our agreement with them, that amount endowed the Herbert Hoover 90th Birthday Fund.[5] "His and Hers," as the students dubbed the two buildings, were complete— or so they thought on campus.

Thanks to Rita's excellent work in planning, decorating, furnishing, and landscaping the new building, it has 30 percent more floor space than we initially planned. And thanks to our continued fundraising, after 1964 we received many more generous contributions for what, on my recommendation to the Hoover family, would be named the Lou Henry Hoover Building. After the building was completed Dr. Ricardo-Campbell received from the staff a scroll which read:

> In appreciation of our decorator par excellence
> *Dr. Rita Campbell*
> whose impeccable taste, unfailing good judgment,
> and devoted work have helped create
> a beautiful building that is a delight to work in.
> The Hoover Institution Staff
> in the Lou Henry Hoover Building

The Chinese calligraphy on the scroll was done by Chinese scholar Dr. K. N. Chang, a public servant and founder of the Bank of China in Shanghai, who was at the Hoover Institution from 1960 until his death. He was, as noted earlier, instrumental in providing fundraising contacts

---

5. Market value, over $1.6 million as of August 31, 1989.

in Taiwan and Hong Kong, and he was equally helpful with his Chinese-American friends in the USA.

Herbert Hoover and the Uncommon Man Award

On July 22, 1965, the degree of Uncommon Man was awarded posthumously to Herbert Hoover at a ceremonial dinner given by the Stanford Associates at the Mark Hopkins Hotel in San Francisco. In the twelve years since the degree had been initiated, it had been awarded only four times. In 1953, the first award went to Paul Edwards, a long-time president of the Stanford Board of Trustees. The fourth award was given posthumously in 1959 to Lloyd Dinkelspiel, Stanford Board of Trustees president and loyal friend of the university.

Stanford Associates is an organization founded by a small group of Stanford supporters in 1934. By 1953 its numbers had grown to nearly six hundred, and it had created the Uncommon Man degree to honor those who have given unique and outstanding service to Stanford. (The university does not grant honorary degrees.) The Associates' degree acquired its name from one of the most widely quoted statements ever made by President Hoover. Rejecting the popular "cult of the Common Man," he said: "... most people are holding fast to an essential fact in American life. We believe in equal opportunity for all, but we know that this includes the opportunity to rise in leadership—in other words, to be uncommon."

At this ceremony, Stanford President Wallace Sterling reviewed Mr. Hoover's long and varied services to the university he had entered when it first opened in 1891. Other speakers included Dean Richard Jahns of the school of the earth sciences; Professor William Jones, director of the Food Research Institute; Dean Ernest Arbuckle of the graduate school of business; Richard Guggenheim, president of the board of trustees; and myself as director of the Hoover Institution. Mr. Hoover played key roles at all the above-mentioned schools, starting with geology, which is now part of the school of earth sciences. He was a student from 1891 to 1895; he founded the old Student Union in 1915; he founded the Hoover Institution in 1919; he initiated the Food Research Institute in 1921; and he started the graduate school of business in 1925.

Here are Herbert Hoover's own words from volume 1 of his 1951 memoir *Years of Adventure, 1874–1920,* concerning the founding of the Old Union:

> In an address to the student body in 1912, I proposed the erection of a "Union" for the centralization of student activities, for eating and other clubs and general purposes. Subsequently, I gave the Trustees $100,000 for the Union on condition that they lend it an additional $150,000, to be repaid to the University out of its earnings. The students raised still more money. The debt to the Trustees has long since been repaid. The students have enlarged the Union over the years until it is today one of the most beautiful and effective of such institutions among our universities.

Today the old Student Union houses a number of administrative offices and student organizations, and the $100,000 he gave in 1915 would be worth several million dollars today.

Our fundraising efforts continued to pay off, but several members of the Advisory Board did not trust the officials of Stanford University to handle contributions made to Stanford for the Hoover Institution. They were afraid that Stanford might simply keep some of our gifts, or that the Stanford administrators might charge us a large handling fee. To assuage this concern, Allan Hoover sought a legal opinion on the matter. The opinion we received in December 1965 persuaded many members of the Advisory Board to propose that our donors contribute to the Hoover Foundation, which would pass the money along to the Hoover Institution. In reality, however, I found this arrangement much too cumbersome and never actually implemented it. In my years as director, I was critical of Stanford in many respects, but never of the way our funds were handled. Not once did we pay an overhead charge to Stanford on private gifts.

Hoover's First Information Officer

A 1965 grant from the Scaife trusts enabled us to appoint James Hobson as information officer for the Hoover Institution. The purpose of the grant was to enable our Hoover scholarly studies to reach a larger audience, and the amount was sufficient for us to invite newspaper reporters and editorial writers to Hoover as media fellows. In this way journalists could take advantage of short conferences with our scholars. The program was working very well until the assassination of Martin Luther King, Jr., in April 1968. The killing coincided with one of our journalists' gatherings, and we had to cancel the remaining day or two of the seminar. For the next couple of years, my colleagues and I were so busy that we did not get the program fully reinstated. Hobson did, however, continue disseminating the findings of Hoover scholarly studies to newspapers and news magazines.

Ups and Downs with Hoover Appointees

Theodore Draper had been working on a history of American communism for several years. Two volumes were finished, but he had at least one more to go. Professor Sworakowski was very anxious for this project to be completed because he was convinced of its importance for scholars studying communism and its evils. At Sworakowski's behest, I had agreed to give Ted Draper an appointment at the Hoover Institution in May 1963, and under the Hoover aegis, he wrote *Castroism—Theory and Practice* (1965), *Abuse of Power* (1967), and *The Rediscovery of Black Nationalism* (1970). However, he never wrote the third volume of his history of the American Communist party. In 1969, amid divorce proceedings, he left us and went to the Institute for Advanced Studies at Princeton. After several years there, he gave us no indication that he would ever finish the third volume, so in 1974 his grant from the Hoover Institution was terminated.

Sometime after 1974, Associate Director Richard F. Staar learned that Draper had sold some of his papers to Emory University. Dr. Staar called him to discuss this, but Draper became defensive. Staar pointed out that it was not really an ideal arrangement, having part of his papers on the West Coast and part on the East Coast, but Draper simply stated that Emory had paid him more money than we would have (though he did not talk to us about it). It's my recollection that, when he was given his grant by the Hoover Institution, he had promised to donate all his papers to us.

In 1965 Dr. Dennis Doolin, a former Ford Foundation Fellow in Asian studies, was appointed research curator of the East Asian

Collection, and John T. Ma was appointed curator librarian for the East Asian Collection. Ma replaced Eugene Wu, who became librarian of the renowned Yenching Collection at Harvard in 1964. Having worked for Mary Wright at a very low salary for many years, he was skeptical that Hoover would continue my policy of generous salary increases if he decided to stay.

Doolin took a leave from Hoover in 1966 to work for the CIA and never returned, so John Ma was made curator of the East Asian Collection and remained in that position until 1975, when I found it necessary to request his resignation for sexual harassment of female employees. That resignation was on my desk fifteen minutes after I asked for it, so perhaps my request was expected. Nevertheless, I was soon invited to the office of Iris Brest—the university attorney who handled personnel issues—to discuss Ma's departure with her and some faculty members. They claimed, in effect, that I got the resignation under duress and that the Hoover Institution should pay for a lawyer to represent Ma so that he could sue us. I found this preposterous, and told the professors and Ms. Brest they could hire a lawyer themselves if they were so interested in Ma's welfare. Of course, there never was a John Ma lawsuit against either the Hoover Institution or me. The "Brest committee" apparently didn't equate devotion to principle with monetary support. I had learned through painful experience that every time I allowed the Stanford Legal Office to handle anything for us we ended up paying out a lot of money, whether because of bad legal advice or because of hostility to the Hoover Institution, I know not.

On the plus side, we appointed Bertram D. Wolfe to the Hoover Institution in 1965. Wolfe, as I've said, had become disillusioned with communism after the deadly purges of Joseph Stalin and others. Convinced that communism was, in fact, an evil doctrine, he established himself as one of the world's foremost authorities on the subject. The following extracts are from an excellent description of his career issued by the Stanford University News Service at the time of his death, on February 21, 1977:

> He was best known for his book, *Three Who Made a Revolution* [1948]. Translated into 28 languages, it was a study of Lenin, Trotsky, and Stalin

which literary critic Edmund Wilson once called "the best book in its field in any language."

A former public high school teacher in New York City, Wolfe strongly opposed America's entry into World War I, then became an organizer of the American Communist Party, serving as its educational director in 1926–28. He was an executive committee member of the Communist International in 1928–29.

After engaging in a five-month-long fight with Stalin, he was imprisoned for nearly two months in the Soviet Union, "then released with every effort made to keep me from returning to my native country." He also stated, "Stalin had not yet perfected his technique for cutting short discussion."

Wolfe next helped the Spanish Loyalists and wrote *The Fabulous Life of Diego Rivera,* the revolutionary Mexican muralist. After the Hitler-Stalin pact of 1939 he spent nine years researching *Three Who Made a Revolution.*

"It taught me the unreliability of witnesses and even documents, the need to master the Russian tongue, thought, and culture, to search for the truths of the defeated, check them against the truths of the victorious, the available documentary records, and the inherent probabilities of each person and each event."

Once called "the greatest detective among scholars, and the greatest scholar among detectives," he warned that "the production of false reminiscences and inside stories concerning the Soviet Union is growing into a big and sinister industry."

Elected a fellow of the American Academy of Arts and Sciences in 1974, he authored 15 books, mainly on Soviet affairs.

A former distinguished visiting professor of history at UC-Davis, he received an honorary doctorate from the University of California in 1962. He taught at the summer institute of comparative politics at the University of Colorado for several years, and was named adjunct professor of advanced foreign affairs at the University of Miami.

"Only the fact that the City College of New York was tuition-free and that I worked after hours in the Post Office enabled me to go to college," he once said. After graduating Phi Beta Kappa there in 1916, he earned two master's degrees in Romance languages, from the University of Mexico (1925) and Columbia (1931). He received three Guggenheim fellowships during his lifetime.

In his last major address, Wolfe noted that the American Revolution was the only great revolution that did not devour its own children.

"Our Founding Fathers did not try to make a total clean sweep of the past," he said. "We didn't think we knew it all—that all of the wisdom of the ages and all the things that our fathers had learned from the days of Magna Carta on should be swept away.

"On the contrary, Parliament seemed good to us. The doctrine that every man's home is his castle and shall not be violated by search and seizure without a warrant seemed good to us. The American Revolution did not sweep away the past, it built upon it."

Unlike other major revolutions, all its leaders died in bed. "This is something we should be proud of. When we get into arguments with each other, we should remember how these men fought and, when the fight was over, clasped hands and became all together Americans again."

During the summer of 1968, Vice Provost Brooks and I, with the approval of President Sterling, agreed to name as Senior Fellows (a title, I believe, first used by the Brookings Institution) effective September 1, 1968: Richard V. Allen, Milorad Drachkovitch, Peter Duignan, Roger Freeman, Lewis Gann, Stefan Possony, and Rita Ricardo-Campbell. Berkeley Tompkins was also made a Senior Fellow, for a three-year term.

The Defection of Janos Radvanyi

On May 16, 1967, a high-ranking communist diplomat, Janos Radvanyi, defected to the United States by seeking refuge in the Hungarian embassy in Washington, D.C. After he had been debriefed by the CIA on the information he possessed about the operations of the communist regimes in Hungary, North Korea, the Soviet Union, and elsewhere, his story was carried in many newspapers in the United States and abroad.

The CIA then sent him to Stanford University with a two-year Ford Foundation grant (as far as I know, the last time the Ford Foundation assisted a communist defector). It no doubt helped that Bill Bundy, former Secretary of State Dean Acheson's son-in-law, was a high-ranking official in the CIA, and his brother McGeorge Bundy was president of the Ford Foundation.

Dean Carl Spaeth of the Law School, chairman of the Committee on International Studies at Stanford and the person to whom Dr. Radvanyi was assigned, called me to ask if the Hoover Institution had office space for Dr. Radvanyi. We were pleased to provide space for such a courageous person, and we assigned him a small office on the second floor of the Hoover Tower. Radvanyi enrolled in classes in the history department to prepare for his doctoral dissertation, "Hungary and the Super Powers," under the direction of Profs. Gordon Craig and Ivo Lederer.

He spent two years working on grants from the Hoover Institution until he received his doctorate in history in June 1971. When he came to me for career advice, I suggested that his wealth of experience in communist countries and his ability to compare that life to life in a free society like the United States would make him an invaluable teacher. He agreed enthusiastically, then promptly discovered that a job search in the United States was very different from a "job search" in a communist country. There he would have been assigned a position by a powerful commissar. Instead, he wrote scores of letters to various universities and received an offer of an associate professorship in history at Mississippi State University. He began his teaching career there in September 1971 and is now a professor of history and the director of the Center for International Security and Strategic Studies at Mississippi State. He continues to publish internationally recognized books.

The Selection of Kenneth Pitzer as President of Stanford

In 1966, pressure from powerful Stanford trustees forced President Sterling to announce his retirement, effective August 31, 1968. In return for his capitulation to their wishes, they made him chancellor for life with pay and a house, and they approved his appointment of Richard Lyman as provost. The trustee search committee consisted in part of Roger Lewis as chairman, Gardiner Symonds of Houston, and David Packard. They were determined to choose a president more reliable than Wallace Sterling, and they considered a number of candidates, including David Truman, the number two person (provost) to Grayson Kirk at Columbia University. However, the administrative mishandling of the demonstrations at Columbia weighed against him.

They also considered me, and David Packard told William J. Baroody, Sr., that I was his favorite candidate. When my name was presented to the Faculty Advisory Committee, however, there was strong opposition, and the trustees gave in. This led to one of the few disagreements Dave Packard and I ever had. In my view, if they let the faculty veto their choices, there was no point in having a trustees' search committee, and Packard was irked by my opinion. In any case, the search was still going on at the time of the June 1968 trustees' meeting, so they named the dean of the Medical School, Robert J. Glaser, MD, as acting president, effective September 1. In late summer the Stanford trustees announced that Kenneth Pitzer, the president of Rice University in Houston, would become president of Stanford on December 1, 1968.

Shortly after his installation, Pitzer invited me to become a member of what he called his advisory group. In addition to President Pitzer, the members were Provost Lyman, the deans of the various schools, Vice President Alf Brandin, Vice President Kenneth Cuthbertson, and Fred Glover as secretary. The principal memory I have of our few meetings is of asking President Pitzer what he intended to do about the flagrantly illegal behavior of Prof. Bruce Franklin (the Franklin saga will be discussed later in this chapter). Immediately, I felt like a skunk at a lawn party. Pitzer said we couldn't discuss a faculty matter that might end up in a lawsuit. Only Alf Brandin had the courage to support me.

Unfortunately, Dr. Pitzer's appointment turned out to be a disaster, and the faculty committee was at best unenthusiastic about his appointment. From then on, the Stanford trustees had very little, if any, influence on the selection of a president of Stanford while I was Hoover director. The faculty committee preferred Provost Lyman, which is undoubtedly why he became president shortly after Pitzer was forced to resign in the summer of 1970.

Lawrence Kimpton, a former president of the University of Chicago who had resigned in the early 1960s to become a vice president of Standard Oil of Indiana, tried to persuade the trustees on the search committee, and David Packard in particular, that the faculty would quickly change their minds about me once I was in charge of their salaries and perquisites. He failed to persuade them, but I learned a valuable lesson from that experience: businessmen, even the most successful, are in awe of professors. I still do not fully understand this, but I made frequent use of the knowledge in building the Hoover Institution. From then on I never hesitated to call important foundation and business CEOs for appointments or contributions. Businessmen also suffer from a real disadvantage in dealing with professors—they have full-time jobs, employees, stockholders, and directors to satisfy, while tenured professors can spend much of their time scheming.

Meanwhile, the founding president of Claremont Men's College, Dr. George C. S. Benson, was scheduled to retire at the end of the 1968–69 academic year. Benson asked Bill Baroody whether he thought I would be interested in succeeding him as president, but Baroody opined that I had a better job already and probably would not be interested. He was correct.

Making the Hoover Institution a Leading International Center

In the meantime, we were obtaining a series of grants to support and enhance the work of the Hoover scholars. Our first $50,000 grant came from the Louis Calder Foundation in 1963 to build our Latin American Collection, and we received additional grants from Calder on a regular basis until 1984, for a total of $510,000. Louis Calder himself was involved in the first two contributions, and we owe a large debt of gratitude to Calder Foundation Trustee Reinhold Dreher for continuing them. Mr. Dreher became a member of our Advisory Board in the late 1960s, then served on the Board of Overseers when it was established in 1971. Mr. Hoover was highly pleased with the Calder contribution because he considered Latin America vitally important. He was a strong believer in the Monroe Doctrine, and after he was elected president in November 1928, he and Mrs. Hoover traveled to Latin America and inaugurated the Good Neighbor policy, which essentially remains in effect to this day.

Dr. Yuan-li Wu became professor of international business at the University of San Francisco in 1960, and that year began consulting for the Hoover Institution. In the latter capacity he directed three studies of arms control problems in East Asia and produced books on steel production, energy resources, and transportation in mainland China. Dr. Frank Hoeber and I arranged to have these published—in 1963, 1965, and 1967, respectively—under three contracts, totaling about $100,000, the costs to be divided between Stanford Research Institute and the Hoover Institution. From 1964 to 1968 the arms control project was supported by two grants from the U.S. Arms Control and Disarmament Agency.

In those days, as now, 25 percent to 35 percent in overhead went to Stanford University, but recently Stanford tried to raise the rate to 78 percent, the highest rate for any school in the country except the Harvard Medical School (78.1 percent). After navy auditor Paul Biddle and his associates discovered outrageously wrongful charges and other shenanigans on the part of Stanford University, the overhead rate was reduced to 55.5 percent.

Over the years my colleagues and I had often discussed whether we should keep the Hoover Institution small or attempt to build a more powerful international and domestic think-tank. By 1966 the decision had essentially been made by virtue of the excellent scholars we had appointed, their research output, and our success in raising funds for a second building and for expanding the library and raising the scholars' salaries.

In 1967 Susan Louise Dyer bequeathed an endowment fund of $176,746 for a Research Fellowship in the Lou Henry Hoover Memorial Collection on Peace. The market value of this fund as of August 31, 1989, was $677,013, but there was a problem with the bequest—there *was* no Lou Henry Hoover Memorial Collection on Peace. When he donated the Hoover House to the university as a residence for the president, Mr. Hoover had insisted that the Stanford trustees make $62,500 available for creating the Lou Henry Hoover Collection. Instead, my predecessor Dr. C. Easton Rothwell had spent the money, primarily on trips and research assistants for himself and his left-wing friends. Dr. Sterling was embarrassed when I informed him of this difficulty, because he and Rothwell were personal friends.

Fortunately, we were able to go a long way toward correcting this situation. In the 1960s, Mr. Hoover's friend Fred Wickett had recommended that he invite John Crummey, founder of FMC Corporation, to become a member of the Hoover Advisory Board. Crummey demurred, saying that he was too old, but suggested that instead we invite his grandson Paul Davies, Jr., a graduate of Stanford and the Harvard Law School. Davies accepted and obtained $100,000 from FMC Corporation to establish the John Crummey Memorial Collection on Peace.[6]

Appointment of Herbert Hoover III

When Mr. Hoover resigned from the Stanford Board of Trustees in 1962 after fifty years of service, he became a trustee emeritus. Thomas Pike, board president, and immediate past president David Packard tried to get Herbert Hoover, Jr., to succeed his father. Herbert Jr. gave Packard a number of reasons for declining, including his position as a trustee of the University of Southern California, but Packard was sure he knew the real reason. Before becoming president of Stanford University, J. E. Wallace Sterling had headed the Huntington Library. Naturally, he'd had to resign that post when he accepted the Stanford position, but he remained a library trustee. When Mr. Hoover resigned as a Huntington Library trustee, Sterling made a special trip to Southern California to oppose the election of Herbert Hoover, Jr., to replace his father and he succeeded. In addition, rightly or wrongly, Sterling had allowed Herbert Hoover III (Pete) to be dismissed from Stanford for poor grades. Mr. Hoover's friend W. B. Munro, a fellow trustee of the Huntington Library, was furious over Sterling's actions and reported them to the former president Hoover. Munro resolved to change his will and leave his fortune to the Hoover Institution, but he died before he could do so and Stanford remained in his will.

Treasury Secretary George Humphrey was a good friend of Herbert Hoover, Jr., and had spoken very highly of my work on the Goldwater campaign for the presidency. On the strength of that recommendation I tried both in 1965 and 1966 to get Herbert Hoover, Jr., to join the Hoover Institution's Advisory Board. He refused, giving his usual reasons—his trusteeship of the University of Southern California, the various corporate boards he served on, and several other activities. Finally he suggested that his son Herbert Hoover III be appointed, and I agreed. At the

---

6. The market value of this fund as of August 31, 1989, was $310,000.

urging of several members of the Advisory Board, President Sterling dropped his opposition, and Pete accepted the trusteeship on September 13, 1967.

Amid all this I had several job offers, including a professorship and a corporate executive position, but I turned them all down. Building the Hoover Institution into a think-tank of international eminence was an absorbing challenge and far more fulfilling—particularly since I was able to do it in partnership with my scholarly spouse, Rita.

South Africa

In late April 1968, after my second meeting as a University of California Regent, Rita and I took our one and only trip to South Africa as guests of the government. The trip was arranged by John Mills, then the South African consul general in San Francisco. We flew South Africa Airways to Johannesburg with one stopover in London. It was a particularly interesting time to be in South Africa. Apartheid was still in force, mandating separate beaches, separate dining facilities, separate communities—such as the Transkei, which we visited—and even such absurdities as separate toilets and separate lifts (elevators). We visited a modern separate university for blacks, the University of the North, which was then under construction.

Johannesburg was a beautiful modern city, the largest city in South Africa, and we also visited the two capital cities, Pretoria and Capetown. At that time Prof. William Hutt was still teaching in Capetown. An Englishman who had received his Ph.D. from the London School of Economics, Professor Hutt was an ardent and outspoken foe of apartheid. We had a very interesting visit with him and his artist wife Grethe, then stopped at Stellenbosch University near Capetown. The South African government arranged appointments for us with several cabinet officers and members of parliament. I remember two in particular: One was Piet Botha, the minister of defense who subsequently became prime minister. He gave me a hard time regarding the arms embargo President Johnson had imposed on South Africa. Later he told me with a twinkle in his eye that I would be surprised if I knew how many European governments were happy to sell the same arms to them, not to mention how the embargo had stimulated their own arms industry. The other memorable appointment was with Helen Suzman, the only female member of parliament and an open opponent of apartheid. We then met with several faculty members at Witwatersrand University.

We had enough time before the May U.C. Regents meeting to spend one night at Kruger National Park. This game preserve was much more impressive to see than to read about. The variety of animals and birds was astonishing, but the most impressive were the lions and the elephants. Clearly, South Africa was doing an excellent job of both conservation and controlling poaching. We returned home via Rio de Janeiro.

Our trip cost the Hoover Institution nothing because we were guests of the South African government. The South Africans had entertained us well while trying to educate us about the advantages of apartheid—a wasted investment in that regard, but a valuable trip for us nevertheless.

When we returned, there was much to do. Professor Sworakowski had reached sixty-five, the mandatory retirement age for both professors and administrators. On July 2 Prof. Richard Staar of Emory University arrived to be interviewed for the post of Senior Fellow and associate director for library operations. The U. S. Health, Education and Welfare Department gave the Hoover Institution a $100,000 grant under the Higher Education Act of 1965. Witold Sworakowski and I had set up, with the assistance of the cooperating universities, the Western Consortium of Colleges. The consortium facilitated growth in specialization by each library and fostered interlibrary exchange of books and other materials. In 1969 HEW gave the consortium a grant of $125,000.

Specific gifts for our International Studies Program continued. The Scaife Family Charitable Trusts and the Scaife Foundation started to support the program in 1969 with a grant of $100,000, and by August 1989 they had provided over $4 million for the International Studies Program at the Hoover Institution. The story of this world-renowned program is told in later chapters.

More Appointments, More Controversy

John Lewis, professor of political science, came to me with an interesting proposal in early 1969. Could we offer former Secretary of State Dean

Rusk a joint appointment to the Hoover Institution and the Stanford political science department? Because of Rusk's distinguished career, I was immediately interested. Dean Rusk had been a Rhodes Scholar at Oxford University in 1933, associate professor of government and dean of the faculty at Mills College from 1934 to 1940, an army officer from 1940 to 1946, assistant secretary of state for Far Eastern affairs from 1950 to 1952, president of the Rockefeller Foundation from 1952 to 1961, and secretary of state from 1961 to 1969.

A few weeks later, a chagrined Professor Lewis informed me that his colleagues in the political science department did not think Rusk would have any knowledge of value to impart to the students. I was surprised. I had already decided that he would be a most valuable addition to the staff of the Hoover Institution. After Dr. Lewis and I discussed the matter, however, it was clear that his colleagues fell into two groups—those who believed that Rusk should have resigned as secretary of state in protest against the Vietnam War and those who opposed any and all joint appointments with the Hoover Institution. The Stanford political science department has not changed in twenty-five years.

Dr. Eric Voegelin, prominent political theorist and philosopher and former Max Weber Professor at the University of Munich, came to Hoover in 1969 as the Henry Salvatori Distinguished Scholar. Voegelin had written *The New Science of Politics* (1952), *Order and History* (three volumes, 1956–57), and *Anamnesis,* (1966), among other works. His appointment was made possible by a $250,000 gift from Henry Salvatori, a Los Angeles geophysicist and industrialist, whom Richard V. Allen and I visited in 1968.

The Bruce Franklin Saga

On May 1, 1969, Stanford's self-styled Maoist English professor Bruce Franklin and his followers broke into Encina Hall where the university kept its salary and personnel records. Provost Richard Lyman, who was acting president while Pitzer was out of town, called the police—the first time in the history of Stanford the police had been called onto campus. They quickly got the situation under control.

On Tuesday afternoon, May 27, I had my own confrontation with

Professor Franklin on the steps of the Hoover Tower. I credit the dedication of my executive assistant, Alan Belmont, a former high-ranking FBI official, for the fact that, although Franklin and his ragtag army had broken the windows of the Lou Henry Hoover Building, they had never managed to occupy either that building or the Tower. The group gathered in front of the entrance to the Tower and demanded admission. We told them they could pick five or six representatives, and we would be pleased to have those men and women enter to discuss their "demands." Franklin's followers refused and insisted that I meet with the entire group. At that very tense moment I realized that they had made a fundamental error: They had set the one and only microphone on the steps of the Tower so I could answer their questions.

I accepted the invitation with enthusiasm, and later that day the Stanford News Service issued the following release:

> W. Glenn Campbell, director of the Hoover Institution and a regent of the University of California, engaged in a free-swinging discussion with students about activities at both places Tuesday afternoon.
>
> Shortly after he left the 90-minute session, about 50 students gathered around the steps of Hoover Tower and ignited a fuel-soaked effigy of Campbell.
>
> About a dozen students and Associate Prof. H. Bruce Franklin of the English Department questioned Campbell sharply about the UC and Hoover. Their audience of about 250 included 100 supporters of the April 3rd Movement and Students for a Democratic Society who came to the Tower from a White Plaza rally, several passersby, and quite a few members of the Hoover Institution staff. When students pressed Campbell verbally on his feelings about Berkeley's "People's Park," he replied: "I intend to vote my best judgment and I do not intend to be intimidated by you."
>
> Campbell said "I'm not opposed to parks" and indicated Berkeley planned another park a few blocks from the controversial site. The land, Campbell noted, belongs to the University of California. While he is willing to discuss its use with students, "we cannot tolerate unauthorized groups taking over land for which we have a responsibility to the State of California."
>
> Audience members said the "People's Park" would be open to all citizens, and a speaker from Berkeley charged that Campbell and his fellow regents,

through the use of police and National Guard, were the ones who perpetrated violence there.

Earlier, Campbell said: "I regret the violence and disturbances" in Berkeley. "I regret the death of Mr. Rector, I regret equally deeply the death of the caretaker at the UC-Santa Barbara and two black students at UCLA. Violence and disruption have no place at a university, and I hope it will cease as soon as possible at Berkeley."

Fred Cohen, a junior and SDS leader, demanded to know why communist scholars are not appointed to the Hoover staff, since "one-third of the world is communistic." Hoover scholars, he said, "are studying to stop communist movements; we want to study it to create more communist movements."

Bertram Wolfe, 73-year-old scholar and author on Hoover's staff, who had been sitting on the steps listening, shouted an answer: "How the hell do you know where I stand? You don't do your homework."

Campbell commented that "we do not have political tests; we do not appoint a person because he is a communist or anti-communist." Hoover's documents, he said, are available "to anyone who has the scholarly interests to use them."

Prof. Franklin, who has been active in the A3M, quoted from a newspaper article which said that in Africa, when opposition leaders are arrested, their documents are stolen and sent to Hoover. He asked if the article was true.

Peter J. Duignan, curator of African Studies at Hoover, said that there was an opposition leader arrested, but that "he was a library agent, not a secret agent. He has written articles exposing police brutality, and at grave risk to himself had them filmed and sent to Hoover, for no pay.

"If he had not done this, those documents would have been lost to history."

Campbell said "we have people who collect documents; if someone wants to call them a network of agents, that's their business."

Michel Nabti of the Hoover staff said "scores of distinguished officials" from around the world "beg us" to take their documents. "This session would indicate you know very little about Hoover," he added.

Franklin also asked Campbell why neither UC nor Stanford has any blacks or other minorities on its governing boards, and how present members are selected.

"I would hope there would be (minorities) appointed in due course," replied Campbell. "The governor appoints those he considers the best qualified to govern the University of California, and I assume Stanford trustees are appointed on the same basis."

At the end of our confrontation that day, I told Professor Franklin that I wanted him to know that I didn't think much of my own judgment on one matter.

Before reporting that exchange, I should fill in some background. The American Enterprise Institute for Public Policy Research was holding a "rational debate series" in Washington, D.C. John Howard, president of Rockford College in Illinois, had agreed to argue the case for keeping our colleges and universities engaged in traditional scholarly activities. Dr. Warren Nutter, the moderator, could not find a university president willing publicly to defend the attempts to politicize campuses in opposition to the Vietnam War. I told AEI about Stanford's self-described "Maoist" professor, and suggested that Bruce Franklin would probably be willing to debate. He was, and he did. So that day on the steps of the Tower, I said I had a question for him and, since he had been urging "openness," I was sure he would not mind answering it: How much was he was paid for participating in a debate in Washington, D.C.? He hesitated briefly, and then said he was paid $3,000. I hadn't known the exact amount of his compensation, but I was sure his honorarium had been generous for those days. And, of course, he'd also received his airfare and coverage of his other expenses for two return trips to Washington. Clearly, his motley crew of followers were stunned that he had pocketed the money personally instead of using it to promote the "cause."

Franklin promptly launched into a tirade, reminding the crowd that Lenin and Mao had both urged revolutionaries to steal from capitalists if necessary. I replied that, though I didn't count myself an expert on Lenin or Mao and their ethics, I did know a budding capitalist when I saw one. The crowd, which by then consisted of at least as many spectators as followers of Professor Franklin, roared with laughter and the meeting broke up. In my experiences with Marxists, Maoists, and other assorted leftists both at U.C. Berkeley and Stanford, I found that the one thing they could not take was ridicule. They are good at handing it out, but aren't gracious about receiving it.

In the fall of 1970 the Hoover Institution had another visit from Professor Franklin and his entourage. They announced that they were going to visit the Hewlett-Packard Company at noon to confront that "war criminal" David Packard, who was on leave as deputy secretary of defense. Then they were going to visit the "war criminal" in the Hoover Tower. Since Stanford did not show much concern about this assault on Hoover, I felt I had no alternative but to inform Alan Belmont that we were going to use our own security—baseball bats, clubs, and rocks wielded by any Hoover employee who volunteered. By about 11 AM Belmont had lined up a large number of volunteers, including several librarians and such scholars as Richard Staar, Dennis Bark, Peter Duignan, Lewis Gann, and Witold Sworakowski.

Soon a representative from President Pitzer's office appeared and asked Mr. Belmont whether we were planning to let Franklin and his militants—who had already occupied nearly every other building on campus: the Business School, the Engineering School, the president's office (which they burned), and Encina Hall—into the building. Belmont's immediate answer was no. We were, he said, prepared to fend them off ourselves. The potential for lawsuits resulting from Belmont's plan finally got the university to act on our behalf. It promised that by 1 PM twenty Santa Clara County sheriff's deputies would arrive to take over the defense of the Hoover Tower.

I was so reassured that I kept my off-campus luncheon appointment. Meanwhile, our visiting scholar William Hutt from the University of Capetown approached the Lou Henry Hoover Building. The students massed in front of it and in front of the Tower prevented him from entering. Professor Hutt, a lifelong opponent of apartheid, believed strongly in free speech and abhorred the obstructionist behavior of professors like Bruce Franklin. Spotting a policeman, Hutt protested this behavior and proposed to bring charges against Franklin's group. The policeman was so delighted to find someone at Stanford willing to take a stand that he took Hutt's name and telephone number. (After the confrontation, however, Alan Belmont had to go to Professor Hutt and ask him to withdraw his charges. Without strong support from Stanford University, we could never win a case against Franklin, and we doubted that such support would be forthcoming.)

By the time I returned, about 1:30, the protesters were walking down

Page Mill Avenue, having been rebuffed at Hewlett-Packard. When I got to the lobby of the Hoover Tower, I was greeted by Alan Belmont and the twenty Santa Clara County deputy sheriffs in full riot gear. Each time Franklin and his followers started rattling the front door and demanding entrance, the deputies would move into the lobby and the demonstrators would retreat. Finally, Franklin's army got discouraged and departed, leaving behind only some high school students who were yelling epithets at the police. Just as Dr. Ricardo-Campbell was returning to her office after teaching a class, the police lined up close to the doors, threw them open, and charged out with a loud yell. She barely escaped being knocked over, and the young students scattered in all directions and were not seen again.

In November 1969 the Hoover Institution hosted a very successful conference titled "Peaceful Change in Modern Society." Eleven essays were presented, beginning with Sir Anthony Eden's call for reconvening the Geneva Conference on Indochina and ending with a warning from the Reverend William Pollard, physicist and priest, that we riders on "spaceship Earth" were coming to the end of the Industrial Revolution and entering an age of enforced austerity. We scheduled a second conference, "The United Nations at 25: Performance and Prospect," to be held January 11–13, 1971, the twenty-fifth anniversary of the first meeting of the United Nations General Assembly in London in January 1946. Participants were to include a former U.S. ambassador to the U.N., Henry Cabot Lodge, and three past presidents of the world body's General Assembly: Charles H. Malik of Lebanon, Carlos P. Romulo of the Philippines, and Edvard I. Hambro of Norway. Mr. Romulo was unable to attend the meeting but he did submit his paper for publication.

This conference was to be opened by Henry Cabot Lodge, who had been ambassador to South Vietnam at the height of the Vietnam War in the late 1960s. He was to deliver his speech in Dinkelspiel Auditorium, which seats about seven hundred people, and Alan Belmont had received no advance information that it was to be disrupted. When Henry Cabot Lodge, Berkeley Tompkins, and I entered, the audience booed. Bruce Franklin and fifty to one hundred members of his goon squad were scattered through the audience. The booing was mild when I briefly introduced Dr. Tompkins, the chairman of the session, but he took too much time introducing Ambassador Lodge. He also reacted whenever the crowd hissed or booed. By the time Lodge got to the podium, boos were coming from everywhere, and I had to intervene several times to ask the audience to be polite to our distinguished visitor. In the meantime, Lodge was lecturing me on how disruptions were handled when he was in the Senate: when a Senate session was disrupted, the sergeant at arms and his aides removed the disrupters. This Boston Brahmin informed me that he had fulfilled his part of the agreement—he had written his speech and was ready to deliver it—so it was up to me to enforce order.

I persuaded Ambassador Lodge to make a second attempt to speak, but the booing became even louder. Lodge was threatening to leave, and I knew that a riot would ensue if I called on the six hundred or more serious attendees to throw the "bums" out. All I could do was step quickly to the podium and announce, "Since you cannot behave properly toward our distinguished guest, the meeting is canceled." Later that afternoon Ambassador Lodge delivered his talk to a considerably smaller group in Annenberg Auditorium—Professor Franklin and his henchmen were not present.

By now Richard Lyman was president of Stanford, and he announced his intention to dismiss Professor Franklin. The Advisory Board to the Academic Council—whose chairman that year was Prof. Donald Kennedy—scheduled a hearing on the matter. Before the hearing, Franklin called and asked me to be what he referred to as a "hostile witness." He acted as his own counsel, and when I appeared he asked me several outrageous questions about my political views. Professor Kennedy intervened only when I told him that I was not on trial and I would walk out if he allowed any more such questions. Sympathetic to Franklin—he voted against discharging him—Kennedy was obviously enjoying my discomfort and clearly had no desire to interfere until I forced his hand. At another point during the hearing, Kennedy stated that the people in charge of the Lodge speech had not exercised proper "crowd control." I often wonder what *he* would have done if he had been on that platform, caught between the haughtiness of Henry Cabot Lodge and the boorish bullying of Franklin and his goons.

When the vote was taken, it was five to two (Chairman Kennedy and Prof. Robert McAfee Brown, a professor of religion who was also an anti-Vietnam War activist) in favor of discharging Franklin. On February 12, 1971, President Lyman dismissed Professor Franklin for inciting "occupation of the university computer center, urging defiance of a police order to disperse, and calling a nighttime rally for violent action." Donald Kennedy has ever since tried to defend his vote as necessary to protect free speech at Stanford. In fact, Professor Franklin was encouraging destruction of property and inciting violent action. On the basis of his words and actions in the Franklin case alone, I have never understood why the Stanford trustees later made Donald Kennedy president of the university or why President Lyman recommended him.

Gift Record for the 1960s

Because of the gifts mentioned earlier in this chapter and many other generous bequests, by 1970 our endowment and reserve funds had increased from approximately $2 million to more than $12 million, a sixfold increase in endowment. In addition, the Lou Henry Hoover Building had been constructed and the Tower renovated. We did not then recognize that this record would not be surpassed under my direction, or that it was highly unlikely *ever* to be surpassed. For the first time since the 1920s, when Mr. Hoover obtained the initial funds from the American Relief Administration and the Committee for Relief of Belgium, the Institution had raised a sizable amount of new endowment.

In his remarks to the Hoover Institution Board of Overseers on July 16, 1987, George Nash, Mr. Hoover's official biographer, summarized the progress made by the Hoover Institution:

> Shortly before Mr. Hoover died, he told David Packard that the founding of the Hoover Institution was probably the most important thing he had done in his life. He had great hopes for the didactic purpose that this Institution could serve in enlightening the American people about Communism and about the wars and revolutions of our time. The question of the relationship of the Institution to its larger community, as you can see, has been with us for a very long time. In fact, I would say that the tensions that beset this "think tank" are of two kinds and are inherent in the Hoover/Stanford relationship as it has evolved to this point. First, regard-

less of one's politics, there is an inevitable *structural* tension surrounding an institution that is called "independent within the frame of Stanford University." Secondly, there is a deep-seated *ideological* component that has existed now for about forty years. The Hoover Institution was not meant to be simply a library or simply an archive. Instead, it has become, as its founder wished it to be, an interdisciplinary research center. But more than that, it is perceived today as being predominantly if not monolithically conservative in its public policy thrust in an academic environment where the ideological winds blow fiercely from the opposite direction.

6

The Silver Seventies

ON JANUARY 11, 1971, THE STANFORD UNIVERSITY BOARD OF Trustees adopted a series of resolutions:

That the Committee recommends approval of the proposed revised provisions for the Advisory Board of the Hoover Institution and for the selection and appointment of future directors of the Hoover Institution, as follows:

1. The name of the Advisory Board shall be changed to Board of Overseers of the Hoover Institution on War, Revolution and Peace. The duties of the Board include reviewing the effectiveness of the Institution's operations, advising on new policies and programs and helping to maintain interest in and support of the Institution.

2. In view of the fact that the Hoover Institution is a national institution with an international standing and reputation, the Board must be a national Board and not be limited geographically in its membership or to graduates of Stanford University. No limitation shall be placed on size of membership except to keep it within reasonable limits.

3. Present members of the Hoover Institution Board may continue to serve without limit as to term.

4. New members of the Board shall be appointed to three-year terms, with a limit of two consecutive three-year terms. A period of at least one year must elapse prior to reappointment after two consecutive terms.

5. Members will automatically cease to be included on the Board if they do not attend at least one meeting during a three-year period.

6. The Board of Overseers shall elect its Chairman, Vice Chairman, and

its Executive Committee. New members of the Board shall be recommended by the Executive Committee and after approval by the Board of Overseers and by the President and Trustees of Stanford University they shall be invited to join the Board by the Chairman of the Board of Overseers of the Hoover Institution.

7. The Board of Overseers shall make an annual report to the President and Trustees of Stanford University.

With respect to the selection and appointment of future Directors of the Hoover Institution:

1. A search committee shall be constituted consisting of four nominees of the Senior Fellows of the Hoover Institution, three nominees of the Board of Overseers and three nominees of the President of Stanford University. The Chairman of the Committee shall be selected by the President from the nominees of the Senior Fellows.

2. After the President of Stanford University has selected a candidate from the nominees of the search committee, he shall submit the name of the person so selected to the Board of Overseers for their approval and then to the Board of Directors of the Herbert Hoover Foundation for their approval.

3. After such approval, the recommendation shall then be submitted to the Board of Trustees of Stanford University for approval of the appointment as Director of the Hoover Institution.

4. Whenever the directorship of the Hoover Institution is vacant or the Director is absent on leave, the Associate Director shall be Acting Director.

The seeds of these provisions had been sown months earlier. At the January 1970 meeting of the Hoover Institution Advisory Board, President Pitzer recommended changes in the composition and operation of the board to make it more consistent with newly adopted standards for university visiting committees. The Advisory Board responded by appointing a committee chaired by Allan Hoover to consider the president's recommendations and recommend a response to the full board.

John Swearingen, chairman and CEO of Standard Oil of Indiana, presented the Allan Hoover committee report at the summer meeting of the Advisory Committee. Its recommendations went well beyond Pitzer's original proposals and were directed toward greater autonomy for the

Hoover Institution. President Lyman and I engaged in several discussions through the autumn of that year, discussions which led to agreement on the committee's proposal. We also sought and won the concurrence of the Faculty Advisory Committee on the Hoover Institution and the Hoover Advisory Board.

The proposed new policy covered two subjects that had been dealt with ambiguously, if at all. First, the Hoover Advisory Board itself: Under the proposed new arrangement, that group would become the Board of Overseers of the Hoover Institution, and its responsibilities would be spelled out more clearly. The procedures for selecting members of the board were similar to the earlier method, but the terms of office and the election of board officers were more clearly defined.

Second, the procedure for selecting a new director: The key element was, of course, the search process to narrow the field of possibilities. Under the new arrangement, the search committee would reflect the Hoover Institution's variety of interests by including the Senior Fellows of the Institution, those outside the Institution whose support and interest were important sustaining elements, and the president and faculty of the university. This committee would produce a list of nominees from which the president would select a candidate to be approved by the Board of Overseers and the Board of Directors of the Herbert Hoover Foundation. (This provision was consistent with the 1959 action of the Stanford board.) Finally, the candidate would be approved by the Stanford Board of Trustees. In effect, the Allan Hoover committee recommended that Stanford University have very little involvement in the activities at the Hoover Institution, except to provide monetary support for the library. The director was to be selected by the Advisory Board with the prior approval of the Hoover Family Foundation.

When John Swearingen made his presentation in the de Basily Room, Stanford trustee Morris Doyle was very upset, as was Richard Lyman (who became Stanford's president that summer). They were concerned that the Hoover director and the Advisory Board would not be sufficiently accountable to the Stanford Board of Trustees. This was particularly disturbing to them because, at the same time, the Stanford Research Institute bought its freedom from the university in order to continue doing classified research for the federal government.

Had we firmly supported the Allan Hoover committee's proposal instead of cooperating with President Lyman, the Hoover Institution would have been spared much grief at the hands of Stanford's eighth president, Donald Kennedy. Under our proposals the Stanford trustees could still remove the Hoover director for not satisfactorily discharging his duties, but the trustees would have to *explain and defend* their reasons for termination. Therefore, the trustees would have been required to offer legitimate reasons for my dismissal in May 1988. Board President Warren Christopher and university President Donald Kennedy could not, in that case, have used my age as a pretext for their actions.

Successes in the '70s

Early in 1970 Ruth Lane of *Sunset* magazine observed that many well-educated women put off developing careers in order to raise their children. When those children reached high school and the family anticipated college expenditures, the mothers needed to go back to work, primarily for monetary reasons—but they did not necessarily know *how* to go about finding a job, or even know *what jobs* were available. Mrs. Lane, who had two sons herself, thought that this was a terrible waste of talent. Rita Ricardo-Campbell agreed, and they put together a conference on second careers for women. Jane D. Fairbank, wife of Stanford professor William Fairbank, and Susan G. Bell assisted Dr. Ricardo-Campbell. Mrs. Lane contributed $3,000 and Rita got approximately the same amount from Richard Scaife to create a one-day course for women who wanted to go back to work. In a campus-fair setting, they presented potential jobs in particular areas and offered opportunities for attending community college courses that would prepare women for those jobs.

On May 2, 1970, 700 women attended the conference, and its proceedings were later published. Fifteen occupational fields—for example, computer science, medicine and biology, library administration, environmental planning, and business and finance—were represented by 150 women and men from the San Francisco Bay Area. This was, I believe, the first such conference held in the United States, and it became a prototype for conferences all over the country. Using the same format, the University of California at Riverside held a similar workshop in 1971, and Duke University followed suit in 1975. So widespread was the influence of that original conference that today community colleges regularly offer courses that acquaint women with the kinds of jobs available and often train them for those jobs.

The National Public Affairs and Peace Fellows Program

The new National Fellows Program proved to be a great success. In 1968 David Packard and I were discussing what to do with income from the special trust fund containing his and his wife's Hewlett-Packard Company stock (set up when he became Nixon's assistant secretary of defense). He suggested funding our fledgling "national fellows" program. The name immediately struck me as ideal for the infant program, and it was so christened.

From 1969 to December 1971 the Packards contributed $340,000 out of their special trust fund to the National Fellows Program. Packard had originally stated that *all* the income should go to the Hoover Institution, but Stanford's vice president for development, Kenneth Cuthbertson, tried to keep it all for Stanford. Finally, Mr. Packard asked his friend Trustee Morris Doyle to handle the matter, and Doyle divided the funds (approximately $700,000) about equally between Stanford and Hoover. In 1970, the Scaife Family Foundation boosted the program with a matching gift of $500,000.

The Hoover-financed National and Peace Fellows programs were created primarily for academics with Ph.D.s. Our first National Fellow was Dr. Dennis Bark in 1970–71, and the first executive director was Dr. Lawson Pendleton, appointed in May 1970. From 1967 to 1976 the Vivian Bilby Noble Foundation gave $155,000 to the Public Affairs Fellowship Program, begun in 1967 under the direction of senior staff member Richard V. Allen. Our first Public Affairs Fellow was Edwin J. Feulner, Jr., who is now the president of the Heritage Foundation in Washington, D.C.

In 1972 the Scaife Family Foundation provided a lead-off grant of $750,000 to expand the Domestic Studies Program. After lengthy internal discussions with the Senior Fellows, I asked Senior Fellow Martin

Anderson to outline the program for presentation at the December 1971 Board of Overseers meeting at the American Enterprise Institute in Washington, D.C.:

1. The current program of library acquisitions and research work in the international field will continue, and provision will be made for expansion as circumstances permit.

2. The domestic program will be expanded, with the goal of making it comparable in size and quality to the international area.

3. In both the foreign and domestic areas emphasis will be placed on analytical studies, as well as the traditional historical studies for which the Institution is well known.

4. While continuing to focus on basic, fundamental research, special attention will be given to research with policy implications.

5. Efforts will be made to develop relationships with other research institutions, when such actions would complement and strengthen the Institution's own work.

Stanford President Lyman attended this meeting. When assured that we intended to build only a working library for domestic studies, not a research library as we had for international studies, he supported our initiative. David Packard was also at the meeting, and was so favorably impressed that he told me I could, if I wished, designate for the Domestic Studies Program the shares of stock he'd given to the Hoover Institution when he resigned as deputy secretary of defense.[1]

Endowment Funds Honoring Our Predecessors

In the early 1970s Wayne Vucinich, professor of history, and I agreed that we should have a dinner in honor of Harold Fisher, former chairman of the board. Vucinich handled the arrangements and invited people he thought were both friends of Professor Fisher's and potential contributors. Many of those present knew that I had criticized Fisher's left-wing views, so I decided that Hoover ought to contribute to the fund. I announced at the dinner that the Hoover Institution would match the amount received

---

1. The market value of this fund as of August 31, 1989 was $310,000.

from other donors to the Harold Fisher Fund. The total amount, including the Hoover contribution, was \$13,500,[2] the income from which would be used to purchase books on the Soviet Union and Eastern Europe.

Around 1973 Fred Glover called me on behalf of President Lyman. He explained that, because of expenses associated with his wife's long illnesses and the fact that he received a rather small pension, Fisher was effectively destitute. Would the Hoover Institution contribute to a fund for his support? I agreed at once and instructed our finance officer to send \$10,000. Whatever our differing opinions, Harold Fisher was an honorable man and a gentleman. He passed away in 1975 at the age of 85.

As director, I believed in honoring my predecessors and colleagues—Prof. Ralph Lutz, the second director (I never knew the founding director, E. D. Adams), for whom we established a special acquisition fund;[3] Professor and Associate Director Witold Sworakowski, for whom we established an endowment for the collection of Polish books;[4] and my first assistant, Edith S. Fabyni, for whom we established an endowment for the collection of Hungarian books.[5] All my predecessors were given good offices in which to work. Fisher kept his office on the second floor of the Tower until his death. Easton Rothwell, my immediate predecessor, who left to become the president of Mills College, received gifts of \$15,000 donated to us through the San Francisco Foundation for work on his book *Changing Great Power Relations in the Pacific Region* (unpublished because it was lost by a Hoover staff member). All these funds were established during the lifetimes of the honorees.

Because I benefited greatly from Professor Lutz's knowledge of the history of the Hoover Institution, I moved him—with his pleased concurrence—to the corner office on the eleventh floor, directly across from Mr. Hoover's, and he remained in that office until his death in 1968.

As an indicator of the progress we had made, on October 22, 1973, I received this letter from Fred Terman:

---

2. The market value of this fund as of August 31, 1989, was \$310,000.
3. The Ralph H. Lutz Special Acquisition fund had a market value of well over \$315,000 in August 1989.
4. The Witold H. Sworakowski fund had a market value in excess of \$149,000 in August 1989.
5. The Edith S. Fabyni fund had a market value of \$68,000 in August 1989.

Thank you for sending me a copy of the three-year report (1969–72) of the Hoover Institution.

This is an impressive story of accomplishments. As a one-time Provost who wrestled with budgets, I was particularly impressed with the two pages of charts detailing expenditures and income. The record pictured there is a tribute to your personal effectiveness in developing worth-while programs and in obtaining financial support for them.

Although the university funds going into the Hoover Institution in 1971–72 were more than four times the corresponding amount in 1959–60, such an increase in income, taken alone, would barely have kept the Hoover Institution afloat on a custodial basis. What has transformed the Hoover Institution under your leadership is the large increase in endowment earnings, and gifts, which have resulted from your well-planned and aggressive fund-raising efforts.

Another factor that does not escape my notice is the more than one-hundred fold increase in publications and microfilm sales. This is the real payoff, as it provides tangible evidence that the Hoover Institution is productive in scholarly terms and that people are reading what it produces.

Our Soviet Visit

On the morning of January 16, 1972, we were visited by the Soviet minister of culture, Madame Yekaterena Furtseva. I met her in the Nicolas de Basily room with a former associate director, Witold Sworakowski. Madame Furtseva had been brought in through the back door that morning to avoid demonstrations protesting the policies of the Soviet Union in respect to Jewish immigrants. Sworakowski was seated next to her so they could talk in Russian and he could interpret for me. During the course of the discussion, she asked if I had ever been to Moscow. When I told her I had not, she invited Rita and me to come as her guests. Noticing our painting of the old Winter Palace, she declared unequivocally that it belonged back in the Soviet Union. After I left, Sworakowski showed her some of our major collections on imperial Russia and the Okhrana.

Rita and I planned our trip to the Soviet Union for early April. We were duly warned not to say anything affecting national security because of my association as a U.C. regent with the Lawrence Livermore and Los Alamos Laboratories. Our trip began in England, where we visited Peter Bauer and Ralph and Josie Harris before proceeding to the Netherlands for a luncheon with Ambassador and Mrs. Middendorf. After that we took an American plane directly to Moscow.

We were met by the State Department's deputy chief of mission, Mark Garrison, who had spent the previous year at the Hoover Institution. He helped us clear immigration and customs and check into the Hotel Rossya. This hotel had over three thousand rooms, the biggest hotel in the world then. When we were shown to our room, however, I found it extremely small. My friend from the State Department assured me that we were getting VIP treatment: "This is a *suite!*" The "suite" consisted of a small second room where the bed was situated. If you jumped over the bed, you were in the "living room." The furniture looked ready to collapse even though the hotel was then only about four years old. The toilet was in an alcove off the living room, and Rita had trouble getting it to work. Luckily, I found that I could make it work with a good swift kick.

Once settled, we visited Red Square; Lenin's Tomb (Stalin had been removed and buried elsewhere, then brought back to lie in the line of important communists behind Lenin); St. Basil's Cathedral, a former Russian Orthodox church used by the communists as a tourist attraction; and the crown jewels. The next day we called on the head of the Russian Archives, a KGB agent, because we were trying to set up an exchange program with him. The KGB agent seemed to know little about the archives, so at the end of our conversation—which appeared to go very well—I asked if someone could *show* them to us. He was accommodating, but instead of seeing the documentation relating to people Stalin had killed, we were shown twelfth- and thirteenth-century church archives. Despite the lack of air-conditioning, they seemed quite well preserved. In any case, the KGB agent might as well have shown us the *other* archives, because neither of us could read Russian.

We also visited the Soviet Academy of Sciences to see Georgi Arbatov, head of the Canadian-American section. Arbatov had visited the Hoover Institution and I had hosted a luncheon for him at the Stanford Faculty Club. I believe he had visited Hoover largely because Richard Nixon had recently been elected president, and some of our Fellows were working for the new administration. He knew that Nixon and I were campmates at the Bohemian Grove, and wanted to discuss American policies in economics, foreign affairs, and military matters. We continued those discussions in Moscow with frequent disagreements over how fast the Soviet economy was growing versus the U. S. economy.

One evening we went to the Bolshoi Theatre to see the famous Russian ballet. A KGB agent seated next to me started a conversation in English, emphasizing how bad conditions were in the Soviet Union and hinting that he would like to get out. I grunted noncommittal answers until he lost interest. We were also regularly approached by people in the streets for favors, all of which we ignored. We did not want to end up in prison like other Americans who had made the mistake of sharing American currency or otherwise dealing with these supplicants.

In the Soviet Union at that time most women worked outside the home. Rita was curious to see how they managed it, so Mark Garrison and his wife arranged a dinner party with mid-level Soviet officials. When Rita asked how the women managed to work, keep house, and cook the meals, they answered that it was easy: "We just call the commissary and have meals delivered!"

One afternoon, we attended a cocktail party at Spasso House, the home of the American ambassador. The guests included some naive visitors from various newspapers and magazines who were sure the Soviet Union was a pleasant, progressive place with a thriving economy and an enviable standard of living.

Perhaps they did not visit the Moscow department store, Gum, to find out how few goods were for sale and how long the many lines were. Even then, people got their fruits and vegetables, meat and poultry, from stalls set up by peasants who were selling their produce privately.

After about four days Mark Garrison got us to the airport and onto the plane without interminable waiting. When we landed at the airport outside Leningrad, we were treated as VIPs, met by a car and driver, plus a guide. On the way to the hotel, our guide said we would definitely like our accommodations, but we didn't know what she meant until we arrived at the luxurious Europa Hotel. The huge pre-Soviet hotel had been built in the late nineteenth or early twentieth century. Our suite had three large rooms—a living room, a bedroom with a bathroom with a pull-chain toilet, and a study with a grand piano. By then, ready to have a little fun with the KGB, I walked into the living room, looked up at the ceiling, and said, "This is more like a U.S. hotel, but I wish they'd get rid of this crummy nineteenth-century furniture!"

In Leningrad we were taken to what had been the czar's Winter Palace, which housed the Hermitage Museum. Peter the Great and Catherine the Great had sent agents all over Europe to buy valuable art, so that Russia's art collection would rival the much older French, Italian, and British collections. The Winter Palace itself was basically a copy of Versailles with high ceilings, enormous chandeliers, etc. The art collection was indeed impressive, and we spent nearly a full day there. Overall, however, it was eclipsed by the Louvre in Paris, the Prado in Madrid, and the British Museum in London. We spent part of another day at the Russian museum and found it very poorly maintained, with portraits less impressive than those in the Hoover Institution's de Basily Room.

An American consulate had been recently established in Leningrad in exchange for a Soviet consulate in San Francisco, and one evening, we were invited to the home of the new American consul-general. The food was good and the conversation interesting, but one thing stands out in Rita's mind and mine: a young Soviet college woman there wanted *very* much to visit the West, because she had been told that the West was much more prosperous and interesting than Leningrad. Such candor in the Soviet Union was extraordinary.

When our Russian visit was over, we paid our bill at the Europa and proceeded to the airport, accompanied as always by a KGB agent, to board Scandinavian Airlines for Copenhagen. Both of us heaved sighs of relief at leaving the USSR. As a memento of the occasion, I bought Rita a beautiful necklace which has now been passed on to our youngest daughter, Nancy.

An Important Innovation

The Domestic Studies Advisory Committee was founded in 1973. George Stigler, Walgreen Professor of American Institutions at the University of Chicago, was appointed chairman, so he became a regular visitor to the Hoover Institution. He and I put together what we considered a distinguished group—including Moses Abramovitz of Stanford, Edward Banfield of Harvard, William Baxter of the Stanford Law School, Gary Becker of Chicago, Jack Hirshleifer of UCLA, Hendrik Houthakker of Harvard, and William Meckling of the University of Rochester. Over the years the membership of the group rotated, but Stigler remained chairman (and Becker remained a member) until the committee was discontinued in 1990. George Stigler deserves much of the credit for the quality of the Hoover Institution Domestic Studies Program. As a result of his and the committee's advice, we brought several excellent economists to the Hoover Institution, including Thomas Moore, Thomas Sowell, Robert Hall, Kenneth Judd, Edward Lazear, Thomas Sargent, and finally Gary Becker himself as a part-time Senior Fellow.

Martin Anderson, the first coordinator of the Domestic Studies Advisory Committee, was succeeded in 1974 by Thomas G. Moore who, in turn, was succeeded by Edward Lazear in 1985 (when Moore was appointed to the President's Council of Economic Advisors). Stigler and the Domestic Studies Advisory Committee were also very helpful in selecting top-notch National Fellows. Every autumn when the committee met here, the National Fellows who were also Domestic Studies Fellows appeared to discuss their projects. They were frequently trembling and nervous because Stigler had a biting wit and was not known for suffering fools gladly, but the best of the Fellows found that the experience ultimately improved their projects.

Rita and I found Stigler thoughtful and kind, and we looked forward to his annual dinner at our home. Stigler was also an ideal adviser, and we met frequently. Every year just before he returned to Chicago, we held a longer meeting in which he shared his impressions of both the National Fellows and Domestic Studies programs and suggested changes that Hoover might consider. His advice was invariably excellent, and I virtually always took it. Nevertheless, at the end of the meeting he would say, "I am just your adviser, and you are the director; and, as you know, you are the one who has to make the final decision and take the responsibility."

From 1973 through 1989, we held an annual dinner in honor of the Domestic Studies Advisory Committee to which all Senior Fellows, their spouses, and several donors were invited. Over the years our distinguished speakers included Stanford President Richard Lyman; Nobel Prize winners in economics George Stigler, Milton Friedman, Friedrich von Hayek, James Buchanan, and Gary Becker; and James Coleman. We also invited professors from related Stanford departments and received many compliments for bringing distinguished persons and their spouses together with members from other departments and from the Hoover Institution.

In 1976 Associate Director Richard F. Staar and I decided to institute an International Studies Advisory Committee. At that time the International Studies Program included analytical, documentary, and bibliographic research, as well as the publication of works on social, economic, and political movements in the twentieth century. The program was placing greater emphasis on major issues currently facing policymakers or issues that might emerge in crises. Staar, with the help of the area curators, coordinated the International Studies Program.

The purpose of the International Studies Advisory Committee was to assist these efforts by commenting on the scope of current programs and by helping to initiate additional policy-oriented projects. Seven prominent scholars were named to this committee, including committee chairman Robert A. Scalapino, professor of political science at the University of California at Berkeley, and Harry G. Johnson, a professor of economics at the University of Chicago. Scalapino, my Harvard office mate at Leverett House while we were attending graduate school, is a distinguished scholar and an expert on both Chinese and Japanese politics. Like the Domestic Studies Advisory Committee, Scalapino and his colleagues helped us find and select excellent National Fellows, and Fellows in the international field also discussed their projects before the committee, whose criticisms and suggestions were generally beneficial.

From 1976 through 1989, we held an annual dinner in honor of the International Studies Advisory Committee. As at the Domestic Studies Committee dinner, many distinguished speakers appeared, including President Lyman, Professor Scalapino, Honorary Fellow Friedrich von Hayek, Senior Research Fellow Milton Friedman, and Prof. Samuel Huntington. This committee was dissolved in 1990.

From January 1, 1960, through August 31, 1989, we raised $54.9 million in funds to endow the Domestic Studies Program. During the same period, we raised $4.1 million in endowment funds and $10,883,125 in expendable funds for the International Studies Program.

Library Gifts

Large gifts continued to come in for our library collections. It is usually more difficult to raise money for book acquisitions and processing than for buildings and programs (which can be named after donors), but *if* you have an outstanding research and publications program—plus distinguished visiting scholars from all over the world—and *if* the director and his associates work on it continuously, the money *will* come in. A gift of $50,000 came from the Kresge Foundation in 1970 for use in special library acquisitions. Between 1970 and 1975, we also received $700,000 from the S. H. Cowell Foundation for our Special Acquisitions and Collections fund. We owe much to the late I. W. Hellman for arranging these gifts, because Stanford had placed us last on the priority list. In fact, we were not supposed to approach a possible donor until he or she had turned down several of Stanford's appeals for funds! Mr. Hellman was determined that the money should go to the Hoover Institution because he was disappointed with the way Stanford had dealt with anti-Vietnam War demonstrations. He liked the "no nonsense allowed" approach taken by Governor Reagan and a majority of the U.C. regents toward the U.C. Berkeley demonstrations inherited from former President Clark Kerr and Governor Edmund G. (Pat) Brown.

In March 1970 Mr. Hellman and I were walking back from lunch at the Faculty Club when he asked me what I thought of his cousin Eleanor Heller, my fellow U.C. regent. I replied in a way for which I've often been criticized—I told him the unvarnished truth: "Since you asked, not much." I qualified that by saying that Mrs. Heller was a very conscientious and well-informed regent—but she usually voted against Governor Reagan and a majority of the regents when it came to controlling Berkeley's campus radicals. Mr. Hellman said he felt the same way about her, and then added with a twinkle in his eye, "You will get your $500,000." I had passed his test.

The Andrew W. Mellon Foundation awarded the Institution a $150,000 grant in 1973, covering a three-year period. This was part of the foundation's program to enable a select number of universities in the United States and Canada to increase their library resources on East Asian studies. In 1974, then, Richard Staar and I decided to appoint a scholar to take charge of the Eastern European Collection, as we had already done for the African, the Middle Eastern, and the Far Eastern collections. Karol Maichel, curator of the Eastern European Collection, resigned effective December 31, 1974, and was replaced on a half-time basis by a Stanford professor of history, Wayne S. Vucinich.

One of the projects Vucinich started during his year as curator was a series of studies of nationalities in the USSR. For the first study, we paid the author $500. Over the years, the payments steadily increased, first to $1,000, then to $1,500, and finally to over $2,000. I enthusiastically supported this project because, like Mr. Hoover, I was certain that some day the Soviet Union would be composed of free people. These studies might help those people gain their freedom and would also be useful to them after they did so. In the foreword to his first publication, Professor Vucinich describes the series:

> In most surveys of the history of Russia and the Soviet Union, the more than one hundred non-Russian peoples receive far less attention than their histories and cultures merit. Moreover, such general works tend to give only superficial attention to such important topics as the Russian conquest of foreign nationalities and lands, the development and administration of ethnic minorities under Tsarist and Soviet rule, Russia's role in transmitting both Russian and West-European ideas and institutions to their own Asian and non-Slavic groups, and Russia's character as a melting pot of different ethnic peoples and cultures.
>
> *The Crimean Tatars* is the first in a series of volumes that discuss the history and development of the non-Russian nationalities in the Soviet Union. The subject of this book is especially appropriate for the opening volume of the series, because a study of this particular people vividly illustrates a number of the problems encountered by Soviet leaders in their attempt to create a multi-national society. Except for the Volga Germans, the Crimean Tatars are the only one of the component nationalities of the USSR who, having once been granted an autonomous territory, appear to have had this privilege permanently revoked.
>
> The problems discussed here have parallels which are examined in the remaining volumes of the series. Since the beginning of the rapid industrialization of the Soviet Union, the requirements of economic development and political control have transformed the ethnographic map of the Soviet

Union and created in many national autonomous territories situations nearly as acute as that in the Crimea. Many of the nationality groups have found themselves outnumbered and politically displaced by immigrating Great Russians, Ukrainians, and others. This movement of peoples and its results have called into question the functioning of the Soviet federal solution and have created discontented local nationalisms to plague the rulers in the Kremlin.

A new pattern, however, is now emerging. The difference in birth rates between the dominant Slavs and the non-Russian nationalities is changing the ethnographic balance more and more in favor of the latter. It appears possible or even likely that in the relatively near future the Great Russians will be outnumbered by the other nationalities.

As a result of these dynamics of development the study of the past and present of the non-Russian nationalities is extremely important. It is also significant in what it portends for the future. Thus, studies such as the one presented here, and those that follow, should provide the Western reader with a fuller understanding of the complexities of Soviet reality. Comparable volumes on several other major nationalities, a total of seventeen, are currently in preparation. Included are separate studies of the principal nations of Soviet Central Asia, the Caucasus, the Baltic region and the Ukraine, as well as special groups such as the Jews and the Crimean Tatars. Each volume examines the history of a particular national group in both the Tsarist and Soviet eras with an emphasis on determining its place in the Soviet federation as well as its impact on the evolution of Soviet society.

The following is a list of the seven studies in this series written by different authors and edited by Wayne S. Vucinich and published by the Hoover Institution Press:

The Crimean Tatars by Alan Fisher, Studies of Nationalities in the USSR Series, 1978.

The Volga Tatars: A Profile in National Resilience by Azade-Aysy Rorlich, Studies of Nationalities in the USSR Series, 1986.

The Kazakhs by Martha Brill Olcott, Studies of Nationalities in the USSR Series, 1987.

Estonia and the Estonians by Toivo U. Raun, Studies of Nationalities in the USSR Series, 1987.

Sakartvelo: The Making of the Georgian Nation (Co-publication of Indiana University Press and Hoover Institution Press) by Ronald Grigor Suny, Studies of Nationalities in the USSR Series, 1988.

The Modern Uzbeks: From the Fourteenth Century to the Present—A Cultural History by Edward A. Allworth, Studies of Nationalities in the USSR Series, 1990.

The Azerbaijani Turks: Power and Identity Under Russian Rule by Audrey L. Altstadt, Studies of Nationalities in the USSR Series, 1992.

When the Soviet Union broke up, this series was one of the few available studies on many of its ethnic groups.

In 1974 Prof. Richard Atkinson, associate dean for the Social Sciences and Humanities, called to ask if we could meet. When we did, he mentioned that he and his colleagues would like to ask Seymour Martin Lipset to leave Harvard and come to Stanford. He did not think Lipset would come, however, unless he was offered a joint appointment to the Hoover Institution. Since we had already discussed an appointment for Professor Lipset, I assured Dean Atkinson that my colleagues and I would be delighted to have him at the Hoover Institution. Together, we brought him to Hoover and Stanford as a "target of opportunity" appointment.

We also discussed joint appointments for Alex Inkeles and James March to the Hoover Institution and the Stanford School of Education. In due course, all these appointments were arranged, and Dean Atkinson later remarked that the Hoover Institution seemed to have higher academic standards than the rest of the university. One reason he had originally asked to meet with me was that he had heard so much about Hoover's "low scholarly standards" and the "difficulty" of working with Director Campbell.

To commemorate the hundredth anniversary of Mr. Hoover's birth, we established the Hoover Associates program in 1974. The associates were to be individuals who, in cooperation with the Board of Overseers, actively promoted the Institution's programs and general welfare. Co-chairmen of the Founding Committee of the Associates were Joseph J. Burris, Paul L. Davies, Jr., and Jack S. Parker. The initial contributors to this program at the Hoover Associate level (which required a donation of $10,000 or more) included these co-chairmen, along with Henry T.

Bodman, Alf Brandin, D. Tennant Bryant, Gordon Hampton, Wallace Hawley, Eleanor Howard, Jacqueline Hume, Emil Mosbacher, Jr., Fred Russell, Dan Throop Smith, Richard Staar, Darrell Trent, Dean Watkins, and James T. Wood. Rita and I contributed an additional $200,000. These donations and others totaled over $600,000 in expendable funds, and the Hoover Associates program became a solid contributor to the Institution's advancement.

The William H. Noble bequest of 1973 totaled $6.6 million, unrestricted and expendable.[6] This was the largest unrestricted bequest to Stanford to that date. Some $3.6 million was allocated for a library endowment and $3.0 million for Domestic Studies research projects and publications.

The genesis of this generous gift was a telephone call from Morris Doyle on the morning of April 3, 1973. Doyle explained that Mr. Noble had had Stanford in his will for years for one third of the residue of his estate—that is, several million dollars. However, he had cut Stanford out because of his disgust at the university's failure to control campus disruptions in the 1960s and early 1970s. Since I always respond quickly to donor possibilities, I sent Doyle the following letter that very afternoon:

> I think the best way to begin to tell someone of the program and plans of the Hoover Institution is by having him look at our new Three Year Report (two copies enclosed). As promised, I am also sending you, on a confidential basis, copies of the letters written by David Packard and Arthur Burns [chairman of the Board of Governors of the Federal Reserve System at that time] in support of our plans to expand the Institution's Domestic Studies Program.
>
> I find that most of our donors are interested in the Institution's relationship to Stanford University, and after the rather unusual organizational relationship is fully explained to them they are quite impressed with the extent to which the Hoover Institution at one and the same time both enjoys an independent status within the frame of Stanford University and is still legally

---

6. As of August 1989 the market value of the Noble bequest for library endowment was just over $10.4 million, and the market value of the Domestic Studies endowment was over $9.3 million.

a part of Stanford. Copies of the two key Trustees' resolutions of May 1959 and January 1971 covering these matters are enclosed.

Since I gather that the prospective donor is interested in economics, I want to point out that for the past three years an anonymous donor has been making substantial contributions varying from $60,000 to $75,000 per annum for the following purpose: to support Fellows in the National Fellows Program who are interested in research and instruction on the American economy.

The Roush endowment, which is now approaching $500,000, states: "To establish The Emma and Carroll Roush Fund for American Studies in the Hoover Institution on War, Revolution and Peace. The purpose of this Fund is to expand research and instruction by the Hoover Institution on the American economy, with primary stress on the private economy and its contributions to human well-being, including an evaluation of public policies that preserve and foster free enterprise."

I received a response from Morris Doyle, dated April 11. Mr. Doyle wrote that "Ham" Enersen, a partner of his, had informed him that Mr. Noble had undergone surgery and was suffering from an inoperable malignancy. The prognosis was not good, and Doyle did not know when Enersen would have an opportunity to speak about the Hoover Institution. The next call from Doyle came on June 4, informing me that a codicil to Mr. Noble's will would give one third of the residue—which would total in the millions—to the Hoover Institution. Mr. Noble's will was reported in the July 30 *San Francisco Chronicle:*

> The talk of the bridge tables is Bill Noble's will, which was filed for probate on July 16. Bill died on June 26, four weeks after the will was written, though most of his friends weren't even aware that he was ill.
>
> Always a man of definite tastes, he left $50,000 to the San Francisco Opera Association, but that can only go toward production of operas by Verdi and Puccini.
>
> Everything that's left after specific bequests will go in equal shares to the California Academy of Sciences (but nothing can be used for an aquarium or any marine life), the Fine Arts Museums of San Francisco (nothing to be used for modern or contemporary art) and the Hoover Institution on War, Revolution and Peace (no restrictions).

This was the largest bequest that Hoover received in place of Stanford during my directorate.[7] Further gifts or bequests would follow from people angry about the changes President Donald Kennedy and his coterie made in the Western civilization course, and also about the loss of the Reagan Presidential Library. During the 1990–91 fiscal year, for example, about $1.3 million in bequests testified to that anger.

The Herbert Hoover Federal Memorial Building

The Herbert Hoover Federal Memorial Building was born of careful planning, teamwork, quick decision-making, and choreographed bypassing of the usual Stanford committees. With the hundredth anniversary of President Hoover's birth approaching in 1974, Sen. Mark Hatfield of Oregon introduced a bill in early 1972 that created a committee of distinguished citizens to plan an appropriate memorial to the late President Hoover. The following fall I called on him to suggest that he replace his bill with one that would situate the memorial at the Hoover Institution.

Senator Hatfield had worked at Hoover on his master's thesis, which concerned Mr. Hoover's labor policies as secretary of commerce. While there he had met his future wife, Antoinette, who was working on her master's degree in education, and he had gotten to know and admire President Hoover. Mr. Hoover, in turn, recognized Hatfield as a man with a great future in either the academic or the political world. At least once in the 1940s he invited the future senator to be his guest at the Bohemian Grove. Hatfield readily agreed to my proposal and—even though Congress was nearing the end of its second session—introduced the bill my colleagues and I had drafted. Having served for several years on the committee planning a memorial to Franklin D. Roosevelt, Hatfield was well aware of how little progress such a committee would make unless conditions were propitious.

In the meantime I consulted with Allan Hoover, the sole surviving son of the late president, and had his approval, as well as that of Mr. Hoover's grandson Pete, for building the memorial at the Hoover Institution. I also consulted David Packard, Bryce Harlow, and William Baroody, Sr.

---

7. Its market value totaled about $19.7 million in August 1989.

Senator Hatfield and I testified before a subcommittee of the House Education and Labor Committee in 1973—and got absolutely nowhere. The chairman of the subcommittee, Congressman O'Hara of Michigan, blamed the Depression on President Hoover. On the other hand, we had no difficulty finding Senate sponsors for the bill. The bipartisan list of sponsors included William Brock of Tennessee, Alan Cranston of California, Barry Goldwater of Arizona, Edward Kennedy of Massachusetts, George McGovern of South Dakota, Majority Leader Mike Mansfield of Montana, Minority Leader Hugh Scott of Pennsylvania, and John Tunney of California. The bill passed the Senate with ease, but our problem in the House of Representatives remained. Charles Gubser, who then represented the Stanford area, approached Wayne Hayes of Ohio, chairman of the House Administration Committee, who agreed that Mr. Hoover should have a memorial and arranged for me to testify before the subcommittee chaired by Frank Thompson of New Jersey.

Hurriedly, with Rita's assistance, I got the Stanford Planning Department to prepare an architectural drawing that showed a twelve-story building. At that time the Stanford administration was planning a gargantuan new main library building, so there was not enough space for the sized building we really needed. As it turned out, Stanford was unable to raise sufficient money for the proposed library, so we ended up with plenty of space available for the beautiful building architect Ernest J. Kump designed for us. The Stanford planning office staff was reluctant to cooperate until I assured it I would take full responsibility for the drawings if Stanford's president and trustees objected.

I gave my presentation to Congressman Thompson's subcommittee that summer. By then the question was whether we would receive $5 million with no matching requirements or $7 million on a one for one matching basis. Congressman Thompson believed that if it was hard to raise funds for the FDR memorial, it would be much harder to raise funds for a memorial to Herbert Hoover. I considered this argument for a moment, then replied that, with all due respect, the Hoover Institution would take a $7 million grant on a one for one matching basis. The committee agreed and wished me well. If I had followed Stanford's usual bureaucratic procedures, I'd have had to consult the appropriate university authorities before making that decision. I probably would not have got an answer in time to appear before Thompson's committee again during that session, and the funds would almost surely have been lost to us. (This take-charge approach was effective for the Hoover Institution, but it also contributed to the resentment against me on the part of Stanford's administration.)

So far, so good—until the Truman Memorial came up. The bill to create a $30 million Truman Scholarship Program could not be considered without a special ruling because it came to the floor *after* the Rules Committee was allowing discussion of anything but major legislation. Still, Mrs. Truman was not in good health, and it seemed appropriate to establish a memorial to her late husband while she was still alive. Unfortunately, when the bill came to the floor it failed to muster the two-thirds majority vote necessary to obtain the special ruling. I nearly despaired of our bill passing under those circumstances, because several Republican congressmen had voted against the Truman bill—as had many Democrats. Luckily, the Truman bill was brought up again a few days later and passed. House Minority Leader John Rhodes of Arizona made a personal plea to Speaker Carl Albert, who graciously agreed that the Hoover Memorial bill should also be brought to the floor.

Discouraged by the prospects for the bill, I had left with my wife and three daughters for a long-planned Christmas vacation at our condominium in Maui. An unusually heavy dust storm had hit the island just before we arrived, and we worked all day, washing windows and clearing away the dust. In the midst of our labors, a messenger came from the clubhouse to say that Senator Hatfield wanted to speak to me as soon as possible. I called the number in Washington, D.C., and got both Senator Hatfield and Richard Burress on the telephone. Hatfield proudly informed me that, while the Senate remained in session awaiting the swearing-in of Gov. Nelson Rockefeller as vice president to President Ford, the bill had arrived from the House—and the Senate had passed it *unanimously*

On January 4, 1975, the White House issued the following statement:

> S. 1418, the Herbert Hoover Memorial Bill, authorizes the Secretary of the Treasury to make available $7 million in matching grants to the Hoover Institution at Stanford University for the construction and equipping of a

new memorial building. This memorial building will complete the Hoover Institution's library and research complex.

The addition of this building will make the dream of Herbert Hoover in 1919, when the Institution was founded, a reality. With expanded facilities, the Institution will be strengthened as a national and international center for advanced research on the problems of the 20th Century. It will make available to scholars and students from each of our states and every country in the world the research facilities essential to academic scholarship.

The terms of the government grant required the Hoover Institution to report on the use of the building for twenty years after it was built and to agree, in keeping with the constitutional separation of church and state, that the facility would not be used for religious services.

Because of excellent work of Darrell Trent and Rita Ricardo-Campbell in supervising the planning, construction, decorating, furnishing, and landscaping of this building, only $500,000 of the matching funds were needed for construction and furnishing. Over the next five years, with the permission of the Pew trusts president Allyn Bell, their $1 million contribution (the $750,000 grant from the Pew Memorial Trust plus $250,000 from the Joseph N. Pew Jr. Trust) was used for library acquisitions and cataloguing. Other matching funds were used for other purposes, such as the Teller and Swain National Fellows endowments.[8]

The William Volker Fund

The Hoover Institution had come very close to receiving *all* the assets of the William Volker Fund in August 1964, but the arrangement fell through, and we did not receive another grant from the Volker Fund until August 14, 1970, when Roger Freeman managed to obtain several grants in succession for his work on *The Growth of American Government*. Between 1970 and August 31, 1977, the Hoover Institution received a total of $585,270 from the Volker Fund in grants to Roger Freeman and to other Hoover staff members. Some donations were for the National Fellows Program,

---

8. The market value of the remaining funds, which we called the 60th Anniversary Fund, totaled over $7 million in August 1989.

some went to Richard Burress for a conference on regulation, and others went to support the work of Martin Anderson and Rita Ricardo-Campbell.

Morris Cox had taken over as president of the Volker Fund during the 1970s, and he and the trustees were determined to carry out the wishes of the founder: that the fund be dissolved after the required period of years. He and his fellow trustees, particularly John Burkhardt of Indianapolis and Joe Carter of the Clorox Company in Oakland, started negotiations with the Hoover Institution.

The situation became immensely complicated and staggeringly expensive, involving numerous lawyers and a lawsuit filed in Missouri on behalf of several Kansas City charities. Both Richard Burress and I were required to give depositions under oath in the fall of 1977. We could undoubtedly have settled the case well before we did if the Volker lawyers had not persuaded their clients *not* to give the Kansas City charities the additional $1 million they were seeking. Finally in late May 1978, about an hour before the case was scheduled to go to trial in Jefferson County, Missouri, the very able John Shepherd of St. Louis managed to reach a settlement—under which those charities got an additional $2 *million*. What's more, the various lawyers involved—except for John Shepherd—gave self-serving advice that increased their fees and cost us several hundred thousand dollars.

In the end, when the William Volker Fund was dissolved in the spring of 1979, the Hoover Institution received approximately $7.5 million. Except for the $25 million grant from the Ford Foundation in the early 1960s, this was the largest foundation grant in Stanford history to that date. Because of an excellent investment performance by Grantham, Mayo, Van Otterloo and Company, and because over the years we spent very little of the income—since the return was much higher than the Stanford rate of return—the market value of this fund for domestic studies was over $36.5 million in August 1989.

This was the first time that the Hoover Institution was able to invest its funds separately from those of Stanford University. Associate Director Darrell Trent and I had been trying to do this for years. We succeeded this time largely because President Lyman and Board President Peter Bing were so anxious to have a successful conclusion to their campaign to raise $300 million for Stanford. Since Grantham, Mayo's rate of return was several percentage points above Stanford's for the time period in question, we got about $7 million extra for the Hoover Institution. (If we had been able to do this for all Hoover funds beginning in 1960, the Hoover endowment would probably have been about $50 million larger in August 1989.) During my last year as director, thanks largely to the efforts of Darrell Trent and the other members of his committee, we finally got the Stanford trustees to agree to separate investment of virtually all the Hoover endowment. This should greatly assist my successors.

Honorary Fellows

Ronald Reagan became the first Hoover Institution Honorary Fellow on February 1, 1975, when he deposited his gubernatorial papers with us. My colleagues and I gave a reception and dinner for Governor and Mrs. Reagan at the Stanford Faculty Club. In the course of my after-dinner remarks, I told the governor that my only criticism of his performance in office was that he had not gotten rid of any of the U.C. professors who had threatened to leave when he was elected. He was, according to them, "anti-higher education." Since Ronald Reagan was president of the United States from January 20, 1981, to January 20, 1989, his papers are now much more valuable than those of a former governor would be. It is always difficult to put a valuation on such a collection, but $50 million is probably not an unreasonable estimate.

Alexander Solzhenitsyn became an Honorary Fellow on June 2, 1975, when he honored the Hoover Institution by making it the first place he visited in the United States after his expulsion from the Soviet Union. President Lyman and I had cabled our support to Solzhenitsyn on February 14, 1974, shortly after he left Russia:

> Please know that should you desire to continue your research and writing, we will do all that we can to facilitate your work and to accommodate you and your family.
>
> The Hoover Institution has one of the world's largest collections of Russian materials.

This press release then announced Solzhenitsyn's appointment:

Alexander I. Solzhenitsyn has accepted an appointment as an Honorary Fellow of the Hoover Institution on War, Revolution and Peace at Stanford University, Institution director Glenn Campbell announced Friday, June 6.

The Nobel Prize laureate, after a week of intensive work at the Hoover Library researching his new book on Russia in 1917, said, "The documentation I have examined at the Hoover Institution is outstanding and, in many respects, unique. Materials dated prior to 1922 are especially well represented here. It is the kind of original source material that the Soviets, in order to rewrite history, either destroyed or refuse to make available to scholars. I look forward to utilizing your collections and library materials for the rest of my life."

Solzhenitsyn hopes to return to the Hoover Institution for extended research, and while he is at his home in Switzerland, the Institution will supply him with research materials by mail.

Director Campbell said, "We are delighted that Alexander Solzhenitsyn, whose moral courage and literary accomplishments are probably unexcelled by any living person, is affiliated with the Hoover Institution. We look forward to a long and fruitful relationship."

Solzhenitsyn's wife, Natasha, assisted him with his research during his visit to the Hoover Institution.

A friendly crowd of about 200 gathered on the steps of Hoover Tower to hear Solzhenitsyn.

As translated by Richard Staar, associate director of Hoover Institution, he said:

> I am very grateful for the invitation which I received from the Hoover Institution during the first days of my expulsion from the Soviet Union.
>
> It was impossible for me to accept this invitation earlier, but I did realize what a wonderful opportunity this would have been for me.
>
> There is a Russian proverb, "In every unhappiness, there is also happiness."
>
> It is a delight to work here in these rich Russian archives.
>
> I would not have had this opportunity if it were not for two different unhappy circumstances. The first such unhappy circumstance was that all of our archival materials were strewn throughout the world. The second circumstance, of course, was that I was expelled from the Soviet Union.

In my own country, Russia, I had no access to any archival materials. And when I was working on various topics dealing with the First World War, namely the year 1914, the military archives administration of the Soviet Union began an investigation to establish who had given me access to these materials.

Here I have had open access to the richest archival material dealing with Russia, and I can work without any interruption or interference.

Unfortunately my stay at this time must be very brief, but I do hope that in the future I can come and spend more time at the Hoover Institution.

During their stay, Rita and I gave a small dinner party for the Solzhenitsyns. It was attended by President and Mrs. Lyman, Richard and Jadwiga Staar, and Senior Research Fellow Dimitri von Mohrenschild, editor of the *Russian Review,* among others. During our dinner conversation, Mrs. Solzhenitsyn confided to me that she did not mind serving as her husband's research assistant, even though she had a Ph.D. in mathematics and had taught at the University of Moscow. She had, she explained, always been interested in history. In that case, I asked her, why hadn't she majored in history instead of mathematics? She looked at me as if to ask whether I was stupid or simply crazy—study *history* in the Soviet Union!

In May 1976 the Solzhenitsyns returned to the Hoover Institution a second time to do further work on a book about the Bolshevik Revolution of 1917, the fourth volume in a series on Russian history. At a dinner in their honor, Rita was seated between Solzhenitsyn and David Packard. Toward the end of the dinner, they got into an argument about trade with the Soviet Union. Basically, Packard favored more trade and Solzhenitsyn favored much less or no trade, as he felt that any trade only helped the Soviet military and not the Russian people. At this point, my wife came over to my table (it was a sizable dinner party) and urged that I get Mr. Solzhenitsyn's speech under way before the disagreement became any stronger.

In his speech, Solzhenitsyn spoke of the obstacles to Western scholars in gaining a historical perspective on Russian and Soviet history. Concerning the library, archives, and staff, he stated, "No serious Western scholar of Russian and Soviet history can bypass the Hoover Institution

... the help of your Hoover collections and of the staff of your Institution is of inestimable value."

During a June 1, 1976, ceremony held in the Nicolas de Basily Room of the Hoover Tower, Solzhenitsyn received the American Friendship Award from the Freedoms Foundation. His perceptive acceptance speech on the fragility of human freedoms received nationwide attention.

The South Pole

In early 1970, Dr. Guy Stever, president of Carnegie-Mellon University in Pittsburgh, became a director of the National Science Foundation. In May 1972 President Nixon got his first chance to nominate eight new directors to replace those appointed by Lyndon Johnson. I was one of the eight, and after some opposition from Democratic senators, I was confirmed in early September. Our six-year terms would end in May 1978, and Jimmy Carter defeated President Ford in November of 1976, so we would not be reappointed. Fortunately, I had already planned and gotten approval for a January 1977 trip to the South Pole.

Our party—including Grover Murray, Bill Nierenberg, and the longtime secretary Vernice Anderson—left San Francisco for Auckland, New Zealand, where we changed to a New Zealand Airlines flight direct to Christchurch on the South Island. At the National Science base in Christchurch, we were outfitted with the proper socks, underwear, boots, hats, jackets, trousers, and other gear, and were scheduled to make the trip from Christchurch to McMurdo the next day. Unfortunately, our C-130 cargo plane had to turn back not once but twice because of engine failure. While we waited for the repairs to be done, I had time for a picnic with Rita's M.D. friend William Wardell and his wife at the University of Christchurch. I was struck by the great resemblance of Christchurch to Oxford University in England.

On the third attempt, our plane made it to McMurdo, where we visited Capt. Robert Falcon Scott's cabin. Some of his food was still frozen and theoretically edible. The next day a ski plane took us to the South Pole, a much safer and easier journey than Captain Scott's in 1912. At the Pole we were taken to the winter quarters built by the navy soon after World War II. They had been converted for the use of scientists who stayed from late January to October or early November.

We enjoyed seeing penguins in their natural habitat; so many visitors were feeding them they were becoming lazy and little interested in diving for fish. The commissary sold glasses marked "South Pole," from which I still sip my evening cocktail, and coffee cups, from which I frequently enjoy my morning coffee. When it was time to leave, we all piled into the C-130—whose engine *still* didn't work all that well—and flew back to Christchurch. The next morning we had to part, and headed home our separate ways.

Completion of the Herbert Hoover Memorial Building

In July 1976 Jack S. Parker of General Electric was chairman of the Hoover Board of Overseers. By then sufficient progress had been made both in fundraising to match the $7 million federal grant and in completing the architectural plans of the building. We were able to hold a groundbreaking ceremony considerably earlier than we had anticipated, at the time of the Board of Overseers meeting.

President Ford sent a message noting that the expanded library and research facilities would serve as an outstanding educational center for scholars from many countries; keynote speaker Hugh Seton-Watson, professor of Russian history at the University of London, called the Hoover Institution's resources "a unique treasure" for scholars; and Allan Hoover foresaw that the building would "be a living memorial utilized by thousands of students and scholars from this country and abroad who will make many contributions to my father's abiding lifelong interest—the promotion of peace."

Several scholars new to the Hoover Institution were working in the domestic policy area that year: Senior Research Fellow Geoffrey H. Moore of the National Bureau of Economic Research was continuing his work on national and international economic indicators; Ronald Coase, who won the Nobel Prize in economics in 1991, spent the spring and winter of 1977 at the Hoover Institution conducting research on the political/economic aspects of the U.S. broadcasting industry; and Professor Everett Carll Ladd, Jr., of the University of Connecticut spent the year with us as a Visiting Research Fellow, collaborating with Senior Fellow Seymour Martin Lipset. In addition, Robert Conquest, former United

Kingdom diplomat and well-known author of *The Great Terror* and many other books on Russia, was appointed a Senior Research Fellow.

Meanwhile, the library and archives, already among the largest in the United States, were enriched by a number of new collections, such as those of Jay Lovestone, who was secretary-general of the U.S. communist party from 1927 to 1929 and by 1976 had become a prominent labor leader. We also received the papers of R. Allen Griffin on American technical and economic assistance missions to China and Southeast Asia; of former U.S. Marine Corps Commandant David M. Shoup on World War II campaigns in the Pacific and on the Vietnam War; of Army General Albert C. Wedemeyer on the World War II grand strategy for Europe and the Pacific; of Air Force General Edward G. Lansdale on service in Vietnam and on counterinsurgency operations in the Philippines; of French army officer Yves Godard on World War II military and resistance operations, on the Indochinese war, and on terrorist activities during the Algerian independence struggle; and of David Middlemas on Portuguese Africa and on the 1974 revolution in Portugal.

Among the many honors received by Hoover Fellows was a National Endowment for the Humanities Senior Fellowship awarded to Dr. Rita Ricardo-Campbell, the first woman at Stanford to receive such an appointment.

The Herbert Hoover Memorial Building, which would cost about $30 million if it were built today, was dedicated on July 20, 1978. Speakers at the dedication ceremonies included Paul L. Davies, Jr., Allan Hoover, Richard W. Lyman, Mark O. Hatfield, Peter S. Bing, Gerald Ford, and me. After our first Board of Overseers meeting in Stauffer Auditorium in the Federal Memorial complex, I received this letter from Allan Hoover:

> Sorry to have left in such a hurry. There were several things I would like to have talked to you about:
>
> Item No. 1 was that the meeting was first class! The members really enjoy listening to what makes the trouble spots in the world. Those talks are real drawing cards.
>
> Item No. 2. The new building certainly makes the mechanics of the meeting day far more enjoyable, and with a minimum of rushing around.
>
> Last, but by no means least, you are doing a magnificent job and we are

all proud of your handiwork. You have built a tremendous operation and opinion force, under the most difficult circumstances.

Recently a disturbing trend has appeared in the use of this facility. The government grant and the matching funds were solicited for offices and seminar rooms for scholars, but sizable parts of the second and third floors were turned into office space for a growing administrative bureaucracy. This is clearly contrary to the spirit of the grant. The Pew gifts, for example, were given for a Center for Domestic Studies on the second floor of the Memorial Building, not for offices for the director, deputy director, associate director for operations, and all their administrative assistants and secretaries. Office space was redesigned and original research office walls were torn down, so visiting annual National Fellows and others had to move to the adjacent Lou Henry Hoover Building. This arrangement separated the visiting staff from the permanent Fellows in domestic policy, handicapping the informal daily interchange of ideas between visitors and permanent staff. This interchange was maintained to some degree by the afternoon coffee hour in the Senior Commons Room, a time we initiated when the building opened in the fall of 1978, but it took permanent staff much longer to meet and exchange meaningful ideas with visitors. About two years ago this situation was corrected in response to complaints from Senior Fellows.

Another Stanford Faculty Attack

In June 1978 Leon Seltzer, director of Stanford University Press, called to invite me to lunch at the Faculty Club. He chaired a committee consisting of undergraduate student Sally Brazil, history professor and Hoover Senior Research Fellow Alexander Dallin, emeritus professor of history George Knoles, and several others. Seltzer informed me that the committee was recommending that the library of the Hoover Institution be placed under the jurisdiction of the Stanford University Library system, and he hoped I would support this recommendation. Taken completely by surprise, I gave my usual answer in such situations: I would have to think about it.

Over the summer I met with President Lyman to clarify the current relationship between the Hoover Library and the university libraries. When the Stanford Faculty Senate met in October, President Lyman completely disavowed the report of the Seltzer committee, thus aborting another attempt by a small group of university faculty to bring the Hoover Institution Library under university control.

In 1979 Lyman approached me to ask whether the various Pew foundations might contribute to Stanford—particularly in the area of the humanities—apart from the Hoover Institution. I agreed with him that the Pew trusts had plenty of money, and I had no objections to his soliciting donations. In due course, the university received a Pew Memorial Trust Grant of $500,000, expendable over three to five years, to provide general support for the Stanford humanities program. Two additional grants of $250,000 each from the Pew Memorial Trust, also expendable over three to five years, were given to support scholarly research in the humanities.

These are just two examples of how President Lyman and I managed to work together in the best interests of the Hoover Institution and Stanford University. They demonstrate that conflict is not a necessary component of the relationship.

Showing my blue-ribbon foal Rosie.
(Ontario, 1937)

University of Western Ontario, debate team, 1943–44. Back (L to R):
Jack Cram, George Peters, Bob Davis. Front: Elizabeth Galbraith,
James Gillies, Glenn Campbell.

Graduation ceremonies,
University of Western Ontario.
(1944)

Rita and Glenn returning from Europe aboard the new luxury liner, the S.S. *United States*. Upon arrival Glenn met with Herbert Hoover to discuss the directorship of the Hoover Institution. (1959)

The Campbells with Generalissimo Chiang Kai-shek on the embattled island of Quemoy. (1963)

Campbells on camels. (Egypt, 1965)

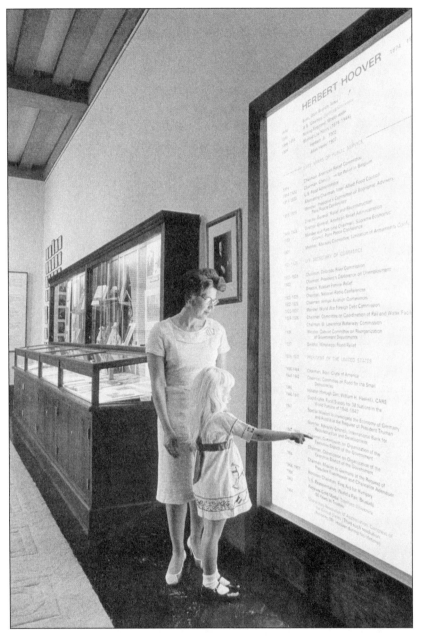

Our daughter Nancy, age 4, gets a tour of the Hoover Exhibit Room. (1964)

A gathering of the Campbell clan (L to R):
Alfred, Evelyn, Milton, Glenn, Marjorie, Graham. (1968)

Madame Yekaterena Furtseva (gesturing), Soviet Minister of Culture,
visits the Hoover Institution. (1971)

Confrontation: Leftist professor Bruce Franklin, leading a group of radical students, tries unsuccessfully to occupy the Hoover Tower. Director Campbell faces and addresses the hostile throng.

Director W. Glenn Campbell under the Hoover Tower. (Mid-1980s)

Post-retirement photo: W. Glenn Campbell, Director Emeritus, the Hoover
Institution on War, Revolution and Peace. (c. 1990)

The Campbell grandchildren. David Porter (top left), Glenn Bizewski (top right), and Caroline and Thomas Yaeger (bottom).

Aerial view of the Stanford campus. The Hoover Tower looms at the center.

The landmark Hoover Tower, center, is flanked by the two new facilities added
during my directorship, the Herbert Hoover Memorial Building, dedicated in 1978
(left), and the Lou Henry Hoover Building, dedicated in 1967 (right).

Dr. Rita Ricardo-Campbell addressing the Hoover Advisory Board on the subject of Social Security in President Hoover's office in 1966.

SUPREME ECONOMIC COUNCIL
OFFICE OF
THE DIRECTOR GENERAL OF RELIEF

Paris 19 June 1919.

Prof. E. D. Adams,
Hotel Montana,
Paris.

My dear Prof. Adams:-

       This is to confirm the offer which I made
to Dr. Wilbur to find $50,000 at his demand or the de-
mand of anyone he appointed to undertake the work for
the purpose of sending a representative to Europe for
the collection of historical material for the Stanford
University Library. This fund to be entirely at the
disposal of Dr. Wilbur or his agent for any purpose of
expense for purchase of documents or otherwise that will
contribute to the library's strength with regard to a
documentary history bearing on the war.   The fund is
available at any time on demand.

                   Faithfully yours,

                   Herbert Hoover

Herbert Hoover was the 31st president of the
United States of America.

President Hoover's handwritten inscription reads, "To my good friends Glenn and Rita Campbell—the good wishes of Herbert Hoover."

"... President and Mrs. Reagan invited us to a dinner for the queen and prince in San Francisco ..." Nancy Reagan, Queen Elizabeth, President Reagan, W. Glenn Campbell (1983). This was actually our third meeting with the royal visitors that week. The queen showed no signs of recognizing me, but Prince Philip clearly remembered Rita: "Not the descendant of that dismal economist David Ricardo again!"

Nobel laureate economist, Hoover Honorary Fellow Friedrich A. von Hayek. His seminal 1944 work, *The Road to Serfdom,* was a body blow to socialist theory. Hayek was co-founder and president of the prestigious Mont Pelerin Society, and addressed Hoover gatherings many times.

David Packard, co-founder of the Hewlett-Packard Corporation, led the Hoover Board of Overseers with strength and wisdom, and donated generously to its endowments as well.

Nobel laureate Alexander Solzhenitsyn made Hoover his first stop in the United States in 1975, after his expulsion from the Soviet Union, and was named an Honorary Fellow. Solzhenitsyn delighted in Hoover's Russian archival collections, saying, "It is the kind of original source material that the Soviets, in order to rewrite history, either destroyed or refuse to make available to scholars."

Nobel laureate economist, Hoover Senior Research Fellow, colleague, genial friend: Milton Friedman was one Hoover scholar who never needed introduction, no matter where in the world my duties took me. His work at Hoover helped "sell" the Institution, and thus contributed greatly to its health and growth.

President Richard Nixon's handwritten inscription reads: "To Dr. Glenn and Rita Ricardo-Campbell — With warm regards from one who *is not* a male chauvinist! 2-22-'89 Dick Nixon."

President Reagan's handwritten inscription reads: "Dear Glenn — Look!
You let me upstage you! Thanks for all the other things you do and
Warmest Friendship. Ron." (c. 1980)

Herbert Hoover. Fisher Leyes, Sculptor

George P. Shultz by Bruce Wolf, sculptor. 1997. Lost wax bronze.

Herbert Hoover, 1887–1964 by Haig Patigian, American sculptor. The bust was donated by Gertrude Margaret Gregory in remembrance of the friendship of Thomas Tingey Craven Gregory and Herbert Clark Hoover.

Oil portraits of Drs. W. Glenn Campbell and Rita Ricardo-Campbell specially commissioned for exhibit in the Campbell Conference Room (Herbert Hoover Memorial Building).

7

The (Almost)
Golden Eighties

THE MOST AMBITIOUS RESEARCH WORK UNDERTAKEN BY THE
Hoover Institution to that time sought fresh answers in a time
racked by inflation, domestic confusion, and weakness in foreign relations. Published in January 1980 and the highlight of the academic year, *The United States in the 1980's* was edited by Senior Fellows
Peter Duignan and Alvin Rabushka, and coordinated by Dennis L. Bark.

Thirty-two experts addressed major domestic and foreign policy
questions facing the United States at the beginning of that decade. The
real importance of the book, however, lay in the contributors' and editors' recognition that the major problems of the 1980s would be inter-
related, that no problem could be resolved in isolation, and that differ-
ing perspectives could establish a clearer and more balanced understanding
of problems that are often viewed as separate from one another. The
authors analyzed the central issues, described policy options, and recommended specific courses of action to address or mitigate specific problems. Their findings added up to a comprehensive study of ways the
country could govern itself more effectively and could restore people's
faith in the United States as the leader of the free world.

The United States in the 1980's was addressed to all those concerned
with the formation of public policy—to opinion leaders at the federal,
state, and municipal levels of government; to members of the academic
and business communities; and to the public in general. The authors of
the essays wrote additional articles to explain and elaborate their findings for newspapers and magazines before and following publication of

the volume. The individual essays themselves were reprinted for wide distribution by the Hoover Institution Press.

The response to the project was excellent. The book was translated into six languages (Chinese, German, Italian, Japanese, Korean, and Spanish) and went into four printings. The book's co-editors and contributors logged more than fifty speaking engagements in major U.S. cities, including two one-hour telecasts on William F. Buckley's "Firing Line." The book was reviewed in many syndicated columns and in newspaper articles throughout the United States and abroad. It was also well received by members of the House and the Senate, and fifty-two copies were ordered in May for all members of President Carter's Commission for a National Agenda for the Eighties. The book was distributed in Great Britain by Croom Helm of London and was the featured selection of the Macmillan Book Club for the month of July. In a letter announcing the book's selection, Richard Kelley, director of the club's Library of Political and International Affairs, wrote:

> As you know, we review hundreds of books every year for the Library of Political and International Affairs and it's rare that we come across a book that has as many strong selling points as Duignan and Rabushka's: exhaustive, authoritative, and handsomely produced. It's a source book that I'm sure our members will be referring to for years to come, whether their interests lie in the domestic or foreign policy spheres.

Interest in the book was particularly intense just before and after the 1980 presidential election because eighteen of the contributors served on policy study groups advising President Reagan. Extensive electronic media coverage included a video segment on the "CBS Evening News with Walter Cronkite." Correspondent Barry Petersen reported that "not only have Reagan's top aides read it—some helped write it: a blueprint for the years ahead." In 1980 more than fifty major media representatives visited the Hoover Institution. News commentators and journalists were particularly interested in Hoover's research capacities, current and future, in both domestic and international studies.

Because of the public policy orientation of much of the research, special efforts were made to disseminate the results to public officials in innovative ways. By drawing on the expert capabilities of its scholars and their broad backgrounds in public policy analysis, the Institution was able to inaugurate its "Washington Seminars" in 1980 under the direction of Associate Director and Senior Fellow Richard T. Burress. These seminars, held both at the Hoover Institution and in Washington, D.C., played an important role in the dialogue between scholars and policymakers that is crucial to effective implementation of responsible government action. (Many important congressmen and senators and their staffs praised the Hoover scholars, and this greatly assisted Hoover fundraising. Thus, it came as a great surprise to me when my successor terminated the program after the February 1990 Hoover Board of Overseers meeting in Washington, D.C.)

On January 7, 1980, my colleagues held a party in the lobby of the Tower to celebrate my twentieth anniversary as director of the Hoover Institution. Senior Fellow Peter Duignan, something of a prankster, arranged for a lively performance by a belly dancer, whom I studiously—and stoically—ignored.

The Early 1980s

This extract from the 1981 Annual Report suggests the status that the Institution had achieved by 1980:

> In September 1980 the Institution hosted the biennial general meeting of the Mont Pelerin Society. Approximately 600 members and guests, including 22 former national fellows, attended the week-long conference. It was the first general meeting to be held in the United States in more than two decades; the only previous general meeting was held at Princeton University in 1958. Speakers on subjects related to "Constraints on Government," the general theme of the conference, included Senior Research Fellow Milton Friedman; William E. Simon, former Secretary of the Treasury; Lord Harris of High Cross, General Director of the Institute of Economic Affairs, London; and Sir Keith Joseph, Secretary of State for Industry in Great Britain.

Ronald Reagan at the 1981
Hoover Overseers Meeting

On January 6, 1981, President-elect Ronald Reagan was the principal speaker at the Hoover Institution Board of Overseers meeting at the Sheraton-Carlton Hotel in Washington, D.C. In addition to the overseers and their spouses, many of the people present were already important—or about to become important in the Reagan administration: Presidential Counselor Edwin Meese and his wife, Ursula; Attorney General Designate William French Smith and his wife, Jean; and Sen. John Warner of Virginia and his wife, Elizabeth Taylor. Reagan's speech was characteristically generous:

> Dr. Glenn Campbell, my own teammate—as you all know—and you, Ladies and Gentlemen:
>
> It is a privilege to address you—the members of the Board of Overseers of the Hoover Institution, and your guests. It is also a pleasure to do so because of my association with both the Institution and its director, Glenn Campbell. This association has spanned many years. I have been privileged to have a great deal of advice and help from the Institution, and tonight I would like to talk to you about the Hoover Institution and Glenn Campbell's two decades of success.
>
> Since its founding in 1919, the Hoover Institution has become a national and an international center for documentation and research on social, political, and economic change in the twentieth century. It enjoys a reputation for excellence that is a direct reflection of the efforts of Glenn and his staff to maintain the highest traditions of its distinguished founder, former United States President Herbert Hoover.
>
> Indeed, in 1978, the *New York Times Magazine* called the Institution "the brightest star in a small constellation of conservative think tanks ... operating from a base of honorable conservatism, first-rate scholarship, sharp wits, acute perceptions and clear reasoning."
>
> Well, I'm happy to say that, as I mentioned before, I've experienced this conservatism and scholarship, these wits and perceptions, and this reasoning personally through my association with the Institution as an honorary fellow. During my visits there, I have had the opportunity to discuss public policy issues with a staff made up of Nobel laureates, members of

the American Academy of Arts and Sciences, and other distinguished thinkers.

Moreover, during the recent campaign, I called on more people from the Institution to help with my campaign than from any other institution. Some, such as Glenn and Rita Ricardo-Campbell, served on my policy task forces. Others, such as Martin Anderson, Darrell Trent, and former Senior Fellow Dick Allen, worked on my campaign staff. All are now assisting me in the transition to a new administration. That's why, when the press was having at me about my so-called gaffes, I wasn't frightened for one minute. I knew that everything I said was true.

Hoover's excellence has emerged in large part because of Glenn Campbell. It is he who has worked so hard and planned so well. It is he who has maintained such high standards of academic excellence in finding the best scholars available. It is he who has worked to provide a challenging and stimulating environment in which superior scholarship can take place. It is he who has raised the financial resources necessary to develop a fine research institution. And, it is he who has effectively and fairly administered this "brightest star" in the constellation of think tanks.

I'm happy to report that Glenn's talents haven't gone unnoticed by others. In fact, his dedication to superior scholarship and his reputation as an effective and fair administrator led me to make him my first appointee to the University of California Board of Regents in 1968. And, there was no combat pay at that time! During the 1980 campaign, he chaired my Education Policy Task Force and my International Economic Policy Task Force. He is now serving on the Personnel Advisory Committee, which is responsible for making cabinet- and sub-cabinet-level recommendations.

Glenn has also served on the Board of the National Science Foundation, as a member of President Ford's Committee on Science and Technology, and as a member of the President's Commission on White House Fellows.

I am deeply grateful to Glenn and the Hoover Institution staff for the support and the expertise that they provided me in the past and are providing now. And, I would say that I am looking forward to receiving such advice in the years ahead, for superior scholarship and research will be critically important in making the hard policy choices that are necessary to turn our country around.

The Reagan Administration and the Hoover Institution

Shortly after that Board of Overseers dinner, Dr. Rita Ricardo-Campbell was offered a position on the Council of Economic Advisors. If she accepted and we moved to Washington, members of the Personnel Advisory Committee were quite confident that I could be appointed a special ambassador. In fact, Michael Deaver assured me that President Reagan would name me as undersecretary of state for economics if I wanted the position.

I knew, of course, that if I went to Washington, Donald Kennedy would impose his policy of six-months-maximum leave for public service before I would have to resign as the director of the Hoover Institution. During those halcyon days when he hoped I would leave Hoover, he always greeted me cordially and enthusiastically. Once in the early 1980s, he even brought a carton of tea to my office. He rarely visited me there, and even more rarely brought gifts. I thanked him, but I could see that he was looking the office over and planning to move into it himself if I left to work in the Reagan administration. I sometimes wonder what would have happened if I had resigned, gone to Washington, and arranged with Kennedy to return as a Senior Fellow. Whom would he have finagled in as director? And when would the Hoover Institution buildings and endowment have been taken over by Stanford's imperial president?

The Nixon Papers

Former President Richard Nixon called me late in 1981 to ask if the Hoover Institution would be interested in having his presidential papers. I remember the call vividly because he called me at home while I was getting dressed and said, "Glenn, this is Dick Nixon." I was stunned, but recovered enough to reply, "Yes, Mr. President." When he offered his papers, I told him we were also negotiating for the Ronald Reagan Presidential Library, and he said he wasn't surprised. We agreed to talk further, and I told him I would get back to him.

I discussed the matter with Dick Burress, and we agreed there was no way we could handle two Republican presidential libraries at once, especially given Stanford President Kennedy's negative attitude toward

Republican presidents. I asked Burress to call President Nixon's assistant, whom he knew well, so he could inform the president of our decision. Later that day, during an appointment with Kennedy, I told him what we had done, but added that there was still time for us to get the Richard Nixon Library if we wanted it. In reply, he grumbled, "You know how to make my day!"

Actually, President Nixon was willing to give us his papers on very reasonable terms— no new building and only minimal staff requirements. When I told Sen. Mark Hatfield about this offer, he was appalled at Kennedy's attitude. He wanted to reopen the matter, but we finally agreed that with Donald Kennedy at the helm, we would be wasting our time. Subsequently, I discussed the possibility of locating the Richard Nixon Presidential Library at the University of California, Irvine, with a representative of former President Nixon and with Chancellor Dan Aldrich. Since I was the chairman of the U.C. Board of Regents for 1982–83, I placed the matter before the regents at the March meeting, and they unanimously approved placing the Nixon Library at Irvine, the closest campus to Yorba Linda, where Nixon was born.

Early the next week, I was packing to leave for Sydney, Australia, to meet Rita and then proceed to Canberra, where we were to be guests of the American ambassador. A telephone call came from Chancellor Aldrich to inform me that he and his cabinet had decided to present the proposal to the Faculty Senate one more time. I warned him that this foolish move would lose them the Nixon Library, because the former president did not want it publicly known that another university, in addition to Duke, had refused his presidential library. And so it turned out: President Nixon was so understandably annoyed that he decided to build his own presidential library in Yorba Linda. This library was dedicated several years ago and is now open for use by scholars and for public tours.

White House Reception
for the Board of Overseers

These were President Reagan's remarks on the Hoover Institution at a 1982 White House reception:

Welcome to all of you. And may I say how wonderful it is for Nancy and me to see so many old friends again. I see faces that bring back memories of battles gone by.

It is fitting that we are brought together because of the Hoover Institution. All of us are concerned about the future, or we would not be here. Over the years, the Hoover Institution has made enormous contributions to the future freedom and prosperity of mankind.

Laying the intellectual foundation for change is absolutely essential if a free society is to be maintained. Unlike totalitarian and authoritarian regimes, change is a way of life in a free society. Where there is academic freedom and freedom of speech and press, it is scholarship and research that plant the seeds of change. Whether our children will reap a harvest of liberty or suffer tyranny and deprivation depends on what is planted today in the minds of those who will create the reality of tomorrow.

Over its distinguished career, the Hoover Institution deserves to be singled out for its service, its standards, and its contribution. Since its founding in 1919 by former President Herbert Hoover, the Institution has been a preeminent center for the advanced study of domestic and foreign policy. Its library and archives are a valuable national resource and a tribute to what dedicated individuals can do—without tax dollars. I have reason to know nothing is impossible to the Hoover Institution.

In my inaugural address, I quoted from a diary found on the body of a young soldier killed in the First World War, Private Martin Treptow. Well, someone over at Hoover dug through the archives and found a Liberty Loan poster from 1918 quoting Private Treptow's diary. Marty Anderson presented that poster to me in the cabinet room as a gift from Hoover, and I just want you to know how appreciative I am.

Many of us who have chosen politics as a career—in my case it was a second career—I had to do something after Bonzo lost his life in an accident— but seriously, those of us who are involved in government owe so much to the Hoover Institution. Under the leadership of your able director, Glenn Campbell, and with hard work and diligence, you built the knowledge base that made the changes now taking place in Washington possible. Dr. Campbell attracted some of the world's best scholars to the Hoover Institution. I'm glad he did, because we've borrowed some of them to serve in top spots in this administration. Glenn . . . to you a personal thanks.

I am proud to be an honorary fellow of the Hoover Institution even though that compounds the feeling of guilt I've carried since getting my diploma at Eureka College; I have always felt that was honorary, too.

Thank you for being here today and for all you are doing to support this indispensable bulwark of liberty.

Mixed Blessings

On January 5, 1983, I received the following letter from world-renowned philosopher Sidney Hook:

> Dear Glenn—
>
> Of the sixty years that have elapsed since I graduated from College at the age of twenty, I have now spent one-sixth of them (16 2/3%) at Hoover. These sunset years of my life have been among the happiest and most rewarding not because of the material perks but because it has given me a congenial place for creative dissent and cooperation in a common cause.
>
> I owe that to you.

Sidney Hook became a Senior Research Fellow on January 1, 1973, when he was seventy years of age. After a long and distinguished career as a professor and departmental chairman at New York University, he was famous for the number of controversies he had engaged in, including one with Lord Bertrand Russell. He had written scores of books and articles, and was famous for his anti-communism, even though he continued to insist he was a Marxist philosopher until the day he died.

It was unbelievable that, in all that time, he was never invited to teach a course in Stanford's philosophy department, even though he was far more distinguished and internationally renowned than the other professors. At one time, the chairman of the department said rather huffily, "If Hook wanted to teach, all he had to do was ask." He had to take that position because the department did not want publicly to admit its opposition to—not to say *bias against* —Sidney Hook. Many doctoral students did come to him privately, and he spent hours talking to them and helping them. He also published about a dozen books while he was here, including his autobiography.

The Manley-Rebholtz Petition

On April 21, 1983, a petition was circulated at Stanford by John R. Manley, a professor of political science, and Ronald Rebholtz, an English professor. The petition spelled out why, in their opinion, the Stanford faculty opposed—and should oppose—the Hoover Institution's independence. The Manley-Rebholtz petition was so outrageous that many Stanford professors were disgusted by its obvious attempt to curb free speech. As a result, Alphonse Juilland, a distinguished professor of French and Italian, drafted a counterpetition. Signers of *that* petition said that they "deplore and oppose the investigation of the political orientation of the Hoover Institution, although we have no objection to an impartial assessment of the scholarly excellence and achievements of Hoover appointees."

Professor Juilland felt so strongly about the matter that he bought his own stamps and addressed the envelopes himself. When he got the returns, he showed the professors' names to President Kennedy, who studied them carefully, then told Professor Juilland that they were much more distinguished than the professors who had signed the Manley-Rebholtz petition. I believe he also told Juilland that he could not find a right-wing kook in the whole lot. His comment about "distinguished Stanford professors" obviously referred to professor of geology Richard Jahns, professor of law John Kaplan, professor of computer science John McCarthy, professor of economics (and subsequently provost) James Rosse, professor of history Lewis Spitz, professor of philosophy Patrick Suppes, and professor of chemistry Carl Djerassi, among others.

VIP Visitors

During 1983 Hoover hosted a number of important visitors. I met with Queen Elizabeth and Prince Philip when they visited the Scripps Institute of Oceanography at the University of California, San Diego, and Rita and I were invited to the luncheon President Kennedy gave for them at the Hoover House. The queen and the prince were interested in the history of the Hoover Institution.

Later President and Mrs. Reagan invited us to a dinner for the queen and prince in San Francisco. When I went through the receiving line, the queen simply gave me the "royal handshake and stare" for the third time in a week, but when Rita followed me to greet Prince Philip he clearly remembered her: "Not the descendant of that dismal economist David Ricardo again!"

It was a most interesting dinner. Deputy Chief of Staff Michael Deaver was in charge of arrangements, and the staff had ostensibly invited representative Americans from all walks of life. The two I remember best were Joe DiMaggio and Willie Mays, representing baseball. I never got to talk with Mays because he was surrounded by too many fans, but I had a nice conversation with DiMaggio. We debated whether he or Ted Williams had been the better player. DiMaggio, a very modest man, insisted that Williams was a better player because he was a better hitter.

In April, on my first trip to Japan as the new chairman of the Japan-U.S. Friendship Commission, I was scheduled to meet with Prime Minister Nakasone. Before we arrived our Japanese hosts explicitly expressed their desire that "the other Dr. Campbell" behave like a Japanese wife that day. Rita agreed, but I had barely met the prime minister and was about to sit down when he said, "Where is Mrs. Dr. Campbell?" I pointed to her and he got up, went to her, and brought her over to sit next to him. Since the prime minister spoke excellent English, he took us into his office after the formal greetings were over and dismissed all his aides. Rita made him very happy when she innocently asked who had done the fine Japanese paintings on the wall. Nakasone is an amateur artist, and the paintings were his own.

In May former Governor Jerry Brown was in the area and asked to meet with me, so Senior Fellow Martin Anderson and I had a lengthy discussion with him in the de Basily Room. In July former President Carter was on a fundraising trip to the San Francisco area. He had agreed to build his library and a public affairs center at Emory University in Atlanta. Acting Deputy Director John Moore and I had almost an hour-long talk with Carter, who was particularly interested in how Hoover had become an independent institution within the framework of Stanford University. What, he wanted to know, had Herbert Hoover done to protect the Institution's independence after his own death? After he returned to Georgia, Carter sent me this letter:

August 1, 1983

I appreciate your concern for the details of our development as a center and will continue to welcome your advice. There is no doubt that some of the problems facing the Hoover Institution will also face the Carter Center over time. Your willingness to share your views certainly is important as our Center must benefit from the experience of those that have preceded it.

Thank you for your time and advice. I trust I can call upon you for your suggestions in the future.

Sincerely,
Jimmy

A New Program for the 1983–84 Academic Year

The Board of Overseers recommended that we undertake a new initiative directed specifically at national security affairs. The gravity of our national security problems was evident, and the challenges in this area were likely to grow in the coming decades. The Institution's unique library, its archival resource base, and the expertise of its scholars in the strategic, economic, social, historical, and political dimensions of national security made it an ideal agent of change.

In response to this suggestion, President Reagan sent this message to a January 1984 meeting of the Board of Overseers in Washington, D.C. He recalled

> the pleasure it gives me to be an Honorary Fellow of the Hoover Institution and to be a colleague of some of the most distinguished scholars of our nation. I am sure members of the Board are very proud of the role they have played in developing such a unique and influential national institution.

We, in turn, were delighted that President Reagan had accepted the Stanford Board of Trustees' invitation to locate "the Ronald Reagan Presidential Library at the University in affiliation with the Hoover Institution." His library and museum would be a priceless academic resource for scholars, students, and others engaged in the study of American government and history. By selecting Stanford University as the site for his library, Reagan would place his presidential papers in close proximity to his gubernatorial and other papers, which would assure the unity of his papers for scholarly research. The president's interest in Stanford grew out of his close ties with the Hoover Institution, ties strengthened in 1975 when he became an Honorary Fellow and also by his many visits to the Institution and discussions with resident Fellows on domestic and international policy issues.

Bouquets and Brickbats

On July 18, prior to the 1984 Board of Overseers meeting, Emil (Bud) Mosbacher, Jr., Jeremiah Milbank, Jr., and Andrew Hoover went to see David Packard. They had told me about this visit the night before, and I urged that they be very careful in what they said to him because he was becoming deaf and might misunderstand them. In fact, they inadvertently did exactly what I feared. David Packard understood that they wanted me fired, so my August appointment with him turned out to be less than pleasant.

In the meantime, though, the Board of Overseers sponsored a twenty-fifth anniversary tribute to me at the Stanford University Faculty Club. A letter of congratulations from President Reagan was read by Ed Meese. David Packard, Donald Kennedy, and University of California President David Pierpont Gardner spoke. I was presented with a unanimous California State Assembly Resolution of congratulations, signed and presented by Robert Naylor, minority leader of the state assembly, and co-sponsored by Speaker Willie Brown. Robert Naylor conveyed Brown's regrets that he could not attend the dinner since he was at the Democratic National Convention in San Francisco. The compliments were gratefully received, but more important, I was extremely proud of the work we were doing and eager to see it continue.

Before the mid-1980s, the country witnessed a profound transformation in national policies. It began with a series of innovative public policy proposals in the 1960s and 1970s, and spread by the 1980s to virtually every aspect of government policy. Monetary policy, taxation, government regulation, strategic defense, and federal social welfare and health policies had all been reviewed, reconsidered, and reformed.

When new laws are enacted in our nation's capital, the basic research on which the new policies are built is often ignored, but Senior Fellow Martin Anderson stressed the importance of those ideas to the policy determination process: "The real power now lies in the intellectual world, while the apparent power lies in the policy world, and the world of presidential campaigns serves as a catalyst."

Few were more qualified to make this judgment than Martin Anderson. Few had his depth of experience in the political arena, government, and academia. He was research director in three presidential election campaigns, served as an assistant to the president for policy development, and taught and pursued research at several universities and research institutes. It was a source of immense pride to know that the ideas developed by scholars at the Hoover Institution had greatly influenced the new policy agenda, and I was and am confident that historical analysis will increasingly recognize the key roles played by these scholars.

Anderson had taken a leave of absence from the Hoover Institution in early 1979 to become an adviser to former Governor Ronald Reagan. In August of that year, he penned Policy Memorandum No. 1, establishing the groundwork for what would later be known as "Reaganomics." Theodore H. White, in *America in Search of Itself: The Making of the President, 1956–80,* wrote: "Anderson's policy memo ... was a montage of minority ideas percolating among intellectuals around the nation. What makes it so fascinating as a campaign document is that two years later, so much of its thinking had become the law of the land."

To cite one example, the 1981 tax cut on the Anderson blueprint became economic policy. That tax cut helped give the nation four years of economic recovery without inflation, and has contributed to subsequent, largely sustained economic growth throughout the 1990s, all thanks largely to the ideas of Senior Research Fellow and Nobel laureate Milton Friedman. As the founder of the monetarist school of economic thought, Dr. Friedman had impressed on the minds of policymakers the critical role of monetary policy in determining the inflation rate. His teachings and writings contributed greatly to the Federal Reserve Board's significant shift in monetary policy in 1979, which produced the first sustained period of noninflationary growth in two decades. The need for tax reform had been evident for some time. The radical revision of the tax code under President Reagan could be traced to the writings of Milton Friedman almost two decades earlier and to the more recent work of Senior Fellows Robert Hall and Alvin Rabushka.

The contributions of Hoover scholars continued to be sought and offered throughout the Reagan years. The writings of Senior Fellow Thomas Sowell on poverty in America dramatically changed the focus of the social welfare policy debate. His numerous articles and books provided theoretical and empirical underpinnings for the Reagan administration's reform of ineffective and costly social welfare programs. In addition, Dr. Sowell's ideas on affirmative action and racial quotas, probably more than those of any other person, inspired the social policy of the Reagan administration.

As a member of President Reagan's Economic Policy Advisory Board, Senior Fellow Rita Ricardo-Campbell helped shape health policy in the 1980s. The *Annals of Internal Medicine,* in its review of her book *The Economics and Politics of Health,* said: "The chapter titled 'Policy Recommendations' seems to convey a precis of the direction taken by the Reagan Administration concerning health care. This alone is adequate reason to read the book." Another reviewer referred to Rita as "one of the most influential unofficial policy advisers to the Reagan administration on health care."

One important element in the policy agenda of the late 1970s and 1980s was deregulation of American business, based partly on the research of Senior Fellow Thomas Gale Moore. Moore served on the President's Council of Economic Advisors for the last half of the Reagan administration. His demonstration of economic inefficiencies caused by government regulation contributed significantly to the deregulation of the airline and trucking industries in the late 1970s. More generally, his work and that of Milton Friedman contributed to deregulation of other industries, such as banking, in the 1980s.

In defense and national security matters, the president's most innovative and potentially most important proposal was the Strategic Defense Initiative (SDI). Perhaps this initiative, more than any other, illustrated the power of ideas in the policy sphere. Hoover scholars—from Senior Research Fellow Edward Teller, called "the scientist probably most responsible for Mr. Reagan's decision to seek an actual defense against nuclear weapons," to Martin Anderson—played a crucial role in the development of SDI.

Hoover scholars strongly influenced the rebuilding of our nation's defenses, beginning in the late 1970s and continuing into the 1980s. Senior Research Fellows William R. Van Cleave and Henry S. Rowen received special commendation for their work in this area.

None other was more qualified than the president himself to testify to the influence of scholars from the Hoover Institution on the policy revolution of the 1980s and on determining the course of the Reagan Revolution. The policy revolution had sprung from deep wells, and there was reason to believe it would continue into the next decade. Consider the federal budget deficit. This problem could not be solved without substantial reductions in government spending and/or increased taxation. John Cogan, Hoover Senior Fellow and principal associate director, was coordinating a study of the growth of government spending. The findings and recommendations of this study were expected to answer many difficult questions that plagued efforts to reduce the deficit.

In international affairs, "uncooperative allies" are always a problem. After forty years, the United States needed more help from its allies to defend the West against Soviet expansionism. Senior Fellow Melvyn Krauss wrote an important book on this subject—*How NATO Weakens the West*. The development of an effective policy toward the Soviet Union was of critical importance to the United States. After Henry S. Rowen wrote his article "Living with a Sick Bear," he was invited to the White House to meet with President Reagan and his foreign policy advisers. The interplay between economics and national security was at the core of Dr. Rowen's work, of Dr. Krauss's, and of Senior Fellow Bruce Bueno de Mesquita's. Formerly chairman of the department of political science at the University of Rochester, Dr. Bueno de Mesquita was concerned with the role of incentives in foreign policy decisions.

At the Hoover Institution scholars conducted research on economic, social, and political movements, as well as on basic public policy issues. At the heart of this research and policy analysis were such notable scholars as Senior Research Fellows Sidney Hook, James Stockdale, and Senior Fellows Peter Duignan, Alex Inkeles, Seymour Martin Lipset, and Richard Staar. Another research institute director once said that the Hoover

Institution housed the "upstream scholars" who produced seminal works on which others "downstream" depended.

No control whatsoever was exercised over the freedom of inquiry of Hoover scholars. The Hoover Institution never took policy positions, and its scholars were free to write, speak, and testify on any policy matter. Ideas have no political boundaries. Whatever political party is in power is inevitably influenced by the continuing revolution of ideas that started before President Reagan took office and continued after he left.

A Major Misunderstanding

Amid all this positive input, I was unprepared for my August 1984 confrontation with David Packard. After some brief pleasantries, he got up, shut the door, and informed me that I was finished as director of the Hoover Institution. I was stunned, and I started to question him. He informed me that the chairman of the Board of Overseers (Mosbacher) was behind my removal, as were Jeremiah Milbank, Jr., and Andrew Hoover. When I asked him if Dean Watkins approved, he replied that, knowing that Dean and I were long-time friends, he had been very careful to get Dean's approval. I asked whether this plan had been engineered by Donald Kennedy, but Packard contended that, while Kennedy favored my dismissal, he did not want to be involved. He didn't want me to be able to blame him.

Toward the end of the meeting Packard offered to set up a chair for me at the American Enterprise Institute. Annoyed, I informed him that Rita and I had sufficient savings and did not need his charity. Since our relationship had taken such a sour turn, I said, we would probably not meet again till we gave depositions in the lawsuit for defamation of character and attempted illegal dismissal that I would file against Packard, Kennedy, and the Board of Overseers all of whom approved my discharge—not to mention the Stanford Board of Trustees if it approved the action.

The next day I began calling various people Packard and I had discussed. The first person I reached was Dean Watkins, a member of the California delegation to the 1984 Republican Convention in Dallas. He returned my call a day later. When I told him about my conversation with Packard, he said it was the most nonsensical thing he had heard in a long time. The day after he got back from the convention, Watkins was seated next to David Packard at a luncheon and told Packard he was not with him on this one. Packard replied, "It was probably not a very good idea anyway." I got the same reaction from everyone I spoke to, including Bud Mosbacher.

In the meantime, Kennedy had been busy trying to line up an acting director to take over after I was discharged. He invited Dennis Bark to lunch in early August at a Japanese restaurant. Bark consulted me, and I urged him to go, to order an expensive meal, and to listen carefully to Kennedy. During the meal Kennedy asked whether Bark could serve as acting director during the search for my replacement. Bark replied that, unfortunately, he was heavily involved in writing a book about Germany.

At roughly the same time, I met Paul Davies, Jr., for lunch at the Pacific Union Club. He had already received a call from Kennedy's office (as had Dean Watkins) indicating that there would soon be an important meeting in David Packard's office. Of course, the meeting was canceled when Kennedy found no support for my dismissal.

In late September Mosbacher, Milbank, Hoover, and I met at the Hoover Institution. I had fallen while playing tennis the day before, and my broken wrist was badly swollen. All three men assured me that they had visited Packard only to ask that he lend his good offices to help them find a qualified successor to me *when the time came.* They also wanted his assistance in seeing that proper procedures were adhered to in selecting a new director. They certainly had not intended to convey any loss of confidence in me as director. Indeed, they thought I had done an excellent job of building a unique, world-renowned Institution, and they expected that I would continue to provide such leadership for many years to come. I enjoyed, they told me, strong support from both the Executive Committee and the Board of Overseers as a whole. Finally, they regretted any misunderstanding about the directorship and were pleased to report that President Kennedy and the trustees did not intend to challenge the agreed-upon procedures when the time did come to select a new director.

Hoover-Stanford Relations, 1985–86

There had actually been considerable improvement in Hoover-Stanford relations. The attacks against the Hoover Institution and its scholars, which increasingly and publicly brought into question Stanford's commitment to academic freedom, had substantially subsided. Talk of a Hoover-Stanford "divorce," initiated by the Dornbush Report of the Stanford Faculty Senate Committee on Relations Between the Hoover Institution and the Stanford Professoriate, disappeared. Stanford had agreed to be the site of the Reagan Library, and the cordial feelings that action indicated toward President Reagan seemed sufficient evidence that the Hoover-Stanford crisis truly was "the crisis that should never have been." We intended to continue making every effort to ensure continued improvement in Hoover-Stanford relations, leading to a new and prolonged period of mutual cooperation and trust.

In July 1986 the open-air courtyard at the heart of the Hoover Institution complex was dedicated in honor of U.S. Senator Mark Odom Hatfield. In 1978, at the dedication of the Herbert Hoover Federal Memorial Building, Mark Hatfield had said, "Herbert Hoover has inspired my life . . . his words, his life, his philosophy have been my inspiration. Would that I could emulate him." Those words are inscribed on the plaque designating the Mark Hatfield Court.

Contemplating the Future

As I reflected on my approaching retirement, my concern for a smooth transition was greatly alleviated by the appointment of Richard Lyman, former Stanford president, to a five-year term as director of the Center for International Studies. Lyman had always been an enthusiastic supporter of joint appointments between the Hoover Institution and the departments and schools of Stanford University. On the other hand, I was mindful of the warning the late President Hoover had given me on several occasions. Though Hoover had succeeded in keeping the Hoover Library from being taken over by Stanford, he had lost faith in the willingness of the Stanford administration to protect the independence of the Hoover Institution. That was essentially why, instead of establishing his presidential library at Stanford, he located it at his birthplace in West Branch, Iowa.

At the time, the firmness of the Stanford trustees made it clear that President Sterling had no chance of removing me, but President Hoover had warned me that there was no specified retirement age for the director, and that I should be wary of "sneak attacks." The first attempt to retire or fire me (I was never sure which) took place in the summer of 1984, just after I celebrated my sixtieth birthday and my twenty-fifth year as director. The attempt was made by people who wanted to set up an outside committee to evaluate the present programs and future plans of the Hoover Institution. This plan was killed when Trustee William Kimball was named to chair the Trustee Committee on the Hoover Institution. Ironically, the second attempt, which came in January 1985, was *led* by Kimball, and shortly thereafter I expressed a desire to retire by December 31, 1986—or as soon as my successor was in place. Rita and I were both interested in working in the second Reagan administration. Unfortunately, the university would not meet my first condition by reaffirming the 1959 trustee resolution.

When I was asked what part of my job gave me the most satisfaction, I always answered that it was neither the buildings nor the large endowment. My real satisfaction lay in the work of the remarkable scholars we were able to attract to the Hoover Institution. These scholars have made many important contributions to both the theoretical and practical aspects of national and international policy.

I also derived deep satisfaction from the opportunity to engage in meaningful public service, whether it involved international agencies; the federal government; state and local governments; large foundations, such as the National Endowment for the Humanities and the National Science Foundation; or boards of trustees of other colleges and universities. I was and am especially proud of my years as a regent of the University of California. It is naturally satisfying to be involved with the work of the world's leading public university system, but beyond that I found two issues especially rewarding. First, because of the firmness of the Board of Regents, the University of California still had ROTC on five campuses (Berkeley, Davis, UCLA, Riverside, and San Diego). A few Stanford students were able to take ROTC at Berkeley despite the fact that Stanford had "offed" it well over a decade earlier. Second, I was serving as chairman of the Board of Regents when David Gardner was elected president and was able to observe him skillfully and rapidly lead the university to outshine even its own illustrious past.

In December 1987 I announced the appointment of Secretary of State George Shultz as an Honorary Fellow. He took up residence at the Hoover Institution in February 1989, at the end of the Reagan administration. At the same time, he resumed his post as the Jack Steele Parker Professor of International Economics at the Stanford Graduate School of Business and remained there until he was seventy.

The Reagan Library

When the ten-person Reagan Foundation Board of Trustees was put together in early 1985 to organize work on the Reagan Library, Mrs. Reagan objected to only two people: John Herrington and Judge William Clark. Ed Meese, however, had convinced the Reagans that both Herrington and Clark should become trustees and that the officers should be Glenn Campbell (chairman), Edwin Meese III (vice chairman), William P. Clark (treasurer), and Martin Anderson (secretary).

As chairman of the Ronald Reagan Presidential Foundation from 1985 to 1987, I helped raise a total of $38 million in cash contributions and pledges,[1] as well as contended with disagreements over the architect, the location, etc. At a September 1985 meeting in Washington, the trustees agreed to choose one architect for both the library and the Center for Public Affairs. The same day, architects' presentations were made to the trustees by Hugh Stubbins, Jr., of Stubbins Associates, Inc.; Gyo Obata of Hellmuth, Obata and Kassabaum; MacDonald Becket and Lou Naidorf of Welton Becket Associates; and Dale Sprankle and John Lynd of Sprankle, Lynd and Sprague. Architects' presentations were made to the trustees in Palo Alto on October 14 by Cliff May of Clifford May Associates; Fred Hummel of Daniel, Mann, Johnson & Mendenhall; John C. Warnecke of John Carl Warnecke & Associates; Charles Davis of Esherick, Homsey, Dodge & Davis; Howard Elkus of Architects Collaborative;

---

1. But for Donald Kennedy's vehement opposition to keeping the Reagan Library attached to the Hoover Institution, we would have raised at least an additional $9 million per annum from 1985 to 1989.

John Stypula of Spencer Associates; Derek Parker of Anshen and Allen; Goodwin B. Steinberg of Goodwin B. Steinberg Associates; and Rush Hill of Hill Partnership, Inc.

Then on October 18 Martin Anderson informed the trustees that, in the opinion of the interview group, the architect should be Hugh Stubbins. He also urged the trustees to consider Hoover Associates as the local architect, primarily for its knowledge of local requirements and its experience in obtaining necessary construction inspections and approvals. The trustees asked for a budget from the architect before any commitment, then agreed to recommend Mr. Stubbins to President and Mrs. Reagan as the primary architect, Mr. May as a consultant to Mr. Stubbins, and Hoover Associates as the local architect. President and Mrs. Reagan approved the recommendations.

Stubbins had designed a wide variety of buildings in this country and abroad—the Citicorp headquarters on Park Avenue in New York City; the Federal Reserve Bank of Boston; the Pusey Library, Loeb Drama Center, and Countway Library of Medicine at Harvard University; academic buildings at Mt. Holyoke and Bowdoin colleges; the Seely G. Mudd Library at Princeton; the Graduate School of Business and the School of Law at the University of Virginia; plus buildings in Japan and Germany.

I arranged with Michael Deaver for Stubbins' sketch of the proposed building to be shown to Nancy Reagan at the White House on December 14. When Deaver, Rita, and I arrived in the upstairs living room, Mrs. Reagan was there with Christmas punch and cookies. After President Reagan joined us, he and Mrs. Reagan reviewed and approved the architect's sketch. Our opening banquet for the Ronald Reagan Foundation the following evening was attended by the President and Mrs. Reagan, long-time Reagan supporter Sen. Paul Laxalt of Nevada, all the trustees of the foundation, most of the cabinet, and several members of the board of governors. The architectural sketch, which consisted of two renderings, was prominently displayed that night at the dinner and the next morning in the East Room of the White House when President Reagan, Hugh Stubbins, and I met for a brief discussion. Mr. Stubbins described his concept of the library to the trustees and members of the board of governors of the foundation, and explained the major features of the two renderings on display. At that same meeting Stubbins was named as the architect for the library.

To my great surprise, at a trustees' meeting on January 8, 1986, John Herrington began to criticize Stubbins' work. He led off by alleging that there had not been a sufficient search for an architect, and that Stubbins was charging too much. Actually Stubbins was charging only his costs since he was a great admirer of President Reagan. His regular fee would have been about twice what we had agreed on. Herrington's only building experience was in commercial construction where architects use the same plans several times. But because he had been a commercial builder in Walnut Creek, he fancied himself an expert on architecture. Only when he was referred to a top San Francisco architect who told him what a bargain the foundation was getting did he finally admit he was wrong.

Judge Clark supported Herrington, referring to some criticism he had heard about a roof that collapsed on a Stubbins building in Berlin, Germany. (The Berlin Congress Hall was finished in 1957, and its problem had to do not with architecture, but with building materials and roof supports that the West German government insisted be used. Of course, at the time of the meeting none of us knew all this.) Former Attorney General William French Smith was also negative—but much more subtly so—and a new trustee, Mary Jane Wick, appointed at President Reagan's request, supported the nay-sayers.

In the event, the trustees agreed—the chairman abstaining—to conduct a small-scale competition to select the architect. Messrs. Elkus, Stubbins, Obata, Hummel, Becket, and May were all to be asked to present four building elevations, a site plan, a rendering, and a statement of probable construction costs. These were to be delivered to the Hoover Institution by February 20 for a presentation on February 22. Mr. Elkus declined to participate and was replaced by the Hill Partnership, Inc.

I arranged a January 14 telephone conference to try to reverse the decision. I reviewed the architect selection process from its inception through the January 8 meeting, but the trustees voted to affirm the January 8 decision. (For: Clark, Deaver, Herrington, Meese, Wick. Against: Anderson, Campbell. Mr. Smith did not participate in the call and did not vote.) At the end of the call, Michael Deaver stayed on the line to assure me that I really had nothing to worry about—Stubbins was a class act as an architect and was bound to win.

Meanwhile, Hugh Stubbins came to Stanford for a site visit, and I told him what had happened. I could tell he was shaken. When his plane back to Florida landed in Pittsburgh, he called to tell me that if he were a Japanese architect, he would be expected to commit hara-kiri. The next day he called again. He told me that, since I had been honest and forthcoming with him, he was going to be the same with me. Deaver had informed him that the second architectural contest was a phony, arranged only to embarrass Campbell, and that he—Deaver—was sure Stubbins would win. Stubbins said he was shocked by the action and by Deaver's attitude, but he had replied, "I will proceed to do what I normally would—complete the design schematics phase and present it to the foundation as scheduled in February." I agreed he had done the right thing.

I next called Dr. Gary Jones, executive director of the Reagan Foundation, to make certain no other architectural firms had been informed of the competition. When Jones assured me that nothing had been sent out, I asked him to hold off until I, as chairman, gave the go-ahead. Then I started calling key trustees, all of whom were shocked at what was going on and deeply concerned about potential lawsuits against the trustees. Deaver had left on a trip to the Far East, instructing Herrington to see that the contest announcement was sent out. Late one afternoon Herrington came into the foundation's Washington office, ignored Dr. Jones, and ordered Deaver's assistant to forge Deaver's signature and mail the announcements. When the assistant protested that that exceeded his authority, Herrington allegedly said that he would be responsible. Mr. Obata of Hellmuth, Obata and Kassabaum in St. Louis called to ask whether this second contest was for real. Out of loyalty to the foundation, the executive director had to tell him it was.

On February 22 the judging took place as scheduled in Room 130 of the Herbert Hoover Federal Memorial Building. The various firms—Welton Becket Associates; Daniel, Mann, Johnson & Mendenhall; Hellmuth, Obata and Kassabaum; Stubbins Associates; Hill Partnership, Inc.; and Cliff May—had obviously spent many thousands of dollars preparing their architectural drawings, renderings, and models. The trustees selected the Becket firm, the Obata firm, and the Stubbins firm as the finalists.

I could not be present in Washington, D.C., on March 10 when the drawings, models and renderings were reviewed by the President and Mrs. Reagan, but Stubbins was indeed selected to design the library. The president's first response, I understand, was, "Haven't I seen and approved this once before?"

Meanwhile, the site of the library was still in dispute. President Reagan's wealthy friends and supporters in Los Angeles had never wanted his library to be located at "elite and snobbish" Stanford in Northern California. They packed the trustees with people opposed to the Stanford site, including Mary Jane Wick, Walter Annenberg, Lew Wasserman, and even third-generation Stanford alumnus John Herrington. Former Interior Secretary William P. Clark, who attended Stanford briefly in the 1950s, eventually joined the Southern California bloc.

Then in February the Stanford Faculty Senate insulted President Reagan by voting that acceptance of his library did not "represent a collective position either endorsing or condemning the person or policies of Mr. Reagan." Of course, the Faculty Senate was neither required nor expected to endorse President Reagan's "person or policies." The intent of the statement was perfectly clear. Like Donald Kennedy, James N. Rosse, provost and acting president, would not disavow the faculty statement. In early April—despite my repeated entreaties and a belated plea from Board President Warren Christopher—the Stanford Faculty Senate voted 26 to 4 to require changes in the plans for the Reagan Library at Stanford, changes that the National Archives could not possibly accept.

On April 2 Stanford's Faculty Senate passed, by an overwhelming vote, a resolution asking the Stanford Board of Trustees—which had already approved the library's design and site—either to reduce the scope and size of the Reagan Library or to move it to a remote part of the campus. In effect, the Faculty Senate was asking for a building that it knew in advance the foundation would be unwilling—and the National Archives, under its statutory requirements, unable—to construct.

During the April 23 foundation meeting I made it very clear that the vote of the trustees for the Southern California site would *not* be unanimous. By the end of that long and contentious meeting I was so exhausted that I asked Smith to apprise Warren Christopher of our decision. I did not at the time realize that stress had torn the mitral valve in my heart.

On July 14 I was operated on at the University of California at San Francisco Health Center, and the badly damaged mitral valve was replaced by a mechanical substitute.

The decision to change the site of the library was not without sizable costs. It separated the Reagan gubernatorial and related materials owned by the Hoover Institution from the presidential papers, and it sacrificed the twenty-acre Stanford site and the thirty-five acres of committed open space around it, valued by Stanford at $41,250,000. Clearly, Donald Kennedy did not want the Reagan Library located at Stanford University. Indeed, in a 1990 interview covering his first ten years at Stanford, Kennedy confirmed his preference for ideology over scholarship when he said he had no regrets over losing the Ronald Reagan Presidential Library: "Stanford did exactly the right thing on that one."

The Southern California group also paid a high price for the move. They lost about $6 million in pledges, including $2 million of a $2.5 million pledge from David Packard, $2 million from Ross Perot of Dallas, and $1.5 million from the Bradley Foundation of Milwaukee. I had $4 to $5 million more in contributions or pledges pending when the Southern California trustees pulled the plug on the Stanford location.

In September I resigned as chairman of the trustees of the Ronald Reagan Foundation, because I felt that, since the library was going to be in Southern California, the chairman should be from there as well. I was replaced by former Attorney General Smith, President Reagan's personal lawyer, who had rejoined his Los Angeles law firm, Gibson, Dunn and Crutcher. On October 21, 1987, I sent this letter to all members of the Board of Governors of the Ronald Reagan Presidential Foundation:

> I am writing to all members of the Board of Governors to report that effective September 2 of this year former Attorney General William French Smith was elected Chairman of The Ronald Reagan Presidential Foundation Board of Trustees. With the Presidential Library and Center for Public Affairs now planned for a location in Southern California, it seems particularly appropriate that the Trustee Chairman should come from Southern California.
>
> It has been a great privilege for me to serve the President and Mrs. Reagan for over two years as Chairman of the Board of Trustees of the Reagan Foundation. I also want to take this opportunity to thank the many mem-

bers of the Board of Governors who either contributed generously themselves to the Foundation, or were instrumental in obtaining contributions to it.

During my tenure as Chairman, the Foundation raised a total of $38 million in a combination of cash contributions and pledges. This amount is well in excess of the $31 million that was estimated for the cost of the Presidential Library when it was scheduled to be located at Stanford University, but not sufficient to also cover the cost of the Center for Public Affairs as originally planned.

As you know, the Reagan Foundation Trustees decided on April 23 that it was essential that the Presidential Library and affiliated Center for Public Affairs be located at the same site and, since regrettably this could not be accomplished at Stanford University, these facilities would be located in Southern California.

In answer to the numerous questions that I have received on the subject of the move, I can say that a number of factors played a role in the decision of the Foundation Trustees. One important one was the February 1987 action of the Stanford University Faculty Senate in passing a resolution stating that Stanford's acceptance of the Library did not "represent a collective position either endorsing or condemning the person or policies of Mr. Reagan." No one argued that Stanford did or should endorse President Reagan's policies. The Senate, however, went beyond this and insisted that Stanford not endorse or honor the person of Ronald Reagan. To his supporters, the Senate appeared to be saying "We'll accept your papers and your library, Mr. Reagan, but we will not accept you."

1988

The year opened on an optimistic note. On January 6, the senior staff of the Hoover Institution wrote a letter to the Honorable John C. Shepherd, chairman of the Board of Overseers, and another to the Honorable Warren Christopher, president of the Stanford Board of Trustees, to communicate some general concerns in advance of the forthcoming meeting of the Institution's Board of Overseers. In the letter, they praised me generously and urged the boards to do everything necessary, financially or otherwise, to ensure that I remain director of the Hoover Institution:

Since we hope that Dr. Campbell will carry on as Director, we were disheartened to learn of Hewitt Associates' findings on relative compensation. Dr. Campbell, whose achievements place him at the top of directors of national research organizations, receives compensation only two-thirds the average of heads of these institutions, with no indication that the situation is improving. Further, Dr. Campbell's job has been made more difficult by the less than enthusiastic support that he has received from the Stanford administration. We hope that this situation can be remedied, since it is in Stanford's interest that Dr. Campbell continue his superb leadership of the Hoover Institution.

We continue to be frustrated by implicit criticism from other individuals at Stanford of the Director and of the Institution he has led. The attacks are made without evidence and are irritating and time-consuming. We trust that the Boards will continue to support the work and integrity of the process at the Hoover Institution so that a movement toward separation, alluded to in the Dornbush report, does not become a reality.

In April 1988 I released a statement indicating that I believed Hoover's premier position would endure, irrespective of its connection to Stanford, but that my strong personal preference was that Hoover remain an "independent institution within the frame of Stanford University." I stated that I stood ready, as I had throughout my tenure at Stanford, to cooperate fully with the rest of Stanford University. I simply wanted to ensure cooperation and support in place of attack and harassment and to maintain the independent status of the Hoover Institution. Despite this offer of an olive branch, on May 17 Board President Christopher and University President Kennedy, with the complicity of Provost Rosse, struck without warning. Christopher delivered the following letter to my office:

May 16, 1988

Dear Glenn:

Dean Watkins, with whom I discussed the subject matter of this letter, suggested that I write directly to you.

The Stanford Trustees hold the Hoover Institution in high esteem and recognize the importance of its continuing scholarly contributions. You have had a major role in the Institution for 28 years. Under your Directorship, it has achieved an enviable reputation as an independent institution within the frame of Stanford.

The Institution has flourished under the Trustees' Resolutions of 1959, 1969 and 1971. We believe that these resolutions provide a proper charter for enhanced cooperation between the University and the Institution, with promise of even greater achievement in the future. In the exercise of our fiduciary responsibilities, we see no basis for the separation of the Institution from the University, and indeed we are committed to building and strengthening the relationship in the future.

The basic provisions regarding the Director are contained in the May 21, 1959, Resolution of the Board of Trustees. This Resolution calls for a retirement age of 65 for the Director. The provision to this effect, which was approved by President Hoover and antedates your appointment as Director, has now been in place for almost three decades. Moreover, it is customary and we believe it is generally appropriate that top administrative positions at Stanford are relinquished at 65. Accordingly, we have concluded that the 1959 Resolution should be respected and that a search for the new Director should begin now. While we have determined that the time has come for us to begin the process of transition in the Directorship of the Hoover Institution, we are determined to do so as constructively as possible, and we solicit your cooperation to that end.

With respect to the selection of a successor, the Trustees intend to proceed in full compliance with the Trustees' Resolution dated January 12, 1971. This Resolution calls for a Search Committee consisting of four Senior Fellows, three Overseers, and three Members appointed by the President of the University, with the Chairman to be appointed by the President from among the Senior Fellows. This Search Committee will be promptly activated.

Looking to the future, we hope that your service to the Hoover Institution will continue as Senior Fellow and Director Emeritus. We are prepared to enter into an agreement providing that in this new status you would (1) receive compensation of $125,000 a year for five years with annual increases equal to the average annual Stanford faculty salary increases; (2) be entitled to sabbatical leave of one year with full pay or two years with one-half pay, with a special stipend of $100,000 for research and travel during the sabbatical; (3) retain health and life insurance benefits, parking privileges, travel allowances, and other current benefits; (4) be provided research and clerical assistance and an appropriate office; and (5) upon retirement as Senior Fellow, receive $25,000 per year in addition to your retirement compensation. Regarding an office, we want to respect the understanding that President Hoover's office, currently occupied by you, will be preserved because of its historical importance. Accordingly, we would not expect the office to be used by anyone other than you and we look forward to working with you and the Hoover family to determine the best way to recognize its historical importance. We appreciate all that you have done for the development of the Hoover Institution, and we reiterate our hope that we can look forward to your continued participation as Senior Fellow and Director Emeritus.

Sincerely yours,
Warren Christopher

Once again the senior staff of the Hoover Institution reacted, and on June 8 sent statements to the president and to members of the board of trustees. My forced retirement was protested not only by the Hoover scholars, who themselves had often been victims of discrimination at Stanford, but by other friends of Stanford as well. Sen. Mark Hatfield sent this message to the Stanford Board of Trustees:

> As a Stanford University alumnus I am surprised and dismayed to learn of the arbitrary action that you took concerning a forced retirement of Dr. Glenn Campbell as Director of the Hoover Institution. I strongly urge you to meet with the Institution's Board of Overseers and Dr. Campbell as soon as possible to reach an agreement on his status as Director. Having admired President Hoover all my life and having known him well ever since I was a graduate student at Stanford in the late 1940's and worked with him often up until his death in 1964, I am confident that Mr. Hoover would approve this course of action which, in my opinion, is also the wisest course of action.

In July 1988 I thought everything had been settled, but I soon found that it was not. James C. Gaither, new board president, told me that Kennedy would not allow him to offer me a salary higher than $125,000, well below what Hewitt Associates had recommended I receive (but well above the $106,112 that Dr. Kennedy had awarded me). Apparently, President Kennedy wanted to pay both former President Lyman and me the same salary—even though the Center for International Studies, which Dr. Lyman directed, was relatively small and undistinguished and had a budget about one seventh the size of the Hoover Institution's.

On July 27 Acting President James N. Rosse sent me a letter that in essence confirmed both the forced-retirement decision and the conditions and compensation stated earlier (see above) by Warren Christopher.

> Dear Glenn:
>
> I am pleased to confirm the discussions which Jim Gaither has had with you, with respect to your appointment as Counsellor of the Hoover Institution. I am writing to appoint you to that position, effective August 31, 1989, when you retire from the Directorship, on the following terms . . . .
> Here followed a lengthy list of essentially the same terms offered by Warren Christopher.

Distressing as the situation was, I hardly had time to worry about it just then. The world at large does not stand still in the midst of personal disruptions. In July I received a distress call from Edward Teller about the Strategic Defense Initiative (which Sen. Edward Kennedy called "Star Wars"). SDI was threatened by opposition from the generals and admirals. I asked, "Edward, can it wait till Monday? On Monday I will call the national security adviser, Colin Powell, and see what can be done." I called Powell on Monday, and he said he would arrange a meeting with the president as soon as possible. In the meantime, I should ask Teller and Martin Anderson to come to Washington. I think we arrived late Tuesday.

The next morning the president's science adviser, Bill Graham, met us at the White House Mess. After lunch Martin Anderson, Colin Powell, Lowell Wood, Edward Teller, Ron Lehman, General Abrahamson, Bill Graham, John Nuckols, Ken Duberstein, President Reagan, Vice President Bush, and I gathered in the Situation Room. At the end of the meeting we agreed that the president should be urged to proceed with SDI as fast as possible because of the Soviet threat.

Meanwhile, Back on the Campus . . .

By the early fall many Hoover Institution Fellows were petitioning the president of the Stanford Board of Trustees to keep me as director—at least through the end of the calendar year 1989—and to make the trustees and president aware of the excellence of Hoover's documentation and research program. Excerpts follow from some of their letters to James Gaither.

From Senior Research Fellow Robert Conquest:

> . . . Dr. Campbell has been, in one way or another, shabbily treated by the University authorities . . . We have already seen deplorable actions like the denial of normal salary raises. . . . Such actions, petty in themselves, represent an attitude which (it seems to me) make it particularly necessary to prevent all attempts by the University bureaucracy to encroach further on the Hoover's status. . . . there is also the strange tendency of some on the left to believe that their style of "liberalism" should be the central ideology of academe. . . . My impression of the faculty members I meet is that a large number of them, even of strong "liberal" views, are not fanatically anti-Hoover. But they are inclined to give in, on this as on other issues, to a vocal minority, and to the less vocal, but not always equitable, moves of the University leadership.
>
> . . . In conclusion, I think I should say that all of us at the Hoover have been deeply indebted to Dr. Campbell, not merely for defending the status of the Institution as a whole, but also for securing the individual scholarly autonomy of the Fellows. . . .

From Senior Fellow Robert Hall:

> . . . As an on-campus organization, Hoover has a strong advantage over independent research organizations. For example, Hoover offers far superior working conditions to the Brookings Institution, and Hoover's success in attracting and retaining top scholars is far better. The Hoover Institution is a place where basic, original scholarly research is carried out.
>
> . . . The Hoover Institution has achieved a higher degree of academic freedom than any other research organization known to me. At Hoover, scholars are supported to carry out research of their own choosing. There are no directives from the administration on research topics.

From Senior Fellow Milorad Drachkovitch:

... Hoover's academic staff is solidly behind the man who has been instrumental in building over the decades Hoover's academic excellence—recently fully recognized by the Board you preside over ... If you treat Campbell fairly we shall all rejoice. If the contrary happens, I am convinced we shall be as one man behind our Director.

From Senior Fellow Peter Duignan:

... The continued unseemly battle the University is waging against Glenn has reached me here even in the quiet and isolation of the Princeton Institute for Advanced Study ... Let Glenn stay on until December 31, 1989, even if a new Director is found before that date. Nothing is lost and a great deal will be gained. The Senior Fellows do not want a hasty transition . . . .

From Senior Fellow Martin Anderson:

... I think it would be especially important if the Trustees could agree to making Dr. Campbell's retirement date the 31st of December 1989. We have a long and difficult search ahead of us and this would give us an additional small cushion of time. It would also allow Dr. Campbell to complete 30 full years in service as the director of the Hoover Institution.

From Associate Director Charles Palm:

... Just as Herbert Hoover predicted in the beginning, separate identity of the Hoover Library has been a vital factor in attracting important collections and the attention of scholars around the world. Internationally, the reputation of the Hoover Library and its world-renowned collections is quite independent of that of Stanford. It is a tribute to Stanford that it has permitted, indeed supported, an independently operated library that serves scholars far beyond the university's own borders. By tolerating separateness, Stanford has encouraged the development of a great national and international treasure.

... If the selection process for the new director has not been completed by August 31, allowing Glenn to stay on until the actual arrival of his successor would be a gesture by the Trustees that would be well received by all at Hoover and would go a long way to insure a peaceful transition.

The Stanford trustees ignored these and many similar letters of support, and I assumed the title and position of counselor on August 31, rather than December 31, 1989, even though a new director had not yet been found. Rather than extend my tenure until my successor was in place, the trustees named John Raisian acting director as of September 1. The insult to me was calculated and obvious.

Counselor for Life—?

Being forced to retire at sixty-five—when at least five other Stanford administrators were older—was bad enough. Naming an acting director added insult to injury and aggravated the grossly unfair manner in which my salary had been kept down. The way the trustees proposed to repair that damage did not make sense. Using their approach, my salary would be approximately $177,000 when I reached seventy and approximately $237,000 when I reached seventy-five. In other words, the less I worked, the more I'd be paid.

The position of counselor was not administrative. What's more I'd been repeatedly promised—in one on one discussions with both Warren Christopher and James Gaither—that I had been made counselor for life, under both state and federal legislation. With hindsight, it was a great mistake for me not to demand this in writing. That would have protected me from any claims that no such promise had been made and/or that a shortage of funds required my removal from the payroll. The closest analogous position at Stanford is chancellor for life, and three Stanford presidents—David Starr Jordan, Ray Lyman Wilbur, and J. E. Wallace Sterling (all deceased)—have held that position after retiring.

Hewitt Associates is one of the leading experts in the field of executive remuneration for the heads of nonprofit institutions such as colleges, universities, and think-tanks. Its recommendation to the president of Stanford University on my salary was unanimously approved at the July 1987 meeting of the Board of Overseers—and then totally ignored by the administration. If Donald Kennedy and Warren Christopher had acted objectively instead of vindictively, my salary would have been set at an appropriate level on September 1, 1987. In that case, the trustees would never have had to confront this unfortunate issue, and I would also have been happy to forget the long history of previous salary discrimination.

Another matter could also have been straightened out before my successor was in place. For many years the majority of Hoover Senior Fellows—at least twenty—had been kept from teaching at Stanford University, although they were very distinguished scholars, many of whom had held important positions in federal and state government. They had much to offer Stanford students, including a better balance in the educational program in the social sciences and some of the humanities. There were ways to change this situation, but the prime requirement would have been for Kennedy and the board of trustees to encourage various departments or schools to act in a professional and objective manner.

If Kennedy had simply asked me when I wished to retire, I would—for family and personal reasons—have told him December 31, 1992, at the outside, but preferably December 31, 1991. I believe that by the end of 1991 we would have successfully completed the campaign to raise $100 million.

A Financial Summary

During the twenty-nine and two-thirds years of my directorate, my colleagues and I raised $98,340,005 in endowment gifts, living trust gifts, and expendable gifts; $7,558,000 in receipts from sales of publications and duplicate books; and $1,454,000 in receipts from sales of microfilms, for a total of $107,352,005.

Recently, Don Meyer, Stanford's associate director for development, reported that the various Scaife trusts plus the Carthage and Sarah Scaife Foundations had given Hoover approximately $45 million in 1996 dollars, well over $40 million of it while I was director. The gifts of other large contributors such as the Pew trusts, the Olin Foundation, and David Packard would also be adjusted considerably upward using 1996 price levels. The university budget supported library and administration expenses in the amount of $11,437,351, but nearly all of this was covered by overhead funds from federal grants to the Hoover Institution which went to Stanford University, and by staff benefits included in paragraph 8 of the 1959 Board of Trustees Resolution:

The Director and members of the staff of the Institution:

(a) shall be eligible for retirement benefits made available by the University to the non-faculty members of the University staff. The Director, Assistant Director, the Librarian, and the Curators may be eligible, alternatively, to retirement benefits made available to regular faculty members of the University, and if so, may opt for this eligibility;

(b) shall be eligible to participate in the benefits of health and insurance programs sponsored by the University;

(c) shall be eligible, under University regulation, to lease University land on which to build and own private homes for their own occupancy.

For the academic year ending August 31, 1969, staff benefits totaled a little over $109,000; for the year ending in August 1980, almost $520,000; for the year ending in August 1985, almost $1,290,000; and for the 1988–89 academic year, over $2.2 million. Add staff benefits for all the years I was director and they approximately equal the $11.4 million we received as university budget support for library and administration.

The overhead funds the university received on Hoover grants of $6.1 million during my directorate shows that the university got a very favorable deal in 1969–70, the year that Vice Provost Howard Brooks and I agreed that Hoover would not receive the overhead funds on its grants, but would instead receive increased funding for library and administration. When I was appointed director on January 1, 1960, the Hoover endowment was under $2 million, no more than half the endowment of the Brookings Institution. As of 1970, the Hoover endowment had grown to about $12 million and by 1980 to approximately $40 million. Both these figures were considerably higher than the comparable figures for Brookings.

The total value of the Hoover complex (buildings, archives, and books, plus endowment) undoubtedly far exceeded $300 million, and many of our books, documents, and archives are really priceless because some are the only copies in existence.

Introduction to the 1988 Annual Report

I opened my report that year with some personal reflections:

> December 31, 1989 would have marked my 30th year as Director of the Hoover Institution. During this period, the Institution grew from an important, but specialized library and archives, plus archival research, to a national and international institution of major research and policy making significance. The Hoover Institution was especially dear to me and I regarded it as part of my family. I had watched it grow from a small and struggling child into a mature adult, and its scholarship, relevance in the public policy arena and general reputation gave me great pride, much like the satisfaction that parents feel when their offspring's success exceeds their dreams.
>
> I can look back on my tenure at Hoover as a happy and rewarding career. My relationship to the scholars, to the staff, and to our many friends and supporters had always been one of mutual respect and confidence. We learned a great deal from each other and we continued to grow as we moved toward the 1990's. There were many that I could thank for this, but none was as important as my wife and colleague, Dr. Rita Ricardo-Campbell. Without Rita's invaluable support and advice during my long tenure, Hoover's success undoubtedly would have been greatly diminished.
>
> This, I should note, had been noticed by more than just a grateful husband. In his excellent book on the Reagan Revolution, my colleague Dr. Martin Anderson generously stated: "Glenn Campbell is without peer, the premier intellectual entrepreneur of this century. His partner in this life-long work is his wife, Rita Ricardo-Campbell, a descendant of David Ricardo, the 19th century English economist. Better known for her work as a public policy scholar, she advised and counseled the director on everything from personnel to policy."
>
> As I looked back on my nearly 30 years at Hoover, several high points came to mind. First was the vast increase in the number of volumes in the library and in archival holdings. As a repository devoted solely to 20th century social, economic, and political change, the Hoover Institution Library and Archives was the largest in the world. Among all libraries, it was among the largest in the United States. With 1.6 million volumes, the Hoover Library was ranked in size with such major academic libraries as Notre Dame University Library, Purdue University Library, and Dartmouth Uni-

versity Library, which collected in many fields and in all historical periods. At Stanford, the Library of the Hoover Institution was larger than the Stanford Law School, Business School, and Medical School Libraries combined. In fact, the Hoover Institution Archives, which held over 42 million documents, was the largest private archival repository in the United States, if not in the world.

An equally gratifying high point was the significant improvement in the quality and scope of the scholarship at Hoover, both internationally and domestically, during my tenure as director. There could be no doubt that Hoover's pre-eminent scholarship could be traced to the success my colleagues and I had in protecting the integrity of the academic process at the Hoover Institution from a small, but significant, cadre of intolerant left-wing professors at Stanford. Former President Richard Nixon wrote me on July 1, 1988: "Congratulations on your fight to prevent the left wing liberals on the Stanford faculty from taking over the Hoover Institution."

Protecting Hoover's independence was a sacred trust requiring constant vigilance. Indeed, my role as protector of the Institution's independent status, as mandated by President Hoover, often placed me at odds with some of the Stanford faculty and administration. I regretted this undesired side-effect of my duties, but I believed that friction was the inevitable cost of maintaining academic freedom at Hoover. That the benefits far outweighed the costs was evidenced by the quality of the Hoover scholars and by the value of the scholarly work produced over the years.

Of course, great scholarship does not take place in a vacuum. It must be generously supported. I am proud of the fact that during my tenure as Director the Hoover endowment went from $2 million to about $125 million. (With the improved investment procedures that were put in place during the 1988–89 academic year, the Hoover rate of return should go even higher in the future.)

For purposes of comparison, it should be noted that as of August 31, 1988, the Graduate School of Business had an endowment in excess of $66 million; the School of Earth Sciences, one of $31 million; the School of Engineering, about $37 million; the School of Law, about $46 million; and the University Libraries, almost $40 million. In fact there were only about 75 universities and colleges in the United States that had an endowment larger than that of the Hoover Institution.

Given Hoover's ample material resources, I was always on guard against the possibility that the Institution would be targeted as a "takeover candidate" by certain avaricious Stanford professors and administrators. In this, the University did not disappoint me.

Yet greed, and envy, by themselves, cannot fully explain the continuous barrage of criticism and harassment Hoover was subjected to over the years by disgruntled Stanford faculty and administrators. My colleagues and I never liked the media description of us as the "conservative" Hoover Institution. When confronted with this inaccuracy, our rejoinder was that we were not conservative; we merely looked conservative because we were located at a university which had become more and more left wing. Despite our repeated attempts to correct this unfair label, its frequent usage persisted through the years—much to our chagrin and frustration. We always suspected that Stanford's politics—not Hoover's—was the root cause of the unwarranted attacks on us, but we could never prove it.

However, one of the Hoover fellows, George Marotta, researched the extent of the left-wing bias of the Stanford faculty. For example, in May 1988, 57 Stanford professors signed a petition urging that the University Trustees bring Hoover under "normal academic governance" or failing that to "end connections between the University and the political arm of the Hoover Institution, as distinct from the library and archives." Examining public voter registration data, Marotta discovered that 94 percent of these professors were registered Democrats, only 2 percent were Republicans and 4 percent were independents.

On the other hand, a 1987 Gallup Poll showed that 39 percent of the American public were registered Democrats, 32 percent Republican, and 29 percent independent. Scholars at the Hoover Institution were 34 percent Democrat, 52 percent Republican and 14 percent independent. Although Hoover was relatively close to the general population, we apparently looked much too conservative to an unrepresentative and liberal faculty.

Press Conference—July 1988
Board of Overseers Meeting

There was so much press interest in my retirement status that after the Board of Overseers meeting, Robert Malott, James Gaither, and I held a press conference. Many interesting questions were asked, most of which I had to answer. One was: Why wasn't I suing the trustees as I had threatened to do? My answer was that they had awarded me so many benefits that, according to my lawyers, Edward Bennett Williams and Edwin Meese, I no longer had a case. Williams had explained that the law provided no relief for people in my position after the age of sixty-five. He had discussed the matter with Clarence Thomas, then head of the EEOC, and Thomas had confirmed his opinion. He concluded that my only hope lay with a board that would overlook the age issue.

Another question was, Had the Hoover Institution received most of its money from conservative "fat cats"? I replied that most leading universities had been founded by rich, conservative fat cats like the Stanfords; John D. Rockefeller, Sr., who founded the University of Chicago; and James B. Duke, the tobacco magnate who had donated millions to Trinity College on the condition that it take his name. I pointed out that Harvard received much support from conservative fat cats, enough to become the richest private university in the world. Harkness of Standard Oil had given Harvard President A. Lawrence Lowell the money to build the Harvard houses, and had given even more money to his own alma mater, Yale, to build its college system.

What was I planning to do after I was no longer director? I said that I hoped I would continue to have considerable influence at Hoover, but I would transfer most of my attention to the University of California because I had many years to serve as the senior regent.

The Dedication of the East Asian Reading Room

One very happy event in the ensuing months of 1988 was the dedication, on October 14, of the East Asian Reading Room of the Hoover Institution in honor of Dr. Chang Kia-ngau, recognizing his great contributions to China's modernization and his scholarly accomplishments. Located in the Lou Henry Hoover Building, this magnificent room contains Chinese, Japanese, and Western reference materials and periodicals, and desks for scholars.

The program that day included testimonials to Dr. Chang Kia-ngau by his widow, Mrs. Pihya C. Chang, by his grandnephew Professor P. H.

Kevin Chang, and by distinguished scholars and friends, as well as my own remarks. A reception attended by more than fifty guests followed. Both the room itself and the fund for maintenance and support of the collection were named for Dr. Chang. This description of the Chang Kiangau endowment appeared in the dedication program:

> The Hoover Institution's East Asian Collection possesses the most unique holdings on modern China in the twentieth century of any library in the world. These materials include pamphlets, newspapers, periodicals, government reports, survey findings, monographs, literary writings, and so forth. Rich source materials pertain to the Chinese Revolution of 1911 and describe the warlord period of the teens and twenties, the brief period of nation building under the Kuomintang Party, the civil war and rise of the Chinese Communist Party, the period of socialism after 1949, and the developments of a modern economy and polity in the Republic of China on Taiwan.
>
> In the decades ahead, major developments will occur in the People's Republic of China, Hong Kong, and the Republic of China. The East Asian Collection must continue to acquire important primary and secondary documents to record these impressive events and transformations and preserve them for future generations of scholars.
>
> To that end, the Hoover Institution on War, Revolution and Peace wishes to honor Dr. Chang's name and memory by establishing a fund that will endow the acquisition of modern research materials. This act will provide an enduring tribute to his achievements and the humanist ideals he stood for.
>
> This fund-raising effort was launched in 1985 and will continue until $1 million has been collected. To date, collection for this fund has come to $375,000, with another $80,000 pledged. We hope that the friends of Dr. Chang will assist the Hoover Institution in its efforts to develop the collection on modern China in the decades to come.
>
> Interested donors may contact Dr. W. Glenn Campbell, Director, Hoover Institution, Stanford, California 94305.

The $1 million was finally collected a few years ago.

Title VIII Program

Legislation introduced in Congress in 1981 was passed and signed by President Reagan in 1983 establishing the Department of State's Soviet-Eastern European Research and Training Act of 1983, Public Law 98-164, Title VIII. Funding was appropriated in the 1984–85 fiscal year to be available for the 1985–86 academic year. The program was to run for ten years, and Hoover was recognized as a national institution and given the maximum grant each year.

Dr. Richard F. Staar, coordinator of the International Studies Program, was to obtain the funds and find the scholars. The first grant was for $180,000 per annum, to be administered by the Hoover Institution. All succeeding grants were for $200,000. The State Department allowed Stanford to charge only 10 percent overhead, and Stanford allowed the Hoover Institution to accept the grants on this basis. The first five grants were obtained by Dr. Staar while I was director, and he has obtained two more since my retirement. Fortunately, the ten-year limit has been removed, and I am hopeful that Dr. Staar will continue to receive these funds indefinitely.

At my last Board of Overseers meeting as director in July 1989, Chairman Bob Malott, addressing the board, applied a quotation from George Bernard Shaw to me: "The reasonable man adapts himself to the world. The unreasonable man persists in trying to adapt the world to himself. Therefore, all progress depends upon the unreasonable man." William E. Simon, former treasury secretary, had two plaques engraved with the quote, one for himself and one for me.

At that meeting we tested the TV system under development by Associate Director Annelise Anderson. She and her assistant devised a way for Sen. Pete Wilson to speak from his office in Washington to Chairman Malott and me in the Hoover courtyard. The hookup could also be seen in the Stauffer Room by all the board members. Malott and I talked to Wilson primarily about why he was leaving the Senate to run for governor. I heard later that the whole process blew the mind of Donald Kennedy, who vowed to kill the whole system. In this, he apparently succeeded. True, he is no longer president of Stanford, but the Hoover Institution is only now putting together a state-of-the-art TV system.

Many overseers did not recognize the value of such a system for fundraising—perhaps we had spoiled them by raising so much money without one—but Senior Fellow Martin Anderson and I foresaw that without high-tech tools fundraising would fall off. We were correct. Now, nearly ten years later, virtually every one of our fundraising competitors uses TV. At last, under the direction of Richard Sousa, Hoover will have the TV facilities we hoped for.

Fundraising at Hoover

I have often been asked about my fundraising strategy. In a sense, I borrowed from the fundraising approach of successful politicians: it is easier to raise a large sum of money from, say, four wealthy donors than from four hundred small ones. But to garner a large contribution one must have a good product to discuss. In our case, that meant being able to demonstrate that important subjects were being researched and written about by fine scholars whose work would influence public understanding and policy. It also meant that our scholars must present their research findings—or have those findings rewritten—in language readily understood by an educated person rather than in the sometimes arcane jargon of a particular discipline. I cannot overstate the value of articulate scholars who can discuss their subjects in clear and simple English. The director then, alone or with colleagues, gets on a plane, visits the potential donor, explains the project, and—having "made the sale"—leaves. This process is the same whether the donor is an individual, a foundation, or a corporation. Successful fundraising requires travel.

But if fundraising for a public policy research institution is in some ways similar to political fundraising, in other ways it is more like corporate marketing or advertising. In that sense, the "products" are published research and newspaper op-ed pieces. These can be marketed to government officials; to congressmen, senators, and other office holders; to prospective donors; and to the media. Donors like to see some tangible results of their generosity, and they enjoy meeting and interacting with the director of the institution and/or with scholars from their area of interest.

As a general rule, potential contributors, regardless of the size of their donations, are wary of directors of development bearing charts. They want to deal with the institution's director or with a scholar who is knowledgeable about particular programs. Letters and meetings held in the director's office are poor substitutes for one-on-one visits to donors. This is especially true when, as is the case with Hoover, yours is not a conventional teaching institution with a broad alumni base.

Still, although we traveled widely to the sources of our funds, my colleagues and I always tried to get our contributors to visit the Hoover Institution where they could see for themselves our impressive collections and our extensive archives, and could meet with the Hoover scholars. In the 1960s those scholars included Prof. Witold Sworakowski, Stefan Possony, Roger Freeman, Peter Duignan, Milorad Drachkovitch, Lewis Gann, Richard V. Allen, and Rita Ricardo-Campbell. In the 1970s visitors met Richard Staar, Martin Anderson, Dennis Bark, Alvin Rabushka, Ramon Myers, Robert Wesson, George Marotta, Robert Conquest, and Senior Research Fellows Edward Teller and Milton Friedman. In the 1980s Adm. James Stockdale, Edward Lazear, Melvyn Krauss, Bruce Bueno de Mesquita, Kenneth Judd, Chiaki Nishiyama, John Cogan, and George Shultz were added to the roster, and Charles Palm usually showed visitors the collections and the archives. Shultz, by the way, joined our staff in 1989 after serving as secretary of state, secretary of treasury, secretary of labor, and director of Office of Management and Budget.

Did these visits help in our fundraising? Early in 1964 Richard Scaife, Dan McMichael, and Charles Ford of Pittsburgh came to the Hoover Institution, and their $750,000 matching grant built the Lou Henry Hoover Building. A return visit in 1966 brought us a $1 million pledge that carried us a long way on our campaign to raise $5 million in endowment funds. Donations following visits in 1968 and 1970 provided grants with which we started the National Fellows Program and greatly expanded the Domestic Studies Program. The Scaife trusts and the Scaife Foundation were the largest donors to Hoover during my tenure, contributing over $14 million from the Scaife trusts, the Sarah Scaife Foundation, the Allegheny Foundation, and the Carthage Foundation. Because many of these donations came to us in the 1960s and early 1970s when the dollar was worth more (before the inflationary Carter years), their value maintains the Scaife family's ranking as our largest contributor. Stefan

Possony, Richard Staar, Dennis Bark, and Martin Anderson played crucial roles in my visits to Pittsburgh to meet with the Scaifes and their representatives. And, incidentally, the Hoover Institution is the only part of Stanford that Richard Scaife will support.

In my thirty years as director, Hoover received almost $13.3 million from the Pew trusts of Philadelphia. From 1982 to August 1989 alone, we received more than $7.8 million. Again, Martin Anderson and Dennis Bark, this time along with John Moore, were instrumental in garnering these gifts. Pew Foundation officials—including three of its presidents: Allyn R. Bell, Jr., Robert I. Smith, and Thomas W. Langfitt, M.D.— also visited us, either to attend July Board of Overseers meetings or to meet various Senior Fellows in domestic studies: Martin and Dennis, along with Milton Friedman, Thomas G. Moore, Alvin Rabushka, Thomas Sowell, Rita Ricardo-Campbell, and others.

Between 1970 and August 31, 1977, the William Volker Fund contributed $585,000, most of it in the form of grants for Roger Freeman's magnum opus *The Growth of American Government*. Richard Burress, Martin Anderson, and Rita Ricardo-Campbell also received smaller grants. Then late in the 1970s Morris Cox became president of the Volker Fund, and he and the other trustees acceded to the wishes of the fund's founder, who had asked that it be dissolved after a certain period of years. In 1979 the fund's remaining assets—$7.5 million—were turned over to the Hoover Institution. Apart from the $25 million Ford Foundation grant in the early 1960s, Volker's was the largest foundation grant in the history of Stanford University.[1] The total gifts for the year 1978–79 were about $12.5 million, equivalent to $30 million in 1998 dollars.

In 1973 Hoover was given an unrestricted and expendable William H. Noble bequest of $6.6 million, the largest unrestricted bequest to Stanford to that point. Of that sum, $3.6 was allocated for a library endowment[2] and $3 million for domestic studies research projects and publications.[3] Between 1975 and August 1989, the John M. Olin

---

1. By August 31, 1989, the market value of the expendable Volker Fund was over $36.5 million, and it was to be spent solely for domestic studies.
2. Valued at $10.4 million as of August 31, 1989.
3. Valued at $9.3 million as of August 31, 1989.

Foundation pledged $3.7 million to Hoover. From 1975 to 1986, it gave over $622,000 to the Domestic Studies Program. From 1976 to 1981, it gave $348,000 in unrestricted funds. The Olin Foundation was so impressed with the National, Peace, and Public Affairs Program that in 1983 it established the John M. Olin Public Affairs Fellowship Program, and from then till August 1989 it contributed $900,000. Between 1987 and 1989 the foundation added $400,000 for the John M. Olin Media Fellows Program. Further impressed by our world-renowned collection of Soviet and East European documents, it donated $750,000 between 1986 and 1989 to increase the utilization of these resources and to fund the John M. Olin Program for Soviet and East European Studies.

From August 1988 to August 1989 the Olin Foundation pledged more than $700,000. Half a million of those dollars were earmarked for a television project, "Statecraft," planned by former Secretary of State George Shultz. I neither approved this expenditure in advance nor objected to it. The project was important to Shultz. Nevertheless, he was eventually forced to cancel it because he could not raise the $5 or $6 million he needed. Olin also gave us $150,000 for the Hoover television project and $100,000 for the Rose and Milton Friedman Endowment Fund.

During his tenure as secretary of defense from 1969 to 1971, David Packard and his wife contributed $340,000 to the National Fellows Program. The money came from a special trust fund they were required to set up under the tax laws then governing public service. When he retired from the cabinet in December 1971, Packard donated Hewlett-Packard stock valued at slightly over $1.5 million to the Domestic Studies Program,[4] and the Packards have made several other generous donations, including more that $1 million for the National Fellows Program between 1975 and 1986. During my directorship, Packard's gifts totaled over $3.3 million.

The largest corporate gift to the Hoover Institution during my directorate—$2.2 million—came from the Nomura Corporation of Japan in May 1989, after Dr. Chiaki Nishiyama and I met with Nomura CEO Tetsuya Tabuchi to seek funding for our Center for International Monetary Studies.

The division of our efforts in the 1970s into a Domestic Studies

---

4. In August 1989 that gift was worth over $4 million.

Program, an International Studies Program, a National Fellows Program, a Media Fellows Program, and a Visiting Scholars Program was an asset to our fundraising. In my thirty years as director, we combined individual programs in various ways, according to whatever structure or strengths we believed would attract both distinguished scholars and prospective donors. These broad categories of research and study enabled us to be flexible, and I espoused and maintained them throughout my directorate. I never had to worry about who took or got credit for a donation.

The success of any fundraising, however, is determined not solely by the amount of money raised, but also by the *cost of raising it.* Working with Richard Staar, Martin Anderson, Dennis Bark, Rita Ricardo-Campbell, and, after 1982, Dr. Thomas Henriksen, I was able to keep our costs at 2 to 3 percent of gifts. Stanford University, with its huge development office, spends 7-plus percent of its gifts.

My Final Report

In my final report as director I was able to say that the Hoover Institution was excellent by every measure.

- *Scholars.* The most important asset of any organization is the quality of its people, and Hoover was unequaled in that regard. In the combined fields of economics, political science, international relations, sociology, history, and law, our appointments included seven Nobel laureates— Alexander Solzhenitsyn in literature, and Kenneth Arrow, Milton Friedman, Friedrich von Hayek, George Stigler, James Buchanan, and Gary Becker in economics; fourteen members of the Academy of Arts and Sciences; seven members of the National Academy of Science; and winners of the Congressional Medal of Honor, the Presidential Medal of Freedom, the National Medal of Science, and the Jefferson Award. What's more, their scholarship was often applied to public service.

  My assessment of the quality of Hoover's scholars is supported by an article entitled "The Good Think-Tank Guide" in the December 21, 1991–January 3, 1992 issue of *The Economist* which ranked the Hoover Institution #1 among think tanks worldwide:

"The Hoover Institution on War, Revolution and Peace . . . the highest overall score."

- *Staff.* Resident and visiting scholars are supported by an effective and efficient staff of librarians, archivists, and researchers; by a major scholarly press; and by administrative and clerical personnel.
- *Documentation.* The Hoover Institution library contains 1.6 million volumes and its archives—the largest private collection of its kind in the world—consist of some four thousand collections. Together the library and archives make up the world's largest research organization.
- *Facilities.* The three buildings constitute an attractive setting for the pursuit of scholarship. Together they offer both quiet places for private study and thought, and common rooms for intellectual interaction.
- *Fundraising.* When I came to Hoover as director in 1960, its endowment was two million dollars. By 1970 it had grown to twelve million. That sixfold increase plus the addition of our second building was never equaled, and many believe it will not be equaled in any future period.

At my first Advisory Board meeting in July 1960 I outlined my vision and strategy for the decade ahead, including my plans to appoint several scholars to the staff and to raise $5 million dollars in new contributions. Clearly, we exceeded those objectives, and I never again devoted time and energy to "the vision thing." Thereafter, I presented an annual report to the Advisory Board (later renamed the Board of Overseers) that updated our strategy as the annual reports of corporations and universities do. Apart from that, I concentrated on providing leadership and the backbone needed to keep the Hoover Institution independent.

By 1980 our endowment had reached $40 million and the Herbert Hoover Federal Memorial was constructed. In September 1981 a letter came to me from Nobel laureate and Hoover Institution Senior Fellow Milton Friedman: "May I say how happy Rose and I have been with our relation with Hoover. . . . Credit for much of that must go to your management."

That letter meant a great deal to me. Friedman, after all, is undoubtedly the best-known economist in the world. He has traveled and lectured widely in Japan, Hong Kong, Taiwan, Communist China, India, Africa, the former Soviet Union, Eastern Europe, Germany, and Great Britain. When his book *Free to Choose* was translated into Japanese, it sold more copies in Japan than it had in the United States and was the basis for a very successful television series. Indeed, when Dr. Chiaki Nishiyama and I met with Tetsuya Tabuchi of the Nomura Corporation, we were most interested to find that the only Hoover economist whose name Tabuchi recognized was that of Milton Friedman.

Looking Back

On September 1, 1989, I became a counselor of the Hoover Institution. At that point, our endowment and living trusts totaled $125,702,023 (at market value) in addition to expendable funds of almost $3,000,000. We had gift commitments of roughly $5,000,000 and were named as a beneficiary in wills for between $10,000,000 and $12,000,000. These numbers exceeded the amounts raised by most of the schools at Stanford—including the Business School, the Law School, the Engineering School, the School of Earth Sciences, the School of Education, and the University Library. Only the Schools of Medicine and of Humanities and Sciences could claim larger endowments. If this same rate of increase continued over the next thirty years, Hoover's endowment would reach about $3.8 billion, and two more buildings would be erected. That's a very unlikely prospect.

Where did the money come from?

- $98,340,005 in endowments, living trusts, and expendable gifts
- $7,558,000 in receipts from sales of publications and duplicate books
- $1,454,000 in receipts from sales of microfilm
- $886,207 in Ford Foundation funds allocated to strengthening our library system 1962–72
- $7,000,000 in a federal grant for construction of the Herbert Hoover Federal Memorial
- $6,100,000 in other government grants
- $11,437,351 in university budget support for library and administration expenses

Our fiscal relationship with Stanford meant that the university received a considerable amount in overhead funds on government grants to Hoover. Then, during the 1970–71 academic year, Hoover research became what Stanford terms a "formula unit," and in return the university agreed to increase its funding of Hoover's library and administration costs. Vice Provost Howard Brooks and I agreed that (a) Hoover would not receive the overhead funds on grants to the Hoover Institution, and (b) the institutional costs of providing retirement benefits for research scholars would be borne by Hoover rather than by Stanford. (Stanford had initially taken on that obligation in the 1959 Trustees Agreement.) The six Senior Fellows, therefore, who retired in August 1995 receive their benefits from Hoover and only technically from Stanford.

Hoover Institution Budget, 1989–90

Hoover's financial situation at the end of my tenure is a tribute to both the vigor with which my colleagues and I raised funds and the wisdom with which we husbanded and spent them. The budget for fiscal year 1989–90 was estimated at $17.1 billion, up more than $1.4 million from 1988–89. Projected revenue sources were listed as:

- Individual, Foundation, and Corporate Gifts   44%
- Endowment Earnings   29%
- University Funds   23%
- U.S. Government Grants   2%
- Publication Sales and Miscellaneous Income   2%

Those endowment earnings were estimated at almost $5 million. Until fiscal 1988–89 there had been no fixed payout rate for our $80 million in endowment funds. That year I agreed to a 4.75 percent payout rate in exchange for separating our investment procedures from those of Stanford. It is absurd to suggest that, having accumulated $80 million in expendable funds, we have created a deficit of $4 million by agreeing to a future payout percentage. Of course, I could have taken $4 million *out* of the endowment fund before agreeing to the percentage, but my goal in agreeing to the 4.75 rate was to maintain the real value of the endowment. It is worth noting that Harvard University has the largest endowment of any private university in the world—$11 billion as of June 30, 1997—and that endowment provides less than 30 percent of the school's operating budget. The payout rate is kept at about 4.5 percent to maintain the real value of the endowment.

In 1989–90, Stanford contributed some $4 million in partial support of Hoover's library, which houses a third of the volumes available to Stanford students and faculty. That constitutes 23 percent of the Hoover budget. In 1959–60, Stanford's $125,000 input represented about one third of Hoover's annual budget.

Ninety-four percent of Hoover's 1989–90 budget was allocated for research, library and archives, and the Hoover Press. The remaining 6 percent covered administrative and fundraising costs. My salary, for example, totaled $1,462,042 from January 1960 to August 1989. (Labor economists John Raisian and Edward Lazear calculated that I was eligible for salary discrimination compensation in the amount of $942,358 in 1989 dollars.)

National Think-Tanks

James A. Smith's *The Idea Brokers*, published in 1991, is the first comprehensive study of think-tanks and their role in American society. Following are excerpts (pp. 184–91, *passim*):

Mr. Hoover's Legacy

The Hoover Institution on War, Revolution and Peace, as it is now known, is decidedly different from the other conservative institutes. It is more a center for advanced study than a participant in day-to-day policy debates. During more than twenty-five years as Hoover's president, (Director) Campbell assembled a group of roughly seventy social scientists and historians, including Milton Friedman, George Stigler, Kenneth Arrow, Thomas Sowell, and Seymour Martin Lipset.

It is the best endowed of the policy research organizations and the only major one that operates autonomously within the framework of a university, although Hoover's emergence as a focus of the conservative revival has sometimes proved nettlesome to members of the university community. . . .

For nearly forty years, the Hoover War Library operated quietly, often in straitened financial circumstances, as a division of Stanford University.

Research fellows performed curatorial duties, and the publishing program was tied closely to the archival collection. In the 1920's, with support from the Rockefeller Foundation, the library began the nation's first systematic studies of the Soviet Union.

In the late 1940's and early 1950's, the Carnegie Corporation provided funding for studies of revolution and international relations. In sheer quantity over the years, scholarly bibliographies and edited collections of documents have far outweighed research that is of immediate relevance to policymaking.

In the late 1950's, however, Hoover and some of his associates began to plan a more active political role for the institution, and Hoover declared that the institution's research and publications must "demonstrate the evils of the doctrines of Karl Marx—whether Communism, Socialism, economic materialism or atheism—thus to protect the American way of life from such ideologies, their conspiracies, and to reaffirm the validity of the American system."[2]

This declaration sparked the first of a series of controversies over the propriety of housing a research institution with an ideological mission in the university community. An ad hoc faculty committee protested that Hoover's statements violated the basic principles of scholarly investigation. Questions about the institution's relationship to Stanford have simmered ever since.

In 1959 the library's status was formally redefined, and the library became an independent institution, operating without reference to faculty or faculty committees and reporting directly to Stanford's Board of Trustees through the university's president. Much of the controversy between Stanford and the institution over the years has focused on questions of governance and control, but these problems have been aggravated by the uncompromising conservatism of the institution's longtime director, W. Glenn Campbell. . . .

Campbell cannot be called a charismatic leader. "Dour" and "prickly" are adjectives often used to describe him. But, over the past thirty years, he has also been the most effective institution builder in the conservative movement. Like Wesley C. Mitchell of the National Bureau of Economic Research

---

2. Hoover, quoted in *Stanford Daily* (March 29, 1960).

or Robert Brookings of the Brookings Institution, Campbell has left an enduring institutional legacy and has won the admiration of fellow conservatives by confronting liberalism within the university. Just as Baroody made an adversary of Brookings to win support, Campbell could argue that the Hoover Institution was creating a principled alternative to a mindlessly tolerant, "anything goes" campus liberalism.

Campbell's immediate task was to continue to build the research collection and stabilize the library's finances. Having come from Washington and AEI, he was also committed to Hoover's plan to make it a major conservative voice in public policy circles. Drawing on the former president's conservative friends and associates, he began to raise the necessary funds. The institution was also an early beneficiary of wealthy western conservatives, many of whom had been drawn into politics by the surge of activity surrounding the Goldwater campaign. Campbell convinced these conservatives that an intellectual center, such as the Hoover Institution, could keep the conservative faith alive through hard times. Given its locale at Stanford University and the presence of so many leading conservative economists, the institution was also an early favorite of conservative foundations.

An admiring colleague fondly describes Campbell as a "penny-pinching Scot," saying that his success in raising an endowment was a matter of appealing to conservatives early on and managing programs tightly with an eye to the long term. In that respect, Campbell differed markedly from Baroody, whose organization fell deeply into debt in the mid-1980's. Campbell deserves full credit for building the Hoover Institution into a major national research center. The institution's corps of scholars increased from six in 1960 to about seventy in residence in the late 1980's. It has grown from a financially pressed library and archive with a $2 million endowment and an annual budget of about $370,000 (only $50,000 of which supported research) to a research institution with an endowment of over $125 million and a $17 million budget, over $7 million of which supports research. Roughly 25 percent of the budget is supplied by the university, while 75 percent comes from endowment and outside contributions. The institution's growing wealth has been no small part of the controversy on the campus, with Campbell complaining in 1988, the last year before his not-altogether-voluntary retirement as the institution's director, that Stanford was attempting another takeover of the institution. Certainly, the institution was slipping from his control after nearly three decades; as the 1989 academic year began, John Raisian took over as acting director.

The Ronald Reagan Foundation

On December 8, 1989, I received from Ronald Reagan a letter in which he thanked me for my years of service and friendship. He concluded by informing me, regretfully, that my service as a trustee of the Ronald Reagan Presidential Foundation would conclude at the end of 1989. I accepted his decision and sent my resignation to the foundation's chairman, William French Smith, on January 2, 1990. I requested only that I not be held responsible for decisions made after my effective resignation date in any suits brought against the foundation trustees by third parties, and that my contribution as the founding chairman of the Ronald Reagan Presidential Foundation be duly noted among the names listed on the wall of the presidential library. I then replied directly to President Reagan on January 29, 1990:

> Dear Mr. President:
>
> Your letter of December 8, 1989 reached me just before Christmas.
>
> Let me apologize for not replying sooner, but Christmas and the New Year is a very busy time at the Hoover Institution, involving fundraising, a meeting of the Hoover Overseers, and carrying out my duties as the Senior Regent of the University of California where I have served since you first appointed me on March 1, 1968. In addition, I serve on several advisory committees to President Bush.
>
> When the Foundation Board of Trustees made the decision in April of 1987 to change the Library location, the Trustees unanimously agreed to refund or forgive a pledge from any party whose commitment was made with the understanding that the Library was to be built at Stanford University. I have heard recently that this led to the loss of several million dollars in pledges for the Presidential Library and affiliated Center for Public Affairs. If there is anything that I can do to be helpful in this matter, particularly with those persons from whom I obtained pledges, please feel free to call on me anytime.

Since you have been involved with Pepperdine University at various times, you will be pleased to know that I was awarded an LL.D. on December 16; and last week I received The Order of the Sacred Treasure, Gold and Silver Star medal from the Japanese government.

Rita joins me in best wishes to you and Nancy.

Sincerely,
/Glenn/
Glenn Campbell

cc: The Ronald Reagan Presidential Foundation Board of Trustees.

President Reagan's December 8 letter was approved and signed by him, so I cannot agree with those who suggest that the decision was made by Mrs. Reagan or by Trustees Mary Jane Wick and Fred Ryan. On November 15, 1991, three trustees and long-time supporters of President Reagan were fired: Edwin Meese III, vice chairman of the foundation; Martin Anderson, secretary; and William P. Clark, former treasurer. A *Los Angeles Times* story dated January 1, 1992, reported on a trustee resignation:

Associate of Reagan Quits Post

Library board: John Herrington's departure follows that of three other longtime advisers to the former President.

The last of Ronald Reagan's closest political associates has quit the board that built Reagan's presidential library, expressing disappointment that other longtime advisers who were squeezed out in April would not be reappointed.

In a letter to the former President, former Energy Secretary John S. Herrington resigned from the Ronald Reagan Presidential Foundation that raised $60 million for the library near Simi Valley.

Herrington was the only longtime Reagan associate spared last April when former U.S. Attorney General Edwin Meese III, former Interior Secretary William P. Clark and domestic policy adviser Martin Anderson were quietly dropped from the board.

Disgruntled loyalists, who requested anonymity, contend that the ouster was orchestrated by Nancy Reagan without the knowledge of the former President. Reagan has denied it, remarking at one point that "this is part of the picking on Nancy that goes on."

In the Dec. 19 resignation letter Herrington told Reagan that he hoped that these three loyalists would be reappointed. But, he wrote, if "they are gone from the Reagan Foundation board for good, and I now realize that is your intent, I must go also.

"Bill, Ed, and Marty are my friends, and no President ever had stronger supporters than these three," Herrington wrote. "I'm sure you can understand my feeling of loyalty to them, Mr. President."

Neither the Reagans nor their spokeswoman could be reached for comment Tuesday. Reagan Foundation Board Chairman Lodwrick M. Cook was vacationing out of the country and unavailable for comment, said Scott Loll, a spokesman for Cook, who is also chairman and chief executive officer of Atlantic Richfield Co.

In an interview in October, Cook said that three board members were released in April because their six-year terms had expired. He said the former President asked him to limit all members to one term to bring new faces to the board and broaden support for the library.

Herrington's term also expired, but Cook said he asked him to stay on as treasurer to maintain continuity of the books until the foundation reached its goal of raising $75 million to pay off debts and launch a conservative think tank.

On Nov. 4, 1992 nearly all the Reagan library—with its 55 million pages of White House documents and its public museum—was turned over to the National Archives during a dedication ceremony that featured a historic meeting of President Bush and four former Presidents (Nixon, Ford, Carter, and Reagan).

The foundation has retained control of a suite of offices for the Reagans, foundation staff, and the proposed think tank, which would be called the Ronald Reagan Center for Public Affairs.

Herrington's departure leaves the foundation board without any member of the Reagan Administration except Frederick Ryan, who was President Reagan's White House scheduler and is now his chief of staff.

In a flurry of letters and phone calls that followed that shake-up, many Reagan loyalists lamented that the board and public affairs center would lack the vision of conservatives who helped wage "the Reagan Revolution" in Sacramento and Washington.

Herrington, who could not be reached for comment, told Reagan in his letter that Meese, Clark and Anderson "were key implementors of your vision for America.

"We along with many others, fought the fights together and took the heat when your popularity was not high; we strategized and worked days and nights to bring about what you believed in and what we still believe," Herrington wrote.

"I had hoped to change your mind regarding their appointment, and barring that, I had hoped we might structure a public affairs board with their talents, ideals and loyalty that could carry on your legacy. I finally understood Tuesday at the Foundation meeting that that is not to be."

Herrington wrote his letter a quarter of a century after he began working for Reagan "as a volunteer in Ventura County in 1966" during Reagan's first gubernatorial campaign.

Herrington, who was an assistant Ventura County district attorney at the time, served as Reagan's assistant secretary of the Navy and energy secretary. He now practices law in Walnut Creek and until recently was chairman of the publishing company Harcourt Brace Jovanovich, Inc.

It was my understanding from reliable sources that the Reagan Foundation owed at least $6 million on the library at the time of its dedication on November 4, 1992. This amount has apparently now been raised or pledged. On the other hand, the foundation trustees were either unable or unwilling to raise the $15 million they had budgeted for a public affairs center, and that project was canceled as of June 29, 1993.

Originally, a much larger public affairs center was to have been the centerpiece of the library, museum, and public affairs complex. However, Mary Jane Wick (whom I once described as a "boutique" fundraiser), and Fred Ryan knew little or nothing about what a public affairs center does. The center had been proposed by Martin Anderson, Edwin Meese, and me when the whole complex was to be located at Stanford in association with the Hoover Institution. Now only former Presidents Jimmy Carter and Lyndon Johnson have public affairs centers or schools of public affairs. There is also the well-endowed Kennedy School of Government at Harvard University. (The Kennedy Presidential Library was originally to be situated at Harvard, but many objections were raised about the traffic congestion it would create in Cambridge. The library was built instead on the South Boston campus of the University of Massachusetts.)

The Deukmejian Papers

George Deukmejian, former California governor, donated his gubernatorial papers to the Hoover Institution in January 1991. He had already deposited his papers as a member of the state assembly (1962–66), a state senator (1966–78), and an attorney general of California (1979–83). During his campaign and governorship he visited the Hoover Institution several times and met with Martin Anderson, his chief of staff. Twice he met with me while he was governor. Hoover scholars briefed him both before he ran for governor and after he was elected, and he reappointed me to the University of California Board of Regents in March 1984.

Board of Overseers Chairman Malott, with the acquiescence of the other members of the Executive Committee and my successor, fired Steven Merksamer, the governor's first chief of staff, from the board after a minimum three-year term and did not reappoint him. Fortunately for them, Merksamer is not a vindictive man, because he could easily have persuaded his boss to donate the papers elsewhere.

People who were not at Hoover during my thirty years may not realize the extent to which we were always faced with the jealousy of many faculty members. My predecessors in the directorship had all been historians. I was the first Ph.D. in economics to head the Hoover Institution, and I always did my best to keep a good balance between scholars of economics and those of history, and to support other social sciences when we built and stocked the library and archives.

My successor, John Raisian, was a UCLA Ph.D. in labor economics, and things have gotten somewhat out of balance. Virtually all our historians have retired or are close to retirement, and only economists and political scientists are currently being appointed. Once again, as when I first came to Hoover, the library is used primarily by visitors.

8
Library and Archives

W HEN HE WAS CROSSING THE NORTH SEA LATE IN 1914, Herbert Hoover read an article by Andrew Dickson White, president of Cornell University, lamenting the difficulty of studying the French Revolution because of the disappearance of contemporary documents and fugitive materials. Mr. Hoover resolved not to let this happen to the records of the vast war that had just burst forth in Europe. His vision of collecting contemporary materials on World War I (as it was called much later) became a reality in 1919, first through his personal enterprise and later through a cooperative effort with Stanford faculty and friends, and with assistants all over Europe. Here began the Hoover Institution, and in the next seventy-five years it would become the preeminent national and international research library in the United States for the study of twentieth-century political, social, and economic affairs.

Since World War II, the United States government has made extensive use of the Hoover Institution's facilities. Because the collections on political and economic affairs frequently provide materials not available elsewhere in the country, federal departments have entrusted the Institution with special research projects. Hoover records, for instance, permitted the United States to map the location of Soviet forced labor camps for presentation to the United Nations in 1951. The collections are used by agencies such as the Department of State, the Central Intelligence Agency, the Department of Justice, the Federal Bureau of Investigation, and the military services. Congressional committees, members of Congress, and senators also request information or documents available only at the Institution. The microfilming of rare books and other materials for the research organizations of federal agencies has become a routine job for the Institution's staff. Much of Hoover's research material (journals, monographs, documents, and newspapers) has been microfilmed by the Institution for sale to libraries and scholars. This microfilm program began in the late 1960s and by 1989 offered seven hundred titles. The microfilm program greatly expanded the use of Hoover's research material, hitherto restricted only to people who visited the library—and what's more, it made money.

In another field of public service, the Hoover Institution has continually assisted public schools and civic organizations that request speakers or materials for programs on international relations or foreign countries. Hundreds of foreign visitors—scholars, political and trade-union leaders, government officials, businessmen, and journalists—come to the Institution every year. The government and foundation administrators who sponsor these trips often comment on the favorable impression foreign dignitaries carry away from their visits to the Hoover Institution.

Through research, publications, fellowships, reference assistance, and public service, the Institution carries out its functions, collecting the living documents of international affairs, organizing them, and making them available for use; fostering their use by qualified persons; and encouraging and aiding the spread of knowledge. The name of the Institution and the history of its development indicate in general what its interests are, but it is appropriate to stress those areas in which the holdings of the Institution are most distinguished.

The first is war—not only its military aspects, but also its political, economic, and social causes and consequences. Modern strategy, nuclear war, and arms limitation are an important part of the Institution's collection. The fields of propaganda and psychological warfare, and of the means of influencing public opinion, both in war and in peace, have long concerned the Institution.

The second major area is revolution. This embraces all the most important revolutionary movements of this century—nationalism, imperialism, socialism, communism, fascism, and national socialism.

The third area of great significance is peace—the whole range of diplomatic, economic, and cultural relations, and the achieving of peace through international administration and law.

A number of American libraries have been named after the men who donated their collections either to start the library's holdings or to give them a central focus. Notable among them are the Bancroft Library of the University of California, Berkeley, named for bookseller and scholar Hubert H. Bancroft, who collected material on the Western United States and Mexico; the Clements Library of the University of Michigan, named for American industrialist William L. Clements; and the Huntington Library at San Marino, California, named for Henry E. Huntington, a railway executive and financial expert who collected early English literature and Americana. But Hoover's donations outrank all of them in size, coverage, and importance.

American university libraries and public libraries did not generally collect contemporary manuscript material until the 1930s and 1940s, a decade or more after Hoover began his historical manuscript collection in 1914. No individual contributed as much material to a library or financed as much of the acquisition expenses to build a great library as did Herbert Hoover. He himself largely assembled the greatest private library and archive the world has ever seen. By 1989 it contained over 1.6 million volumes and millions of archival items.

Throughout his life Herbert Hoover was one of the Hoover Institution's greatest collectors, and he and his friends financed the library and its various research programs from the beginning. In January 1960 the entire Institution, especially the library and archives, was without the funds necessary to operate efficiently because Mr. Hoover had lost confidence in the director and in the Stanford faculty. I followed Hoover's own guidelines and those of previous directors in running the library. Once we had sufficient funds, I broadened the collecting activities of the library and archives according to the curators' suggestions for documenting new crises or awakened interests. By collecting materials on World War II and the postwar period, Agnes Peterson (who first joined the Institution in 1952) was able to turn the earlier Western European Collection into an internationally known resource which covered the early years of the twentieth century. In 1961 a full-time African curator (Peter Duignan of the Stanford history department) was appointed to collect on colonial Africa, the end of colonialism, and newly independent Africa. Then in 1963 the curatorship of the Middle East Collection was upgraded to a full-time position, and the Latin American Collection was expanded.

Takeover Attempts

From about 1920 on, two ambitious directors of the Stanford Main Library system tried to take over the Hoover Library. The first was librarian George Clark, who believed that a librarian's job was to buy and catalog books. He was succeeded by another librarian, Van Patten. When I was appointed director on January 1, 1960, I was a thirty-five-year-old economist with a doctorate from Harvard who had directed research at the American Enterprise Association. I was also an unabashed nineteenth-century liberal and free marketeer at a time when Keynesian economics and twentieth-century liberal-left ideas dominated academia. At that time, the Stanford Main Library staff still coveted control of the Hoover Library. I managed to fend off their takeover attempts while greatly increasing the size and the importance of Hoover's library. All these librarians were empire builders, jealous of the international reputation of the Hoover Institution.[1]

In 1998 the Stanford administration, under strong pressure from the expansion-minded head of the Main Library (renamed the Green Library after a major donor), tried to cut some $2 million from the total university funds earmarked for the Hoover Library and to stop the Hoover Institution from collecting anything but archives. It failed, but I view this as the opening stage of another attempt by the university to take over the whole Hoover Institution, lock, stock, and endowments.

Collecting for the Library
and Archives After 1960

As our financial resources grew, we budgeted more funds for acquisitions, staff, and collecting trips by the curators. The Special Acquisitions

1. The references to George Clark and Van Patten as librarians come in part from Charles B. Burdick, *Ralph Lutz and the Hoover Institution,* chap. 5: "Struggle and Stimulus."

Fund, established through the generosity of the Andrew Mellon Foundation, allowed us to buy important collections when they came onto the market. Just as Hoover himself had done, we raised monies for curatorial acquisition trips, the primary means of procuring large private collections and political ephemera (which seldom fall into book dealers' hands). Throughout my tenure as director, I encouraged curators to travel and to renew or establish contacts in the changing circumstances of, say, Africa or Taiwan or the Middle East. Thanks to Hoover's reputation, we were even able to send collectors into Communist China, Russia, Taiwan, and South Africa under apartheid.

I depended on the curatorial staff to make the case for collecting trips, which were always expensive and often long (averaging four to six weeks). They reported that they were usually under surveillance in communist countries and in South Africa, and some collections were actually stolen before they could be shipped. One collector, Latin America and Brazil scholar Donald Chilcote, was arrested in Angola by Portuguese officials for having in his possession political literature of African liberation groups. It took a letter from Mr. Hoover to get Chilcote out of jail— but he could not salvage the political ephemera he had collected for us. In the event, we collected more and published a documentary history, *Emerging Nationalism in Portuguese Africa,* along with a bibliography of Hoover's large collection of liberation literature.

A curator's reception, of course, was likely to vary with the political temperature of the Cold War or the particular foreign government's attitude toward the United States. We learned from Hoover and his "historical sleuths" to anticipate important political developments and to collect wherever trouble broke out. For example, in 1946 President Truman appointed Herbert Hoover to coordinate the world effort to relieve the famines that followed World War II. Hoover visited thirty-nine countries, and as on previous humanitarian trips, he acquired important documents (for instance, on the Chinese Nationalists' war against the communists). Again, local representatives were appointed to collect materials in troubled areas—Africa, the Middle East, Latin America. We increased our acquisition budgets and curatorial trips, and encouraged curators to enlist locals to collect on our behalf. We usually had to pay only purchasing and mailing costs, but in some cases we left money with our agents so they could buy important collections and cover their expenses. In South Africa, much political writing was proscribed, so purchases had to be made clandestinely and the material shipped out in diplomatic pouches or under false labels. Microfilm of the records of the South African Communist party was shipped as "missionary journals"!

Collecting for the library was not passive, not a matter merely of awaiting the donation of manuscripts and files. Documents were not acquired to be stored and to gather dust. Hoover curators were always alert to collect records of important contemporary events and eager to publish documentary histories based on these collections. My job was to find funds for this collecting and publishing. The Hoover Institution developed the most effective collection in the United States on Western colonialism in sub-Saharan Africa. In 1961 Curator Peter Duignan began saving the records of black resistance to white rule that led, between 1972 and 1977, to the production of the four-volume *From Protest to Challenge: A Documentary History of African Politics in South Africa, 1882–1964*. This effort was acclaimed by the *Times Literary Supplement* as "a feat of such distinction that it is hard to call to mind a single parallel or precedent." During a trip to South Africa in 1961–62, Duignan had established a network of agents for collecting materials for the project. Books, pamphlets, typewritten and handwritten items, and thousands of pieces of political ephemera on South Africa were collected and became the basis of his four-volume documentary history, dedicated to the African people of South Africa. In 1962–63 Hoover provided a grant for Thomas Karis, a professor at CCNY, to index twenty-five reels of film—18,500 text pages—of the first "treason trial." This project was subsequently joined to other collected material and became a full documentary history, with Prof. Gwendolen M. Carter of Northwestern University joining Karis as general editor of the series. Sheridan Johns III and Gail M. Gerhart edited individual volumes. All four editors made repeated trips to American, British, and South African collections, libraries, and archives for additional source material. In 1987 these valuable volumes were brought out in paperback to make them more available to the South African reading public, which was so concerned with the ongoing struggle for black rights in South Africa. The costs of editing and printing these complex volumes were so high that the University of California Press declined an invitation to co-publish the series.

The expansion into the African field did not lead us to neglect the other collections. Notable acquisitions in Western European documentation included the resources of the Allied Commission for Austria during the period 1945–55; the stenographic protocols of the congresses of the French Mouvement Republicain Populaire, 1945–62; a microfilm copy of the NSDAP Hauptarchiv, the main historical archives of the Nazi party; and the papers of Louis Loucheur (1871–1931), one-time French minister of war, armaments, and reconstruction. Documents on the Third International included the unpublished papers and memoirs of former communist leaders such as Henri Barbé, a member of the Presidium of the Comintern (1928–30), and Albert Vassart, a representative of the French Communist party to the Comintern (1934–35).

In 1960, thanks to Mr. Hoover's reputation and some vigorous fundraising, the Honorable Chen Cheng, vice president of the Republic of China, permitted the Hoover Institution to microfilm some 1,170 documents on the period of the Kiangsi Soviet (1931–34). At the time this collection was the most important file of Chinese Communist party (CCP) records in a Western library. In addition, 150 Chinese communist publications relating to the 1945–49 period were microfilmed in Taipei. These unique records, issued for use only within the CCP, contain a wealth of data on the communist struggle for power.

Hundreds of gifts have enriched the collections each year. We received an extensive collection of books, pamphlets, and files on the Far East and communism from Mrs. Alfred Kohlberg in 1961. Her late husband, a long-time student of Chinese affairs, was an American business executive, national chairman of the American Jewish League Against Communism, chairman of the American China Policy Association, and member of the board of the Institute of Pacific Relations. His collection includes correspondence, newsletters, clippings, and other printed matter relating to communist influence in the United States, China, and other parts of Asia, and to the anti-communist movements in the United States.

In 1963 we raised funds for the systematic collecting of material on Latin America, a process that had been interrupted in the 1940s and

1950s. Our searches focused on Cuba, Argentina, Bolivia, Brazil, Chile, Colombia, Mexico, and Venezuela. Theodore Draper was made a research fellow in May 1963 so he could complete his monumental history of the U.S. Communist party. Though he never finished that history, he did write a brilliant book on Castro and Castroism and helped us collect rare Cuban material. In fact, it is thanks in part to Draper that we became the leading collecting center on Castro and on Castroism in Latin America.

During most of the 1950s and the early 1960s, Witold S. Sworakowski was both an assistant director and a curator of the Eastern Europe and Soviet Union Collection. Professor Sworakowski was one of the great collectors and bibliographers of the Hoover Institution. Perhaps his most impressive feat was obtaining, in 1963, Boris Nicolaevsky's library on European socialist revolutionary movements—notably Menshevism, Bolshevism, and communism—in the face of intense competition from Harvard, Columbia, and Indiana universities. We outbid them, and Boris Nicolaevsky was paid $70,000 for his collection, with an additional $100,000 set aside to bring Nicolaevsky and Anna Bourguina to the Hoover Institution as curators of the collection (at $20,000 per annum for five years). The Nicolaevsky Collection included more than twenty thousand books and other publications, plus scores of archives, manuscripts, and letters dating from 1901. In the collection are papers of Trotsky's and Bukharin's; letters of Lenin's, Zinoviev's, and Andreev's; and a collection—discovered in 1983—of over thirty linear feet of correspondence between Trotsky and his son, Lev Sedov. These letters, previously thought to be lost or stolen by the KGB, were identified by Jan Van Heijenhoort, then translated and annotated.

Because processing all these acquisitions is costly and time-consuming, we don't always know exactly what we have. That is why it was twenty years before we fully realized what a treasure the Nicolaevsky Collection was. The announcement of this discovery in 1987 attracted scholarly interest from around the world and was described by Hoover archivists as "an exceptionally important new historical source." The most significant single work is Trotsky's draft of his *History of the Russian Revolution,* published in 1931. The collection also contains 485 family letters, including 254 from Trotsky to his son, which provide a rare window on the author's private life. It also includes extensive drafts of more than five hundred books, articles, and circular letters written by Trotsky, amounting to a substantial manuscript record of most of his major and many of his minor writings from 1929 to 1936. One "remarkable portion" of the manuscript is 1.5 linear feet containing drafts of chapters omitted from the published version of his *History of the Russian Revolution.* The single most important item is a completed chapter, "Soglashateli" ("The Compromisers"), dealing with the abortive Kerensky-Krasnov counterrevolution of November 1917. In an article published in the April 1987 issue of the *American Historical Review,* assistant archivist Dale Reed and archival specialist Michael Jakobson note that almost all the material at Hoover "clearly passed, directly or indirectly, from Sedov to Nicolaevsky." But "for whatever reason, neither Nicolaevsky nor his wife, Anna Bourguina, made known during their lifetimes the existence of the Trotsky-Sedov papers in their custody." Only after Bourguina's death could the archives staff, with the support of the National Endowment for the Humanities, undertake a comprehensive arrangement and description of all the rich material in the collection. As part of the purchase agreement, we received permission to sell duplicates of Nicolaevsky's books in our possession. These brought in so much money that we nearly recouped the total cost of the collection, $170,000. This was key to our establishment of the Ralph Lutz Special Acquisitions fund.

The vast Nicolaevsky Collection occupies more than 330 linear feet, and has been the source of several documentaries in a series on the Menshevik movement. Prof. Vladimir Brovkin has discovered and edited a series of letters and reports by leading Mensheviks, describing how the Bolsheviks censored and suppressed opposition movements between 1918 and 1922.

Witold Sworakowski's collecting genius was not confined to Eastern Europe and the Soviet Union. He bought or received as gifts numerous archives on Western Europe, Turkey, and the United States. Sworakowski retired in 1969 and died in 1979. Dr. Richard F. Staar replaced him as associate director for Library and Archival Operations and served in that position until 1981, when he became U.S. ambassador to the Mutual and Balanced Force Reduction Negotiations in Vienna, Austria.

Growth

The 1960s and early 1970s were a troubled period in Stanford's history. The Hoover Institution, like other organizations, had to cope with bitter hostility from the militant left and suffered physical damage and verbal abuse from radical faculty and students. Nevertheless, the Institution grew remarkably during this period. The archives grew as well. The gubernatorial papers of Ronald Reagan came in 1975, followed by the papers from his 1976 and 1980 presidential campaigns, and the papers from the 1980–81 presidential transition teams. The collection consists of papers accumulated while he was governor of California, including correspondence, cabinet proceedings, speeches, notes, legislation, campaign material, press releases, printed matter, videotapes, films, and phonotapes relating to California politics and government. They cover the period between 1967 and 1975. The collection also includes matter relating to Reagan's candidacy for the 1976 Republican presidential nomination, with records of Citizens for Reagan and of various California state executive agencies.

After receiving Governor Reagan's gift of his papers, the archives received many new collections. In 1975, a $30,000 donative sale was made to the Hoover Institution of Jay Lovestone's papers. Lovestone was the secretary-general of the U.S. Communist party from 1927 to 1929 and secretary-general of the Communist party opposition, later known as the Independent Labor League of America, from 1929 to 1940. Subsequently, he became the executive secretary of the Free Trade Union Committee of the American Federation of Labor. His papers consist of correspondence, reports, memoranda, bulletins, clippings, serial issues, pamphlets, other printed matter, and photographs relating to the Communist International, the communist movement in the United States and elsewhere, communist influence in foreign trade unions, and organized labor movements in the United States and abroad from 1906 to 1989.

Meanwhile, relations with Stanford University grew closer on one level through joint appointments to the Hoover Institution and various academic departments. Some Hoover curators also served as curators for corresponding programs in the university library system. From 1969 to 1977 G.K. Hall and Company of Boston completed the filming and publication in eighty-eight volumes of the Hoover Institution's entire library catalog. Publication of the catalog reduced the need for special bibliographies of Hoover's rare holdings, and fewer bibliographical publications were produced after that. Hall's filming of the Institution's card catalog was in part a security measure. During the student unrest in the late 1960s, the university library's card catalog was damaged when honey and red ink were poured over drawers and cards were ripped out. Student radicals, led by Maoist faculty member Bruce Franklin, tried on several occasions to occupy the Hoover Tower in which the public catalog was located. They did not succeed in taking over the building, but fires were set in some of the lavatories.

Amid these troubled times a new Hoover collection was begun, covering national, regional, and local publications of the various movements and coalitions known as the New Left. A member of the local radical group Venceremos was given a budget of $25,000 a year to collect New Left material. He did a good job but left after two years to set up his own radical institute in Palo Alto. (I withhold his name in case the knowledge that he worked for the Hoover Library would detract from his standing in leftist groups.)

In 1969 the Institution also initiated a consortium of fifteen western colleges and universities to coordinate library acquisitions policies. The Hoover Library was to be the central site in the western United States for international studies. Unfortunately, after receiving two grants from the federal government, the consortium failed to secure continued support and was disbanded in the mid-1970s. Yet the concept was farsighted and has now become a reality through computer networking. Hoover's library continued to serve historical scholarship by further expanding its archival collections, especially those on the United States, Africa, and the Middle East.

The Raymond Moley Collection was acquired as a donative sale in 1968 for $140,000, paid off at $14,000 per annum over the following ten years. Moley was an adviser to Franklin D. Roosevelt from 1932 to 1933, U.S. assistant secretary of state, editor of *Today,* and contributing editor of *Newsweek.* His collection includes correspondence, diaries, reports, memoranda, speeches, notes, printed matter, and photographs relating to criminology, the administration of justice in the United States, the assimilation of immigrants, U.S. politics, the presidential campaign of 1932, the FDR administration, and correspondence between Mr. Moley and Richard M. Nixon.

By 1989 Hoover Library contained the most extensive collections on modern China and the Soviet Union to be found in the Western world, as well as impressive resources on almost every major region. Only the Indian subcontinent and the Pacific Basin (aside from China, Taiwan, and South Korea) remained outside the library's sphere of operations. Hoover curators, archivists, and librarians continued to deal with a large and varied body of manuscripts, archives, books, serials, and ephemeral materials in some thirty-five languages.

General funds supported the library, but my associates and I continually worked to raise endowment funds for library operations. The William H. Noble bequest, over half of which was put into library endowment, is the largest endowment fund supporting the library. Income from it has been crucial to the development of library programs at the Hoover Institution, especially to the acquisition of special collections. The Herman Axelbank Film Collection on Russia and the USSR, 1890–1970, is one such collection.

The Hoover Institution drew worldwide attention when it acquired Axelbank's films. According to one film expert, it is "undoubtedly the largest and most valuable film collection devoted to the subject of revolutionary and pre-revolutionary Russia in the Western Hemisphere, and probably in the Western world." Over 250,000 feet of film document activities of the czar, his family, and his associates; the two Russian revolutions of 1917 and their leaders; the Provisional and Soviet governments; Soviet military forces in World War II; and Russian culture and economy. The collection includes film of the March 1921 Kronstadt mutiny, the first purge trials of social revolutionaries in June 1922, and many political figures of the time (for example, Kerensky, Lenin, Trotsky, Zinoviev, Kamenev, and Stalin).

For the library and archives, the late 1970s and the 1980s were a period of expansion. The 1987–88 budget anticipated an annual expenditure of $13.9 million, a fivefold increase over the 1971–72 figure, at a time when many other American academic institutions were wrestling with financial difficulties. The bulk of this income derived from individual, foundation, and corporate gifts (37 percent), and endowment income (30 percent). About 26 percent came from Stanford University, and only 4 percent from the federal government. In that budget, 93 percent of the Institution's funds was dedicated to research, library, archives, and the Hoover Press. Only 7 percent was allocated to administrative costs.

In 1988 the Far Eastern Foundation of the Republic of China pledged $3 million to establish the Sun Yat-sen Endowment for Advanced Chinese Research Studies at the Hoover Institution. This gift was an important step toward significant expansion of the Hoover Institution's program of studies on Northeast Asia, East Asia, and the Pacific Rim countries. Douglas Ton Hsu, director of the Far Eastern Foundation, wrote to me, "I believe that this program under your supervision, will certainly improve the mutual understanding between the United States and the Republic of China."

As a result of archival solicitation efforts in the late 1970s, many collections were received from cabinet officials and other prominent members of the Ford and Reagan administrations. We were given the papers of George P. Shultz, secretary of state 1982–89 (the first secretary of state to place his documents in a California library), secretary of the treasury 1972–74, director of the Office of Management and Budget 1970–72, and secretary of labor 1969–70. Shultz's collection includes correspondence, photographs, and memorabilia relating to American domestic policy and foreign relations, especially during the presidential administrations of Richard M. Nixon and Ronald Reagan. He also donated records he accumulated as president of Bechtel Corporation.

Carla A. Hills deposited her papers with us in 1977 and added to them in 1986. Hills, a 1955 Stanford graduate, served as a U.S. assistant attorney general, as secretary of housing and urban development from 1975 to 1977, and as a trade ambassador for President Bush from 1989 through 1993. Her papers include correspondence, reports, memoranda, speeches, and printed matter relating to housing and community planning and development in the United States, along with material on civil litigation involving the U.S. government—especially lawsuits involving President Richard M. Nixon—and the activities of the Republican party, the American Bar Association, and the Alliance to Save Energy.

Other collections include:

- The papers of Robert T. Hartmann, a 1938 Stanford graduate, who was a counselor to the president from 1974 to 1977.
- The papers of Milton Friedman, covering the years from 1930 to 1988, originally acquired in 1977. Friedman taught economics at the University of Chicago from 1946 to 1976, and his papers include writings, correspondence, notes, statistics, printed matter, sound recordings, and motion picture film relating to economic theory, economic conditions in the United States, and government economic policy.
- The papers of Warren Nutter, an American economist who became assistant secretary of defense for International Security Affairs from 1969 to 1973. An expert on the Soviet economy, he was the first scholar to prove Soviet economic data were false. His papers were given to the archives in July 1981 as a gift from his widow, Jane Nutter.

In 1977 I obtained endowments for two subject collections: the John D. Crummey Peace Collection and the Paul and Jean Hanna Collection. The Crummey Collection, named after the founder of FMC Corporation, contains a vast number of books, periodicals, newspapers, and two million pages of archival documentation relating to peace, peace conferences, the founding of the League of Nations and the United Nations, pacifism, disarmament, isolationism, conscientious objectors, and antiwar activism. The Hanna Collection on the Role of Education in 20th Century Society was started in 1976 by the Hannas with the objective of explaining how education—both formal and informal—powerfully influences the development of societies and the interaction between societies. The Hanna Collection has become one of the most important collections of its kind in the United States. Its holdings include papers of U.S. government officials and education groups; the records of the International Council for Educational Development dealing with international education and education in developing countries; and the papers of the American Educational Research Association, the largest and most important U.S. scholarly organization concerned with research on education.

Dr. Paul R. Hanna was the Lee L. Jacks Professor of Education at

Stanford University and a Senior Research Fellow at the Hoover Institution. He was the founder and first director of the Stanford International Development Education Center (SIDEC) and undertook numerous missions abroad for Stanford, the U.S. Departments of State and Defense, UNESCO, foreign governments, and private foundations and agencies. He participated in national efforts to create educational policy. Jean S. Hanna was for many years a teacher of English in this country and abroad, and was co-author and editor with her husband of several widely acclaimed textbook series. The endowment they established in 1979 provides funds for both a curatorship and a secretary.

Successful fundraising enabled the Institution to expand its staff. In 1983 important additions were made to the library staff: Dr. John B. Dunlop served as associate director for the library and archives until 1987. Middle East bibliographer Edward Jajko and conservation officer Judith Fortson were also added. Latin American curator Joseph Bingaman retired in 1985, and William Ratliff replaced him. Ratliff received his Ph.D. in Chinese and Latin American history from the University of Washington and has been affiliated with the Hoover Institution since 1968. For more than two decades he has written on Latin American politics and U.S.-Latin American relations, taught courses at Stanford and other Bay Area universities, and—as scholar, curator, journalist, and government consultant—and made fifteen trips to Latin America. Charles Palm, head librarian and archivist, was appointed associate director for the library and archives in 1987. A graduate of Stanford, Palm has been a member of the Institution's staff since 1971.

Conservation and Preservation

Herbert Hoover was especially concerned with the collection of material that might otherwise disappear forever. This farsighted interest in saving ephemeral materials was even more important than he might have realized. Throughout this century, especially during politically difficult times, most published materials have been printed on paper of poor quality, subject to acid hydrolysis which causes brittleness, discoloration, and sometimes disintegration of the paper. The Hoover Institution's library and archival holdings are particularly vulnerable to such problems of deterioration because they were produced largely during the twentieth century—"the era of bad paper."

For this reason, the Institution made conservation one of its programmatic priorities. The Hoover Memorial Building included a carefully designed conservation laboratory, an indication of the Hoover Institution's recognition of the problems of preservation and of its commitment to preserve its holdings and make them available for scholarly researchers, both present and future. The foremost concerns of the conservation program, which began in 1983 with the hiring of Judith Fortson, have been: (1) preventive measures, such as basic repair of papers and bindings, proper housing and handling, and environmental controls; and (2) the transfer of information to more permanent media through microfilming and preservation photocopying.

In addition to these ongoing programs, in the late 1980s several special projects furthered the program's goals and extended the useful life of significant segments of the collections. The first of these projects, funded by the U.S. Department of Education, addressed the needs of the Institution's poster collection and its rare newspaper holdings. The first stage of the poster work consisted of preparing photographic slides of all unique and variant posters. The posters themselves were then sealed in polyester and stored in specially constructed boxes of acid-free corrugated cardboard. Selected items received applied treatment in the lab, and all photographed posters are also being cataloged and indexed. Individual entries will be available on-line.

The second component of the Poster and Newspaper Preservation Project was the microfilming of many rare newspapers in the Institution's holdings. Newspapers filmed in this and other projects have full on-line catalog entries in RLIN (Research Libraries Information Network) as well as in the public catalog of the Hoover Institution, and they are listed in *Newspapers in Microform*. Used copies of the film are available both in-house and through interlibrary loan.

Another project funded by the Department of Education was designed to preserve and catalog the Institution's rare collection of contemporary published sources on the Russian revolutions, covering material on the first revolution of 1905, the 1917 revolutions, the Provisional Government (1917), and the civil war (1921–23). Published during an era of intense political turmoil, these items are on paper of *very* poor quality.

The general Russian collections are the concern of another special project. Funded in part by the National Endowment for the Humanities, its major focus was the microfilming of unusual and fragile materials. This project included, for example, the Okhrana Collection, which consists of the records of the Paris-based branch of the imperial Russian secret police responsible for intelligence operations abroad in the period 1883–1917. Over a thousand Russian pamphlets were also selected for filming, including the Russian Mass Education Collection—most of which was published between 1919 and 1925—and pamphlets from the Soviet Minority Languages Collection of the 1920s and 1930s. Some runs of émigré publications were also filmed, as were Russian/Soviet newspapers chosen from the Hoover Institution files. In addition to microfilming, the NEH-supported project included rehousing the photographic holdings on Russia and copying the nitrate negatives.

The National Endowment for the Humanities also provided support for a cooperative Research Libraries Group project in which the Hoover Institution participated. This microfilming of endangered Chinese research materials included monographs and serials published between 1880 and 1949 in four major areas in which the Hoover Institution is particularly strong: modern Chinese history, economics and land agriculture, education, and literature. All microfilmed items have been cataloged on-line in the Research Libraries Information Network, a national computerized database.

Adding to the Collections

During the 1980s we collected the papers of many men and women who helped shape the modern world. In 1987 the papers of Sir Karl Popper, internationally acclaimed philosopher on natural and social science, were acquired for $75,000. Born in Vienna in 1902, Popper was widely regarded as one of the greatest living philosophers. "The papers reflect the breadth of Popper's scholarly interests and his profound influence on political philosophy, history and philosophy of science, and art criticism," noted W. W. Bartley III, a former Senior Research Fellow at the

Institution and Popper's designated biographer. Bartley referred to the Popper archive as "one of the two or three most important intellectual archives of the century, one whose acquisition will benefit many members of the Stanford community." Popper, professor emeritus of logic and scientific method at the University of London. was knighted in 1965. His major published works include *The Open Society and Its Enemies* (1945) and *The Poverty of Historicism* (1957). His first book, *Logik der Forschung (The Logic of Scientific Discovery)*, was published in 1935. His works have been translated into twenty-five languages.

The Popper Collection contains extensive correspondence with philosophers, historians, physicists, biologists, mathematical logicians, and classicists. There are exchanges of great historical value: Popper and Erwin Schroedinger debating the "arrow of time," letters on the early versions of the Einstein-Podolsky-Rosen experiment, and an extensive cache of letters between Popper and Sir Ernst Gombrich regarding cultural history and psychology. Other correspondents include Bertrand Russell, G. E. Moore, Rudolf Carnap, Hans Hahn, Kurt Goedel, Fritz Machlup, and Gottfried von Haberler. The acquisition of the Popper Collection presents exciting possibilities for students of British social and intellectual life, in particular the enrichment of scholarship that resulted from the emigration of European intellectuals fleeing the Nazi menace. The presence of the Popper Collection at Hoover will further enhance Stanford's ability to document the traditions of contemporary scientific thought.

One of the largest files in the collections is an exchange of letters between Popper and F. A. Hayek (the Austrian-born English economist and philosopher) that extends over fifty years. The letters record debates between Nobel laureate Hayek and Popper on the limits of rationality, the methodology of the social sciences and economics, the conditions for the creation of a free and open society, and political science. Other major acquisitions in the 1980s include the papers of Hayek, Sen. S. I. Hayakawa, and Dixie Lee Ray, Washington State governor; the papers of Gleb Struve; the papers of Pierre Marie Gallois, chief adviser on national defense to Gen. Charles de Gaulle; the papers of Maj.-Gen. Edward G. Lansdale, special assistant on counterinsurgency to Ambassador Henry Cabot Lodge, 1965–67; and the papers of Ellsworth Bunker, ambassador to South Vietnam, 1967–68.

Governor Ray's collection was given in March 1982. Ms. Ray was a member and chairman of the U.S. Atomic Energy Commission during the early 1970s; assistant secretary of state for oceans, international environmental and scientific affairs in 1975; and governor of the state of Washington from 1977 to 1981. Her large collection includes papers, slides, phonotapes, videotapes, motion picture reels, phonograph records, and other memorabilia.

Samuel Ichiye Hayakawa was a Japanese-American educator and semanticist who served as president of San Francisco State University and was a U.S. senator from 1976 to 1982. His papers were received in November 1982 with increments added till May 1988. They consist of correspondence, memoranda, reports, government documents, clippings, other printed matter, photographs, phonotapes, and videotapes relating to many aspects of foreign relations and domestic politics.

The papers of former California Governor George Deukmejian (discussed in chapter 7) were deposited at the Hoover Institution in January 1983, and will remain a restricted collection until February 28, 2041.

Albert Coady Wedemeyer—general, U.S. Army, and commanding general, U.S. forces in China—originally deposited his papers at the Hoover Institution in 1983. It was increased by increments received until 1991. The collection consists of orders, plans, memoranda, reports, correspondence, speeches, clippings, other printed matter, photographs, and memorabilia relating to Allied strategic planning during World War II, to military operations in China, to U.S. foreign policy in China, and to post-war U.S. politics and foreign relations.

Friedrich August von Hayek, who won a joint Nobel Prize in economics with Gunnar Myrdal of Sweden in 1974, deposited his papers in our archives in January 1986. Hayek was president of the Mont Pelerin Society from its founding in 1947 till 1962, and his collection includes correspondence, conference papers, and conference programs relating primarily to meetings of the Mont Pelerin Society. However, it also includes material on laissez-faire economics and associated concepts of liberty. The material is in English and German.

One of the many distinguishing features of the Hoover Institution program for collections has been its emphasis on revolutionary movements and upheavals. Hoover collectors were quick to develop the largest collection in the United States on African nationalist and liberation movements, on Islamic fundamentalism, and on the Polish Solidarity Movement in the 1980s, including some fifteen hundred underground serial and brochure titles and over ten thousand individual items. For the holdings on Central America, a major new collection on the Mexican Communist party was acquired—internal party speeches and papers, complete runs of major party publications, Comintern documents, and other rare materials relating to communist and other left-wing political organizations in Mexico and to Soviet involvement in Latin American affairs over the past forty years.

The successful acquisitions program of the 1980s was matched by important new initiatives in library automation. Under the leadership of Senior Fellow and East Asian curator Ramon H. Myers, the East Asia Library was one of a few libraries selected to become a site for the installation of a computerized system of bibliographic control of materials in the Chinese, Japanese, and Korean languages. Under the direction of archivist Charles Palm, a leader in the area of archival automation, the Hoover Institution joined the Cornell, Yale, and Stanford libraries, and the Research Libraries Group in a pioneering effort to develop a computerized national database for the exchange of archival information. When the project was completed in 1985, records for all four thousand collections in the archives were available on-line to scholars across the country.

The archives contain more than sixty collections of papers documenting U.S. public opinion and intellectual history: the papers of *New York Herald-Tribune* columnist Mark Sullivan, of *Fortune* editor Herbert Solow, and of *Harper's* editor Lewis Lapham. No treatment of American intellectual life since the end of World II would be complete without reference to Nobel laureate Milton Friedman and distinguished physicist Edward Teller, both of whose collections are in the Hoover Institution Archives. Other major economists whose papers are in the archives include Fritz Machlup, Benjamin Rogge, Dan Throop Smith, Murray Weidenbaum, Roger Freeman, and William Niskanen. The Hoover Institution Archives is also the repository for the files of the Mont Pelerin Society, an international organization of economists, public figures, and journalists dedicated to the study of free market economics. (See *The History of the Mont Pelerin Society* by Max Hartwell of Nuffield College, Oxford.)

Documentation on American radicalism is older but equally extensive and includes the papers of Jay Lovestone and Bertram D. Wolfe, and
those of Benjamin Gitlow, co-founder of the Communist Labor party.
These papers and those of Sidney Hook and Joseph Freeman (editor of
New Masses and *Partisan Review*) are also rich sources for materials on
the undercurrents of U.S. intellectual history throughout this century.

The Hoover Institution Press and Library

The Hoover Institution Press, founded in 1962, publishes scholarly books
on a broad range of subjects relating to twentieth-century history and
domestic and foreign affairs, as well as bibliographic and documentary
works. Under the direction of an executive editor assisted by specialists
in design, production, and marketing, the press published or co-published an average of twenty books a year. In 1987, sixty-eight Hoover
Press books were adopted for classroom use in over two hundred eighty
courses. There were over three hundred forty-five books in print from
the Hoover Press, and an additional eighty or so were co-published with
other presses. Since 1960, when I became director, over four hundred
fifty books have been produced by the Institution and some one hundred fifty more have been co-published. Most of these books were based,
wholly or in part, on material collected by the Hoover Library and
Archives.

The Hoover Institution has a long tradition, encouraged by Herbert
Hoover, of publishing books based on documents deposited in the Institution. The first documentary studies appeared in the 1930s and dealt
with Germany and the Soviet Union. In the late 1950s and early 1960s,
documentary studies appeared on Occupied France in World War II and
on the 1917 Kerensky government in Russia. In the 1970s two major
documentary series appeared on Portuguese African nationalist movements and on African political opposition to white rule. Then a new
series was begun called Hoover Archival Documentaries. Its purpose was
to shed new light on important events concerning the United States and
the history of the twentieth century. Several volumes in the Hoover
Archival Documentaries series are autobiographies, diaries, and letters
deposited with us for safekeeping. According to series editor Robert

Hessen, deputy archivist, these materials might otherwise have been censored or suppressed. An eyewitness diary of the Russian Revolution was entrusted to Frank Golder in 1922 when he was there to gather materials for the new Hoover War Library. The author, Iurii V. Got'e, was a young historian who feared the Bolsheviks would confiscate his manuscript. It lay unread until Prof. Terence Emmons discovered it in 1982. His translation, *Time of Troubles,* was published by Princeton University Press and sponsored by the Hoover Institution.

Another recent discovery is the autobiography of Edward Osóbka-Morawski, premier of the coalition government in Poland after World War II. He wrote his memoirs in 1951 at the urging of the Polish Military History Institute. When he realized they would be suppressed, he arranged to have a copy smuggled to the West. Prof. Andrew Michta of Rhodes College translated the manuscript, to which annotations were added from the papers of deputy premier Stanislaw Mikolajczyk (also in the Hoover Archives).

A unique inside look at Soviet-Chinese relations is found in the diary of Chang Chia-ao, the chief negotiator with the Soviet Union for the return of Manchuria to Chinese control. The translation of *Last Chance in Manchuria* was edited by Donald Gillin and Ramon H. Myers.

American diplomacy and foreign policy are the subjects of several volumes in the archival series: *Negotiating While Fighting: The Diary of Admiral C. Turner Joy at the Korean Armistice Conference,* edited by Allan E. Goodman; *The Diplomacy of Frustration: The Manchurian Crisis of 1931–33 as Revealed in the Papers of Stanley K. Hornbeck,* edited by Justus Doenecke; and *Berlin Alert: The Memories and Reports of Truman Smith,* edited by Robert Hessen. This last book revealed that during Col. Charles A. Lindbergh's famous visits to Berlin during the 1930s, he was engaged in intelligence gathering for the U.S. War Department. A volume drawn from the papers of the America First Committee, the leading anti-interventionist group in 1940–41, was refused by the Library of Congress in 1943. The committee's papers were secured for the Hoover Institution Archives through the personal efforts of Herbert Hoover, who wanted to safeguard them and ensure their availability to future historians.

Of American men-at-arms who commanded major theaters of operations in World War II, only one survived in 1989: four-star Gen. Albert C. Wedemeyer. Drawing from the Wedemeyer papers at the Hoover Institution, Keith E. Eiler assembled Wedemeyer's writings in a Hoover archival documentary entitled *Wedemeyer on War and Peace.* The book includes his reports on his training in the 1930s at the Kriegsakademie in Berlin, the 1941 Victory Plan for mobilizing the American war effort by concentrating first on Europe, the famous 1947 Wedemeyer Report on China, and other documents that provide a picture of one of the most talented American generals of this century.

9
Public Service

T HE HOOVER INSTITUTION HAS A LONG TRADITION OF PUBLIC
service. Herbert Hoover himself set its example, spending the
last fifty years of his life in public service. A highly successful
mining engineer then approaching his fortieth birthday, he was in England at the outbreak of the Great War in August 1914. Quickly he helped
Walter Hines Page, the American ambassador to the Court of St. James's,
bring home Americans who were stranded in England without funds.
As Hoover reported in his memoirs, "I did not realize it at the time but
I was on the slippery road of public life."

Tiny Belgium, scene of so much frontline carnage, suffered terribly
during the war. At the invitation of the Belgian government, Hoover took
charge of the Committee for the Relief of Belgium. He and his co-workers
saved millions from starvation. When the United States entered the war
in 1917, he returned to Washington, D.C., to serve as the U.S. food administrator for President Wilson. When World War I ended with an Allied
victory on November 11, 1918, Hoover was asked to take an important
role in Woodrow Wilson's delegation to the Paris Peace Conference. As
noted in Chapter 1, it was here that he personally collected one of the
Institution's most valued treasures, the Paris Peace Conference Collection, and founded what became the Hoover Institution on War, Revolution and Peace.

At President Wilson's request, Hoover went on to direct the American Relief Administration, which functioned from 1919 to 1923. He and
his associates again were successful in saving countless people, many of
them children, from starvation. In addition, his collector/historian

associates Ralph Lutz and Frank Golder and their co-workers collected enormous quantities of rare documents and books.

In March 1921 Hoover was named secretary of commerce in the Warren Harding administration, and he held that post until he resigned to run for president in 1928. He ran for the nation's highest office in 1928, becoming the only Stanford graduate ever to become president of the United States, serving from March 1929 to March 1933.

When the Russians occupied the Baltic states and attacked Finland in the winter of 1940, Hoover organized a food assistance program for these small democracies. It had to be terminated when the United States entered World War II in December 1941.

In the immediate postwar years, Hoover undertook a number of missions for President Truman. After a worldwide trip to study famine conditions in the defeated nations and elsewhere, he urged President Truman to hasten food to Japan, Germany, and Italy. Truman did, and in 1948 he appointed Hoover to chair what became known as the first Hoover Commission. In 1953 President Eisenhower appointed him chairman of the Second Hoover Commission. Hoover's fifty years of public service were thus busy and eventful. Indeed, President John F. Kennedy asked Mr. Hoover to head the newly established Peace Corps, but Hoover declined for reasons of age.

His son, Herbert Hoover, Jr., served as an undersecretary in the State Department under John Foster Dulles while Dwight D. Eisenhower was president. There is no record of Herbert Hoover III engaging in government service, but he is a lifetime member of the Hoover Institution Board of Overseers and has served on the boards of a number of important nonprofit institutions.

The Goldwater Campaign

Rita and I met Barry Goldwater shortly after he was elected to the U.S. Senate in November 1952. We were pleased to be among the advisers invited to his home in Scottsdale, Arizona, when he announced on January 3, 1964, that he would run for the presidency:

Ever since the last Republican convention thousands of Americans have asked me to seek the Republican presidential nomination in November. I have withheld a decision until now, not because of any attempt to be politically coy, but because I have been giving every aspect of such a decision the most serious consideration.

Today, here at our home, in the State I love, with my family and with the people whose friendship and political interest have placed me where I am, I want to tell you two things.

First—I want to tell you that I will seek the Republican presidential nomination. I have decided to do this because of the principles in which I believe and because I am convinced that millions of Americans share my belief in those principles. I have decided to do this also because I have not heard from any announced Republican candidate a declaration of conscience or of political position that could possibly offer to the American people a clear choice in the next presidential election.

One of the great attributes of our American two party system has always been the reflected differences in principle. As a general rule one party has emphasized individual liberty and the other has favored the extension of government power. I am convinced that today a majority in the Republican Party believes in the essential emphasis on individual liberty.

I have been spelling out my position now for ten years in the Senate and for years before that here in my own state. I will spell it out even further in the months to come. I was once asked what kind of a Republican I was. I replied that I was not a "me-too" Republican. That still holds. I will not change my beliefs to win votes. I will offer a choice, not an echo. This will not be an engagement of personalities. It will be an engagement of principles.

I have always stood for government that is limited and balanced and against the ever-increasing concentrations of authority in Washington. I have always stood for individual responsibility and against regimentation. I believe we must now make a choice in this land and not continue drifting endlessly down and down toward a time when all of us, our lives, our property, our hopes, and even our prayers will become just cogs in a vast government machine.

I believe that we can win victory for freedom both at home and abroad. I believe that we can be strong enough and determined enough to win those victories without war. I believe that appeasement and weakness can only bring war. I have asked and will continue to ask: Why not victory—why not victory for sound, constitutional principles in government—why not victory over the evils of communism?

I am convinced that in this year 1964 we must face up to our conscience and make a definite choice. We must decide what sort of people we are and what sort of a world we want—now and for our children.

My candidacy is pledged to a victory for principle and to presenting an opportunity for the American people to choose. Let there be a choice—right now and in clear understandable terms. And I ask all those who feel and believe as I do to join with me in assuring both the choice and the victory.

The second thing I want to tell you is that I will continue with all my strength to work for America and for Arizona in my service in the Senate. I have previously announced that I will file for reelection to the Senate. I find no incompatibility in these two candidacies.

Senator Goldwater clearly showed the same concern for a competition of ideas that animated the Hoover Institution, and took his stand for principle and victory over communism. Former President Hoover endorsed Barry Goldwater, and Herbert Hoover, Jr., served as a member of his Foreign Policy Advisory Committee, chaired by former Vice President Richard M. Nixon. Other persons already—or subsequently—associated with the Hoover Institution who served in the Goldwater campaign included Henry T. Bodman, William J. Baroody, Sr., Milton Friedman, John Lawrence, Warren Nutter, Dan Throop Smith, Lewis Strauss, and Edward Teller. Two others, Jeremiah Milbank, Jr., and J. William Middendorf II, subsequently became overseers. George Bush's father, Sen. Prescott Bush, was a campaign adviser, as were Gen. Lucius Clay; George Champion, CEO of Chase Manhattan Bank; and George Humphrey, former secretary of the treasury.

Although Karl Hess was supposed to be Goldwater's speechwriter, most of his speeches were written by Warren Nutter. He and I shared an office in the Republican headquarters on I Street next to the office of Research Director Ed McCabe. On our office door was the slogan From Soup to Nuts. Stanford graduate William Rehnquist was an adviser in the 1964 campaign. (He also served briefly on the Board of Overseers, and went on to become a Supreme Court justice and, in 1986, chief justice of the United States—the only Stanford graduate ever to attain that office.)

On September 1, 1964, I took a two-month leave of absence to work on the Goldwater campaign. A *Palo Alto Times* article reported:

> W. Glenn Campbell, director of the Hoover Institution on War, Revolution and Peace at Stanford University, has left his post temporarily to join Sen. Barry Goldwater's campaign staff.
>
> Campbell, 40, left for Washington, D.C., Monday night. He will work in the Goldwater campaign committee's research department, and advise the Republican presidential nominee on economic matters.
>
> Before leaving, Campbell said he has given advice to Goldwater from time to time in the past, and will now work full-time for the Arizona senator until November.
>
> The Hoover Institution is in no way involved in the campaign, and has no political point of view, he said. Campbell added he will be working for Goldwater as an individual—"That's why I'm taking a leave of absence."

Milorad Drachkovitch, Roger Freeman, Stefan Possony, Rita Ricardo-Campbell, and Yuan-li Wu also participated in the campaign as part-time unpaid advisers. I took leave without pay for this effort because I believed that President Johnson could not be trusted, that he was already maneuvering the country into an unwinnable war in Vietnam, and that his bloated Great Society would be the disaster that it turned out to be. Over the course of his presidency, Eisenhower had managed to reduce greatly the budget deficit, which was over 100 percent of the gross national product when World War II ended. Johnson's Great Society cast aside all such efforts at fiscal responsibility and revived large government expenditures, budget deficits, higher taxes, and lower productivity.

During the 1964 campaign I spent most of my time working with the advisory task forces. Former Secretary of Defense Neil McElroy was in charge of the Defense Task Force, and former Vice President Richard Nixon was in charge of foreign policy. George Humphrey was chairman of the Task Force on Taxation and Economic Policy, and Lewis Strauss headed the Task Force on Science and Technology. At least twice during the campaign members or potential members of an advisory committee withdrew their names because of intimations that the Johnson administration might be looking at their income tax returns. Toward the end of the campaign, William Baroody and I learned from FBI official William C. Sullivan that George Humphrey's hotel room had been bugged. I was instructed to go to a pay telephone and inform Humphrey about the situation. He was extremely grateful.

Several of us at headquarters were worried that Ronald Reagan's campaign speech would mention Goldwater's alleged support for voluntary Social Security. Instead, it included all the points that Goldwater himself could not get the electorate to listen to, particularly the tax and expenditure reductions that would later become known as "Reaganomics." Senator Goldwater was vilified by the liberal press for supporting an all-volunteer military—but by 1968 many of his strongest opponents were adopting the idea as their own. The senator also favored a 5 percent per annum reduction in income tax rates over a five-year period. He further pledged to build up a strong military to prevent the further spread of communism.

Interestingly, the *Stanford Daily* endorsed Senator Goldwater for president, the only major campus paper to do so. The editor, a very intelligent young man named Robert Naylor, went on to the Yale Law School and became the minority leader of the California State Assembly.

Goldwater carried only Arizona and four southern states, but George Humphrey called us and said, "Don't feel sorry, boys. All you have to do is get one in four of the voters to switch and you'll win." When Richard Nixon ran for president in 1968, he did exactly that.

The Nixon-Ford Years

After Richard Nixon was elected president in November 1968, Rita and I were faced for the first time with the opportunity to serve in a national administration. Some Hoover scholars took extended leaves for that purpose:

- Richard V. Allen was principal associate to National Security Adviser Henry Kissinger.
- Dr. Yuan-li Wu was deputy assistant secretary of defense for policy plans and national security affairs, 1969–70.

- Dr. Dennis Doolin was deputy assistant secretary of defense for Far East affairs, 1969–74.
- Dr. Martin Anderson was appointed a special assistant to the president and, in 1971, was named a special consultant to the president for systems analysis. In 1972 Anderson became a Senior Fellow at Hoover. From 1973 to 1975 he was a member of Gov. Nelson Rockefeller's Commission on Critical Choices for Americans, and in 1975–76 he served on the Defense Manpower Commission.
- Senior Fellow Roger Freeman served for a short period, 1969–70, as a special assistant to the president.
- Richard T. Burress was appointed deputy counsel to the president and became chairman of the Renegotiation Board in the early 1970s. On July 1, 1973, he was appointed a Senior Fellow and associate director of the Hoover Institution. He took a leave in 1974 to serve as an assistant to President Ford.
- Dr. Annelise Anderson was a program director in the Law Enforcement Assistance Administration in the Department of Justice, 1970–71.
- Darrell Trent was appointed deputy director of the President's Office of Emergency Preparedness in 1970 and was acting director when he resigned in 1974 to become a Senior Research Fellow at the Hoover Institution.
- Research Fellow James Noyes was deputy assistant secretary of defense for Near Eastern, African and South African affairs, 1970–76.
- Dr. Sidney Hook served on the Council of the National Endowment for the Humanities, 1972–78.
- Senior Research Fellow Dr. Theodore Eliot, Jr., was named ambassador to Afghanistan in 1973 and served until 1978.

As director, I did not feel free to go to Washington, D.C., on a long-term leave. Instead, we kept expanding our contacts, publishing high-quality studies, and obtaining contributions. On the afternoon of February 29, 1968, Governor Reagan asked me to serve as a regent of the University of California for a sixteen-year term. I was aware that the call was coming, and I accepted the appointment after a short conversation about what he was fond of referring to as "the mess at Berkeley." My first term required no state senate confirmation ("to keep politics out of the system"). When Governor Deukmejian appointed me to a second term in 1984, I did have to seek state senate confirmation (also "to keep politics out of the system"). I was elected chairman of the Board of Regents for 1982–83, and I became senior (longest-serving) regent in March 1988.

In May 1969 I was appointed to the President's Commission on White House Fellows and served until I resigned in January 1974. I was honored to know many Fellows who went on to distinguished careers in academia, government, and industry, but three stand out:

- General Colin Powell, President Reagan's last National Security adviser and chairman of the Joint Chiefs of Staff during the Bush administration
- Dr. Michael Armacost, who became undersecretary of state for political affairs and ambassador to Japan during the Bush administration, and who is now president of the Brookings Institution
- Henry Cisneros, President Clinton's first secretary of housing and urban development

Professor Milton Friedman also served on the White House Fellows Commission. In fact, it was at a staff meeting that he and I discussed his joining the Hoover staff. In 1976 he became a Senior Research Fellow. These were also particularly busy years for Rita:

- In 1969 she was appointed to President Nixon's Committee on the Status of Women and served until 1976. Nixon considered this an important committee and met with its members several times. At one such meeting he remarked (I paraphrase): Brains are not awarded according to sex. To ignore women would throw away half the top brains in the country, which we cannot afford to do.
- From 1970 to 1972 Rita was a member of the Task Force on Taxation of the Council on Environmental Quality, of which Hoover Senior Research Fellow Dan Throop Smith was chairman.
- In 1971 President Nixon appointed Rita to the Health Services Industry Committee where she served until 1973.

- From 1972 to 1974 Rita was a member of the National Drug Advisory Committee and remained there until 1977.
- From 1974 to 1975 Rita sat on the National Quadrennial Advisory Council on Social Security and chaired of its Subcommittee on Equal Treatment of Men and Women.
- The first appointment of a Hoover scholar to an important state government advisory post was Governor Reagan's appointment of Dr. Rita Ricardo-Campbell to the Western Interstate Commission on Higher Education in 1967. She served as vice chairman in 1969–70 and as chairman in 1970–71, resigning in the spring of 1974.

The Carter Years

Several Hoover scholars served in Jimmy Carter's administration:

- Rodney Kennedy-Minott was named ambassador to Sweden. Since 1981 he has served as a consultant to the U.S. government on politico-military matters affecting Northern Europe.
- Sidney Hook became a member of the Council on the National Endowment for the Humanities.
- Theodore Eliot was reappointed ambassador to Afghanistan.
- In 1977 Dr. Alvin Rabushka became a consultant to the U.S. Senate and to the National Center for Health Services Research of the Public Health Service.
- I remained a member of the National Science Board.

I proudly list these appointments because our left-wing critics at Stanford frequently and falsely claim that Hoover scholars serve only Republican administrations.

The Reagan-Bush Years

With the election of Honorary Fellow Ronald Reagan as president of the United States in November 1980, Hoover scholars entered public service in even greater numbers:

- In January 1981 Dr. Martin Anderson became assistant to the president for domestic policy issues.

- Senior Fellow Richard V. Allen became national security adviser.
- Dr. Annelise Anderson became an associate director of the Office of Management and Budget and served there until 1983. From 1985 until May 1990 she was a member of the National Science Board.
- In 1984 Dr. John H. Moore became a member of the National Science Board. He became its deputy director in 1985 and remained so until May 1990.
- From spring of 1981 until 1983 Dr. Richard Staar was U.S. ambassador to the Mutual and Balanced Force Reduction Negotiations in Vienna. From 1983 to 1987 he served as consultant to the Arms Control and Disarmament Agency.
- Philip Habib, who accepted a Hoover appointment as Senior Research Fellow in 1970, requires special mention in view of his long and distinguished career in the State Department. After receiving his Ph.D. in agricultural economics at the University of California, Berkeley, he served as ambassador to Korea and as undersecretary of state for political affairs. In 1981 President Reagan appointed him personal representative of the president to the Middle East and he held that position until 1983. He was appointed presidential envoy to the Philippines in 1986, and received a two-year appointment (1986–87) as the president's special envoy for Central America.
- Dr. Rita Ricardo-Campbell was appointed to the President's Economic Policy Advisory Board, chaired by George Shultz and later Walter Wriston. (During the Reagan administration, Milton Friedman, Alan Greenspan—a member of the Hoover Board of Overseers—and Martin Anderson also served on this board.) Dr. Ricardo-Campbell was also appointed to the Council of the National Endowment on the Humanities in 1982 and served until 1989. Since 1988 she has served on the President's Committee on the National Medal of Science. President Bush renewed her term until 1994.
- Thomas Sowell also became a member of the President's Economic Policy Advisory Board but resigned shortly after his appointment because of the demands of his other work.

- In 1981 Dr. John Cogan became assistant secretary for policy with the Department of Labor, and from 1983 to 1985 he served as associate director for human resources of the Office of Management and Budget. From 1988 to 1989 he was deputy director of OMB.

In the fall of 1981 I was appointed chairman of the President's Intelligence Oversight Board (PIOB) and a member of the President's Foreign Intelligence Advisory Board (PFIAB). I served as chairman of PIOB until March 1990 and was a member of PFIAB until July 1990.

When I resigned from PFIAB I received these letters from President Bush and Ambassador Anne Armstrong:

Dear Glenn:

Serving seven American Presidents, the members of the President's Foreign Intelligence Advisory Board have provided a valuable contribution to the security of the Nation. It is with deep appreciation for your own exceptional years of service that I accept your resignation from the Board. Your wisdom, integrity, and energy have played a key role in the difficult, yet essential, tasks of monitoring and improving the quality of the national intelligence effort and helping to define its objectives for the future.

With your help, we have faced squarely the global challenges inherent in the postwar era, and we have defended successfully the democratic ideals of free nations. Although uncertainties still exist, changing conditions present new challenges and opportunities in our search for a more hopeful tomorrow. As historical changes worldwide foster global interdependence and multipolarity, we must keep a watchful eye on America's interests. Your unique insights and expertise have enabled you to serve this country with great distinction, and I hope we may call on you for further assistance and counsel as the occasion may arise.

On behalf of all Americans, thank you for your dedicated service to our country. I am personally very grateful for your efforts toward achieving our goals. I look forward to continuing our work together on the critical issues of our times.

Sincerely,

\s\ George Bush

Dear Glenn:

For the past thirty-four years, the President's Foreign Intelligence Advisory Board's contribution to the security of the nation has been significant and essential. Together we have faced some of the most challenging times ever to confront the United States and its intelligence establishment. When you first became a member of the PFIAB, America stood face to face with an aggressive and formidable Soviet Bloc adversary. Communism had made deep inroads into Latin America and Africa. Terrorism was soon to reach its zenith. And unprecedented espionage against the United States was on the upswing, marking "the decade of the spy." Today, the Warsaw Pact is crumbling, the Soviet Union is fracturing, and communist parties in most nations are in retreat—changes as gratifying as they are dramatic.

Through it all, this Board has worked hard to help the President and his intelligence community meet the increasingly difficult challenges. The judgments and advice we offered on a number of crucial issues were not always popular, sometimes controversial, but never without reason or responsible deliberation. Your own part in this history is significant. For your help and participation, you have my heartfelt thanks.

As we salute the arrival of the new Board, I take great pride in the legacy we leave behind. And I will long cherish the memories of our shared opportunities in service to the country—the challenges met and victories won.

With deep appreciation,

Sincerely,
Anne L. Armstrong, Chairman

On January 19, 1989, my two colleagues and I sent President Reagan the following report of our years on the President's Intelligence Oversight Board:

During your incumbency, the President's Intelligence Oversight Board (PIOB) has operated under the provisions of your Executive Order 12334, without change. We believe that the charter which you set out for us was farsighted and effective and we recommend that it be continued.

Some well-meaning persons in the White House and outside have, from time to time, recommended changes in the PIOB's structure and method of operation. We have consistently rejected such recommendations with good cause, and that remains our position today.

Some of the recommendations have been:

1. That the Board be given subpoena powers. We consider such powers to be superfluous. We have never encountered difficulty in having responsible members of the Intelligence Community appear before us to testify.

2. That the PIOB be accorded the power to place witnesses under oath. Again, we consider this a superfluous power. If witnesses are willing to practice deception on a direct arm of the President, taking an oath would hardly change matters.

3. That the PIOB—which has consisted of three, plus a counsel and a management/security officer who also serves as our secretary—thinks a case could be made for one additional professional legally trained staff member but in our view this is not a matter of urgency. It should be borne in mind that the staffs of the two Congressional Oversight Committees total a dozen persons and we very much doubt that the Committees members are any better informed on the activities of the Intelligence Community than PIOB. Also, the various Intelligence agencies have built-in investigatory offices to the findings of which we have always had full access.

4. That the Board be increased in size. This we think would be a bad mistake. The Board of three seems to us just right; five would be too many for a truly collegial atmosphere and any greater number would be far too many. One might recall the perceptive words of the greatest governor that the State of New York ever had—Governor Alfred E. Smith—"A board is a long, narrow wooden thing." The controlling word here is "long". . . .

You were wise to make the Board bipartisan—that has been one of our great strengths. Another strength has been the fact that the Board Members receive no compensation of any kind.

Has the Board been effective during your two terms, and how does one measure its effectiveness?

We are confident that the Board has been extremely effective during this period. The question of measurement is a more difficult matter. Some might say that the fact that the Board uncovered only a couple of violations serious enough to be brought to the attention of the President demonstrates that the Board's function was of relatively insignificant proportions. The better argument is that the fewer such violations, the more effective the Board was. During our seven years of operation we received and studied 540 quarterly reports and 56 special reports prepared for us by top officials

of the Intelligence Community. Many of these detailed violations, some triv-
ial, most relatively unimportant, and more than a few requiring corrective
action and in some cases, discipline of individuals which the agencies
involved carried out following our suggestions.

But these measurements do not go to the heart of the principal value of
the Board—its deterrent effect on the Intelligence Community. Our central
value lies in the violations that never took place because of the fact of our
existence. The Intelligence Community is well aware of the function and
powers of the PIOB and particularly of the Board's direct access to the President when needed. Your Executive Order goes even further by providing
that any member of the Board may take a matter directly to you whether
or not the other two agree.

A half century ago President Franklin D. Roosevelt's Committee on Administrative Management recommended that he acquire several administrative
assistants "with a passion for anonymity." Mr. Roosevelt did acquire four
assistants which was the first time in American history that a president had
a professional staff. Since that day, fifty years ago, the presidential staff has
grown to the hundreds, and now to the thousands. Unfortunately, the sound
advice of the Committee on Administrative Management has been increasingly more honored in the breach than in the observance.

Your PIOB has been successful in achieving relative anonymity. As it turns
out, that was not such a difficult thing to do. Early on we drafted a short
memorandum to be used in response to media requests for interviews or
information from the staff or the individual members. It reads as follows:

(X) does not grant interviews on the work of the PIOB or its members.
We have faithfully followed this policy. Thus, in seven years, PIOB has
appeared in the national media only a handful of times and the members
even fewer. There have been no leaks of information on any topics from
the Board.

We are satisfied with and grateful for the cooperation we have received
from the Intelligence Community in carrying out our duties, particularly
from Judge Webster. There has only been one major failure in providing us
with ongoing intelligence briefings and that was on the Iran-Contra finding
and the related diversion of funds. We must be forgiven for believing, as we
do, that had we been privy to such information at an early stage, as we should
have been, that this unfortunate incident might well not have occurred.

It has been a privilege and an honor to serve you these past seven-plus years. Messrs. Campbell and Tyroler were original members of the Board appointed by you, and the late Charles Jarvis Meyers joined us several months later. Mr. Meyers died this past July and was succeeded by Mr. Michael W. McConnell less than two months ago. Thus Mr. McConnell cannot be held fully accountable for our observations and recommendations. However, we have informed him of them and he is in general agreement.

With great respect,

Sincerely,
W. Glenn Campbell, Chairman
Charles Tyroler II, Member
Michael W. McConnell, Member

CC: President-Elect Bush

The Japan-U.S. Friendship Commission

On June 30, 1983, I became chairman of the Japan-U.S. Friendship Commission and served for six years, the first person to serve the maximum time allowed under the law. On July 17, 1989, I sent to interested persons this review of the accomplishments of the commission:

> Now that my term as Chairman of the Japan-United States Friendship Commission has come to an end, I think it is both appropriate and informative to offer a brief review of the Commission's achievements over the past six years, particularly since I am the first Chairman to serve the maximum two terms allowed by law. This summary is addressed to those familiar with the Commission and is designed to emphasize highlights and trends, and to serve as an interpretive supplement to the Commission's annual reports, which provide a complete listing of grants.

> *Program*
> The single most important development in the Commission's program has been the increase in the number and range of grants. In fiscal year 1982, the Commission made 97 grants; over the past six years the average annual total has been 125. More importantly, the scope of the Commission's work has been greatly enhanced. Whereas in the pre-1983 period Commission

support had been largely confined to traditional academic centers of Japanese Studies, since then, the Commission has reached out to new institutions and organizations just entering the field. In expanding beyond "elitist" institutions, the Commission has also achieved greater geographic equity, in that most of the new grantees are in the South and the Midwest.

In the realm of academic research, the Commission has been giving less support for theoretical and historical research and more for applied research in the social sciences. In this connection, a new category of programming—"Policy-oriented Research"—was established to address contemporary problems in U.S.-Japan relations. In my judgment, some important work was undertaken in the economic and security areas through Commission grants to the Carnegie Council on Ethics and International Affairs, Mississippi State University, the U.S. National Council for Pacific Basin Economic Cooperation, the University of Washington, and others.

To meet the increasing American interest in Japan and U.S.-Japan relations, the Commission has expanded its programming with journalists, educational television, professional societies, and world affairs organizations. Noteworthy in this regard is the growth of the Commission-supported network of Japan-America societies, which has grown from 11 in 1983 to 20 in 1989. These societies play a vital role in informing the American public on Japanese affairs and U.S.-Japan issues.

Through its support of research, training, and public affairs, the Commission has been attempting to produce a more balanced assessment of Japan and U.S.-Japan relations, i.e., to counteract the views of a small cadre of self-appointed Japan experts. In a similar vein, the Commission has focused its attention on the training of younger scholars and the needs of the "isolated" scholar who is distant from the major library and research centers. Also, the Commission has encouraged the interest of the non-Japan specialist in law, journalism, business and engineering by providing area and language training in professional graduate programs.

In Japan, the Commission's program has also witnessed growth and greater diversity. While continuing to concentrate on the broad field of American Studies, new and more effective approaches have been tried. The bulk of the program involves "faculty development," whereby Japanese professors are given financial support to develop new courses dealing with some aspect of the United States, e.g., American politics, American economy, American finance, American education, etc. The commitment of the grantee and his university is to offer the course in the regular curriculum upon his return to Japan. Twenty scholars—many from outside Tokyo—have participated in the program since 1984, and Commission resources can no longer keep up with the demand.

The Commission continued to provide major support to the two most important Centers of American Studies in Japan at Tokyo University and Doshisha University in Kyoto, as well as the annual summer seminar in American Studies in Sapporo, Hokkaido, and helped to establish a new center at Sophia University.

New programs include short-term grants for Japanese social scientists to conduct research in the United States, support for up to ten young economists annually to present papers in English at American professional meetings, and a variety of projects involving collaborative research and exchange between Japanese and American universities and professional organizations. In addition to furthering scholarship, a principal aim of the Commission throughout is to create an interest in and understanding of contemporary American affairs and U.S.-Japan relations in Japanese academia.

Finance and Administration

In April of 1985, the Commission held a special "policy" session to plot a response to the increasing demands of projects critical to the urgent problems in U.S.-Japan relations. The Commissioners decided that the situation warranted maximum expenditure of resources, i.e., in addition to spending the annual interest on its Trust Funds, the Commission should draw down on its original principal to the extent permitted by law (five percent). At the end of fiscal year 1983, the dollar fund stood at $18,473,894; at the end of fiscal year 1988 it was $17,793,414. The fact that the fund has suffered an erosion of only $680,000 was due to the Commission's success in obtaining a gift of $3 million from the Government of Japan to support its "outreach" programs with the Japan-America societies and similar organizations. Thus, the Commission has, in fact, been able to carry on the dramatic expansion of its programs at virtually no cost to its basic capital.

At the end of fiscal year 1983, the yen fund totaled 4 billion yen, or approximately $16 million at the exchange rate prevailing at that time; at the end of FY 1988 it was 3.6 billion, or approximately $28 million at the current exchange rate. Again, expenditure of original principal, plus lower interest rates in Japan, account for the decrease in the real value of the yen fund. Changing exchange rates account for the increase in the dollar value of the yen fund.

Above all, the Commission continues to enjoy steady support from the Congress in connection with the annual appropriations process. All in all, the Commission remains in good financial health.

Despite increased public interest in Japan, growing demand on Commission resources and expanded programming, the Commission's staff numbers only five. I believe the Commission to be one of the most cost-effective entities in the Washington bureaucracy. The professional personnel hired during my term of office combine Japanese area and language competence, administrative skills, and familiarity with Japan-related governmental, academic and non-profit organizations. I would like to commend Mr. Lindley Sloan, Executive Director, Dr. Eric Gangloff, Associate Executive Director and Japan Representative, Dr. Robert Marra, Program Officer, and Ms. Roberta Stewart, Secretary, for their capable and loyal service to the Commission.

In closing, I would like to express my appreciation for the opportunity to serve as Chairman of the Commission, and to work closely with three outstanding Vice-Chairmen—Ambassador Robert Ingersoll, Garrett Scalera, and Frank Gibney. I have found the Commission to be a challenging and rewarding experience and ask that you continue to support the important work it is carrying out.

Having left the Friendship Commission I was nominated in spring 1990 by President Bush to the National Science Board. My appointment was held up for months by the staff of Sen. Edward Kennedy of Massachusetts, but I was finally confirmed in late October 1990 to a term that ran until May 1994.

Hoover Scholars in the Reagan-Bush Years

- Darrell Trent served as director of the Office of Policy Coordination during President Reagan's 1981–82 transition and became deputy secretary of transportation from 1981 to 1983. He was then appointed ambassador to the European Civil Aviation Conference and served until 1984.

- Dr. Dennis Bark was appointed chairman of the U.S. Coast Guard Academy Advisory Committee, 1981–84, and was a member of the White House Fellows Commission, 1981–85. Since 1985, he has served on the U.S. Institute for Peace Commission.
- In 1981 Senior Research Fellow Adm. James Stockdale accepted the position of chairman of the President's Commission on White House Fellowships and served until he resigned in January 1989.
- Dr. Henry Rowen joined the Hoover Institution in 1983 as a Senior Research Fellow after serving as the chairman of the National Intelligence Council from 1981 to 1983. He became a Senior Fellow in 1987, and in June 1989 took a leave of absence to serve as assistant secretary of defense for International Security Affairs. He returned to the Hoover Institution in 1991.
- Before joining the Hoover Institution in 1986, Director John Raisian served as director of research for the Department of Labor from 1981 to 1984. He was also a member of the National Advisory Committee on Student Financial Assistance from 1987 to 1989.
- In 1982 Dr. Martin Anderson became a member of the President's Economic Policy Advisory Board. That same year he also became a member of the President's Foreign Intelligence Advisory Board, serving until October 31, 1985, when he and ten other persons— including Alan Greenspan, Adm. Thomas Moorer, Edward Bennett Williams, and Peter O'Donnell—were fired in a controversial incident dubbed the PFIAB Halloween Massacre in those circles. In 1987 he became a member of the General Advisory Committee on Arms Control and Disarmament.
- George Shultz became secretary of state in the early summer of 1982. In December 1987 he became the fourth Honorary Fellow of the Hoover Institution. His service as secretary of state ended on January 20, 1989, and he has since been named a Distinguished Fellow of the Hoover Institution.
- Dr. Alan Greenspan became a member of the Board of Overseers in 1982. In 1983 he chaired a bipartisan Reform Commission on

Social Security, and in August 1987 President Reagan nominated him to be chairman of the Federal Reserve for a four-year term. In 1991 President Bush nominated him for a second term and in 1995 and 1999 President Clinton nominated him for a third and fourth term, with Senate confirmation following each time.

- Senior Research Fellow George Marotta served as a member of the National Advisory Board on International Education Programs, 1983–85.
- Dr. Charles McLure, Jr., served as deputy assistant secretary of the treasury for tax analysis from 1983 to 1985.
- Dr. Milorad Drachkovitch was a consultant on Eastern European and Yugoslav Affairs to the Department of Defense from 1983–84. During 1984 and 1985, he served on the Board of Foreign Scholarships.
- In 1983 Senior Research Fellow John H. Bunzel was appointed a member of the U.S. Commission on Civil Rights and served until 1986.
- Associate Director Thomas Henriksen was a member of the U.S. Army Science Board from 1984 until 1990. In 1987 he became a member of the White House Fellows Commission.
- Overseer Dr. Dean Watkins served on the President's Science Advisory Council from 1986 until 1989.
- Overseer David Packard sat on the President's Science Advisory Council during the Bush administration.
- In 1985 Senior Research Fellow Angelo Codevilla became an adviser to the U.S. Senate and the U.S. Department of Defense.
- Dr. Thomas G. Moore took a leave of absence from the Hoover Institution in 1985 to accept an appointment to the President's Council of Economic Advisors. He served until spring 1989. Martin Anderson and I had worked hard to convince the new chief of staff, Donald Regan, that the council should be reestablished. We accomplished this primarily through our mutual long-time friend Pat Buchanan, whom President Reagan had appointed director of communications. The argument that carried the day was that unless the council was reestablished, the administration would lose the services of the approximately twenty-five staff members

who were a very useful counterbalance to OMB's big professional bureaucracy.

- In 1985 Charles Hill became the executive aide to George Shultz. Before that he was chief of staff, Department of State (1983), and deputy assistant secretary, Middle East (1982). In 1989 he became a Hoover Institution Senior Research Fellow.

It is at least interesting to consider the position Hoover scholars did *not* accept in the Reagan administration:

Thomas Sowell, for instance, could have been secretary of education. I was on the "short list" for that position myself, but I was sure that abolishing the Department of Education—as President Reagan had promised during his campaign—would not be a high priority, so I could never kindle any enthusiasm for the job. It went to Ted Bell of Utah instead, and Bell devoted much of his time to sabotaging the plan to abolish the department. By the time Bill Bennett became secretary of education in Reagan's second term, just about everyone had forgotten the 1980 campaign promise. In fact, by the end of the Reagan administration, spending by the Education Department had approximately doubled.

In early January 1981 Dr. Rita Ricardo-Campbell could have been appointed secretary of housing and urban development. I always joked that she was the only person I knew who had turned down a cabinet post on the basis of lack of interest or lack of qualification—particularly the latter. That same month she was also offered a position on the President's Council of Economic Advisors. After considerable discussion with me, she rejected the position, opting to support my efforts to keep the Hoover Institution intellectually and financially independent and to enjoy her family in California. At the end of Reagan's first term, he promised to make Dr. Ricardo-Campbell chairman of the Council of Economic Advisors if the council was reestablished in his second term. After the reelection, Secretary of Treasury Donald Regan and Chief of Staff James Baker switched jobs, and Regan installed Beryl Sprinkel as chairman of the council. Presidential Counselor Ed Meese could have stopped this, but he was preoccupied with the opposition to his nomination as attorney general. Late on the day of the announcement of Beryl Sprinkel's appointment, Regan telephoned Rita in Boston where she was attending a Gillette Company board meeting. He invited her to become a member of the council, and she refused for the second time. This time, however, her reason was different: she believed that the council under Sprinkel would not be influential, and she thinks she was proven correct.

During their conversation she asked Regan what had happened to the president's promise to appoint her chairman. He replied that Sprinkel would be unemployed if he did not get the appointment. This seemed to Rita not a very good reason and she said so. Regan added that he had had some trouble with Sprinkel the first year he was at Treasury, but that now he would do whatever Regan told him to do. Enough said.

Regan had interviewed Rita at length when he was secretary of the treasury and had implied that she would become secretary of health and human services as soon as the incumbent was forced out. Instead, when that position became vacant in early 1987, he persuaded the president to nominate the ex-governor of Indiana, Dr. Otis Bowen, who was responsible for the ill-fated Catastrophic Health Care Act passed in 1988 and repealed late in 1989.

This brief review of literally hundreds of years of devoted public service by senior scholars of the Hoover Institution above and beyond their immense contributions to the Institution illustrates the quality and integrity of the great team it was my honor to assemble and work with during my directorate.

10
Two Dedications and
Two Anniversaries

FOUR CELEBRATIONS STAND OUT AS LANDMARKS TO THE VISION of Herbert Hoover and to its increasing realization in my thirty years as director of the Hoover Institution:

- The dedication of the Lou Henry Hoover Building on October 9, 1967
- The Hoover Institution's Fiftieth Anniversary Dinner on November 17, 1969
- The dedication of the Herbert Hoover Federal Memorial Building on July 20, 1978
- The dinner held on July 18, 1984, in recognition of my Twenty-fifth Anniversary as director

Each occasion was recognized with speeches and letters from the many friends of Herbert Hoover and of the Hoover Institution. I make many of them public here for what they reveal about Mr. Hoover himself and about the Institution he founded. While there is naturally some repetition, there are also individual insights that say a great deal about the man and his legacy. Indeed, I thought that two or three of the quotations were worthy of inclusion in introducing Hoover's history in Chapter One.

On the Dedication of the
Lou Henry Hoover Building
Speeches
Baron Louis Scheyven, Belgian Ambassador to the United States:

I came especially to Stanford from Washington today to bring on this festive occasion a message from His Majesty, the King of the Belgians:

In 1918, from his headquarters, King Albert, my grandfather, signed a decree proclaiming President Herbert Hoover "friend of the Belgian people."

This exceptional honor was conferred upon him for outstanding services. My people and I remain deeply indebted to President Hoover. Not only did he organize food relief for our long-suffering population during World War I, but he also contributed, in a very substantial way, to bringing closer together the American and Belgian educational intellectual elites.

And may I add a personal word of gratitude to former President Herbert Hoover—a gratitude on two counts.

During the First World War, I was a small child belonging to a large family of thirteen. And every morning, I remember receiving at school—together with other millions of Belgian children—a loaf of white bread, the only white bread my brothers and sisters and I would have received, would have eaten, during the First World War which lasted, as you remember, over four years. For that, especially, I am deeply grateful.

But it is not only the physical part, important as it is, which remains in my mind, in my memory, in my feelings of gratitude for President Hoover. I've also been what they call a C.R.B. (Commission for Relief in Belgium) Fellow. At present there are over a thousand Belgian students who came here for some postgraduate work in your universities, and I am one of those thousand Belgians who came here and greatly benefited from their year-long stay in your country and in your midst.

I feel that in my own job as Ambassador of Belgium to the United States, I have been deeply helped by that year I have spent with American Friends at the University of Chicago and elsewhere in the years gone by. For all that, I am grateful to the memory of the great President, President Hoover.

Herbert Hoover, Jr.:

It's my privilege today to express the great appreciation of my brother Allan and myself and all the members of our family for the dedication of this magnificent building in memory of our mother, Lou Henry Hoover.

And especially we wish to express our gratitude to the many people who have so generously made it possible. A great many friends and distinguished people have worked toward the building of this Institution. The hundreds of names on the wall of the Tower building, as well as on the plaque outside the new building, testify to their number.

Among the many who have been extremely helpful, we particularly wish to thank the family of the late Mrs. Alan Scaife of Pittsburgh. Her magnificent grant sparked a successful campaign which made the building possible. And her continued generous support of the Institution has played a key role in its dramatic growth in recent years. I am delighted that Richard Scaife can be with us today.

Also being dedicated are two handsome new rooms in the Tower building, the Jeremiah Milbank Room and the Nicolas de Basily Room.

Jerry Milbank was one of my father's closest friends for over 40 years. He has also been a most generous benefactor of this Institution. I am sure that everyone here joins me in our deep regret that, for reasons of health, Jerry is unable to be here today. However, we are pleased that his son, Jerry Milbank, Jr., can take his place.

The Nicolas de Basily Room is named in honor of a dedicated statesman and diplomat who, in a brief career in the service of his homeland, Russia, achieved high office at a young age. His promising career was cut short by the Bolshevik revolution. A refugee from his homeland for the rest of his life, Mr. de Basily turned his talents to business and finance and to literary activities—in all of which he was eminently successful.

The Institution is most grateful to his widow for contributing his extensive library, as well as the fine paintings, antique furniture and other objects of art that are exhibited in the room. It is also indebted to her for establishing an endowment for the Russian Collection, and I am sure everyone is delighted that Madame de Basily and several of her family are here today.

It is particularly fitting, I think, that this new building should be named for Lou Henry Hoover. The partnership between my mother and father was an unusually close one. Both graduated from Stanford in geology. During the early years of their marriage, when my father was active in mining, Mother had an intense professional as well as personal interest in his work. She loved to travel and she took a vigorous part in all the family expeditions, no matter what their destinations might be.

It was typical of her that when we children turned up, she took us right along too. In fact, she took me around the world three times before I was four years old.

Throughout her life, Mother had a deep affection for the Stanford campus. And notwithstanding all of her travels, this, to her, was always our home. Whenever possible, she took an active part in campus community affairs. And her benefactions were many and varied, though almost always anonymous.

During World War I days in Europe, she was acutely aware of the necessity of preserving the historical documents of the moment, in order to create a foundation for peace in the future. As a result she had an intense interest in the idea of what ultimately became the War Library here at Stanford. She shared my father's hopes and concerns for its future, and was equally as proud as he of its accomplishments as it grew and flourished.

If she could be here today, I know she would be most deeply moved that this building should be given her name. Again, on behalf of our family, I'd like to express to all those people who have made it possible our great appreciation that this beautiful building should be dedicated to Lou Henry Hoover.

Stanford trustee and Hoover Advisory Board member David Packard:

I am, indeed, very pleased and honored to be able to participate in this dedication here today. I know this is an important occasion for the Hoover family to have their mother as well as their father honored here at Stanford and remembered with this beautiful building. The occasion is, I assure you, also an important and a memorable one for many of Herbert and Lou Henry Hoover's friends and admirers. A number of these friends and admirers across the country have helped to make this building possible. From among these I would like to say a word about two.

You already heard Mr. Hoover say how close Jerry Milbank was to his father over a very long period. Mr. Milbank has also been very generous to the Hoover Institution and to Stanford, and it seems to me then that it is indeed appropriate, and I must say very gratifying personally to me, that the main reading room in the Hoover Tower is being renovated and will hereafter be known as the Jeremiah Milbank Room. Mr. Milbank attended many Advisory Board meetings of the Hoover Institution with Mr. Hoover in that room, and I know the Chief would have been very pleased that Jerry Milbank's name will be permanently inscribed there. I am sorry, too, that Mr. Milbank could not be here today. His health is uncertain, but we are indeed honored to have his son, Jeremiah Milbank Jr., here.

About sixty years ago, a penniless and virtually illiterate Serbian youth named Todor Polich arrived in Los Angeles. He learned English and through hard work and no small measure of innate ability, he became a successful businessman. His two sons graduated from Stanford and both played on the football team. Mr. Polich came to admire Herbert Hoover and what he stood for and what he believed in, and I in turn have been a great admirer of Mr. Polich and of his accomplishments. Through his generosity, Mr. Todor Polich has helped make the Lou Henry Hoover Building possible, and I am certain that both Mr. and Mrs. Hoover would have been very proud to know that the main seminar room in this new building will carry the Polich name.

It seems to me this dedication today is not only an important event to commemorate the memory of Lou Henry and Herbert Hoover and to acknowledge those who have given so unselfishly in their tribute to them. This event also, I believe, has an important significance in the progress of Stanford University. The Hoover Institution here on the Stanford Campus has become one of the strong and prominent segments of this University. The books and documents and archives of the Institution constitute a significant proportion of the University's library collection and in fact have contributed significantly to the nation-wide prestige of the Stanford library. The Institution has also become an important center of scholarly research and study and publication on subjects which have great significance in these troubled times of today. Both Mr. and Mrs. Hoover placed great hope that this Institution would serve well in man's continuing search for a better world, and it seems to me that also is the hope of a great university. In many ways, Lou Henry and Herbert Hoover have reflected the tradition of Stanford. They combined a love of scholarship with the dedication to service of their fellow men. I often marveled at their accomplishment in the translation of Agricola's *De Re Metallica*.[1] Lou Henry Hoover's involvement in help for young people was extensive throughout her lifetime, and Herbert Hoover set the finest example for young people who would seek to serve their fellow men in a career of public service.

---

1. The first textbook ever written on the subject of mining, *De Re Metallica*, established mineralogy as a science. Composed in 1556 by Georgius Agricola (Georg Bauer), a Bohemian physician and mine owner, it remained for centuries the only text on mining and metallurgy.

In Mr. Hoover's case it began with relief work, continued with numerous assignments under five Presidents and of course included his service as President himself. Nevertheless, he always stoutly maintained that the private sector—the professional and private business establishment—made the most important contributions to both the social and economic progress in the world. Every student should read his statement about the profession of engineering. "It is a great profession," he said. "There is a fascination of watching a figment of the imagination emerge through the aid of science to a plan on paper. Then it moves to realization in stone or metal or energy. Then it brings jobs and homes to men, then it elevates the standards of living, and adds to the comforts of life. That is the engineer's high privilege." And if this is not enough to appeal to the socially oriented student of today, Mr. Hoover also pointed out that from works of engineering, new laws and regulations have to be made and new sorts of wickedness curbed. He, the engineer, is also the person who really corrects monopolies and redistributes the national wealth.

Herbert Hoover also had something to say which might enlighten those students who look with disdain on a career in business. He was a businessman as well as an engineer, and during the last fifty years of his life, which he spent in the public service, he had many dealings with the business community. He recognized that the vast majority of businessmen are not motivated by selfish interest. As Food Administrator during World War I, he relied largely on the voluntary cooperation of the business community in solving the many problems of maintaining an adequate supply and distribution of the essential foodstuffs to mount a successful war effort.

In accepting President Wilson's appointment, he responded by saying, "I hold strongly to the view that while large powers will be necessary in the minority of cases, the vast majority of the producing and distribution elements of the country are only too willing and anxious to serve." In his administration of this program, although there were great and serious difficulties, most of these were solved because the business community rose above their selfish interest under his leadership. His leadership toward a higher ethic in business affairs continued as he took charge of the Department of Commerce and introduced many programs in which the business community cooperated to better serve the public welfare.

Now, as we all know, it is an image widespread among students, and I must say some professors too, that service to humanity is not a common characteristic in the world of commerce and industry. Such an image was perhaps justified during the early decades of the twentieth century. Fortunately, however, during the last three or four decades in particular, the social attitudes in the world of commerce and industry have undergone a tremendous change for the better. Mr. Hoover's influence, by way of example, and by way of his constructive thought and action, has had no small effect in contributing to this higher ethic in the administration of business and industry. I am particularly pleased, therefore, that the dedication of the Lou Henry Hoover Building here on the Stanford campus recognized the expanding role of the Hoover Institution in the affairs of this university. It is my hope that this new building will help the Hoover Institution serve well both faculty and students in their scholarly studies, in their search for new understandings and new answers to the perplexing questions of today and tomorrow.

It is my hope also that this new building will serve as a continual reminder to present and future generations of students and faculty that Stanford has a great heritage, a heritage worthy of preservation and one reflected in many ways in the lives of Lou Henry and Herbert Hoover. In particular this heritage includes a tradition in which this University and its graduates have served their fellow men in practical as well as in intellectual affairs in the world. It also includes a strong tradition of involvement in public and social service. And I know my hopes in these matters are shared by the vast majority of the Stanford family, as well as all of those who have helped to make this building possible. On their behalf, it is my privilege and honor to present the Lou Henry Hoover Building formally to the President and to the Board of Trustees of Stanford University.

Congratulatory Messages

From President Lyndon B. Johnson:

I am pleased to express my congratulations on the dedication of the Lou Henry Hoover Building of the Hoover Institution at Stanford University.

It is fitting that the wife of this world renowned statesman and President should be memorialized by the great university that prepared him for public life.

Just as she faithfully stood by him in his trying tasks, so will she now be remembered by all who admire and respect his dedication to duty and the Nation's trust.

From President Dwight D. Eisenhower:

The dedication of the Lou Henry Hoover Building memorializes for generations to come a great American who with her husband represented the finest traditions of America. Her charm, her dignity, her warmhearted devotion to people, won her in foreign lands a lasting affection and at home an abiding love. President Hoover, I am confident, valued the assurance on his 90th birthday that this building would be an enduring monument to his wife, above all material birthday gifts he had ever received.

From President Harry S Truman:

Thank you for your very kind invitation to the dedication of the addition of the new Lou Henry Hoover Building to the Hoover Institution.

I wish that I could be present to again express my respect and friendship for President Herbert Hoover but, to my regret, I cannot undertake extensive travel.

Please give my warm regards and good wishes to the members of the Hoover family.

From Senator Robert F. Kennedy:

I am pleased to have this opportunity to extend my greetings on the occasion of the formal dedication of the Lou Henry Hoover Building—the newest addition to the Hoover Institution. I know that this new facility will bring an increased awareness of and appreciation for President Hoover's contributions to our country as well as continue to foster the goals and high ideals of the Institution. Best wishes for a most pleasant afternoon.

On the Occasion of the Hoover Institution's Fiftieth Anniversary Dinner

Speeches

Admiral Lewis Strauss, Mr. Hoover's long-time friend and confidant:

While no specific topic was assigned to me this evening, Dr. Campbell suggested that I might fill a few minutes with some reminiscences of Mr.

Hoover. When one has been fortunate enough to know such a man for fifty of his most active years, and all of your own, it is practically impossible to sort out just a few recollections. There are simply too many.

In which of his many facets shall I call him to mind tonight? That of the humorist and raconteur? (Despite the public image, he was both.) That of the engineer's engineer? The Latinist? The prolific writer? The fisherman-philosopher? The organizer of the compassion of the world for the starving and the orphaned? The thirty-first president of our country? For he was all of these and many more.

Yet so devastating was his denigration and disparagement by hired defamers in the political wars of the thirties that the general picture of Mr. Hoover was a stereotype—a morose and anti-social recluse. Even the description "humanitarian" so apt that it might have been coined for him—was turned into a sneering word by his detractors.

There could be no more false presentment of a man who was approachable, gregarious, generous with his energies and his means, a patriot in the real and finest sense of the term and—rarest of qualities—a man blessed with an understanding heart.

Of his achievements which survive him—the books he wrote, the engineering standards he established, the foundations for international education he created, the reforms and economies in Federal administration which he devised, to mention but a few—none was so close to his heart as the Institution whose semi-centennial we now celebrate. From its beginning, he never wavered in his conviction that a lighthouse could be built to show a course to peace for mankind. The Hoover Tower on this campus has always seemed to me a symbolic beacon.

"Peace," he wrote, "is not made at the Council table or by treaties, but in the hearts of men." And once, long ago, discussing the War Library, he quoted Washington, who had hoped his fellow countrymen would be able, as he put it, "to derive useful lessons from past errors and to profit from dear-bought experience."

Mr. Hoover had observed that a recurring phenomenon associated with the "dear-bought experience" of war is that in the euphoria of victory, peace is presumed to be permanently achieved. It is mistakenly believed, each time, that the final and ultimate war has been fought—"the war to end war."

In consequence, important records of how wars start are consigned to what George Orwell called the "memory hole." There is no interest in the preservation of such papers and they are neglected and soon are lost or destroyed. (This happens quickly to the archives of the vanquished.) Then, when in the course of time, history begins to repeat itself, there is no remembered way out of the labyrinth, no signs pointing to safe exits. Nations begin once more their dismal slide over the precipice of war.

Half a century ago, Mr. Hoover came to the conclusion that man's best hope of peace would be to have the lessons of previous mistakes constantly before us and never to be allowed to forget them. All other means—alliances, covenants, pacts and solemn treaties—had been abortive. "I have not forgotten," he once wrote regretfully, "that my ardent support of the League of Nations and the World Court, at least as an experiment in preserving peace, had failed." What was needed was a storehouse of blueprints for peace, for while "nations can blunder into war," he said, "they cannot blunder into peace."

From that time fifty-five years ago, as Mr. Allan Hoover has told us, his father began to collect, on a worldwide basis, the original records of men and governments, even while wars and revolutions were raging. He did not intend his growing archive to be a mausoleum of documents but, on the contrary, a place of living research, where the mistakes of governments, so costly in human lives and misery, could be studied and remembered—and where the courageous efforts of a few men to avert wars, would likewise never be forgotten. It is in accord with this concept of Mr. Hoover's that Glenn Campbell and his staff have so brilliantly conducted this Institution.

Happily, Mr. Hoover lived to see the work flourish. In his latter years, when he spoke to the young and restless generation, he did not condemn everything they seemed to be saying. He once commented:

> It may be that the era of growing human freedom and economic materialism which began 400 years ago with the Renaissance is continuing today, and is now in a crisis of change which may bring other concepts of civilization. But, if it does, even then, the prime requisite will be Peace, for only from a lasting peace in this Era of Science and terrible new weapons can we hope to save mankind from utter annihilation.

In my observation of Mr. Hoover over half a century, I saw that he had an obsession with peace beyond all his other concerns, and I came to the conclusion that this dedication stemmed from his earliest upbringing. Those among you who are familiar with his writings, or who have heard him speak in public, will recall his frequent allusions to the Decalogue and to the Sermon on the Mount. He was accustomed to mention them together as the palladium of freedom—the cornerstones of liberty and peace. The chapters in the Old and New Testaments where they occur must have been read and re-read to him by his parents in the little house where he was born, for before their early deaths had left him an orphan, he had been so well taught that he firmly believed, and later wrote, that "the transcendent concept of compassion and of peace among men had been launched into the world by those two inspired passages from Holy Writ."

Early on in our association, he became aware of the fact that I could read a little Hebrew, and presuming a degree of competence I did not possess, he once asked me about the translation of the thirteenth verse in the sixth chapter of St. Matthew which puzzled him, as it had many men before him: "to pray the Lord that He not lead us into temptation." I knew only enough to tell him that the language of the plain people in Palestine of that era was Aramaic, and I knew no Aramaic. Later I found a rabbinic commentary which satisfactorily answered his question for, as he had guessed, the explanation was an error of translation in the King James version. But it was in that conversation and others which followed that I discovered his favorite verses, and that most favored of them all (Matthew 5:9) which begins "Blessed are the peacemakers. . . ."

I hope that a personal aside here may not be out of place. At about this time, 1917, my sainted mother once said to me, "Tell me, Lewis, when you and Mr. Hoover are not talking about the war and food control, what do you talk about?" "Well, Mother," I answered, "only last week we had a very interesting discussion about the Gospel according to St. Matthew." Too late I saw amazement and alarm in the eyes of my Jewish mother. She knew that the Gospels were in the New Testament—a book we did not study. Could this mean that Mr. Hoover was leading her son away from the covenant of Abraham? Quick to reassure her, I pointed out that the chapters of St. Matthew we were discussing dealt with the Ten Commandments and the Lord's Prayer, and that the disciples were believing Jews of their day. She was content. Then I told her that a verse Mr. Hoover had particularly liked began, "Blessed are the peacemakers," and to my surprise, she capped it, saying, "for they shall be called the children of God." She had read more than I knew.

A contribution to practical peacemaking, besides the establishment of this Library, was Mr. Hoover's literary testament on peace. It is the book, written with his friend, Hugh Gibson, on the "problems of lasting peace." Mr. Hoover expressed in its pages his hope of developing among the intelligent public, to which it was addressed, a commitment to the maintenance of peace. The Hoover Institution, his tangible legacy, would be the instrument for disseminating to scholars, to statesmen and to that intelligent public an understanding of the causes of past failures and provide the experience drawn from mankind's many efforts to prevent war.

In his view, the avoidance of war was the most urgent goal of man, and the quest for permanent peace the noblest of human aspirations. To it, Herbert Hoover gave the best that was in him.

Thank you.

Professor William Mosely,[2] distinguished scholar and public servant, professor of International Relations at Columbia University and director of the European Institute there:

> Thank you very much, Dr. Campbell, for that warm introduction. President Pitzer, Admiral Strauss, Mr. Hoover and distinguished guests, I would like to add just a few comments to what has been stated very eloquently, both in Mr. Hoover's own works and in the very vivid and eloquent memories of Admiral Strauss and others, about the role of research on foreign policy.

---

2. During World War II Mosely held a number of important posts in the State Department and served as an adviser to Secretary Cordell Hull and later to Secretary James Byrnes in matters involving Western and Eastern Europe, national boundaries, and the future of European nations. From 1955 to 1963 he was director of studies for the Council on Foreign Relations in New York, directing its comprehensive program of research on major issues of U.S. foreign policy. He has published numerous articles and books on Russia, on Balkan history, on the internal and foreign policy of the Soviet Union, and on U.S. foreign policy.

We have a new environment developing in our universities and among a substantial part of the public which places in question the very efforts to which so many of us—and in particular the Hoover Institution—have devoted so much now for fifty years. It is to me very striking that Herbert Hoover was convinced that peace must be fought for every day. And that means thinking hard about it. It is not something which suddenly appears and descends upon mankind as a blessing, without exertion. I was struck in reading back into the history of the founding of the Institution how even in the midst of World War I and of tremendous exertions for mankind, Herbert Hoover saw the need for gathering the materials, for bringing them together and making them available systematically to scholars who would endeavor to answer some of the previously unanswered questions about the past and, in that way, try to avoid some mistakes in the future.

The growth of this Institution is in itself a proof of the great importance people throughout the world attach to this role of policy study and study of the current situations in the world. I don't need to refer to the activities that are based upon the collections, which themselves are unique in the world, but I do want to bring tribute on behalf of all other institutions— since I'm the only speaker not closely connected with the Institution—for the generosity in making materials available, in soliciting funds for fellowships and travel to enable many of these nearly 1,000 people a year to come and to carry on their work in this unique repository, with the advice of a highly competent and experienced staff. In addition, the Hoover Institution has taken responsibility for a broad program of publication which carries the results of its research and policy study throughout the world. And that is extremely important, and is conducted with great efficiency—as I can say, having been engaged in a number of publishing enterprises and knowing how difficult it is to do it well and to get the books out where they are needed.

The Hoover Institution has pioneered in many important fields. It has an important series on colonialism in Africa. We cannot understand the problems of developing countries unless we re-examine from new points of view the impact of the colonial period, of colonial institutions and habits of thought, upon these countries. This is a very important enterprise. The Yearbook on International Communist Affairs has already, in two yearly volumes, set a very high standard and has made available materials that otherwise would have to be sought out in many obscure sources and checked against contradictory reports. A tremendous amount of work has gone into each of these two volumes of the yearbook, which is well worthy of continued active intellectual and financial support.

Dr. Campbell and President Pitzer have been rather modest about the public service of Hoover Institution people. I haven't time to go into detail, but it is important that people with a background of systematic study and with a tradition of objective research have gone into government service from many of our leading institutions, including Stanford University and the Hoover Institution, and thus have enriched government policy-making and implementation and have returned with a deeper understanding of the practical problems of affairs of our country and of the world.

In all these respects, then, the Hoover Institution is a unique institution of outstanding quality, and I'm very happy to bring this tribute from other institutions. I didn't poll them; I didn't need to. I know over the last thirty or forty years how much the Hoover Institution has contributed to the tradition of objective scholarship, or systematic policy study, and to the broadening of the whole discourse of scholarship and to educating a very important public ...

In a period of detente we are going to need more careful policy study than in the past. We're going to need more discriminating analyses of what we can do and what we probably cannot do. We have to examine more carefully why we have better cooperation from some allies than from others. We have to examine the nature of the relationship with our presumed adversaries, some of whom may in the end turn out to be able to coexist with us in a fairly effective way. The simplicities of the early postwar years are giving way to a very complex period of polycentrism within the Communist world, of rivalries between Russia and China which are far more emotional and far more dangerous in many ways than those between the United States and the Soviet Union. And we are going to have to consider what we can do in that part of the world and to try to make better measurements.

For all of this we need more and not less policy research, more scholars of various ages hard at work studying different countries. We need to do more to develop an international community of policy research. We may not be able a few years from now to carry out studies in some Latin American countries unless there is a growing community of social science research in those countries which understands what we're doing. And this is true of many other areas.

Through the small but important contributions of the universities, of institutions like the Hoover Institution, we fought the Cold War to a stalemate—which was all that we really expected from it. We have as a result of that a whole series of contradictory developments within the nations of the Communist world, in their relations with each other, in individual societies, and this needs much more study. We have new concepts of regionalism in Western Europe and in parts of Africa and Latin America. We must do a great deal more in these fields. In other words, in a period of detente we need more thought, more careful analysis, more reasoned controversy and more of the free inquiry which Herbert Hoover referred to in setting up this Institution.

Thank you.

Letter from President Richard Nixon:

For a half a century the Hoover Institution has carried forward the highest traditions of its distinguished founder and performed an invaluable public service. His compassion for the less fortunate, his dedication to peace, and his untiring efforts to build a better life for all Americans—these are the legacy of Herbert Hoover which you nobly memorialize and perpetuate.

Surely the Institution he founded has proved to be among President Hoover's most farsighted contributions to this nation. Built on the conviction that men cannot forge a successful future without first learning and heeding the lessons of the past, the Hoover Institution has sought to collect and preserve our knowledge of history while applying it to problems of the present and hopes for the future. As a world-famous research library and center for advanced study and research on international and public affairs, it has compiled an outstanding record of academic service and civic achievement.

My warm greetings go to the members of the Hoover family on this occasion, and my congratulations to the highly motivated men and women who have sought, in the truest spirit of all Herbert Hoover stood for, to probe into humanity's perplexing problems and to propose through careful study new and imaginative ways to achieve progress and peace with honor. As

President, I am deeply grateful for the Institution's cooperation in the work of Government and for the scholarly counsel that so assists our leadership.

I can only hope that your second half century will be as productive and as rewarding for the nation as the last.

On the Dedication of the Herbert Hoover Memorial

Speeches

Paul L. Davies, Chairman of the Board of Overseers:

As chairman of the Board of Overseers of the Hoover Institution, it is my pleasure to welcome you to this dedication of our nation's memorial to Herbert Hoover. Legislation for this memorial was approved by the 93rd Congress and signed by President Gerald Ford just over three years ago. Other speakers will tell us more concerning the memorial. We are grateful that Reverend Fiennes has come from England to help us celebrate this occasion. Reverend Fiennes is Dean of Lincoln Cathedral and has graciously arranged for the Magna Carta to be displayed for the next four days in the exhibit pavilion to inaugurate this memorial. We are indebted to Dr. Paul Hanna, senior research fellow, for arranging the loan of the Magna Carta.

It is our privilege to have with us Mr. Allan Hoover, the surviving son of President Hoover and a member of the Hoover Institution Board of Overseers. We appreciate immensely having so many members of the Hoover family present today, their agreement to the initial proposal to locate this memorial at the Hoover Institution, and their helpful suggestions and support throughout.

The cooperation in many relationships between the Hoover Institution and Stanford adds to the richness of both institutions and therefore to the contributions that each makes to the community and nation. We all know of the great advances made at the Hoover Institution over the past decade and a half under the leadership of its director, Glenn Campbell. Today higher education, the private university in particular, is experiencing major challenges and undergoing substantial changes. Stanford University is fortunate to have Dr. Richard Lyman as president and Dr. Peter Bing as president of its Board of Trustees.

Before President Ford cuts the ribbon that officially dedicates this memorial, I must briefly thank a few of the many persons who have made this day possible. Time will not permit me to name everyone.

I have mentioned the Hoover family, and others have thanked the Congress and President Ford. When you see this major building—the two pavilions, the center court and fountain, the memorial plaque, and the sundial—I am sure you will agree that Ernest Kump, the architect, and Dale Sprankle, principal-in-charge, have rendered a memorial that is both handsome and utilitarian and one which blends with the other buildings, providing unity to the whole. You will also understand why, in 1970, Kump's firm received the highest award given by the American Institute of Architects to an architectural firm in the United States. Thanks also go to Dickman Construction Company, the general contractor. Please note the sundial and memorial inscriptions designed by Ernest Born and, as you view the Magna Carta and the other treasures in the new exhibit pavilion, note also the hand-carved door done for us by Stan Dann.

A complex project requires much planning and attention. While many Stanford and Hoover people burned midnight oil to see this project to completion, I would be remiss if I did not mention Senior Fellow Rita Ricardo-Campbell, the principal Hoover Institution staff member concerned with the design, and Associate Director Darrell Trent, who with Rita oversaw planning and construction. As you go through the memorial, you will note that the auditorium and a number of rooms and floors are named in honor of some of the donors. To these, and to the many other donors who provided funds to match the federal grant, we express our heartfelt thanks.

After President Ford cuts the ribbon, the pubic is invited to join us for a cool drink, to view the Magna Carta in the exhibit pavilion, and to tour the memorial buildings.

Adding color and music to today's festivities are the United States Marine Corps Color Guard and the San Diego Marine Corps Recruit Depot Band, under the direction of Captain Harold Whitney, Jr.

Oliver Fiennes (Invocation):

Lord, we thank you for your unchanging goodness to us.

Today, we thank you especially for the life and inspiration of Herbert Hoover and all other men and women who have dedicated themselves to the cause of peace and freedom. We remember too those others whose good lives, touching our own, have helped us on our way.

We commend to your care those whose generosity has made this building possible, those whose skill and labor have created it, and those whose working lives are spent in it. May they be humble in the pursuit of truth, enthusiastic in the discipline of excellence, and happy in all they do.

In the words of the Magna Carta, we wish that "the people shall have and hold all their liberties, rights, and concessions well and peacefully, freely and quietly, fully and completely," and we pray that this institution may ever uphold that ideal and oppose with honesty and courage those who would destroy it. So, Lord, in your name we bless this building and all concerned with it.

O Lord, without whom our labor is lost and with whom your little ones go forth as the mighty, be present to bless all work undertaken according to your will—and especially this Hoover Memorial Building, which we bless in your name—and grant to your laborers a patient faith, sufficient success upon earth, and the bliss of serving you in Heaven through Jesus Christ our Lord. Amen.

Allan Hoover:

Mr. Chairman, President Ford, friends of the Hoover Institution: It is my pleasure today to express the great appreciation of the Hoover family for the dedication of this fine educational facility as the nation's memorial in honor of our father and president, Herbert Hoover.

And especially, we wish to thank President Ford, Senator Hatfield, and all of the officials of the United States government, and the many contributors and friends who have worked toward making possible this magnificent memorial.

My father had a close relationship with Stanford University for over seventy years—from the time he entered Stanford as a freshman in 1891, when the university first opened its doors to students, until his death in 1964. He served as a trustee or trustee emeritus for over fifty years.

Among his numerous contributions to his alma mater, he always considered the founding of this Institution that bears his name to be the most important and lasting one. During his lifetime, he and his friends and associates devoted many hours to collecting and preserving the important documents of contemporary history that form the basis of the Institution's international reputation. My father firmly believed in the importance of higher education and the indispensability of free inquiry. He hoped that the study of the records gathered here would help to reveal to men how war and the ravages of war could be avoided and thus outline the paths to peace.

As I said two years ago when we broke ground for the building, my father was never much of a believer in stone monuments. Thus, it is a source of pride to the members of the Hoover family and myself that Congress decided to locate this federal memorial at the Hoover Institution. It will be a living memorial utilized by thousands of students and scholars from this country and abroad who will make many contributions to my father's abiding, lifelong interest—the promotion of peace.

Also, it is very fitting that the Herbert Hoover Memorial Building should so closely resemble the building dedicated a little over ten years ago to my mother, Lou Henry Hoover. They accurately reflect the close partnership which existed between my mother and father.

Many visitors will come to view this memorial with its rare archival treasures. Let us hope that the scholars who work here will continue to make important contributions for the benefit of society as reflected in the ideas of Herbert Hoover.

To quote my father:

For this fullness of life,
for the chance to serve . . .
I am indebted to my country
beyond any human power to repay.

Richard W. Lyman:

Thank you Paul, President Ford, Senator Hatfield, Allan Hoover, distinguished guests, friends.

It is my happy privilege, which can be exercised with appropriate brevity, to welcome you to this distinguished university on the western rim of the North American continent or, take your choice, the eastern rim of the Pacific basin. Seldom can a university have owed so much to a graduate of its opening class as this university owes to the late President Hoover. I often meet people who seem to assume that either before or after he undertook the real presidency—that of the United States—he must somehow have served as president of Stanford University, so closely is his name associated with this institution and its development. He was in a very real sense a second founder and, I'd like to suggest, did more than any one other person to assure that Stanford would be an institution in and of the world and not removed from it. The three parts of the university that are his special brain children testify to that—the Food Research Institute, the Graduate School of Business, and, of course, the Hoover Institution itself. Each is a source of enormous interchange between the campus and the wide world of human affairs. I am happy then to welcome you to this celebration of a notable extension of Mr. Hoover's vision and am especially happy to have with us, in the persons of Senator Hatfield and President Ford, two who contributed so singly to the realization of this most suitable memorial.

W. Glenn Campbell:

Mr. Chairman, President Ford, members of the Hoover family, ladies and gentlemen:

Today we dedicate the Herbert Hoover Federal Memorial, a fitting living memorial to honor a truly great and compassionate American. But we do more. We celebrate the idea that Herbert Hoover gave birth to back in 1919, almost sixty years ago. He had a dream. Motivated by concern for his fellow men, a love of freedom, and a horror of the devastations of war, he set forth on a lifelong goal whose ultimate aim was to promote peace throughout the world. Convinced that ignorance and lack of understanding were the root causes of war and social unrest, he undertook to put together the resources that would lead to the kind of scholarly research that would probe deeply into the political, economic, and social problems of our time, thereby helping all his fellow men to achieve personal freedom, economic prosperity, and a world at peace.

Today the resources he dreamed of putting together have been largely realized. We have one of the most extensive archival collections in the world, one of the finest libraries, physical research facilities that are among the finest anywhere, and a group of resident and associated scholars of great distinction—all located in the midst of one of the leading universities in the country.

But the purpose of all this, the reason why Herbert Hoover founded the

Institution, is still far from realization. Personal freedoms are still rare throughout the world, economic prosperity is increasingly fragile, violence and acts of terrorism are common, and the threat of devastating war is a real and present danger.

It has been over eighteen years since Mr. Hoover and Dr. Sterling asked me to become the director of this Institution. They have been years of hard work, of frustration, of challenges, and most important, ones of great satisfaction. In the day-to-day operations, it is sometimes easy to lose sight of the real purpose of the Hoover Institution. For its product—the pursuit of knowledge and truth about the important and sensitive political, social, and economic problems of our society—is not easily measured. And sometimes it is not even welcomed. The rigorous probing of a brilliant scholar can, and often does, lead to uncomfortable questions about some of our basic institutions.

Today we are faced with an increasing number of serious problems in our society, both at home and abroad, and the challenges and opportunities for the Hoover Institution to contribute to their resolution are manifold. In fact, I believe we are on the threshold of a new intellectual era. Programs, policies, and institutions that have largely gone unquestioned for the last thirty or forty years are increasingly being subjected to the kind of scholarly inquiry that is essential to the health of our free society.

The years ahead promise to be ones of genuine intellectual excitement, perhaps surpassing anything we have experienced so far; and I look forward to them. They will of course be, in some ways, difficult times. The established ways of doing things will be threatened by the prospect of change, and there always is an emotional reaction to change. Dark motivations will be attributed to the restless, questioning souls who tread on the prevailing wisdom of the establishment. Their findings may be summarily dismissed.

We, as an institution, must remember our basic purpose and mission. We must remember to focus on the search for what is right, for the understanding that will preserve and enhance our personal freedoms, that will increase our economic prosperity, that will help us achieve and maintain world peace. Now, more than ever, we truly need free and open competition of ideas. We need the freedom of research and independence of mind that identifies new alternatives, objectively weighs the pros and cons, and presents the results for everyone to see and evaluate. We need the kind of scholarly research that takes the long view of our society, not just the time between now and the next election, but between now and the time our grandchildren will become adults.

In pursuing Herbert Hoover's dream, we will have to be many more things.

In some ways we shall have to be conservative. We shall have to conserve our traditional respect for truth, for honesty, for rigorous, uncompromising research. We must also preserve our dedication to free and unrestricted inquiry.

In some ways we shall have to be liberal. We shall have to be compassionate to our fellow men. We shall have to be liberal in regard to leaving the individual as unrestricted as possible in the opportunities for self-expression and self-fulfillment. We shall have to be free from prejudice or bigotry of all forms.

And in some ways we shall have to be radical—radical, that is, in the uncompromising search for truth; radical in advocating fundamental reforms that we believe in, and radical in having the courage publicly to express our knowledge and our beliefs and to defend them with vigor. I am sure we all look forward to taking part in the next phase of Herbert Hoover's dream.

Finally, before introducing Senator Hatfield, I would like to say on behalf of my colleagues and myself that we will be eternally grateful to the Hoover family for agreeing to locate the memorial here, to Congress for passing the legislation, to President Ford for signing the authorization and funding, to the architects, Ernest J. Kump and Sprankle, Lynd & Sprague, for their excellent work, to the Stanford University and Hoover Institution staff who worked on the project for their dedicated efforts, and finally, to the many supporters and friends of the Hoover Institution whose financial support made all of this possible.

And now it is my great pleasure to introduce one of the finest persons that I have ever been privileged to know—the distinguished senior senator from Oregon, Mark Hatfield. In a very real sense this memorial to the late President Hoover is Senator Hatfield's creation. He initiated the idea; he introduced the first bill; and as a devoted admirer and student of the late president, he followed its progress through Congress closely and effectively right up to its final passage at about 11 PM on the day of adjournment of Congress. Senator Hatfield, you honor us by your presence today.

Senator Mark Hatfield (R–Oregon):

Thank you very much, Glenn. Mr. Chairman, President Ford, members of the Hoover family, President Lyman, ladies and gentlemen:

Antoinette and I are, first of all, delighted to be back on the campus of our alma mater, and as much as I would like to enjoy the privilege of reminiscing, I shall refrain from doing so on this occasion.

Today, when too many of our politicians and political policies are about as authentic as instant mashed potatoes, I think it is very appropriate that we reflect upon some of the qualities of one of our most multifaceted presidents of all time, Herbert Hoover. President Hoover was a man who was both contemporary and generational. He was one who could see the need to mobilize and interdict the economic cycle with the forces of the federal government; and as the first president in history to do so, he tried to bring relief from the suffering of so many during the Great Depression. But he was also a man who looked to the future generations and their needs, because he sought to develop the tools of employment. He was concerned about the great natural resources of this country. He was one of the first to speak out about the pollution of our great riverways, to establish policies for the wise extraction of our minerals, for the protection of our fisheries, and for the management of our petroleum reserves. Also, Herbert Hoover was a man who could act to meet a local need or a global need. One need but reflect briefly upon his history as secretary of commerce to see how he mobilized again the resources of government and private enterprise to assist the victims of the great Mississippi flood in the twenties. And might we ask today, who in this century could literally be credited with saving millions of lives of people who otherwise would have starved, both during and after World War I—a man who never drew a line as to political ideology, but even responded to the needs of the Soviet Union in their great famine period in the twenties, as well.

Too often we honor those who have been credited with destruction of life, and too infrequently do we honor those who have literally rescued people from starvation and disease. For you see, Herbert Hoover understood his common humanity with the peoples of the globe, and he moved from a sense of we and us, rather than they and them. He was also a man who understood the balances of institutional and personal problems and action.

He once observed, in these words, that "a government that is imbalanced in the direction of business could ultimately lead to fascism, a government that is imbalanced in the direction of labor could ultimately lead to socialism, and a government that seeks power unto itself and centralizes power could lead to bureaucratic tyranny." Then he looked into the future and observed that possibly there would come a day when a system of syndicalism would take over which was, as Mr. Hoover classified, the fusion of the elite of business, labor, and government.

But he was also one who understood that America had to have housing, and he brought together the forces of government and enterprise for his great program of Better Homes for America. He also recognized again the personal when he sought and established the eight-hour working day for working persons, recognized that collective bargaining is the heart of the free enterprise system, and said that labor unions are normal and proper antidotes for the unlimited capitalistic organization—for you see, he recognized the need for individual personal responsibility and not dependence upon organizations.

By the same token, he recognized the need for mediating structures in our society and our culture.

Herbert Hoover was also a man who could respond in a philosophical, as well as a pragmatic way. He philosophized about foreign policy when he rejected an aggressive, militant approach to foreign affairs; instead, he said the pragmatic approach is cooperative, non-coercive, anti-interventionist. He also was one who could philosophize about government. He classified his political philosophy thus: liberalism holds that man is master of a state, not the servant; the sole purpose of government is to nurture and to assure these liberties. And yet he was pragmatic when attacking and launching the great task of reorganizing the federal government's executive branch under the commission that bears his name.

And lastly, my friends, Herbert Hoover functioned as a man representing both the physical world and the spiritual world. The physical world was one of his great professional expertise, when he dreamed of and established the Colorado River Reclamation, the Grand Coulee Dam, and the St. Lawrence Waterway. But he also was a man who sensed the needs of the spirit when he said,

Liberty is a thing of the spirit, to be free, to be free to worship, to think, to hold opinions, and to speak without fear. Liberty conceives that the mind and spirit of men can be free only if the individual is free to choose his own calling, to develop his talents to the best of his ability, to keep a home sacred from intrusion, to rear children in ordered security.

Herbert Hoover has inspired my life—from the time that I was in the fifth grade and distributed "Re-elect Hoover" handbills throughout my neighborhood in 1932; to the time that I was a student here at Stanford and had the privilege of interviewing him on a number of occasions; to the relationship as his friend and invitee, sitting around the campfire at Cave Man Camp at the Bohemian Grove, and visiting with him in his apartment at the Waldorf Towers in New York City.

So his words, his life, his philosophy have been my inspiration. Would that I could emulate them.

President Gerald R. Ford, keynote speaker:

It is a very high honor and a very rare privilege for me to have an opportunity to participate in this magnificent ceremony, and I thank you very, very much. This is what you might call my third close encounter with the Hoover Institution. I'm not only deeply honored by the invitation but greatly gratified to be here on this occasion. When I was vice-president, Dick Burress, whom I had temporarily borrowed from his new assignment as associate director of the Hoover Institution to help out in my confirmation process under the 25th amendment and as my assistant for congressional liaison, relayed Glenn Campbell's invitation to speak at ceremonies here on the 100th anniversary of Herbert Hoover's birth. The date was August 10, 1974, but a funny thing happened on my way to Palo Alto. My bags were all packed; I had a great speech prepared about President Hoover. In fact, it may well have been the best speech that I never gave. I'm sure my friend Mark Hatfield, who sponsored the legislation that made this memorial facility possible for us here today, made a much better speech as a pinch hitter for me, while I spent that weekend taking the oath of office and meeting with congressional leaders, the cabinet, the White House staff and the press corps, the Council of Economic Advisors, the National Security Council, and about a hundred ambassadors and an equal number of friends who wanted to tell me who should be the next vice president.

My second close encounter was just two years ago when ground was broken for this magnificent building, which represents the gratitude of the American people for the long lifetime of service to this nation of Herbert Clark Hoover, our thirty-first president. Again, Glenn Campbell invited me to man the spade and also to speak briefly. He was tactful as always and did not remind me that I stood him up once before. Obviously, I very much wanted to come, Glenn, but in July of 1976, a lot was happening throughout the land. I had learned from the Oval Office that all difficult decisions make more enemies than friends, Congress was in its typical cantankerous election mood; there was a long procession of distinguished bicentennial visitors from abroad; and in my spare moments I was trying to remain president against formidable opposition. Regrettably, I had to decline. I sent my longtime friend, Counselor Bob Hartman, one of the distinguished Stanford alumni in my cabinet and now one of Hoover's Senior Research Fellows, to represent me and to read my good wishes. But today, though it has taken a long, long time, I'm here for my third encounter, live and in person. I thank you, Glenn, for your perseverance and for your patience.

It was a surprise to me, but I'm delighted to have the opportunity of making an observation or comment concerning the great exhibit that's here on this campus. The Magna Carta is an inspiration to all of us and it is a tribute to the stature of the Hoover Institution to have the magnificent Magna Carta of Lincoln Cathedral here in our midst. During our bicentennial, I was once again struck by the degree to which framers of our Declaration of Independence, Constitution, and Bill of Rights depended upon the fundamental principles set down at Runnymede in 1215. Today these century-old guarantees of the rule of law and the respect for persons and property against arbitrary abuses of governmental power are indelibly inscribed not only on historic parchments but in the hearts of free peoples on both sides of the Atlantic and here on the shores of the Pacific.

It's most appropriate for a former president to pay tribute to a former president, especially when both were Californians by choice and held similar fundamental convictions about the superiority of private enterprise over any form of state economics, the worth of individual initiative as against governmental dictation, the obligation of humanity to the hungry and to the helpless, and the challenge to liberty at home and abroad. It's a pleasant privilege to do so on what was once the farm of an early governor of California and in the company of a distinguished former governor.

Former presidents are a fairly small club, though hopefully we may have a new member fairly soon. But one of the wonderful things about America is that future presidents are literally all over the place. They number in the millions, and there is today no class, no religion, no region, no race or nationality that can be excluded. Nor will sex be a barrier to the White House in the near future. Betty will appreciate that. Fortunately, millions more potential future presidents are coming along every year. What prophet was around a century or so ago who would have predicted that a blacksmith's son from a small Iowa town, who had been orphaned since he was eight years old, would quit his job as an office boy in Salem, Oregon, study nights in order to win admission to the exciting new university just opening in California, and pursue his ambition of becoming a mining engineer—the best mining engineer in the world. That is what Herbert Hoover did with the help of Stanford University. He did it long before he scaled the highest peaks of achievement in half a dozen other fields and was elected president of the United States by the largest landslide since George Washington. I don't want to be misunderstood as advocating that working on the farm and studying engineering is the best possible background for the presidency. Seriously, there should be no occupational or professional requirements for the presidency, except the requirement of proven character, demonstrated decisiveness, and a broad vision of the world and the critical responsibility of the United States as the champion of freedom and peace in our time.

Herbert Hoover had all of these qualifications and many, many more, too. His life was an outstanding example of the pursuit of excellence and his birthright Quaker concern for his fellow men and women. Many, if not most, of our presidents have taken pride in their humble beginnings, in working hard for their education, and in the attainments of private and public life both before and after residence in the nation's capital. It's not only true of President Hoover, but I believe it's generally true that Americans have understood, appreciated, and even loved their former presidents more after they have left the White House. The struggles of their successors with the unending dilemmas of democratic leadership have made most past presidents look better and better as years go by. So I suppose there's still some hope for me. But I remember, as a boy in Michigan, hearing the legend of Herbert Hoover as the great humanitarian hero of World War I. I have some youthful collections of his meteoric political rise and fall, but what I know first hand was his dignity and lack of bitterness in defeat, his total devotion to his country, his lifetime dedication to its service, and his tremendous and unique contributions after World War II. It is to the everlasting honor of President Truman, to whom the rule of increasing affection also applies, that among his first official acts in 1945 when he suddenly inherited the awesome burdens was to enlist President Hoover's unique wealth of experience to prevent another postwar famine in Europe by naming him chairman of the President's Famine Emergency Committee. In 1947, two years before I had the honor of going to Congress, Mr. Truman named Mr. Hoover chairman of what was to become known as the first Hoover commission to reorganize and reform the executive branch of the federal government.

Improving the efficiency of the federal bureaucracy and eliminating waste in Washington is, I can testify, a lot easier to promise than to perform. But you can look at Herbert Hoover's monumental recommendations this way— half of them were applauded but tragically never adopted. As for the rest, think how much worse things would be today if they had not been implemented. When President Eisenhower called upon President Hoover to try again with the second Hoover commission, he responded readily at a vigorous 79, and he gave eleven more years of service and counsel to the land that he loved so dearly. He gave his life to America as surely as those like Abraham Lincoln and John F. Kennedy, who were cut down in their prime. Herbert Hoover gave so much.

This place symbolized another quiet but significant facet of Herbert Hoover's greatness. He had a deep concern for history, not as a dry discipline but as an instructor of the present. He had an abiding affection for this great seat of learning established by Governor and Mrs. Stanford, that the children of California may be our children. This audience well knows, and I will not recite, President Hoover's many contributions to his alma mater, of which the Hoover Institution on War, Revolution and Peace is the world-renowned centerpiece.

Beginning in 1919, with his sponsorship of a systematic collection of priceless papers and records from the war and revolutions in devastated Europe, Herbert Hoover, in his own lifetime, helped to build this unique institution into a repository of original resource materials to which scholars of the whole world can turn for enlightenment. I'm told that the Herbert Hoover Federal Memorial Building, which we dedicate today, will complete the so-called Hoover Quad on this beautiful campus. I suppose that in the sense of architectural symmetry, that is correct; but in the larger sense, the accumulation of knowledge about our past and the pursuit of understanding for our future are never, never completed. The legacy of Herbert Hoover herein preserved is the living, growing memorial to a great American and a most uncommon man. A federal contribution to it represents the thanks of a very grateful nation.

Reflecting on the career of another former president, Woodrow Wilson, President Hoover himself quoted the oration of Pericles over the fallen heroes of Athens. It is equally applicable for Herbert Hoover's own eulogy on this occasion. It goes like this:

> So they gave their lives to the commonwealth and received the grandest of sepulchers, not that in which their mortal bones are laid but a home in the minds of men. For the whole earth is a monument of famous men, and their story is not graven only on the stone of their native earth but lives on far away without visible symbol, woven into the stuff of other men's lives.

> No man-made memorial can be everlasting, but here the gifts and the greatness of Herbert Hoover will enlarge the lives of generations of future Americans and the hopes of all humanity for justice and peace.

On the Twenty-fifth Anniversary of W. Glenn Campbell's Directorship

Emil Mosbacher, Jr., chairman of the Board of Overseers, oversaw my Silver Anniversary tribute at the Stanford Faculty Club. He presented me with a silver tray inscribed:

> To Glenn Campbell, whose distinguished leadership of the Hoover Institution and whose extraordinary contributions to the worlds of scholarship and public policy represent a unique achievement. We present our very good wishes on the occasion of his twenty-fifth anniversary as Director of the Hoover Institution, from your friends, July 18, 1984.

At dinner, Edwin Meese read a letter from President Reagan:

Dear Glenn:

I am writing this letter to you both as a friend and as an Honorary Fellow of the Hoover Institution. For Nancy and me it is a special honor to be part of the dinner on July 18 celebrating your 25th year as Director of the Hoover Institution. It is truly a unique occasion, and we are proud to extend to you and Rita our warmest congratulations.

Nancy and I would also like to express to you and to your colleagues at Stanford our deep appreciation for the invitation to locate the Presidential Library and Museum of this Administration in affiliation with the Hoover Institution at Stanford University. We are confident that the collections coming to Stanford will be of great value to future students and scholars.

Under your direction for the past quarter of a century, the Hoover Institution has grown and flourished. As a consequence of your leadership it enjoys today an excellent reputation for scholarship throughout the United States and the world. It has become very simply a unique national asset.

During the past sixty-five years, thousands of scholars from throughout our nation and abroad have experienced first-hand the wealth of the great collections located at the Hoover Institution. We will forever owe a great debt to Herbert Hoover for his foresight in establishing one of the great libraries in the world. In the same way, the scholarly community and the nation owe a special debt to you for carrying on the legacy of Herbert Hoover and creating one of the world's great centers for the advanced study of domestic and foreign affairs. You should be very proud of these achievements, and we are privileged to share this pride with you on this special evening.

Nancy and I send you our best wishes for every future success and happiness.

Sincerely,
Ronald Reagan

Robert Naylor, California assemblyman and minority floor leader, read a resolution cosponsored by Speaker Willie Brown and passed unanimously by the legislature:

Resolution

By the Honorable Robert W. Naylor
Twentieth Assembly District; Relative to Commending
W. GLENN CAMPBELL

WHEREAS, W. Glenn Campbell has served for 25 years as Director of the Hoover Institution at Stanford University, and upon this anniversary, in recognition of his professional excellence, he is deserving of highest honors and commendations; and

WHEREAS, Dr. Campbell received his B.A. degree at the University of Western Ontario in London, Canada, an M.A. degree in economics at Harvard University, and his Doctorate degree in economics summa cum laude from Harvard; and

WHEREAS, He began his professional career teaching economics at Harvard; later he was a research economist for the United States Chamber of Commerce; and then he joined the Hoover Institution after being the research director of the American Enterprise Institute for Public Policy Research; and

WHEREAS, As an economist, Dr. Campbell has served on numerous high level governmental advisory panels, has held seven appointments under five U.S. Presidents, and currently serves as Chairman of the President's Intelligence Oversight Board, as a member of the President's Foreign Intelligence Advisory Board, and as Chairman of the Japan-United States Friendship Commission; and

WHEREAS, He was a member of the President's Committee on Science and Technology and consultant to the Defense Department and to the National Security Council; he is a member of the Board of Directors of the Committee on the Present Danger and the Advisory Board of the Center for Strategic and International Studies at Georgetown University, and a recent appointee to the UNESCO Monitoring Committee; and he has served as a member of many professional and community organizations; now, therefore, be it

RESOLVED BY ASSEMBLY MEMBER ROBERT W. NAYLOR, That he takes great pleasure in honoring W. Glenn Campbell for his exemplary record of professional and personal achievements and dedicated public service, and conveys sincere best wishes for every satisfaction in the future; and be it further

RESOLVED, That a suitably prepared copy of this resolution be transmitted to W. Glenn Campbell.
Members Resolution No. 2758

Dated: July 16, 1984
Signed,
/s Bob Naylor/
Honorable Robert W. Naylor
20th Assembly District

Speeches

David Packard, member of the Board of Overseers:

"This institution should be an independent institution within the framework of Stanford University." Now, this idea was not entirely in accord with the traditional ideas of how a university should be governed, and so this generated a little bit of concern between the faculty and the trustees, and we had to look at this thing in a rather objective way.

I guess I must have visited with The Chief [Herbert Hoover] fifteen or twenty times. Every time we'd go to New York, we'd have a new version of what the relationship would be. I would come back and talk with Wally [Stanford President Wallace Sterling] and other trustees, and we finally worked out a relationship which was acceptable to both. I would like to say a word or two about why I think this was a very good decision, both in terms of the Hoover Institution and in terms of the University. In the first place, it seemed to me that President Hoover, because of his love for Stanford and his very great contribution to his many, many causes around the world and because of his wisdom, deserved some rather special consideration. I also felt that the traditional views about the governance of a university were not necessarily correct, and I say that about the corporate life too, as I think some of you know. So it seemed to me that there could be a logical solution to this, and that it was entirely appropriate to have an institution within the framework of the University that had some independence. So we finally worked this agreement out, and as part of the relationship we were fortunate enough to get Glenn and Rita to come out to take over the Institution in January of 1960.

I felt at the time that the relationship we worked out between the Institution and the University was not only appropriate to meet what The Chief wanted to do at that time, but was a very appropriate relationship in terms of the governance of the University. I still think so. And I want to say to you first that I felt the arrangement we worked out at that time was valid, and I think that same relationship is valid today. I see no reason whatsoever for any change to be considered.

Now about that time—well, I guess it was shortly after—I had the good fortune or maybe I should say misfortune, to become chairman of the Board of Trustees, and at that time we had visions about the future of Stanford. In fact, we talked about . . . that Stanford was teetering on the brink of greatness. I don't know whether it was teetering or tottering, but anyway, that was the common phrase we used, and I guess, as you well know, we fell in. I think without any question, in these last twenty-five years, Stanford University has become one of the great universities—not only of the United States but of the entire world.

And as I think you all know, I have been involved in this in various ways along the line. We have had a great many, very wonderful people working to build the University into one which will make an important and real contribution to the opportunities for our young people and to the future of our country. As I look upon the relationship that has developed over these past twenty-five years, I can honestly tell you that I don't think Stanford University would be where it is today, were it not for the relationship that was developed between the Hoover Institution and Stanford back in 1960 and has continued from then until this time.

Now I think that, as a good many of you know, it was not an entirely warm climate that Rita and Glenn moved into in those days because there was quite a lot of opposition from the faculty and other people. Glenn and I talked about this many times. One of the things I encouraged him to do, and I found that he had already made this commitment, was that if he simply made a commitment to make the Hoover Institution a center of excellence, it would indeed contribute to the progress of the entire University and would justify its own existence. Indeed that is what has happened over these years. I want to join all of you in thanking Glenn and Rita for this commitment to excellence that they made when they first came out here. We ought to thank them for the troublesome times that they have gone through to bring this Institution to the point of greatness, along with the University with which it is associated.

As I came in tonight I saw so many of my good friends, and indeed many people who are here who otherwise would have had no interest whatsoever in Stanford University. I think that any other university in the country would be very hard put to bring together as distinguished a group of people who are interested in the future of our country, who are interested in excellence in education, and who are interested in providing the kind of leadership that is so important for young people today. We really owe Rita and Glenn and the Hoover Institution a great debt of gratitude for making it possible for all of you to be here with us tonight.

I've been involved to some extent in the discussions that have gone on in the last few months, and I'm confident that we will work those out in a mutually satisfactory way. I hope very, very much that we can count on all of you here tonight to continue to support all of us who are in this area and closer to the University than you, in the objective that the Hoover Institution and Stanford University will continue to work together with the goal of building this into one of the great centers of excellence in the entire world. And with that I want to thank you all very, very much for joining us tonight.

Donald Kennedy:

Ladies and Gentlemen:

I'm glad to be able to contribute to this salute to the accomplishments of the Hoover Institution and its Director. I do so amidst some knowledge we all share: that it has been a difficult year and a half for the relationship between the Hoover Institution and the rest of Stanford. I would point out, however, that such difficulties are part of the working life of a great institution, and that controversy is almost inevitably a part of institutional innovation and institutional growth.

At such times, however, it is useful to concentrate on real facts and real accomplishments, and there is much to be proud of. In the last quarter-century, during Glenn Campbell's tenure as Director of the Hoover Institution, there has been extraordinary growth. Since that period almost exactly coincides with my own tenure as a member of the Stanford faculty, the comparison is not a difficult one for me to make. In particular, I would contrast the situation then and now in three areas:

- First, the Hoover Archives—the core resource of this exceptional legacy we have—has been continually and thoughtfully built and expanded, so that it now constitutes an exceptional resource for scholars all over the world.

- Second, Hoover's own roster of distinguished scholars has grown.

- Third, both the number and the proportion of joint appointments between Hoover and academic departments at Stanford have increased, engaging scholars in the two places with one another more effectively.

For all of these accomplishments, we owe Glenn Campbell and his colleagues our thanks and our congratulations.

As for the future, we have a superb opportunity to build on what has already been created. I want to say a couple of things about the prospects for that building. In doing so, I hope I can allay some fears about recent actions of the Board of Trustees with regard to the relationship between the Hoover Institution and the rest of Stanford.

One thing that emerged clearly from the events that began a year ago this past spring is that understanding of and about the Hoover Institution by the Stanford faculty, and vice versa, is less than we should all hope for. It is easy to ignore—or at any rate it should be easy to ignore—the more irresponsible of these charges—and there certainly were some irresponsible ones! But a number of thoughtful, serious, and rather apolitical Stanford faculty members were concerned about Hoover and its relationships to the rest of the University and confessed that they knew less than they would like to both about the policies that link the two and about academic and administrative practices in each place.

An increase in the mutual understanding of Stanford faculty members and Hoover Institution Fellows is one of the objectives of the ad hoc committee on the Hoover Institution set up by the Stanford Board of Trustees. To help in this task, the committee convened a group of equal numbers of Stanford faculty, Hoover fellows, and scholars with joint appointments to examine the appointment process itself and how it might be improved to the benefit of both institutions. A draft report from this group is now in the hands of the committee. It is clear that just in the course of doing the work, members of that group, which was chaired by Professor Robert Ward, came to understand one another and the two institutions considerably better. My own view is that when people sit down and work at problems, things work much better. This exercise, I believe, is no exception.

We shall probably do something quite similar with the various administrative practices and procedures through which the two institutions overlap. In the meantime, the Trustees committee is examining the history and present status of the relationship, with a view to improving the value of the Hoover Institution to the rest of Stanford University and vice versa. I would remind you that those words, explicitly, constitute the charge from the Board of Trustees to the committee. The Board is, after all, no less responsible for the welfare of the Hoover Institution than it is for any other part of Stanford University. It takes that responsibility seriously, and so do I.

But tonight we are gathered to honor Glenn Campbell on his twenty-fifth anniversary as Director of the Hoover Institution. The growth and progress of the Institution over the past quarter-century are impressive and clearly worth celebrating. I congratulate Glenn on his perseverance, his unswerving devotion to the Hoover Institution, and on the accomplishments of the Hoover during his tenure. I think the future holds even more promise for productive and harmonious relationships between Hoover and the rest of Stanford, and I am committed to working patiently and devotedly toward that end.

Dr. David Pierpont Gardner, president of the University of California:

Glenn Campbell's service to the University of California very nearly rivals his quarter-century of service to the Hoover Institution, which makes me especially pleased to join you in honoring him tonight. Appointed to the Board of Regents in 1968, recently reappointed by Governor Deukmejian for a second term, Glenn has been a Regent during sixteen of the most eventful years in the history of American higher education. He has seen the University of California through student unrest, unparalleled expansion, rising and falling economies, three governors, and four U.C. presidents. He has served on virtually every major Regental committee, standing and special, including the pivotal Committee on Finance, which he chaired in 1980–81. In 1982–83 he served in the demanding and time-consuming role of Chairman of the Board. Through his work on no fewer than six search committees, he has been actively involved in the selection of a president, three chancellors, and two laboratory directors. By this time he knows as much about the University of California as he does about supply-side economics, which is saying something.

Obviously, this amounts to an enormous investment of time and energy. But Glenn has also brought to the Board's deliberations an economist's keen eye for the bottom line and an unfailing ability to turn dull discussions into lively ones. He is a leavening influence because his perspective is entirely his own. And because that perspective has been shaped by a professional life spent in the independent sector of higher education, it is especially valuable to the governing board of a public university. For sixteen years, whatever the issue, Glenn has brought that perspective to bear on matters of crucial importance to education and to the University of California.

I should add that the University of California isn't the only organization that has benefited from his presence and his advice: he has served on many educational, cultural, and national boards as well. So even though his primary commitment is to a private institution, public service has been a distinguished and long-standing dimension of his career.

The rewards of serving as a University of California Regent tend to be more ethereal than tangible. But I'm pleased to say that it has brought Glenn at least one modest benefit. I'm told that several years ago the Regents held one of their regular meetings in Los Angeles and most Regents stayed at the Biltmore Hotel, where, as it happened, the Grammy Awards were being televised. Glenn arrived, checked in, and was enthusiastically escorted to his room—which, as it turned out, was the best in the hotel. Encouraged by the warmth of his welcome, Glenn settled in to enjoy a quiet evening. A few hours later, however, came a knock on the door. It was the embarrassed manager of the hotel, who by this time had discovered that his guest was Glenn Campbell the Regent, not Glen Campbell the country singer.

I don't know—at least not from personal experience—whether singing is one of the talents Glenn has contributed to the Hoover Institution. I do know that both the Hoover Institution and the University of California have reason to be grateful for the many other talents he has contributed, as Director and as Regent. On behalf of Glenn's colleagues on the Board, I am delighted to acknowledge his many contributions to the University of California and to convey our congratulations and best wishes on this important twenty-fifth anniversary.

W. Glenn Campbell:

Ambassador Mosbacher, Distinguished Co-Chairmen, Sponsors, and Friends: My father always told me, and he only had an eighth-grade education, that one should always quit while he is ahead. After all this praise tonight, I should quit right now. Being a simple farm boy, my natural inclinations always are to tell a few jokes and speak the truth even if it hurts. However, over the years, I've learned that this is risky business. Thus, tonight I am only going to engage in a few reminiscences and philosophical observations.

First, let me reassure everyone here tonight that this is not a retirement party. As my good friend, Secretary of State George Shultz, said in his telegram of congratulations, "... I am sure that the second quarter century of your stewardship will be as successful as your first."

Forty years ago this month, I first came to the United States as a graduate student at Harvard. The most important event by far that year occurred sometime in late July or early August. My turn had just come to discuss serious economics with the professor whom *Forbes* magazine recently rated as the greatest economist of the twentieth century (better than John Maynard Keynes, that is) when this stunningly beautiful young woman with a magnificent tan, who turned out to have brains and personality as well, came breezing into Professor Schumpeter's office. He immediately ignored me, kissed her hand in the continental style, and said, "How great it is to have you back from vacation, Miss Ricardo." To make a long and pleasant story as short as possible, Rita and I were married two years later—right after she got her Ph.D. and could support me properly. As you can see, I was forward-looking rather than backward-looking even in those days.

If I were to describe Rita's distinguished career fully, we would be here all night—she was probably the first woman to hold a Harvard teaching appointment; after that she held the highest academic rank held by a woman at Tufts College from 1948 to 1951; she was one of the first women to hold a professional staff appointment on the House Ways and Means Committee; she was offered membership on the Council of Economic Advisors in early 1981, and she would have been the second female member in its history if she had not decided to stay with her husband and help him in his trials and tribulations at Stanford University. Above all, she has served as an example and a mentor to our three wonderful daughters, all of whom have either launched or are about to launch professional careers. Furthermore, Rita did all of this without the advantage of an affirmative action program or quotas.

Over the years many people have asked me what part of my job as Director of the Hoover Institution gives me the greatest satisfaction. Let me begin by stating that it is not our magnificent building complex, even though we consider it the best on campus or in the world. And we should all be eternally grateful to the Hoover family for agreeing to locate the Federal Memorial here so that the Stanford Board of Trustees can have a first-class place to meet, and for making the Hoover Tower and the Lou Henry Hoover Building possible. Nor is it the fact that the Hoover endowment has increased from $2 million to $65 million during the past twenty-five years, and that we have raised 5 percent of the total private funds raised at Stanford University since the founding grant without ever engaging the services of a professional fundraiser. We simply consider this to be a recognition on the part of tough-minded charitable types of the high quality of our program.

My real satisfaction comes from the work of the remarkable group of scholars that we have been able to attract to the Hoover Institution and the many important contributions to knowledge and to public policy that they have made. You just have to attend the afternoon coffee to know that at the Hoover Institution the competition of ideas is alive and vigorous and a benefit to all concerned, and not just a theoretical matter. Our scholars, and they are true scholars in the classic sense of the term, gather their data painstakingly and carefully, then try to formulate hypotheses to explain it. Next they do whatever further refining of their data and hypotheses they feel is necessary, and if they are both fortunate and good, they may even end up with a new theory.

Let me cite in this connection the pioneering work of Martin Anderson on welfare policy and on the all-volunteer army; Nobel laureate Milton Friedman's continuing work on money and its relation to economic growth and prices; the well-known work of Bob Hall and Alvin Rabushka on the flat-rate income tax; the important work of Rita Ricardo-Campbell on social security, health policy, and drug regulation—or should I say deregulation; the innovative and pioneering work of Tom Sowell on ethnic differences, affirmative action, etc., along with Jack Bunzel's challenging work on civil rights and affirmative action; Roger Freeman's widely quoted works on the growth of American government; Tom Moore's pioneering work on transportation deregulation—for which he has been commended by Senator Edward Kennedy amongst others; Seymour Martin Lipset's well-known work on American politics and public opinion; James March's research on organizational behavior; and Alex Inkeles' multifaceted investigations of the social structure of the emerging worldwide society and its potential interrelationships with social and cultural aspects of U.S. national development. I cannot discuss our Domestic Studies program without mentioning the fact that one of former Vice President Mondale's principal economic advisers, Dr. Joseph Pechman, spent a lively year with us and, my colleagues and I hope, picked up a number of good ideas for presidential candidate Mondale, not to mention vice presidential candidate Ferraro.

In the international field there are the many contributions of Professor Teller, the most recent being his work on ballistic missile defense, and the important work in the field of national security affairs by Richard Allen and William Van Cleave; the many scholarly contributions of Peter Duignan and Lewis Gann on Africa and the Middle East; those by Bob Conquest, Dick Staar, and Milorad Drachkovitch on the Soviet Union and Eastern Europe. In the field of international economics there is the challenging work of Mel Krauss on international monetary problems and the need for new approaches to Western European defense and economic policy. I want to pay particular tribute to the people who were here during the past twenty-five years and made the achievements of the last decade possible. I refer in particular to Milorad Drachkovitch, Peter Duignan, Roger Freeman, Lewis Gann, and Rita Ricardo-Campbell.

I also want to express my appreciation to the fine members of the staff of the Institution's library, who have done so much to build our great research collections and to encourage their worldwide use. Our Board of Overseers has always been a tower of strength to the Institution and particularly to me personally and its wise counsel and assistance have been indispensable to the Institution's success. However, into each life a little rain must fall, and on more than one occasion during the past two years I have taken comfort from the story told by the late President Lyndon Johnson when he was first rising to prominence—namely, every time a jackrabbit sticks his head above the clover, a bunch of yahoos start throwing stones at him. One cannot work on such emotionally charged issues and activities as the principal campus advocate of the Ronald Reagan Presidential Library complex, Chairman of the Board of Regents of the University of California—particularly when a new president is being chosen—and as chairman or member of several high-level government advisory groups without being on the receiving end of a number of brickbats, sometimes fair but usually foul. As President Truman used to say, "If you can't stand the heat, get out of the kitchen." Frequently the greatest satisfactions come as a result of being unfairly attacked. I refer in particular to a front-page retraction this past February by the local newspaper two days after they libeled me on the front page.

I have already referred to several of the satisfactions derived from the opportunity to engage in meaningful public service, whether it involves international agencies, the federal government, state and local governments, or serving on the boards of the great government foundations such as the National Endowment for the Humanities and the National Science Foundation, or on the boards of trustees of other colleges and universities.

Since our distinguished new president of the University of California has honored us by his presence tonight, I wish to refer to two special satisfactions I have derived in my years as a Regent of the University of California, besides the general satisfaction of being involved with the work of the country's number-one public university system. The first one is the fact that because of the firmness of the Board of Regents—some of my comrades in this action, I am pleased to say, are here tonight—the University of California still has ROTC, and, as a result, because of U.C.'s magnanimity, a few Stanford students are able to take ROTC at Berkeley despite the fact that Stanford offed it over a decade ago. The second was serving as Chairman of the Board of Regents when David Gardner was elected president, and subsequently observing him skillfully and rapidly leading the University to even greater glories than those of yesteryear.

I have had one serious continuing disappointment during my tenure as Director of the Hoover Institution. I refer to my inability, particularly during the *early* years, in spite of continuous trying on my part and that of my colleagues, to get more cooperation and interaction with members of the Stanford faculty and administration. Obviously this would strengthen both the Hoover Institution and the rest of Stanford University. As a very distinguished Stanford alumnus, former dean, and longtime trustee, my good friend Ernie Arbuckle, said in a letter that I just received, which I deeply cherish and from which I know he wouldn't mind my sharing a paragraph with you:

> As you may recall, I was new on the campus when you received your appointment. I remember so well the hurdles that were set up for you to clear before you could achieve your objectives for the Institution and how difficult those early years were. Our friendship was nurtured in that kind of environment and it has been strong ever since.

As a result of persistent efforts over these years, relations have steadily improved. Judging by their fine work to date, I'm encouraged that President Kennedy and the new Trustees Committee on the Hoover Institution are working to remedy this problem once and for all.

Finally, if there is a more challenging, more interesting, and more personally satisfying job in higher education than that of being Director of the Hoover Institution, I have yet to find it.

Emil Mosbacher, Jr.:

Ladies and Gentlemen:

There's no way to follow that except by reading some of the rest of that letter that he referred to from Ernie Arbuckle. Glenn, believe it or not, was modest. He read part of that letter, but I happen to have a copy of it too, and I would like to read to you that which he did not read:

> The quality of the people you have brought to Stanford has made it [Hoover] one of the university's most valuable assets and its research publications and teaching have had a positive and pervasive influence throughout the country. Its close affiliation with Stanford is to me one of its major strengths, and there is no question but that this same association has been an important factor in Stanford's excellence as a university. Without your perseverance, this could not have happened and you should be very proud of your accomplishment, as are your friends.

I'm not going to read all of the letters, and I may be accused of taking them a little bit out of context, but I don't think they are. There is one here from Senior Research Fellow Sidney Hook, who apologizes for not being with us tonight. He said:

Glenn Campbell's achievements represent one of the highest peaks of educational statesmanship in modern times. He has transformed a modest research and archival institution into an internationally famous center for the incubation of seminal ideas in the area of social thought.

And this is the important part:

Glenn will probably be surprised to hear me say, and there are others on the Stanford faculty who will be even more surprised, that his accomplishments are a consequence of his faithfulness to the highest liberal traditions of the past. Never concealing his own conservative allegiance, he has nevertheless taken as his primary criterion of eligibility for membership in the Hoover Institution family, intellectual excellence. Glenn has been far more faithful to the philosophy of Justice Holmes and its stress on the importance of a free market in ideas than have his detractors.

I first got to know Glenn when I was a Fellow at the Center for Advanced Study in the Behavioral Sciences in 1959 and 1960. I soon discovered that his enemies then were my enemies, too. They were the illiberal enemies of the liberal spirit.

I conclude with a toast and a cheer for Glenn Campbell whose stature will grow with the years.

I have another letter, from Federal Reserve Board Chairman Paul A. Volcker, a new Trustee at Princeton University, that says:

Dear Glenn:

I can't be at the dinner, but I also can't let this occasion pass without a note of congratulations. These days anyone keeping at anything important, and sometimes controversial, for twenty-five years—or being permitted to do so—is a special achievement and recognition of its own. The growth of the Hoover Institution in all respects speaks for itself—even if as an old Easterner I resent all that intellectual power moving West. After all, you could teach me all I needed to know about government spending and deficits years ago in Cambridge, when everything was clearer!

Congratulations on a well-deserved tribute to your institution building—only a young curmudgeon could have done it.

And you've heard the letter from the President of the United States, and we have ones from George Bush, George Shultz, Cap Weinberger, and two hundred more people here tonight.

Ladies and gentlemen, thank you for joining in this tribute to a very unique, wonderful guy who has done a super job in a difficult position over a lot of years. Glenn, Rita . . . we love you. Thank you.

Letters

From Gerald R. Ford:

Dear Glenn:

Congratulations on your twenty-five years as the outstanding Director of the Hoover Institution. During this quarter of a century, this superb academic organization has been in the foreground of intellectual research and opinion making in the United States under your fine leadership. We are proud of the work you have done and the achievements of the Hoover Institution during your tenure at the helm. Warmest, best wishes for even greater accomplishments in the years ahead.

From Ambassador David M. Abshire, U.S. permanent representative on the North Atlantic Council in Brussels, Belgium, to Emil Mosbacher:

Dear Bud:

I am deeply sorry that I will be unable to return to the States for your tribute to Glenn Campbell on July 18, but I would indeed be delighted to serve as a "Sponsor" for the occasion.

Glenn Campbell has been a great leader for the Hoover Institution and for the country. The scope of his service, his many and varied contributions to national policy and to national education are a testament to his commitment to the ideals and values this nation represents.

Glenn has been a close friend and colleague for more than two decades. He was deeply involved with Georgetown's Center for Strategic and International Studies from its very beginning. All of us at CSIS benefited tremendously from his knowledge and wisdom.

I have also had the privilege of serving with Glenn in other governmental capacities. There, too, I have seen first-hand the great impact of his insight, good judgment and commitment.

On the occasion of this celebration, please extend to Glenn my warmest and most heartfelt congratulations. He has served as an example to us all, and his contribution to the nation will be long lasting.

From Henry A. Kissinger:

Dear Glenn:

I want to extend my heartiest congratulations to you on the occasion of your twenty-fifth anniversary as Director of The Hoover Institution. Surely for you this is a moment of enormous personal pride in the extraordinary career which you have pursued with such dedication for a quarter of a century. For your friends and colleagues, it is a moment for reflection on and gratitude for the contributions you have made to the intellectual debates of our times, and above all, for your friendship.

While deeply regretting that I cannot be present for the celebration on July 18, I hope you will accept my personal good wishes on this very special occasion.

From Attorney-General William French Smith:

Dear Glenn:

Congratulations on twenty-five outstanding years with the Hoover Institution. I regret that I cannot be with you tonight to join with your many friends and admirers as they fete you on this special occasion. I am delighted, however, to have served as a Sponsor for this unique event.

Your contributions to the Institution are innumerable. During your tenure the Hoover Institution has become an internationally renowned center for the study of foreign and domestic affairs. Many times members of this Administration have turned to the Hoover Institution for an in-depth analysis of a key issue. Your research and documentation are consistently excellent, and it gives me great pleasure to join with your many friends in thanking you, and in wishing you well tonight. Our greatest hope is that you will give us another twenty-five years of excellence in academic research.

From Yvonne Brathwaite Burke to Emil Mosbacher:

It is with a great deal of pleasure that I join as a sponsor of the dinner marking the 25th anniversary of Glenn Campbell as Director of the Hoover Institution. The honor is one that is justly deserved. Glenn has provided impressive leadership in the field of advanced study of domestic and foreign affairs, and the Hoover Institution has been very fortunate to have his direction and leadership over the years.

May I take this opportunity to congratulate Glenn Campbell on his 25th anniversary as Director and wish him many future years of public service.

From Edmund W. Littlefield:

Dear Glenn,

I would like to add my voice to those who honor you in celebration of your 25th anniversary as Director of the Hoover Institution. I only regret that I cannot be there in person but I have just now returned to the area after an extended vacation out of the country. Hence, my delay in writing to you.

During your tenure as Director the Hoover Institution has produced an enviable record for scholarly works. The quality of its Fellows has reached an all-time high and through their consultations and their writings they have had a constructive impact on public policy and on the improvement of human understanding.

You have good reason to be proud of your handiwork and of your personal contribution to the great measure of success that the Hoover Institution has enjoyed under your leadership.

Please accept my very best personal wishes for your continued success.

From Clare Boothe Luce to Emil Mosbacher, Jr.:

Dear Bud:

Glenn Campbell is one of my colleagues on the President's Foreign Intelligence Advisory Board of whom I'm especially fond. Ergo, I'm only too happy to "sponsor" the dinner in his honor, July 18th.

But, darn, I can't be with you as I am planning to leave for Europe in mid-July, not returning until after Labor Day.

Nevertheless, it's true that "the best-laid schemes o' mice an' men gang aft agley." So, if for whatever reason my European plans gang agley, I'll let you know in time to save a place for me at the table.

The Hoover Institute has been a mighty fortress of Historical Truths for many a year, and much of the credit goes to Glenn.

Love N Stuff,
Clare

Excerpts

From James A. Baker III, chief of staff and assistant to the president of the United States: "Your record as Director is impeccable and I know that you have done much to advance the reputation and goals of this fine Institution."

From W. O. Baker, former chairman, Bell Laboratories: "Along with high competency in scholarship and administration, invaluable for our national decision making, you have brought a personal commitment and integrity of highest merit."

From T. H. Bell, U.S. secretary of education: "Your fearless explorations of the regions of conflict and terror have challenged all to face the task of creating a peaceful world. Your hope, intellectual integrity, and goodwill have shown us that it can be done."

From Michael J. Boskin, professor of economics, Stanford University: "The growth in the Hoover Institution's resources, research, and influence is truly remarkable."

From William F. Buckley, Jr., editor, National Review: "What a glorious job you've done, and what satisfaction you must take in what you've done for your country."

From Arthur F. Burns, U. S. ambassador to the Federal Republic of Germany: "I marveled then (when I was at Stanford) at what you were able to accomplish at Hoover, and I have continued to rejoice in your successful efforts ever since. The Hoover Institution, thanks to your leadership, has become a great citadel of significant scholarship and practical wisdom. It is a pleasure to congratulate you and to thank you for what you have done for our country."

From Vice President George Bush: "Twenty-five years ago, you ... resolved to give this country a better base of knowledge and an improved analytic capacity on matters foreign and domestic. You put together a wonderful team of scholars, and you achieved your goal with spectacular success."

From William J. Casey, director of the Central Intelligence Agency: "It is heartwarming to see and realize what you have accomplished in a short quarter of a century."

From George Deukmejian, governor of California: "You can take great pride in your quarter century of service at the Hoover Institution. During your tenure, Hoover's reputation as a preeminent center of study and research has been enhanced, and I commend your dedicated endeavors."

From Morris M. Doyle of McCutchen, Doyle, Brown & Enerson: "You brought strong leadership to the Hoover Institution and have exercised it effectively to the great benefit of the Institution and of Stanford University. Mr. Hoover would be proud of what you have accomplished."

From George V. Grune, chairman of the board and chief executive officer, Reader's Digest: "The visionary work that you have inspired there and the benefits that you have brought to this nation are legion."

From Senator Mark O. Hatfield: "Your leadership and guidance have resulted in a superior organization. We all thank you for your dedication."

From Fred Charles Ikle, U.S. undersecretary of defense for policy: "For a quarter century you have guided the flagship of American political thought to ever higher quality, ever greater strength, ever wider influence..."

From Jeane J. Kirkpatrick, U. S. permanent representative to the United Nations: "During the past twenty-five years the Hoover Institution has become one of the great centers of scholarship, a place where freedom is enjoyed and respected and the life of the mind lived seriously."

From L. W. Lane, Jr., chairman of the board, Lane Publishing Co., and publisher, Sunset *magazine:* "... there have not been very many great leaders worth their salt that have not been controversial as they crusaded with dedication for their goals and beliefs... We have all stepped on a few toes and left a few broken fences—but no one can fault you for your dedication, commitment, loyalty to your troops, and pure hard work."

From Professor Paul W. McCracken, University of Michigan: "Yours has been a career of entrepreneurial creativity in the intellectual domain, and the results have been awesome... Your leadership, re-invigorating the Hoover Institution on War, Revolution and Peace, made a massive contribution toward widening the spectrum for intellectual discussion, and public policy is the better for it."

From Admiral Thomas H. Moorer, U.S. Navy (Ret.): "Your influence has been felt nationwide and the contribution you have made toward maintaining the security and well-being of our great country deserves the highest praise."

From Maxwell M. Rabb, U. S. ambassador to Italy: "The Hoover Institution serves as a continuing source of dynamic thought for those of us who serve overseas. It is an important expression of current thinking in the United States."

From Professor Robert A. Scalapino, University of California, Berkeley: "Under your leadership, the Institution has steadily broadened its interests to encompass the major issues in both domestic and foreign policy."

From Secretary of State George P. Shultz: "Your tenure has been one of our nation's great centers of scholarly endeavor, both because of the scholars on its staff and because of its unparalleled documentary collections."

From Francis A. Sooy, M.C., chancellor emeritus, University of California, San Francisco: "Your insistence on academic excellence in the conduct of the Institution's mission in concert with complete objectivity, both your own, as well as that of the scholars which surround you, has been a source of personal admiration for many years."

From Dean A. Watkins, chairman of the board, Watkins-Johnson Company: "You have taken a small institute of good quality and turned it into a world-class Institution of great excellence."

From FBI Director William H. Webster: ". . . to express my appreciation and affection for Glenn and all that he has done for the country."

From Caspar W. Weinberger, secretary of defense: "You have done such an outstanding job for all of those years that this recognition is much deserved."

From Senator Pete Wilson (R–California): "The impact of the Hoover Institution in guiding American thought and policy has been extraordinary and is directly attributable to you, my friend, who, with inimitable skill, have harnessed the talents of America's intellectual elite into a force which profoundly influences the policy makers of our world."

Reminiscences of the
1980s and 1990s

Chambers of the Chief Justice   March 14, 1990

Dear Glenn,

I was sorry not to be able to be with you at your retirement ceremony dinner on January 16th, and also sorry that I have delayed even more getting around to writing you this letter.

Looking back at your nearly three decades of service as Director of the Hoover Institution, you should feel—you are *entitled* to feel—a good deal of satisfaction. The Hoover Institution under your leadership taught the importance of economic and military strength as the keys to national and international security during the period of the "Cold War." I, like many others, am convinced that it was this approach to American foreign policy— typified by the Hoover Institute and by President Ronald Reagan—that brought about "Perestroika" and "Glasnost." The Berlin Wall went up shortly after you became Director; it is fittingly symbolic that it has come down as you retire. I'm sure no retirement gift could give you more satisfaction than the knowledge that your teachings and your principles have led to such a rich harvest for all of us.

All good wishes to you, Glenn.

Sincerely,
Bill Rehnquist

A MONG THE MANY LETTERS I RECEIVED ON BECOMING A COUN-selor of the Hoover Institution, this is one of the three I treasure most. Another, dated July 2, 1990, came from Professor

335

Paul Gordon Lauren, the director of the Maureen and Mike Mansfield Center at the University of Montana:

> I want to take this opportunity to join my voice with all of the others who have expressed to you their deep appreciation for your leadership at the Hoover Institution for so many years. I have benefited immensely from the library, both as a student and as a faculty member of Stanford University. My years spent as a Peace Fellow also provided enormous personal and professional benefit. Moreover, in your years as Chairman of the Japan-U.S. Friendship Commission, my institution greatly benefited from a grant that helped us create an extremely successful Montana-Kumamoto academic exchange program. For all of these things, among others, I wish to express my deep appreciation to you.

The third letter was written by Dr. Thomas Sowell, long-time Hoover Senior Fellow and friend. It is dated August 31, 1989:

> Although I could not be at your recent dinner, I do not want to let the transition at the Hoover Institution pass without a few words and a token of appreciation for what you have done, both for me and for the larger world of ideas supporting freedom in the United States and in the Western world. My years at Hoover have been the most productive of my career and that would not have been possible without your support. Far more important, in the larger scheme of things, is that you have made the Hoover Institution the world's leading refuge for ideas that were in danger of being stamped out by academic intolerance throughout the Western intellectual world. That these ideas have not merely survived, but flourished, and have become resurgent both in theory and practice, is in part your legacy that will endure after the present controversies have faded and all of us on the stage today have passed from the scene.

I am also grateful to former Secretary of State George Shultz and to former Attorney General Edwin Meese, both of whom were interviewed about my impending retirement. George Shultz said, "[Glenn Campbell has] been very creative, and what you now see here is an impressive and thriving intellectual community . . . It's been fun, interesting and stimulating, and [Campbell] was the driving force behind that. . . ." Then he added, . . . "one of Glenn's endearing qualities is that he loves controversy."

Meese, who became a part-time Hoover Visiting Fellow in 1988, gave his uncensored view of my removal: "This was just another way for the left to stifle the free-flow of thoughts and ideas," he said. "I think this was one of the ramifications of a longtime feud between Hoover and the University from the original days when (President) Hoover was still here."

1989

Because the Hoover Institution changed so dramatically during my tenure, I am frequently asked how a quiet library, used by relatively few scholars, grew into an internationally recognized center for advanced study and research. Professor Robert F. Byrnes, distinguished professor of history at Indiana University, was also director of that school's renowned Russian and East European Institute from 1959 to 1962. He wrote to me in September 1989:

> I thoroughly enjoyed my six months at Hoover. I also completed more work than I had anticipated, even though my expectations were high. The atmosphere there was as ideal as the weather. The support staff was efficient and wonderfully pleasant. This contrasted with the poisonous attitude of some university faculty toward the Hoover Institution, and of some reciprocal feeling from Hoover toward the rest of the University.
>
> I remember well the poor and anemic Institution of 1959, when I spent several summer weeks almost alone in the library. You must look back at your tender age [Professor Byrnes was seventy-two years of age compared with my sixty-five!] to this transformation with a justified sense of achievement. I know that the Hoover Institution has assisted hundreds and perhaps thousands of scholars to advance their work and to push the frontiers of knowledge forward because of what you have done.

The Hoover TV Station

I alluded in chapter 4 to the fact that I felt strongly—given the turbulent times throughout the world—that the proposed Hoover Institution TV station should be functioning as soon as possible. Unfortunately, after August 1989 the program was curtailed.

Money was not the problem. We had excellent prospects for financial support from Chicago (probably good for about half the $1.5 million we needed), and both Associate Director Annelise Anderson and I were ready and willing to make the trip, but Deputy Director Raisian insisted on going there himself to make the presentation. Actually, I would simply have traveled to Chicago on my own if I had not believed his continued assurances that he would take care of it. Surely, I assumed, everyone knew the value of television as the new medium for fundraising. But, Raisian never pursued the funding, probably because Donald Kennedy opposed the plan.

Some years later, Dr. Raisian appeared to have realized that he could not rely on a large fundraising bureaucracy to raise the money he needs. He began to organize the Senior Fellows so that together they could once again expand the program and size of the Hoover Institution. If they are successful, the Hoover Institution will enter the twenty-first century still an independent institution within the framework of Stanford University and still in charge of its financial destiny, rather than merely relying on the rising value of the stock in its endowment.

I was very pleased by John Raisian's tribute to me at the December 8, 1989, dinner for the International Studies Advisory Committee:

> Since January 1, 1960, when Glenn Campbell became its director—the last director to be personally recommended and approved by Herbert Hoover—the Hoover Institution has prospered in every way. The holdings of the Library and Archives nearly tripled in size from 600,000 volumes to 1.6 million volumes in the Library and from 1,300 archival collections to nearly 4,000 collections today. The Library and Archives now constitute the largest private repository of its kind in the world. From a handful of scholars in 1960, the research staff now numbers nearly one hundred resident fellows and dozens of visiting scholars on shorter term appointments. The Hoover Press which in 1960 [we did not establish it until 1962] published one or two books per year now publishes between 20 and 30 books each year.
>
> In 1960, the research program focused only on international studies. While continuing to build this program, Glenn undertook farsighted and challenging new initiatives, including the Domestic Studies Program, the

National, Peace, and Public Affairs Fellow Program, and the National Security Affairs Program—all of which have greatly contributed to the scholarly enterprise and to the formulation of public policy in the United States. The quality of the Hoover Institution scholars is exemplary. They have included five Nobel laureates, fourteen members of the Academy of Arts and Science, and winners of the Congressional Medal of Honor, the Presidential Medal of Freedom, the National Medal of Science, and the Jefferson Award.

One of the essential ingredients of Glenn's success has been his legendary ability to raise funds for support. Building on the base of support developed by Herbert Hoover, he increased the endowment from $2 million in 1960 to over $125 million today. The annual operating budget has increased from $400,000 to $17 million this year. Glenn has inspired loyalty and developed lasting relationships with many generous benefactors.

Successful fundraising campaigns in the mid-1960s and the 1970s led to two prominent buildings—the Lou Henry Hoover Building in 1967 and the Herbert Hoover Memorial Building in 1978. As a consequence, the institution's facilities have nearly tripled in size to more than a quarter million square feet. Very few research centers in the country offer the physical environment that prevails at the Hoover Institution.

While he was building this great institution, Glenn also contributed his remarkable skills to public service. He has held appointments under six U.S. Presidents. He currently serves as chairman of the President's Intelligence Oversight Board, as a member of the President's Intelligence Advisory Board, and as the senior member of the University of California Board of Regents, of which he was chairman in 1982–83. Glenn was a founding member of the Ronald Reagan Presidential Foundation, the first chairman of its Board of Trustees, and continues as a Trustee. Until recently, he served as chairman of the Japan-U.S. Friendship Commission. He was the founding president of the Philadelphia Society, a founding trustee of the Center for Strategic and International Studies at Georgetown University, and a member of the board of directors of many other organizations, including the Mont Pelerin Society, National Science Foundation, Committee on the Present Danger, and Herbert Hoover Presidential Library Association. On November 3 of this year, the Japanese government announced that Glenn was being awarded the Order of the Sacred Treasure, Gold and Silver Star.

By every measurement, Glenn Campbell's professional career has already been a resounding success. Yet, to record the full scope of what Glenn has achieved as director of the Hoover Institution, the historians who write its history for these years will have to do more than simply enumerate a long list of accomplishments. They will have to describe in personal terms what it took to build a world-class international research center—the intellectual effort required to conceive and plan new enterprises; the energy and skill needed to push, persuade, and shape the forces that now undergird this institution; and the personal sacrifices that can never be fully repaid.

The historian will see the spirit of a man who at age 35 took a library of archival treasures, made a career commitment to its distinguished founder, and built up an institution that has had profound impact on the life of the nation. It is the spirit of an "uncommon man."

> Let us remember [said Herbert Hoover] that the great human advances have not been brought about by mediocre men and women. They were brought about by distinctly uncommon people with vital sparks of leadership . . . For the future of America rests not in mediocrity but in the constant renewal of leadership in every phase of our national life.

Were Herbert Hoover among us today, he would join me and all of us who are part of the Hoover Institution family and say to you, Glenn:

> Thank you for all that you have done. Thank you for standing up for the independence of this institution. Thank you for keeping faith with our shared commitment to the purposes of the Hoover Institution. Thank you for being an "uncommon man."

Dr. Raisian also told me that the quarterly Hoover newsletter, inaugurated while I was director, was to feature in its fall 1989 issue my public service career and my accomplishments as director. In fact, no fall 1989 issue was published. When I asked him what happened, he replied that he "blew it." Thus, his laudatory speech, which had been made at a private dinner, would not be heard by President Donald Kennedy or his allies. I was disappointed but not surprised. After all, Raisian needed Kennedy's approval to become director.

The Philadelphia Society Resolution

The unanimous adoption of this resolution (offered by Arnold Beich-man) by the members of the Philadelphia Society at its April 1989 meeting touched me very deeply:

> I rise to ask you to celebrate with me the closing of a 30-year career and the beginning of a new career by one of our members—a distinguished member—in fact the first president of The Philadelphia Society. I refer to Dr. Glenn Campbell, the director of the Hoover Institution on War, Revolution and Peace.
>
> Glenn Campbell, whom many of you know, has served for almost thirty years as director of the Hoover Institution. In that time, he built up that Institution into one of the most intellectually formidable think tanks, not only in the United States, but in the world. Its publications, archives, and library holdings are extraordinarily rich. And were it not for the liberal-left faculty at Stanford, there might well have been another scholarly treasure at Stanford thanks to Glenn Campbell—The Ronald Reagan Presidential Library. But so determined were the left-liberal book burners at Stanford that they forced the Reagan Library to look elsewhere for a home.
>
> Surrounded by such enemies of academic freedom, Glenn Campbell fought for academic freedom—and he succeeded. There are people here who I know would agree that Glenn Campbell contributed immeasurably to the cause of academic freedom without in any way compromising the standards of academic excellence. I refer to Edwin Meese, Martin Anderson, Edwin Feulner, and George Nash, among others, who have known, as I have, at first hand the accomplishments of the Hoover Institution.
>
> I, therefore, would ask the members and guests at this 25th anniversary of The Philadelphia Society to indicate their admiration and support of Glenn Campbell and to authorize the officers and trustees of The Philadelphia Society to suitably inscribe a scroll for Glenn Campbell to be presented to him on a designated occasion.

Other Honors

On November 3 1989, as Raisian indicated, the Japanese government announced that I was being awarded the Order of the Sacred Treasure, Gold and Silver Star.

On December 16, I received an honorary LL.D. degree from Pepperdine University. The resolution conferring this degree was read by Pepperdine Regent Darrell Trent:

> This morning we honor Dr. W. Glenn Campbell, recognizing him for what he has accomplished as the Premier Intellectual Entrepreneur of the twentieth century. All around us we are in the midst of a profound revolution.
>
> Communism is self-destructing before our eyes, Capitalism has won. When historians begin to sift through these periods of change and begin to write about their origins, they will come up with names of prime movers—because all of this has not happened by accident.
>
> One of the prime movers is Glenn Campbell. Dr. Campbell, with his wife Rita Ricardo-Campbell, after Ph.D.s in economics from Harvard and distinguished early careers, built the Hoover Institution into the finest Think Tank in the world, to the point where many of the fellows became and continue to be key players in this revolution.
>
> There have been many accomplishments for Glenn Campbell: (1) Chairman of the President's Intelligence Oversight Board, (2) Founding Chairman of the Ronald Reagan Presidential Library, and (3) Senior Regent of the University of California Board of Regents.
>
> But to sum it all up, one can truthfully say, if it had not been for W. Glenn Campbell, a lot of what is happening in the world today, would not be taking place.

Into the 1990s

On January 16, 1990, at the Metropolitan Club, Rita and I attended a retirement dinner for me. Guests included Federal Reserve Board Chairman Alan Greenspan; Council of Economic Advisors Chairman Michael Boskin; Arms Control Director Ronald Lehman II; Assistant Secretary of Defense Henry Rowen (Senior Fellow on leave); CIA Director William Webster; FBI Director William Sessions; former Joint Chiefs' Chairman Admiral Thomas Moorer; former Attorney General Edwin Meese; Board of Overseers members Gloria Toote, Dean Watkins, and Walter Williams; and nuclear physicist and Hoover Fellow Edward Teller. The master of ceremonies was Edwin Feulner, president of the Heritage Foundation.

Messages came from Oregon Senator Mark Hatfield, California Governor George Deukmejian, California Senator Pete Wilson, and Attorney General Dick Thornburgh. Wilson praised our courageous leadership at Hoover, for making it one of America's (and the world's) foremost bastions of freedom and intellectual integrity. Thornburgh expressed the hope that "continued service in other endeavors would ensure that his valuable contributions to our nation will not cease."

The Search for a New Director

Dr. Gerald Dorfman was named chairman of the search committee for my successor. On June 21, 1989, President Kennedy stated that the search for a new director "is making good progress and will continue its deliberations in the fall but will not be in a position to complete the process before August 31 (1989)."

In the fall of 1989 I wrote to Dr. Dorfman concerning his recommendation to President Kennedy that John Raisian be appointed acting director for one year. He replied as follows on November 22, 1989: "As was publicly announced, the Search Committee decided to recommend the appointment of John Raisian as Acting Director to President Kennedy."

This announcement failed to comply with the 1971 resolution of the Stanford Board of Trustees. There was no provision in the 1971 amendments or in any more recent amendments for such an action by the search committee. The sole function of the search committee was to recommend candidates for the position of director, not to attempt to discharge a director nor to declare the position of director vacant. The appointment of an acting director was justified in accordance with a recent amendment to the 1971 resolution, which provided that the deputy director automatically becomes acting director whenever the director absents himself, resigns, or dies. Since I did none of the above, there was no justification for the appointment of an acting director.

In the meantime, the search continued. This list of finalists for the appointment includes name, age, and position held at the time of consideration:

- Michael Armacost—52—U.S. Ambassador to Japan
- Dennis Bark—48—Senior Fellow and Coordinator of National Security Studies, Hoover Institution
- Michael Boskin—43—Professor of Economics, Stanford University, on leave as Chairman of the Council of Economic Advisors to the President
- Harold Demsetz—58—Professor of Economics, Andersen School of Business Administration, UCLA
- Edward Lazear—41—Senior Fellow, Hoover Institution; Professor of Economics, University of Chicago
- Paul McAvoy—54—Dean of the William E. Simon School of Business Administration, University of Rochester
- Joseph Nye—52—Professor of Government, Harvard University
- Henry Rowen—63—Senior Fellow, Hoover Institution; Professor of Economics, Graduate School of Business, Stanford University
- Darrell Trent—51—Former Associate Director, Hoover Institution; Deputy Secretary of Transportation; and CEO of Rollins Environmental Services
- Paul Wolfowitz—46—Undersecretary of Defense for Policy

Michael Boskin was the Search Committee's first choice, but he had promised President Bush that he would stay at least two years as chairman of the Council of Economic Advisors, and Donald Kennedy was in a great hurry to replace me permanently. The same difficulty affected two other excellent candidates: Michael Armacost had just become ambassador to Japan, and Paul Wolfowitz had just become an undersecretary of defense in the Bush administration. Armacost went on to become president of the Brookings Institution in the fall of 1995, and Wolfowitz is now dean of the Paul H. Nitze School of Advanced International Studies of Johns Hopkins University in Washington, D.C. If the search had been extended for another year, there would have been several other strong candidates. Meanwhile, I could have taught John Raisian how to raise funds, as I had taught Dr. Gary Jones to how raise funds for the Reagan Foundation.

My greatest disappointment of 1989, however, was the continued ban on Hoover Institution Senior Fellows from regular teaching positions at Stanford. At a meeting of the Executive Committee of the Board of Overseers with the Stanford trustees on the afternoon of October 9, 1989, President Kennedy had declared that there had been a sudden and welcome turnaround in Stanford/Hoover relations. On an earlier occasion, Board President James Gaither said that the impediment to cooperation (Director Campbell) had been removed. In light of these statements, it is difficult to understand why there was no action on the matter, because several commonsense remedies were available.

In 1989 George Shultz advised me not to be surprised if Acting Director John Raisian began to turn against me. Thus, it was not entirely unexpected that Raisian induced my very reliable research assistant, Louise Doying, to join his staff while I was away in August 1989. He also sent a memorandum advising me that neither Rita nor I could use student assistants to refill our cars with gasoline (which we had not intended to do). This use of a memorandum was typical of Donald Kennedy's manner of communication, and it was used—as in this instance—when direct personal communication would have been more discreet and more courteous.

I was not even surprised when he required me to pay for my own January 1990 retirement dinner at the Metropolitan Club in Washington, D.C., on the grounds that he had not approved the event. He had, in fact, approved only a reception to be held on the following night. Unfortunately, I was not able to attend that reception because of a long-standing commitment to the University of California Board of Regents. An important topic was scheduled to be discussed and voted on at that regents' meeting—and John Raisian knew about it well in advance.

What *did* surprise me, however, was his treatment of Rita. She had more expertise than any other staff member on Social Security and health-care policy, but after 1989 he never once invited her to take part in conferences on those subjects. Professor Paul Rich invited Rita to take part in a conference featuring Hoover Fellows at the University of the Americas in Mexico in 1995 and once again in 1996, but each time her attendance was vetoed by John Raisian. When we were honored by Board of Overseers Chairman Herbert Hoover III in October 1997, Rita spoke extemporaneously about the fact that—although she herself became a scholar emerita in 1995—in the previous ten years no woman had been appointed a Senior Fellow.

My successor could have invited Rita and me (as others in his position might well have done) to speak at events after he was confirmed as director. He did not do so, even when Gerhard Casper succeeded Donald Kennedy as president of Stanford. Casper is a fine scholar and leader from the University of Chicago, who chose as his provost a former Hoover National Fellow, Condoleezza Rice. I'm confident that relations between Hoover and Stanford will remain excellent as long as the current university team stays in place. Raisian actually waited another five years to recognize our accomplishments—when he was forced to by William E. Simon, Richard Scaife, and Maurice R. (Hank) Greenberg—though he now says he had wanted to do this for years.

Hoover-Stanford Relations

Over the years, in answer to questions about relations between Stanford and the Hoover Institution, I always replied that they were similar to J. P. Morgan's description of the stock market: "They fluctuated." During the 1970s, while Richard W. Lyman was president, we had excellent relationships with the rest of the university, and more joint appointments were made than ever before or since. Compared to more recent Hoover-Stanford relations, our interactions overall were quite good—even while Wally Sterling was president and during Kenneth Pitzer's brief tenure. Not until the 1980s, under Donald Kennedy, did relations deteriorate. Kennedy used every available dirty trick against me, including salary discrimination and allegations about my personal character.

The Investigation

On July 25, 1990, the Office of Federal Investigations conducted a security update on me. Initially, it was a routine matter requested by the Department of Energy in connection with my position as a regent of the University of California. U.C. manages three DOE laboratories: the Lawrence Berkeley National Laboratory, the Lawrence Livermore National Laboratory, and the Los Alamos National Laboratory. The woman who questioned me under oath, however, told me at the end of the interview that, because I had been so forthright in my reactions and in my testimony, she was going to tell me how to obtain a copy of the transcript under the Freedom of Information Act and the Privacy Act. I followed her instructions and received a full transcript of the statements by all persons interviewed, and it is my understanding that this is my property.

Charges had, in fact, been made against me, and the investigators needed to verify or refute those accusations. Our neighbors, the Helgessons, the Sziklaises, and the Youngs all had excellent things to say about Rita and me, and recommended me for a position of trust involving national security. Senior Fellow Martin Anderson, Senior Fellow and former Ambassador Richard F. Staar, Congressional Medal of Honor winner Adm. James Stockdale, Senior Research Fellow Edward Teller, and Dean Watkins (chairman of the board of the Watkins-Johnson Company) all gave me high character recommendations with no reservations whatsoever about my loyalty to the United States—or my use of alcohol.

On the other hand, Donald Kennedy, then president of Stanford University, was complimentary about my ingenuity and the energy I had devoted to the building of the Hoover Institution. He did not question my honesty either, but he *did* allege that I overused alcohol and that he had talked to me when I did not have full control of my faculties. He ended the interview by stating that he would not recommend me for a position of trust involving national security, adding that there was no reason for the government to tolerate what he characterized as my "irrational behavior."

Charles Palm, my associate director, reported that while I was director, he had observed some excessive use of alcohol at social events, accompanied by some slurring of speech. On the other hand, he offered the opinion that this behavior did not interfere with my performance in my job.

John Raisian, my successor, stated—incorrectly—that as counselor I reported to him (I reported to the president of Stanford). He also engaged in amateur psychoanalysis about my "problems" in my new position. He accurately stated that my role was to advise him and said that he found me to be an honorable person—trying at times, but no serious problem.

All my neighbors and close friends were then asked about my alleged character defects—specifically, whether I abused alcohol. Fortunately, the neighbors and colleagues who knew me well did not believe these scurrilous charges, so I was not forced to sue Donald Kennedy. What he and his coterie called "trouble with alcohol" was actually a life-long nervous condition that arises whenever I am under pressure and have to speak in public or on the telephone. Curiously, no other university president (Sterling, Pitzer, Lyman, or Casper) ever accused me of abusing alcohol. When Kennedy raised this issue, Bud Mosbacher said, "Oh, that's just one of the cheap tricks used by lower-level government officials to blacken the character of their superiors." The other charge commonly made in that context was womanizing—and we agreed that Donald Kennedy, of all people, wasn't likely to accuse me of that.

The Trifkovic Matter

On February 18, 1992, a dinner at the Faculty Club honored Japanese Prime Minister Nakasone. Secretary of State George Shultz was the host, and after dinner he and Mr. Nakasone engaged in an exchange of views about various world problems (Nakasone speaks excellent English). It was my misfortune to be seated at the table with a rude and mendacious Serb named Srdjan Trifkovic. Serbia had recently reinvented "ethnic cleansing" in its war against the Croatians and had destroyed the beautiful city of Dubrovnik. Mr. Trifkovic obviously did not like some of my comments, especially my statement that I could not understand why the Serbs seemed to hate the Jews.

He supposedly had a tape recorder on his person which, he claimed, recorded my "objectionable" remarks, but he never produced the tape, not even when he complained to Raisian. Nevertheless, my successor chose to believe him and to censure me with no evidence and no opportunity for me to confront my accuser or anyone who allegedly confirmed my "racist" statements. Except for a local newspaper story or two, the censure was little more than a joke. The Serb collected his grant and left.

I suspected that Dr. Raisian was responding to pressure from Donald Kennedy to find some way to dissolve my contract with the Stanford trustees. Subsequently, Honorary Fellow Dame Margaret Thatcher blasted the Serbs at a breakfast in the Hoover Institution's Stauffer Auditorium—with Raisian present. George Shultz had done the same thing on several occasions. In addition, an open letter to President Clinton in the September 2, 1993, *Wall Street Journal*, signed by Thatcher and Shultz and by several Hoover employees, called for NATO action against the Serbs.

Eventually, this "Letter to the Editor" appeared in the *Stanford Daily* (May 13):

Campbell not a racist, Hoover colleague says

I was shocked and outraged by the irresponsible article on the "Campbell incident" in Friday's *Daily*.

I was not present at the dinner at which W. Glenn Campbell is alleged to have made objectionable remarks to a visiting Serb scholar and I cannot judge the merits or demerits of the objections raised.

However, I have known Glenn Campbell for about 40 years and have worked closely with him much of that time. I have never observed him to behave in an anti-Semitic or racist way, and have never heard him make anti-Semitic or racist remarks. He is not an anti-Semite, a Nazi, or a racist.

To call him one solely on the basis of an ill-reported dinner table conversation is irresponsible in the extreme. Rad Dimitric and the *Daily* should be thoroughly ashamed of publishing such drivel.

Milton Friedman
Senior Research Fellow
Hoover Institution

Fundraising

It had often been suggested that the Hoover Institution organize its fundraising in a manner similar to that employed by the Graduate School of Business, the Law School, the other professional schools at Stanford, or the School of Humanities and Sciences. Unlike these entities, however, the Hoover Institution has no alumni. A large, bureaucratic development office, which may be necessary for alumni appeals, would not be suitable for a think-tank. So when John Raisian adopted the university model and hired a director of development, I was deeply concerned.

A development director cannot undertake the aggressive and continuous fundraising activity that can be managed by the director and his deputy, with the help of Senior Fellows, Senior Research Fellows, and the counselor(s), and geared to the specific interests of potential donors. However, money is always an issue for institutions such as Hoover, and John Raisian raised it in a January 1990 Board of Overseers meeting:

Implementation Issues

The extent of resources devoted to development are not sufficient at the current time. During the 1980s, we have raised about $5 million per year on average (which includes both expendable funds and endowment), and this fundraising effort has been virtually flat over the decade. At the same time, our expenditure budget has nearly tripled. Furthermore, half of our funds raised over the decade have come from fewer than ten donors, and three-quarters of funds raised have originated from around thirty donors.

Until now, Glenn Campbell and Tom Henriksen, in conjunction with a small clerical staff and occasional assistance of other Hoover administrators and fellows, have served as the gatherers of fuel for the Institution. I believe we need to increase and broaden our efforts in this important area, and I propose we do so by first hiring a professional development officer, and then begin with an assessment of how an efficient (i.e., productive, but lean) development office would be organized. At the Stanford Business School, there are eight professional staff and six clerical staff which generate around $11 million, so I believe there is reason for thinking that we need to augment our current staffing in an appropriate fashion.

As we attempt to broaden the base of our support and increase the number of donors, we will need to install an automated information management system for development operations. The system will record donor interests and profiles, track donor giving, produce mailing lists for direct mail appeals and informational mailings, notify staff of follow-up and reporting requirements, and produce other management tools. We intend to survey the available software options in the next few months.

The work of the Hoover development office, when organized, must be properly integrated with the efforts of the Development Committee. Donor contacts must be carefully coordinated to avoid conflicting messages to donors or impressions of disorganization. As the number of Overseers and staff making donor contacts increases, the potential for confusion will increase. Proper guidelines, effective lines of communication, and discipline will be needed. It will also be important to coordinate appropriately our efforts with the Stanford Development Office to avoid conflict. I plan to meet with the Vice President of Stanford's development office to brief him on our development goals and objectives, and to discuss matters of coordination while preserving independence of function.

If he had shown me this statement in advance, I would have corrected several points:

- Many scholars and overseers were engaged in fundraising with Thomas Henriksen and me.
- It is necessary in the interests of accuracy to correct for the price level increases of the 1980s.
- Taking the comparison back to the middle and late 1970s would show that Hoover got $7 million from the federal government for the Herbert Hoover Federal Memorial Building, plus the Noble bequest of $6.6 million and the William Volker Fund gift of $7.5 million, which offers a truer picture of our fundraising results.
- During the 1978–79 fiscal year, the Hoover Institution received almost $12.5 million in private contributions, an amount likely to stand as an annual record for years to come.
- The $12.5 million raised in 1978–79 was equivalent to at least $30 million in 1998 dollars. The amounts raised during 1989–90 and 1990–91, averaging about $8 million, look small in comparison.
- About half the money raised from 1989 to 1991 came from pledges obtained while I was director or from wills drawn in 1987 or earlier.
- In fiscal year 1995–96, the Hoover Institution received slightly less than $10 million in gifts, about $3 million of which came from the dissolution of the Margaret and Herbert Hoover, Jr., Foundation. Given the size of the development office (ten staff members), this is not impressive.
- The market value of the Hoover Institution's endowment as of September 1, 1996, totaled almost $172 million. Only the

increase in stock values saved the Institution from serious financial problems. (This total included the $50 million market value of the fully expendable William Volker Fund, which my colleagues and I obtained in the late 1970s and which is to be used exclusively for Domestic Studies.)

About the only accurate statement Raisian made was that the Business School had fourteen people in its development office. For about twenty-five years, in the 1960s, 1970s, and early 1980s, the school lagged behind the Hoover Institution in donations—even though it had a large development office and many graduates. Thus, its endowment was only about $70 million in August 1989—compared with Hoover's $125 million, plus pledges, expendable funds, and potential bequests. Indeed, the parallel Business School figure at the end of fiscal 1991–92 was still only $92.1 million.

A 1993 increase in the payout rate (from 4¾ percent to 6¾ percent) mandated by the Stanford trustees obscured deficits in the budget and decreases in annual contributions. Fifty percent of the budget of the Hoover Institution was covered by endowment income and only 23 percent by gifts in 1992–93. The Hoover deficit for 1992–93 was estimated at almost $4 million in the February 1993 report for the overseers meeting, but the numbers changed—on paper—when the Stanford trustees increased the pay-out rate in June. For the 1992–93 year administration and development office costs were projected at 10 percent, 4 percent above the 6 percent that held during my years as director.

The market value of the endowment was almost $172 million as of September 1996, so it is difficult to discern what the development bureaucracy did—other than spend money. Since the Dow Jones, the S&P, and the NASDAQ indexes had average increases well over 100 percent, the market value of the endowment should have risen to well over $200 million—some say close to $250 million—by June 1998.[1]

---

1. Despite the recent discouraging news that the market value of the endowment had dropped from $211 million in August 1997 to $207 million a year later, economic tides have moved in our favor and the value in December 1998 was up to $233 million.

At the February 1997 meeting in Washington, D.C., Dr. Raisian said he was about to announce that the Hoover Institution was starting a five-year fundraising campaign which he hoped would garner almost $75 million. He hoped to increase annual support to an amount in excess of $13 million by the end of August 2000. No new building was planned unless some donor gave about $25 million.

The financial position of the Institution constitutes its most formidable challenge. If the stock market levels or falls, the director will either have to raise much more money or stop expanding such questionable research programs as the Eastern European Diplomats Program. This program was fully funded, almost entirely by the Pew trusts (historically the second largest contributor to the Hoover Institution), but it is dangerous in the long run to devote *all* the funds contributed by one foundation to a program that shows little evidence of long-term payoff.

Former State Department officer Charles Hill drew an analogy between the Eastern European Diplomats Program and the "Chicago Boys," a group of Chilean diplomats and scholars who furthered their education at the University of Chicago. Hill initially used this analogy to convince George Shultz of the merits of the program, but it is a flawed comparison. The Chileans had to pay to send their students to Chicago and also to pay the Chicago professors who advised them. Eastern European countries, on the other hand, had no dollar exchange funds, so the Hoover Institution had to cover all costs—about $20,000 per person—when the program was inaugurated in the fall of 1990. Eventually Shultz became convinced that the program was a waste of money, and it has been terminated.

At the time of the Board of Overseers meeting in July 1990, I was invited to meet with John Raisian and Chairman Robert Malott to discuss—I believed—my role at the Hoover Institution in fundraising, financial management, and policy matters. As soon as I arrived, I found out that Malott wanted, instead, to put me in my place. He started by telling me that no one at Hoover was interested in my views any more. I told him I was sorry he had that attitude and left. Of course, I should have realized that Malott would become Kennedy's ally and that John Raisian would join forces with them. I realized then that I had made a huge mistake by not arranging for former Treasury Secretary William E. Simon, instead of Robert Malott, to become chairman of the Hoover Board of Overseers. Malott spent his time selecting successors, primarily lawyers, who, he knew, would not pay attention to my ideas. Thus, it was not until they could no longer keep Herbert Hoover III from becoming chairman that Rita and I were finally honored in the fall of 1997 and in March 1998.

When Wally Sterling retired as president of the university, the Stanford Board of Trustees retained him as a trustee, allowing him to use his knowledge and experience to continue to serve the university. With Richard Guggenheim, Sterling co-chaired a successful campaign to raise $300 million in the 1970s while Richard Lyman was president. Mr. Hoover retained one of my predecessors, Ralph Lutz, as a member of the Hoover Advisory Committee, and I kept him on after Mr. Hoover's death. His services were very helpful to me when I was new to my job. I might, it seemed to me, have similarly been appointed to the Board of Overseers and continued to represent the Hoover Institution.

To the best of my recollection, since 1989 I have been in my successor's office only once, to discuss a possible fundraising trip to Japan. He, in turn, came to my office only once, to discuss my allegedly insulting remarks to Trifkovic. I must have suggested dozens of times that we get together once a month for lunch to discuss issues of mutual interest, but there were no replies to my requests. What I wanted to propose to him was that he make me a member of the Board of Overseers and use me in a $100 million fundraising campaign.

A Stanford/Hoover School of International Studies

In 1988 I was hoping that before I ceased to be director I could organize such a campaign and raise an additional $100 million for the Hoover Institution. I knew that by about 1994 we were likely to need a fourth building for the school of international studies that George Shultz and I envisioned. Part of the $100 million would have gone to construct the building and the rest to expand endowment and reserve funds. I envisioned that the co-chairmen for the campaign would be William E. Simon,

Richard M. Scaife, Peter Bedford, and myself. The committee would include Dwayne Andreas, Phoebe Hearst Cooke, Joseph Coors, Edwin L. Cox, Maurice Greenberg, Thomas Jordan, Payton Lake, William Laughlin, J. William Middendorf II, Roger Milliken, Emil Mosbacher, Jr., Nancy Barry Munger, Rupert Murdoch, David Packard, James Smith, Whitney Stevens, and Peter Thieriot.

Unfortunately Donald Kennedy assumed a negative attitude toward this proposal. A new building across the street from the Lou Henry Hoover Building could have served as the headquarters for a school of international studies. Combining the library and archives of the Hoover Institution with the many distinguished Hoover scholars working in the field of international studies and the scholars at Stanford University in the same field would have created the finest such school in the United States. Presently in that location is a building that houses the economics department plus two small economic research institutes and a public parking area. The land now reserved for Hoover Institution expansion is in a much inferior location, suitable only for library space.

Mr. Hoover was always anxious that Hoover staff members work together, so I was surprised when John Raisian took a negative view of working with me on the Institution's financial problems. But I have come to understand that you cannot render services and offer advice to someone who does not want them.

Another fundraising disappointment in my last year as director came to light in November 1989, when President Gardner of the University of California made an announcement at a regents' meeting. In March of that year Stanford University had applied to the West German government to establish a Center of Excellence for German and European Studies without ever seeking the participation of the Hoover Institution, despite its world-renowned program, its library, and its archives. The German government made three grants of $800,000 per year for a ten-year period to establish such centers. These grants went to three institutions: the University of California, Berkeley; Harvard University in Cambridge, Massachusetts; and Georgetown University in Washington, D.C. None of the many distinguished and highly qualified Hoover scholars was mentioned in the application. That was surprising when one considered the following list of Senior Fellows, Senior Research Fellows, and Honorary Fellows, all exceptionally well qualified in the areas of German and European studies:

Honorary Fellows
Friedrich von Hayek (Nobel laureate)
Ronald Reagan (two-term president)
George Shultz (former secretary of state)
Alexander Solzhenitsyn (Nobel laureate)

Senior Fellows	*Senior Research Fellows*
Richard V. Allan	Mikhail S. Bernstam
Martin Anderson	Robert Conquest
Dennis Bark	Larry Diamond
Gerald Dorfman	Milton Friedman
Milorad Drachkovitch	David Gress
John B. Dunlop	Charles Hill
Lewis Gann	Rodney Kennedy-Minott
Alex Inkeles	James Stockdale
Melvyn Krauss	Edward Teller
Seymour Martin Lipset	William Van Cleave
Peter Paret	
Henry Rowen	
Richard Staar	

Had a spirit of cooperation prevailed and the application been jointly prepared, I am confident that Hoover/Stanford would have received one of these grants. Indeed, Mike Heyman, the chancellor of Berkeley, informed me that this was undoubtedly the case.

The Stanford Student Union and the Food Research Institute

My long-held belief that the university wanted to take over the Hoover Institution was not unfounded. Since President Hoover's death in October 1964, two Stanford organizations of which he was very proud have been totally changed or abolished. The first was the Student Union, for which Hoover contributed $100,000 in 1915 in addition to smaller gifts in subsequent years. The "new Stanford Union" opened in 1921, and the costs above Hoover's donation were ultimately paid by profits from restaurants and residential quarters. Recently, it has been converted to a meeting place for black and Chicano studies and a headquarters for minor administrators.

The much larger Food Research Institute was abolished more recently. Established in 1921 by a contract between the Carnegie Corporation of New York City and the Stanford trustees, it was built up over many years. In 1995 a very ambitious dean of the School of Humanities and Sciences, John Shoven, came up with a plan to abolish the seventy-four-year-old institute and pass its $12 million endowment to the economics department and another institute. It cost Stanford about $8 million to shut down the Food Research Institute. Unfortunately, Herbert Hoover III was not a member of the Stanford Board of Trustees. Had he been, I'm sure the decision would have not been approved.

The Hoover Library takeover attempts actually started about 1920. For that story, I recommend Charles Burdick's *Ralph H. Lutz and the Hoover Institution,* published by the Hoover Press in 1974. There were other attempts while I was director, the first in the spring of 1960, the second in 1979. The third attempt, an effort to take over the *whole* Hoover Institution, was begun by Donald Kennedy in the late 1980s but was derailed when his reckless behavior led to his August 1992 resignation.

More Fundraising Opportunities

At the insistence of Donald Kennedy and John Ford, Dr. Raisian agreed to start a development office, which produced only disastrous results until Don Meyer became director of development in 1997. The root of its failure—the fact that the Institution has no alumni—was finally publicly recognized in July 1995 by Buzz McCoy, chairman of the Development Committee. Raising a lot of money basically requires having a good product—then hitting the road to sell it.

For example, the Heritage Foundation in Washington, D.C., raised approximately $24.3 million a year at the time of its Twentieth Anniversary

Report. It employs a nominal director of development, John Von Kannon, at this writing, but he serves primarily as vice president and treasurer. He also takes part in presentations to Heritage supporters at meetings around the country. In mid-1996 I heard Heritage President Dr. Edwin J. Feulner, Jr., make an excellent presentation. When I spoke to Von Kannon about it, he said that any Heritage senior staff member must know the program, know how to sell it, and be able to answer questions about it. Directors of development whose staffs spend their time on computer searches for potential contributors, on holding meetings, and on writing letters to would-be donors, are supervising a waste of time.

According to Feulner, all of Heritage's top staff takes part in fundraising. Feulner himself plays the primary role, particularly when it comes to the contributions from large donors which constitute a sizable share of Heritage's total gifts. Feulner travels almost constantly, including several foreign trips each year (to South Korea, Taiwan, Europe, and Latin America).

The key to Heritage's success was perhaps summed up best by former British Prime Minister Margaret Thatcher in her keynote speech at its anniversary gala: "Heritage has flown the flag for conservatism over this last quarter-century with pride and distinction." It is that commitment to conservative principles, Feulner says, that has made Heritage the most broadly supported think-tank in America, with more than two hundred thousand contributors.

Actually, Heritage's fundraising methods are like those I used at Hoover. It is reasonable, then, to believe that, had Hoover continued on that course, it would now compare favorably with Heritage in financial terms. When I was chairman of the Ronald Reagan Presidential Foundation from 1985 to 1987, Dr. Gary Jones and I plus a small staff raised a total of $38 million in cash contributions and pledges. If President Donald Kennedy had not vehemently opposed locating the Reagan Library at the Hoover Institution, we would have raised a minimum of $9 million per annum more between 1985 and 1989.

Where We Are Now

I doubt that Donald Kennedy and Warren Christopher thought they were doing me a favor in May 1988 when they offered me an extra $25,000 a year if I would retire at the age of sixty-five. But that money has turned out to be very useful to support my research. Despite my years of successful fundraising, John Raisian claimed he had no money for that purpose. Now I use the $25,000, plus funds from the Olin Foundation and from other supporters, to enable me to continue my research as long as I am so inclined. It was also thoughtful of James Gaither to increase my salary by a sizable amount a year before I retired. He, Kennedy, and Christopher also helped me by wording my contract in such a way that I never report to my successor. The president of the university always sets my salary, which indicates that I report to him. Indeed, none of my predecessors ever reported to me, although I did have the good sense to make use of their knowledge of the Hoover Institution.

Ofttimes people have asked why I stayed at Hoover in view of salary discrimination and criticism of my personal character by Donald Kennedy, not to mention his systematic campaign to force my firing or resignation. I stayed and continued the struggle because of the psychic income I derived from protecting the independence of the Hoover Institution from Kennedy and his coterie, along with my sense of accomplishment in building a world-class center of learning.

A Year's Leave of Absence

On April 1, 1993, I announced my decision to take my year's leave of absence with full pay, plus a $100,000 stipend for research assistance and travel, beginning on April 5. I informed John Raisian that I intended to employ Suzi Kosher as my research assistant. Suzi was highly qualified, having a college degree plus experience as an assistant to major league baseball player Reggie Jackson. I apologized for the short notice and asked for an acknowledgment, adding that during my leave I would be away part of the time and on campus part of the time.

On April 2 I received a response from John Raisian, stating that he needed some time to look into my request for "leave status" as stipulated in Jim Rosse's 1988 contract. He acknowledged my intention of retaining Suzi Kosher for research assistance. My office also employed a secretary, Martha Perez. Raisian said if I wished to retain her services, her salary and benefits would be charged to my stipend. If I wished to go away for part of the time, he would be happy to reassign Martha.

On April 5, 1993, I replied to Director Raisian:

> Apparently, you are under some misconception in respect to my contract with the Stanford Trustees, which is administered by the President of Stanford University... Please note that your name was not mentioned in any of these letters. As a courtesy, I was informing you of my plans.

The matter was settled by President Casper, Director Raisian, and myself so that I received the special stipend for research and travel, less the cost of research assistance and my travel costs. Additionally, I would continue to report to President Casper. However, I remained available to undertake assignments for John Raisian should he request them.

Counselor for Life?

On January 10, 1994, John Raisian wrote to inform me that my position as counselor was being eliminated because the Hoover Institution was running over budget and my services did not warrant the expenditures for the position. He extolled my contributions to the Hoover Institution and offered me the continued use of my office, although he could not pay for my support staff. He mentioned a letter I had sent to Gerhard Casper and stated that no one had been authorized to tell me that my job was "for life." He ended by saying that the Hoover Institution was ready to pay the $25,000 per annum promised by Acting President James Rosse *if* I retired on or before August 31, 1994.

On April 6 Gerhard Casper wrote to explain that employment at the university was conditional not only upon good service, but also upon the university's continued need for the services in respect to its financial situation. He said that if I retired on or before August 31, he would consider that I had been terminated rather than retired, and therefore the university's severance policy (payment of a full year's salary plus the maximum two months' vacation) would apply.

On August 26, Casper wrote to me again to say that a lump sum of $183,457 would be paid to me, along with the $25,000 per annum as promised. I would still have staff privileges on the campus and be eligible for health benefits, but no more cash would be made available to me. He also said that he had no objection to my use of the title director emeritus. Finally, if I wanted to keep my "service vehicle" parking sticker by paying for it, I could do so.

On the Financial Front

The market value of the Volker Fund was roughly $60 million in August 1997, surely more than adequate for funding more Senior Fellows and Distinguished Scholars—the purpose for which the fund was intended to be used. It was Morris Cox who, in accord with William Volker's wishes, dissolved the fund in the 1970s. Largely because of the involvement of Roger Freeman and Friedrich von Hayek—both now deceased, as is Cox—the money came to Hoover.

The Axel Swanberg Distinguished Visiting Scholar Award was first given to Hayek; and the Stella and Ira Lillick Curatorship was for twenty-five years held by Peter Duignan. I sincerely hope that the income from those donations will be passed on to other scholars and to other archivists, librarians, or curators. Funding for the $1 million Will Clayton Endowment for International Economic Affairs is now complete and has, to my great satisfaction, been designated for Melvyn Krauss. Hoover also receives income from the Robert Wesson Distinguished Visiting Scholar Fund (which is to go to a scholar who is also a scientist).

The Rita and Glenn Campbell
Distinguished Scholar Fund

On October 22, 1997, Herbert Hoover III, chairman of the Board of Overseers, announced that:

- The Hoover Institution's National, Public Affairs, and Peace Fellows Program will be named after W. Glenn Campbell and Rita Ricardo-Campbell. The National Fellows Program, begun under

Glenn Campbell's directorship, awards one-year scholarships at the Hoover Institution to junior scholars to pursue their research without routine academic responsibilities. More than three hundred fifty-five fellows have participated in the program since 1971.[2]

- Conference Room 330 in the Herbert Hoover Memorial Building will be named after W. Glenn Campbell and Rita Ricardo-Campbell. Their portraits will be hung in the room.
- An endowment of $1 million will be raised and will be named the Glenn Campbell Endowment to support a distinguished affiliated fellow at the Hoover Institution. The Fellow will hold the title of Glenn Campbell Fellow. The first recipient was Keron Skinner, assistant professor at Carnegie-Mellon University in Pittsburgh, Pennsylvania.
- A bust of Glenn Campbell will be commissioned to commemorate his thirty years of distinguished service to the Hoover Institution. This sculpture will be placed in Stauffer Auditorium in the Herbert Hoover Memorial Building.

Rita and I were elated. Some insist this should have been done years earlier, but Rita and I are of the "better-late-than-never" school.

Rita and I were so pleased by these actions that we established the annual "Uncommon Book Award" by donating $100,000 as a gift to the Hoover Institution. The first recipient was Thomas Sowell in 1998 for *Conquests and Cultures: An International History*. He received $5,000. The second recipient was Keith Eiler for *Mobilizing America,* in 1999. He received $10,000 because my wife and I contributed an extra $5,000. We are planning on endowing this in our will or before. These donations were part of Hoover's $75 million campaign which will obviously exceed the targeted amount at the end of the campaign in August 2000. These types of campaigns exceed their targets as did the companion effort in the 1960s and the decade-long campaign in the '70s with no help from fundraisers.

---

2. As of September 1997 the market value of the National Fellows Program endowment was approximately $35 million.

In Conclusion

In late summer 1962 Rita and I went to Paris and were invited to the ancestral home of the Marquis de Lafayette, La Grange Castle. There we were greeted by the Count de Chambrun, a descendent of Lafayette, and his wife. Since we had a letter of introduction from President Hoover, de Chambrun and his wife took good care of us and showed us treasures they had found when they bought the castle. These included correspondence between Lafayette and George Washington, Lafayette and John Adams, and Lafayette and Thomas Jefferson. At that time, I concluded that no complete history of the American Revolution could be written without those archives. This is of some moment because the letters have recently been made available for limited scholarly use. To me, Lafayette's letters perfectly illustrate the value of preserving documents from the past for the enlightenment of the present. That, in essence, has been my life's work.

Preservation of historically crucial documents was equally the lodestar of President and Mrs. Hoover. In September 1967 David Packard participated in Ray Henle's oral history interview about Herbert Hoover. During that conversation he said he believed Hoover had considered

> ... the founding of the Hoover Institution to be the most important thing he had done in his life. And that, of course, is why he was so very much concerned that it be set up and established properly and continue to be run on the plane that he had hoped it would reach.
>
> ... Dr. Campbell is conducting a number of impressive programs that are going to continue to make great contributions of scholarly works ... Every time I look at the program over there, I'm pleased that we were able to go ahead with the arrangement that we worked out, because the whole Institution has been growing in strength and importance ever since... I've told Dr. Campbell—and I'm sure this coincides with Mr. Hoover's views—that we want to have the most competent scholars and the most competent staff in the Institution that we can bring there. In the long range, the distinction of the Institution and its increasing contribution that Mr. Hoover hoped for will be determined by a competent staff, and we're attracting some very fine people.

David Packard remained a staunch supporter of the Hoover Institution until his death in March 1996. Now Rita and I, along with Herbert Hoover III and his wife, are among the few people still alive who remember President Hoover. Therefore, I intend to go on ensuring that the Hoover Institution is run as he would have wished, and I hope that when I am gone the director—whoever he or she may be—will carry on that mission.

In this task, I believe the most important asset of any organization is the quality of its people, which depends, in my view, on the vision and leadership of its director. I made every effort to attract the best scholars with generous salaries and working conditions. By the end of my directorate, the Hoover Institution was without equal in the fields of economics, political science, international relations, sociology, history, and law, and its scholars had reached outside academia to place their knowledge and experience at the service of the public.

Notwithstanding the bumps and scrapes, my thirty years as director of the Hoover Institution were immensely fulfilling and all the more so in that Rita and I were full partners in the enterprise. It has been my privilege to know six presidents of the United States—Hoover, Nixon, Ford, Carter, Reagan, and Bush—and to hold appointments under six of them. I treasure those relationships and hope to find additional opportunities for public service in the years ahead.

In the late 1980s President Donald Kennedy told a Senior Fellow, who happened to be a Democrat, that he did not care if the new director was *twice* as conservative as Campbell—all he wanted was to get rid of me. He succeeded, and no one would consider my successor even *half* as conservative as I am—or even half as arrogant as Kennedy was.

In any event, the Hoover Institution survived the most serious takeover attempt since its founding in 1919, and it is likely to survive through the twenty-first century—unless Stanford University installs a president who can out-Kennedy Kennedy.

On February 14, 1985, the Hoover Institution received a check for $50,000 to establish the Shelby Cullom Davis Distinguished Visiting Scholar Fund at the Hoover Institution. The only condition was that the funds be managed by Davis's own fund-management firm (Shelby Cullom Davis & Company), an arrangement similar to the separate management by Grantham, Mayo, Van Otterloo and Company of the Volker Fund, and the separate management of the Rittenberry $100,000 gift which President Kennedy agreed to in 1983.

By 1985, however, Kennedy was already well into his campaign to force me out as director, and he refused the grant—even though some twelve other universities and 501C(3) charitable organizations had accepted grants from Dr. Davis on the same terms. The money was returned later in 1985, and the Hoover Institution received no more $50,000 gifts from Dr. Davis. Had we received one each year for the remainder of my directorate, the total sum would have been $250,000 (market value in August 1989 about $600,000). In 1986 Dr. Davis donated $485,000 to a Heritage Foundation fundraising campaign, and two years later—because his firm had been allowed to manage those funds—he sent Heritage a check for $1 million. Scholarship at the Hoover Institution paid a high price for Kennedy's actions, and it has always puzzled me that the Stanford trustees did not object.

I cannot sufficiently thank my friends for their invaluable encouragement, especially in recent years. Indeed, on June 10, 1999, my alma mater, the University of Western Ontario, presented me with an honorary doctorate of laws, bringing the wheel full circle. Rita's and my life can be summed up much as Rose and Milton Friedman describe their own: "Two lucky people." We look forward to many more happy years with our daughters, sons-in-law, grandsons, and granddaughter, and all the time we can make for dear friends.

Two lucky people, indeed.

Appendix 1

National Public Affairs and Peace Fellows Program

Dr. Milorad Drachkovitch visited Harvard University in 1968 to discuss its Society of Fellows program with Wassily Leontief. Leontief, the head of the Society of Fellows, took him to the society's meeting quarters in Eliot House. After conducting additional research, Dr. Drachkovitch submitted this memorandum:

> Among its many contributions to scholarly excellence Harvard University is justifiably proud of its Society of Fellows, organized in 1933 with the purpose "to give young men of exceptional ability, originality and resourcefulness an opportunity to pursue their studies in any department of the University, free from formal requirements." Trinity and Kings Colleges, Cambridge, are equally proud of their much older and in some respects even more prestigious and successful "Prize Fellow" programs.
>
> Over the years Harvard's "Junior Fellows" have compiled outstanding records in academic life, government service and foundation posts, and include such well-known people as McGeorge Bundy, Arthur Schlesinger, Jr., and several distinguished scientists such as Dr. Robert Woodward, who is a world-renowned Professor of Chemistry at Harvard and a Nobel laureate. Former Trinity and Kings College Prize Fellows include a significant percentage of the most distinguished British scholars and scientists plus leading political figures and civil servants.
>
> The successes of Harvard and Cambridge Universities are unique and cannot be simply transplanted elsewhere, but they can serve as an inspiration for similar ventures under different circumstances. In this way, and because of its desire to contribute to the quality of American academic and

public life, the Hoover Institution plans to launch its own Society of Fellows, adapting the Harvard and Cambridge experience to the different conditions existing at Stanford University.

The National Fellows Program was launched on April 6, 1970, when the Scaife family offered a matching gift of $500,000. C. E. Ford wrote:

> This is to advise you formally that through the generosity of the Scaife family a challenge grant in the amount of $500,000 has been approved to Stanford University, Hoover Institution on War, Revolution and Peace. This sum is to be applied to the support of your new National Fellows Program which you outlined in your letter of March 12 to Dick Scaife. The amount is to cover the first five years of this program.
>
> Following the suggestion in your letter, the Trustees authorized a lump sum grant payable this year (but to be applied over the five-year period) with the stipulation that a like amount be secured from other sources either in cash or pledges which also must be applied to the first five-year phase of this program.
>
> As soon as you have met this matching condition, please let us know and we will schedule payment before the end of the year. Needless to say, the Trustees are much impressed with this program and wish you and your associates every possible success in its undertaking.

Dr. Lawson Pendleton, the president of the Textile Institute, a small Pennsylvania college, was appointed the first executive secretary in May 1970. The National Fellows Program surpassed all expectations, and the Scaifes continued to support it by contributing an additional $2.2 million to the general endowment between 1975 and 1985. Mr. and Mrs. Packard donated over $1 million to the general endowment fund between 1975 and 1986. In August 1989 the general endowment for the National Fellows amounted to over $6,633,600.

Our first National Fellow was Dennis Bark, and in the spring of 1973 when Lawson Pendleton became president of the Textiles and Science College in Philadelphia, Dr. Dennis Bark succeeded him as executive secretary of the National Fellows Program. Through the 1970s and 1980s, Bark and I worked closely and effectively to amass the full endowment that would secure the program's future. After 1984 Dr. Thomas Henriksen was added to our team, and in August 1989 the endowment totaled almost $18.9 million—plus $100,000 in a living trust.

In 1975 the National Endowment for the Humanities awarded fellowships to support the program so as "to increase the opportunities for uninterrupted and extended discussion and the interchange of ideas with other scholars, particularly scholars outside of Fellows' own fields." This grant funded four fellowships, and from 1976 to 1980 we received three more National Endowment for the Humanities Fellowships, supporting a total of sixteen National Fellows. The $900,000 in expendable gifts from the Olin Foundation, given from 1983 to 1989, was specified for National Fellows in the field of Soviet and Eastern European studies. Other such gifts totaled $3,113,670.

Since August 1989 I believe no money has been raised for the National Fellows Program except through appreciation in the value of the endowments and expendable gifts. Nevertheless, the program continues to be highly regarded and in some ways the candidates keep improving each year. In other ways the program has deteriorated and lost its original focus. Now most of the fellows are econometricians or of a mathematical bent, and very few are policy-oriented.

For example, we haven't had a Public Affairs Fellow for about eight years, even though we received an endowment for one from the Samuel Roberts Noble Foundation of Ardmore, Oklahoma.[1] The last time I talked to a representative of the Noble family, I was told that they were unhappy that no Public Affairs Fellow had been appointed for so long. Indeed, unless the situation is rectified, they might ask that the endowment be returned.

The Silas H. Palmer National Fellowship is to be given to a student doing Ph.D. research in the Hoover Library, and the John H. Stauffer National Fellowship in Public Policy is definitely intended for a Ph.D. working on public policy. I believe the Institution should also return to the practice of naming fellows to the various endowments—for example, the Edward Teller National Fellow in Science and Technology and the two Bittson National Fellows in Twentieth Century Russian and Eastern European History. Obtaining these endowed fellowships during the

---

1. The market value of that gift was almost $1.3 million in August 1989.

1970s and 1980s required a prodigious amount of travel and planning by Dennis Bark and me. To gain the Starr Foundation Fellowship, for example, I traveled to New York and met with Maurice R. (Hank) Greenberg in order to obtain a pledge of $500,000 from the Starr Foundation.

A request by Richard V. Allen and Ed Noble brought us a five-year pledge—beginning in 1970—of $30,000 a year from the Samuel Roberts Noble Foundation for the Public Affairs Program. In 1976 the Noble Foundation made another five-year pledge of $30,000 a year, and in 1980 it donated $500,000 to endow the Public Affairs Fellowship[2] in the National Fellows Program (as a result of a visit Dennis Bark and I made to Ardmore, Oklahoma, for a discussion with the Foundation Trustees).

The William C. Bark National Fellowship on Modern European History was funded to the tune of over $835,000, largely by $100,000 gifts from Robert Pomeroy, George Jagels, and David Packard, along with contributions from George Hart, Peyton Lake, and others. The two A. John Bittson Fellowships for twentieth-century Russian and Eastern European history totaled over $1,892,000, plus a living trust of $100,000; Dick Burress, Martin Anderson, Rita, and I worked hard to get them. The Susan Louise Dyer Peace Research Fellowship, over $677,000, came in the form of a bequest. Other contributions include:

- The George D. Jagels National Fellowship, over $456,400.
- The John A. McCarthy National Fellowship, over $479,300. We agreed to name the Senior Commons Room for John A. McCarthy.
- The Silas H. Palmer National Fellowship—earmarked for a Stanford graduate student doing Ph.D. research in the Hoover Library—almost $170,000. (Silas Palmer, best known as the owner of the construction company that built Stanford Stadium in the 1920s, made this generous donation on the recommendation of fellow golfer Fred Wickett.)
- The Arch W. Shaw National Fellowship, over $1,068,000. (Shaw was a major stockholder in the Kellogg Company of Battle Creek,

---

2. Valued at over $1,298,144 in August, 1989.

Michigan, and a founder of the Shaw-Walker Company of Michigan. A Harvard Business School graduate, Shaw met Herbert Hoover when the latter was secretary of commerce. Arch Shaw's son John gave approximately $35,000 a year to sponsor this fellowship in honor of his father. I made an annual trip to Chicago to sustain this generosity until 1983, when I turned that job over to Tom Henriksen.)

- The John H. Stauffer National Fellowship in Public Policy, over $1,280,800, was obtained with the help of Joe Burris. In return, we named the combination conference room/dining room in the Herbert Hoover Memorial Building the Stauffer Room.
- The Robert E. Swain National Fellowship[3] was created in 1961 when Robert E. Swain made a gift of Varian stock worth about $100,000. Over the years his son Robert C. Swain also contributed, as did his grandson R. J. Swain. Some matching funds for the Herbert Hoover Federal Memorial Building, which were not needed for construction, were added to those gifts.
- The Edward Teller National Fellowship in Science and Technology, over $1,130,300, was made possible by generous gifts from Arthur Spitzer, David Packard, William P. Laughlin, Shelby Cullum Davis, and others.

In August 1989 sixteen National Fellows and four Peace Fellows were appointed from the Stanford faculty, and an additional twenty-five Fellows were at campuses of the University of California (the majority at U.C. Berkeley).

Six National Fellows were professors at the University of Chicago, six at the University of Michigan, five at Boston University, five at the Massachusetts Institute of Technology, five (plus one Peace Fellow) at the University of Washington in Seattle, four at Columbia University, four at the University of Pittsburgh, four at Princeton University, four at the University of South Carolina, four at the State University of New York, four at Yale University, three at Harvard University, three at the University of Iowa, three at the University of Maryland, three at Marquette

---

3. Valued at over $707,000 in August 1989.

FELLOWSHIP	MARKET VALUE— AUGUST 31, 1989
William C. Bark National Fellowship on Modern European History	$ 835,130
A. John Bittson National Fellowships (2) + Living Trust	$ 1,892,167 + $100,000
Susan Louise Dyer Peace Research Fellowship	$ 677,012
George D. Jagels National Fellowship	$ 456,409
John A. McCarthy National Fellowship	$ 479,353
National Fellows (General Endowment)	$ 6,633,625
Samuel R. Noble Public Affairs Fellowship	$ 1,298,144
Silas H. Palmer National Fellowship	$ 169,754
Arch W. Shaw National Fellowship	$ 1,068,004
Starr Foundation National Fellowship	$ 1,229,965
John H. Stauffer National Fellowship in Public Policy	$ 1,280,881
Robert E. Swain National Fellowship	$ 707,251
Edward Teller National Fellowship in Science and Technology	$ 1,130,356
Total	**$17,958,051**

University, three at the University of North Carolina, three at the University of Pennsylvania, three at the University of Wisconsin, and two at George Mason University.

There were two Fellows each at the University of Colorado, the University of Southern California, Ohio State, the University of Delaware, Auburn, American University, and Clemson; one Fellow each at Ball State, Bowling Green, the Claremont Graduate School, Cornell, Rice, Indiana, Rutgers, Santa Clara, San Jose, Seattle, Southern Methodist, Suffolk, Texas A&M, Kenyon College, Oregon State, St. John's College, Alabama, Florida, Illinois, Kansas, Louisville, Montana, Minnesota, Nevada-Reno, Notre Dame, Oregon, Rochester, Texas, Tulsa, Warsaw, Washington University (St. Louis), and Yeshiva University in New York.

Twelve National, Peace, and Public Affairs Fellows became either Senior Fellows or Senior Research Fellows at the Hoover Institution, and three received joint Hoover-Stanford appointments.

Several National Fellows held important posts in foreign countries: Dr. Yung Wei has held a number of important government posts in the Republic of China (Taiwan); Dr. Ming K. Chan was a professor at the University of Hong Kong; and Dr. Denis Lacorne was at the Foundation Nationale des Sciences Politiques in Paris. Canada has also benefited from the National Fellows Program: four National Fellows were professors at the University of British Columbia, one at Simon Fraser University, three at the University of Toronto, one at Carleton University, and one at York University.

We have also had a number of excellent Public Affairs Fellows over the years. The two most distinguished are undoubtedly Dr. Edwin Feulner, Jr., president of the Heritage Foundation, and Dr. Ronald Lehman, former director of the Arms Control and Disarmament Administration, who also served as ambassador for the Start Negotiations in Geneva and as an assistant secretary of defense. One former National Fellow worked for Vice President Quayle, as did one former Public Affairs Fellow. Two National Fellows worked at the American Enterprise Institute, three at the Brookings Institution, two at the Center for Strategic and International Studies, and one at the Center for Democracy. One National Fellow was employed at the U.S. Department of Justice, one at the CIA, one at the U.S. Information Agency, and one at the Intergovernmental Committee for Migration. One Public Affairs Fellow served at the Center for Naval Analysis, one at Citizens Against Government Waste, one at the United States Chamber of Commerce, and another at the World Bank. One Peace Fellow was at the Woodrow Wilson Center at the Smithsonian Institution.

The first National Fellow to become a Senior Fellow was Alvin Rabushka, who has been at the Hoover Institution for over twenty years. National Fellow Laura D'Andrea Tyson, who came from U.C. Berkeley, was the first woman to chair the President's Council of Economic Advisors and was appointed chair of the National Economic Council with cabinet rank in the first Clinton administration. She holds directorships on the boards of Morgan Stanley, Dean Witter, Eastman Kodak, and Ameritech Corporation. National Fellow Condoleezza Rice became the first woman provost at Stanford and holds directorships at both Trans America and Chevron.

Hoover National Fellows who eventually became Senior Fellows include

- Terry L. Anderson, formerly a professor at Montana State University
- Dennis L. Bark, chairman of the trustees of Earnardt Foundation
- Part-time Senior Fellow Robert J. Barro, professor at Harvard
- Bart Bernstein, professor at Stanford
- Angelo Codevilla, professor of international affairs at Boston University and expert on defense and foreign policy
- John Cogan, high-ranking official in Labor Department and Office of Management and Budget in the Reagan administration
- Gerald Dorfman, associate director of research of Hoover Institution
- John Dunlop, former associate director for library operations, with special expertise in history of Russia
- Williamson M. Evers, Research Fellow at Hoover Institution with special expertise in education reform
- John A. Ferejohn, who holds a joint appointment with Stanford political science department
- Thomas H. Henriksen, VMI graduate who came to Hoover Institution as Peace Fellow in late 1970s and is now associate director for program development
- Senior Fellow Kenneth L. Judd
- Keith Kriebel, professor at Stanford's Graduate School of Business, holds a joint appointment to Hoover Institution
- Lawrence J. Lau, former chairman of economics department, has a joint appointment to Hoover Institution
- Thomas E. McCurdy, Senior Fellow at Hoover Institution and professor in Stanford's economics and political science departments
- John Moore, president of Grove City College in Pennsylvania and trustee of Earnardt Foundation
- Walter E. Williams, professor at George Mason University and member of Executive Committee of Hoover Institution Board of Overseers

Appendix 2

State Department and Military Services Program Associates Fellowships

During my directorate, the Hoover Institution sponsored officers from each of the three military services and from the State Department. This program allowed promising officers to pursue intensive independent research on topics relevant to their careers and important to their services. All three services considered an appointment as a Program Associate as a career-broadening experience, important to professional development. Selection, therefore, was highly competitive. After completion of the Hoover fellowship, these officers became general officers, commanders, and senior high-level staff officers at major commands and on joint and service staffs.

Of the military Program Associates appointees, nine were on active duty in the air force, seven in the army, four in the navy, and five in the State Department. One—Clint Smith—was a program officer with the William & Flora Hewlett Foundation. One of our former State Department Program Associates, the late Ambassador Philip Habib, worked out of the Hoover Institution for many years until his death in 1992. Without his help we would not have had a State Department program at all.

Bill Stanton, a State Department Hoover Program Associate in 1990–91, sent this report on May 22, 1991:

State Department Fellows

In the last 22 years, the Hoover Institution has had a total of 26 visiting fellows from the State Department. While many Hoover associates may be familiar with this long-standing program, most probably do not realize how successful Hoover's diplomats have been. Nine of the 26 fellows, in fact, went on to become U.S. ambassadors. These fellows, their years at Hoover, and their subsequent appointments follow:

John Negroponte (1969–70)
  Ambassador to Honduras
  Ambassador to Mexico and the Philippines
  Assistant Secretary of State for International Environmental and Scientific Affairs
Donald Norland (1969–70)
  Ambassador to Botswana, Lesotho, and Swaziland
Thomas W. Simons (1971–72)
  Ambassador to Costa Rica and Poland
  Deputy Assistant Secretary, Bureau of European Affairs
Francis J. McNeil (1971–72)
  Ambassador to Costa Rica
  Deputy Assistant Secretary, Bureau of Intelligence and Research
Stephen Ledogar (1972–73)
  U.S. Representative to the Mutual Balanced Force Reduction (MBFR) Negotiations
Burton Levin (1973–74)
  Ambassador to Burma
  Consul-General, Hong Kong
Curtis W. Kamman (1974–75)
  Ambassador to Chile
  Deputy Assistant Secretary, Bureau of European Affairs
  Deputy Assistant Secretary, Intelligence and Research
Kent Brown (1974–75)
  Robert Frowick (1974–75)
  Ambassador to Czechoslovakia
  DCM, U.S. Embassy Prague
  Head of OSCE, Bosnia
  Helsinki Accords
Francis Terry McNamara (1984–85)
  Ambassador to Sao Tome and Principe
  Ambassador to Gabon
  Ambassador to Cape Verde

Mary Ann Casey (1986–87)
Ambassador to Algeria
Deputy Assistant Secretary, Intelligence and Research
George Staples (1995–96)

(Phil Habib was already an ambassador and had been undersecretary of state for political affairs when he was a diplomat in residence at Hoover from 1977 to 1978.)

The number of Hoover Fellows who have been ambassadors is even more remarkable when you consider that there are currently some 4,500 active Foreign Service Officers worldwide, only a small percentage of whom will ever reach the rank of ambassador. The State Department Fellows at Hoover have been a select group. Seven have gone on to become deputy chiefs of mission or consuls-general, or to hold comparable diplomatic positions:

- Mark Garrison (1970–71)
  Deputy Chief of Mission (DCM), U.S. Embassy Moscow
- Bruce Amstutz (1971–72)
  Charge, U.S. Embassy Kabul
  Consul-General, Bombayv
- John Knowles (1972–73)
  DCM, U.S. Embassy Kiev
- Alexander Rattray (1973–74)
  DCM, U.S. Embassy Islamabad
- Richard L. McCormack (1978–79)
  Political Counselor, U.S. Embassy London
- J. Curtis Struble (1988–89)
  Consul-General, Bangkok
- David Hess (1993–94)
  Charge,

The outstanding careers of so many State Department Fellows demonstrate the value of Hoover's program, which provides a unique opportunity for scholars to interact with, and perhaps even influence, people who may eventually help to shape America's foreign policy. Conversely, it is also a chance for scholars to learn from diplomats who have experienced the world of foreign affairs first-hand.

The National Fellows Advisory Committee performed the same function as the Domestic Studies and International Studies Advisory Committees. The National Fellows Dinners brought professors from related departments and schools at Stanford together with Hoover scholars, distinguished visitors, National and Public Affairs Program Fellows, and Program Associates from the military services and the State Department. Stanford professors seemed genuinely to appreciate these dinners, and they consistently thanked us for inviting them.

Appendix 3

Publications by National Peace and Public Affairs Fellows

The following list, though incomplete, suggests the depth and breadth of the work done by the National Fellows. Nothing I could say would be as impressive as this bibliography:

1971–1972

Atkinson, Dorothy. *Women in Russia.* Stanford, CA: Stanford University Press, 1977.

Bark, Dennis, ed. *To Promote Peace: U.S. Foreign Policy in the Mid-1980s.* Stanford, CA: Hoover Institution Press, 1984.

Feulner, Edwin J. *Congress and the New International Economic Order.* Washington, DC: Heritage Foundation, 1976.

Heussler, Robert. *British Rule in Malaya.* Oxford, England: Greenwood Press and Clio, 1981.

Kennedy, David M. *Over Here: The First World War and American Society.* London: Oxford University Press, 1980.

Magnus, Ralph H., and Eden Naby. *Afghanistan: Implications for United States Policy.* Stanford, CA: Hoover Institution Press, 1982.

Marshall, Bruce D. *The French Colonial Myth and Constitution-Making in the Fourth Republic.* New Haven, CT: Yale University Press, 1973.

Perinbaum, Marie. *Holy Violence: The Revolutionary Thought of Frantz Fanon.* Washington, DC: Three Continents Press, 1982.

Rabushka, Alvin. *Value for Money: The Hong Kong Budgetary Process.* Stanford, CA: Hoover Institution Press, 1976.

Ratliff, William E. *Castroism and Communism in Latin America, 1959–1976.*

Washington, DC and Stanford, CA: American Enterprise Institute and Hoover Institution Press, 1976.

Rhodes, James M. *The Hitler Movement: A Modern Millenarian Revolution.* Stanford CA: Hoover Institution Press, 1980.

Roberts, Paul Craig. *The Supply Side Revolution: An Insider's Account of Policymaking in Washington.* Cambridge, MA: Harvard University Press, 1984.

Sutton, Antony. *Western Technology and Soviet Economic Development, 1917 to 1930.* Stanford, CA: Hoover Institution Press, 1968.

1972–1973

Ackerman, John G., Ivo Banac, and Roman Szporluk, eds. *Nation and Ideology: Essays in Honor of Wayne S. Vucinich.* Irvington, NY: Columbia University Press, 1981.

Bacciocco, Edward J., Jr. *The New Left in America: Reform to Revolution, 1956–1970.* Stanford, CA: Hoover Institution Press, 1974.

Baer, George W. *Test Case: Italy, Ethiopia, and the League of Nations.* Stanford, CA: Hoover Institution Press, 1976.

Cocks, Paul M., Robert V. Daniels, and Nancy Whittier Heer, eds. *The Dynamics of Soviet Politics.* Cambridge, MA: Harvard University Press, 1976.

Ericson, Edward E., Jr. *Radicals in the University.* Stanford, CA: Hoover Institution Press, 1975.

Fowler, Wilton B. *American Diplomatic History Since 1890.* Goldentree Publishing, 1975.

George, James L., ed. *Problems of Sea Power as We Approach the Twenty-first Century.* Washington, DC: American Enterprise Institute, 1978.

Hessen, Robert. *Steel Titan: The Life of Charles M. Schwab.* London: Oxford University Press, 1975.

Kenez, Peter. *Civil War in South Russia, 1919–1920: The Defeat of the Whites.* Berkeley and Stanford, CA: University of California Press and Hoover Institution Press, 1977.

Lemarchand, Rene. *Selective Genocide in Burundi.* London: Minority Rights Group Pamphlet No. 32, 1974.

1973–1974

Bonnell, Victoria E. *Roots in Rebellion: Workers' Politics and Organizations in St. Petersburg and Moscow, 1900–1914.* Berkeley: University of California Press, 1983.

Burns, Joseph M. *A Treatise on Markets: Spot, Futures, and Options.* Washington, DC: American Enterprise Institute, 1979.

Dingman, Roger. *Power in the Pacific. The Origins of Naval Arms Limitation, 1914–1922.* Chicago: University of Chicago Press, 1976.

Higgs, Robert. *Crisis and the Leviathan: Critical Episodes in the Emergence of the Mixed Economy.* Cambridge, MA: Ballinger Publishing, 1984.

Lauren, Paul Gordon. *Diplomats and Bureaucrats: The First Institutional Responses to Twentieth Century Diplomacy in France and Germany.* Stanford, CA: Hoover Institution Press, 1976.

Lynch, Hollis. *Black American Radicals and the Liberation of Africa: The Council on African Affairs, 1937–1955.* Ithaca, NY: Cornell University Press, 1978.

Pelz, Stephen E. *Race to Pearl Harbor: The Failure of the Second London Naval Conference and the Onset of World War II.* Cambridge, MA: Harvard University Press, 1974.

Turner, Robert F. *Vietnamese Communism: Its Origins and Development.* Stanford, CA: Hoover Institution Press, 1975.

Weinstein, Franklin B. *Indonesian Foreign Policy and the Dilemma of Dependence: From Sukarno to Soeharto.* Ithaca, NY: Cornell University Press, 1976.

1974–1975

Banac, Ivo, John G. Ackerman, and Roman Szporluk, eds. *Nation and Ideology: Essays in Honor of Wayne S. Vucinich.* Irvington, NY: Columbia University Press, 1981.

Bernstein, Barton J., ed. *The Atomic Bomb: The Critical Issues.* New York: Little, Brown, and Co., 1976.

Corning, Peter A. *The Synergism Hypothesis: A Theory of Progressive Evolution.* New York: McGraw-Hill Co., 1983.

Goodman, Allan E. *The Lost Peace: America's Search for a Negotiated Settlement of the Vietnam War.* Stanford, CA: Hoover Institution Press, 1978.

Lapidus, Gail Warshovsky, Dorothy Atkinson, and Alexander Dallin, eds. *Women in Russia*. Stanford, CA: Stanford University Press, 1977.

Martin, Donald L. *An Ownership Theory of the Trade Union: A New Approach.* Berkeley: University of California Press, 1980.

Olorunsola, Victor A. *Soldiers and Power: The Development of the Nigerian Military Regime*. Stanford, CA: Hoover Institution Press, 1977.

Owen, Bruce. *Economics and Freedom of Expression: Media Structure and the First Amendment.* New York: Ballinger, 1975.

Shepsle, Kennneth. *The Giant Jigsaw Puzzle: Democratic Committee Assignments in the Modern House.* Chicago: University of Chicago Press, 1978.

1975–1976

Breslauer, George. *Five Images of the Soviet Future: A Critical View and Synthesis.* Berkeley: University of California Press, 1978.

Deacon, Robert T., and Walter Mead. *Price Controls and International Petroleum Product Prices.* Washington, DC: U.S. Department of Energy, 1980.

Goodman, John C. *National Health Care in Great Britain: Lessons for the USA.* Dallas, TX: Fisher Institute Press, 1980.

Hardin, Russell. *Collective Action.* Baltimore, MD: Johns Hopkins University Press, 1982.

Kingston, Esther. *Lenin and the Problem of Marxist Peasant Revolution, 1893–1917*. London: Oxford University Press, 1983.

Lindsay, Cotton M. *Veterans Administration Hospitals.* Washington, DC: American Enterprise Institute, 1975.

Machan, Tibor. *Introduction to Philosophical Inquiries.* Boston: Allyn & Bacon, Inc., 1977.

Moody, Peter R. *Opposition and Dissent in Contemporary China.* Stanford, CA: Hoover Institution Press, 1977.

Moore, John H. *Growth with Self-Management: The Yugoslav Industrialization 1952–1975.* Stanford, CA: Hoover Institution Press, 1980.

Tierney, John, ed. *About Face: The China Decision and Its Consequences.* New Rochelle, NY: Arlington House Publishers, 1979.

Tulchin, Joseph., ed. *Hemispheric Perspectives on the United States. Papers from the New World Conference.* Westport, CT: Greenwood Press, 1978.

Williams, Walter E. *America: A Minority Viewpoint*. Stanford, CA: Hoover Institution Press, 1982.

1976–1977

Chan, Ming. *Historiography of the Chinese Labor Movement, 1895–1949*. Stanford, CA: Hoover Institution Press, 1981.

Laing, James D., David K. Hildebrand, and Howard Rosenthal. *Analysis of Ordinal Data*. Beverly Hills, CA: Sage Publications, 1977.

Lau, Lawrence J., and Dean T. Jamison. *Farmer Education and Farm Efficiency*. Baltimore, MD: Johns Hopkins University Press, 1982.

Schneider, William, and Seymour Martin Lipset. *The Confidence Gap: Business, Labor, and Government in the Public Mind*. New York: Free Press, 1983.

Vree, Dale. *On Synthesizing Marxism and Christianity*. New York: John Wiley and Sons, 1976.

1977–1978

Anderson, Terry L., and Peter J. Hill. *The Birth of a Transfer Society*. Stanford, CA: Hoover Institution Press, 1980.

Barro, Robert J. *Macroeconomics*. New York: John Wiley and Sons, 1984.

Dorfman, Gerald A. *Government Versus Trade Unionism in British Policies Since 1968*. Stanford, CA: Hoover Institution Press, 1979.

Harding, Harry, Jr. *China and the U.S.: Normalization and Beyond*. New York: The China Council of the Asia Society and the Foreign Policy Association, January 1979.

Raditsa, Leo. *Some Sense about Wilhelm Reich*. New York: Philosophical Library, 1978.

Speed, Roger D. *Strategic Deterrence in the 1980's*. Stanford, CA: Hoover Institution Press, 1979.

Weinstein, Allen. *Perjury: The Hiss-Chambers Case*. New York: Alfred A. Knopf, 1978.

Weitzman, Lenore J. *The Marriage Contract: Spouses, Lovers, and the Law*. London and New York: Collier Macmillan Publishers and Free Press, 1981.

1978–1979

Abrams, Burton A. *Study Guide for Maisel's Macroeconomics.* New York: W. W. Norton and Co., 1982.

Capaldi, Nicholas, Luis Navia, and Eugene Kelly. *Invitation to Philosophy.* Buffalo, NY: Prometheus Books, 1981.

Dunlop, John B. *The Faces of Contemporary Russian Nationalism.* Princeton, NJ: Princeton University Press, 1983.

Shirk, Susan L. *Competitive Comrades: Career Incentives and Student Strategies in China.* Berkeley: University of California Press, 1982.

Tyson, Laura D'Andrea. *The Yugoslav Economic System and Its Performance in the 1970's.* Berkeley: University of California Press, 1980.

1979–1980

Falcoff, Mark, and Frederick B. Pike, eds. *The Spanish Civil War, 1936–1939: American Hemispheric Perspectives.* Lincoln: University of Nebraska Press, 1982.

Henriksen, Thomas H. *Revolution and Counter-Revolution: Mozambique's War of Independence, 1964–1974.* Westport, CT: Greenwood Press, 1983.

Okimoto, Daniel, ed. *Japan's Economy: Coping with Change in the International Environment.* Boulder, CO: Westview Press, 1982.

Pike, David. *German Writers in Soviet Exile, 1933–1945.* Chapel Hill: University of North Carolina Press, 1982.

Rawski, Thomas G. *Economic Growth and Employment in China.* New York: Oxford University Press for the World Bank, 1979.

1980–1981

Garcia, Gillian G., and Thomas F. Cargill. *Financial Deregulation and Monetary Control: Historical Perspective and Impact of the 1980 Act.* Stanford, CA: Hoover Institution Press, 1982.

Lacorne, Denis. *Les Notables Rouges.* Paris: Presses de la Foundation Nationale des Sciences Politiques, 1980.

Paul, Ellen Frankel, and Dan Jacobs. *Studies of the Third Wave: Recent Migration of Soviet Jews to the United States.* Boulder, CO.: Westview Press, 1981.

Zimmerman, Martin B. *The U.S. Coal Industry: The Economics of Policy*

Choice. Cambridge, MA.: MIT Press, 1981.

Zipser, Richard A. "Contemporary East German Poetry." A special edition of *Field.* Oberlin, OH.: Oberlin College, 1980.

1981–1982

Brickman, Ronald, Sheila Jasanoff, and Thomas Ilgen. *The Politics of Scientific Uncertainty: Toxic Chemical Regulation in Four Countries.* Ithaca, NY: Cornell University Press, 1985.

Davis, Eric M. *Challenging Colonialism: Bank Misr and Egyptian Industrialization, 1920–1941.* Princeton, NJ: Princeton University Press, 1983.

Dong, Wonmo. *Imperial Japan in Korea: The Political Economy of Penetration and Colonial Development.* Stanford, CA: Hoover Institution Press, 1985.

Dufey, Gunter, and Ian Giddy. *The Evolution of Instruments and Techniques on International Financial Markets.* Tilburg, Netherlands: Society of European University Financial Research, 1981.

Emmerson, Donald K., and Koentjaraningrat, eds. *The Human Aspect of Social Research.* Jakarta, Indonesia: Gremedia, 1982.

Nelson, Daniel J. *A History of U.S. Military Forces in Germany.* Boulder, CO, and London: Westview Press, 1987.

Page, Benjamin I., and Mark Petracca. *The American Presidency.* New York: McGraw- Hill, 1982.

Solinger, Dorothy. *Chinese Business Under Socialism: The Politics and Practice of Domestic Commerce in the People's Republic, 1949–1980.* Berkeley: University of California Press, 1985.

1983–1984

Berkowitz, Bruce. *Stategic Intelligence and American National Security.* Princeton, NJ: Princeton University Press, 1991.

Bielasiak, Jacob, and Maurice Simon, eds. *Polish Politics: Edge of the Abyss.* New York: Praeger, 1984.

Chubb, John Edward. *Interest Groups and the Bureaucracy: The Politics of Energy.* Stanford, CA: Stanford University Press, 1983.

Collier, David. *Squatters and Oligarchs: Authoritarian Rule and Policy Change in Peru.* Baltimore, MD: Johns Hopkins University Press, 1976.

Fullerton, Donald, C. L. Ballard, J. B. Shoven, and J. Walley. *A General*

Equilibrium Model for Tax Policy Evaluation. Chicago: University of Chicago Press, 1985.

1984–1985

Chang, Maria Hsia. *The Chinese Blue Shirt Society: Fascism and Developmental Nationalism.* Berkeley: University of California Press, 1985.

Moses, Joel. *Regional Party Leadership and Policy Making in the USSR.* New York and London: Praeger Publishers and Pall Mall Press, 1974.

1985–1986

Chapman, Herrick Eaton. *State Capitalism and Working Class Radicalism in the French Aircraft Industry.* Berkeley: University of California Press, 1991.

Rice, Condoleezza. *The Soviet Union and the Czechoslovak Army.* Princeton, NJ: Princeton University Press, 1984.

Roberts, Russell. *The Choice: A Fable of Free Trade and Protectionism.* New York: Prentice-Hall, 1993.

1986–1987

Crawford, Beverly. *Economic Vulnerability in International Relations.* New York: Columbia University Press, 1993.

Marks, Gary. *Unions in Politics: Britain, Germany and the United States in the Nineteenth and Early Twentieth Centuries.* Princeton, NJ: Princeton University Press, 1989.

Rogoff, Kenneth and Gene Grossman, eds. *Handbook of International Economics.* Amsterdam, Netherlands: Elsevier Science Publishers, 1995.

1987–1988

Austen-Smith, David. *Positive Political Theory.* Ann Arbor: University of Michigan Press, 1993.

Cooper, Russell. *Wages and Employment Patterns in Labor Contracts: Microfoundations and Macroeconomic Implications.* London: Harwood Academic Press, 1987.

Eaton, Jonathan. *Four Essays in the Theory of Portfolio Choice.* Garland Publishing, 1979.

1988–1989

Ayittey, George B. N. *Indigenous African Institutions.* New York: Transnational Publishers, 1991.

Calder, Kent E. *Crisis and Compensation: Public Policy and Political Stability in Japan.* Princeton, NJ: Princeton University Press, 1988.

Gold, Thomas Baron. *State and Society in the Taiwan Miracle.* New York: M.E. Sharpe, 1985.

Krehbiel, Keith. *Information and Legislative.* Ann Arbor: University of Michigan Press, 1991.

Index